SARA Title III

INTENT AND IMPLEMENTATION OF HAZARDOUS MATERIALS REGULATIONS

Frank L. Fire

Nancy K. Grant

David H. Hoover

 VAN NOSTRAND REINHOLD
New York

Copyright © 1990 by Van Nostrand Reinhold

Library of Congress Catalog Card Number 89-14742
ISBN 0-442-23803-7

Printed in the United States of America

Van Nostrand Reinhold
115 Fifth Avenue
New York, New York 10003

Van Nostrand Reinhold International Company Limited
11 New Fetter Lane
London EC4P 4EE, England

Van Nostrand Reinhold
480 La Trobe Street
Melbourne, Victoria 3000, Australia

Nelson Canada
1120 Birchmount Road
Scarborough, Ontario M1K 5G4, Canada

FIRE ENGINEERING
250 Fifth Avenue
New York, New York 10001

16 15 14   13 12 11 10 9 8 7 6 5 4 3 2 1

Library of Congress Cataloging-in-Publication Data

Fire, Frank L., 1937–
     SARA Title III : intent and implementation of hazardous materials
regulations / by Frank L. Fire, Nancy K. Grant, David H. Hoover.
        p. cm.
     Includes index.
     ISBN 0-442-23803-7
     1. Hazardous substances—Law and legislation—United States.
2. Chemicals—Law and legislation—United States. 3. Disaster
relief—Law and legislation—United States. I. Grant, Nancy K.
II. Hoover, David H. III. Title. IV. Title: SARA Title 3.
V. Title: SARA Title three.
KF3958.F57 1989
353.0077′2—dc20   89-14742
                                                   CIP

PREFACE

SARA Title III is and will continue to be the topic of much discussion. Its impact on industry, local and state governments, and the community is far-reaching, as each of these entitles must participate in the planning process and in the right-to-know provisions. Currently, there is much confusion concerning the appropriate actions to be taken and the exact nature of the responsibilities assigned. This book addresses the confusion by explaining not only what is required, but why.

SARA Title III is purposely vague on the exact method of implementation of required activities in order to allow for local adaptation to particular circumstances. This has caused misunderstanding and confusion. A number of texts have been written about SARA in an attempt to alleviate this confusion by presenting specific plans of action to fulfill the requirements of the law. While these guides are helpful, many communities are unable to use them because they do not fit their specific situation. In order to adapt the forms and procedures of SARA Title III, the industries, governmental units (fire departments, medical facilities, police, etc.) and citizens need to understand the purpose and intent of the law. Once the reason for an activity is understood, it is possible to adapt procedures to achieve its intent.

This book provides that understanding. The chapters which follow not only describe the letter of the law and offer specific suggestions on how to comply, they also explain why the law requires what it does—the intent of the law. Once the intent of legislation is clear, the methods of implementation become self-evident. Guidance on implementation activities is helpful at this point because adaptation to specific situations can be made once their purpose is understood.

This focus on the spirit of the law has been recognized by a number of organizations working in the field of hazardous chemicals. For example, the Chemical Manufacturer's Association, through its Community Awareness and Emergency Response (CAER) program, encourages emergency response planning at the local level. This program can be interwoven with the SARA requirements in order to meet not only the letter of the law but also its spirit by facilitating close working relationships with individual communities to account for their unique characteristics. Thus, each CAER and SARA emergency preplan is tailored to the specific nature of the community. At the same time, however, all of these plans share certain common components.

The spirit of the law encompasses a variety of municipal and private organizations within the community. Although each of these organizations has its own area of responsibility and expertise in the response planning system, the plan itself transcends these organizational boundaries. The result of this blending of expertise and sharing of responsibility is a comprehensive hazardous materials response system which benefits all. This book describes not only the individual responsibilities but also the integrated interactions which comprise the requirements of SARA Title III.

The implementation requirements of SARA affecting communities is detailed in Chapters 8 and 9, which deal with the local emergency planning committee and preparation of emergency response plan. These chapters discuss not only the requirements for the community, but how the community will be better prepared and organized to deal with emergencies. It presents the roles taken by some of the various municipal and community organizations.

Industry is not only a partner in the community planning process, it must also provide information and resources to implement the law. These requirements and their intent are detailed in Chapters 2, 3, and 4, which deal with legislative impacts, regulated hazardous materials and how industry should comply. The last chapter of the book is a basic overview of hazardous materials which can serve as a guide and reference source to Facility Coordinators, community planners, fire service personnel, and other emergency response personnel.

Training is a key feature of SARA Title III, and Chapters 5 and 6 deal with this issue in detail. The training is not just for those individuals who are first responders. It also includes community, municipal and business leaders who are charged with the responsibility of managing an emergency hazardous materials incident and with designing and implementing the system. The book suggests a format for developing successful employee and first responder training programs and describes specific criteria for effective training.

Given the goal of this book—to facilitate the understanding of SARA—Chapters 1 and 10 present the background which led to the passage of Title III, as well as concerns raised and changes which may come about as a result of the experiences of the first years. This aids the reader in putting the specific areas of interest into the context of the whole. Although users of this book may not need to read every chapter, it is recommended that everyone read these two chapters in order to place their specific area of interest into the proper perspective.

This integrated approach and emphasis on understanding the intent of the legislation was chosen on the basis of the experiences of the three authors. Each of the authors has worked and continues to work with SARA in the field. Each has a specific area of expertise. Discussions showed very quickly that in order to best fulfill the requirements of any given areas, be it local community planning, industrial compliance or fire service preparation, it was necessary to have a holistic understanding of the system and to relate to the other participants in the process. It was this realization that led to the conception and completion of this book.

The authors approached this project with the goal of educating and informing the reader. Since the law is so complex and involves so many different components of the community, it is not possible to give one-step solutions to different problems. This book provides a guide and suggestions which, when understood in the context of the other information presented, can successfully be used as needed.

As practitioners, the authors operate within the planning, hazardous materials, and training environments on a regular basis. They are not outsiders investigating the question from a theoretical perspective. Their insights are based upon direct experience and applied study of legislation and other information. Rather than lecturing the reader, the authors are sharing insight, information and experience.

CONTENTS

About the authors

Frank L. Fire is Director of Marketing at Americhem, Inc., and an Instructor of Chemistry of Hazardous Materials at the University of Akron.

Nancy K. Grant is an Associate Professor of Public Administration at the University of Akron, and an adjunct faculty member at the National Fire Academy.

David H. Hoover is an Assistant Professor of Fire Protection Technology, and Director of the Training Center for Fire and Hazardous Materials at the University of Akron. He is also a member of the Ohio State Emergency Response Commission.

PART I

INTENT AND IMPLEMENTATION OF THE LAW

Chapter 1

THE COMING OF SARA

BACKGROUND

There is a history of federal legislation which has directly influenced the daily operation of municipal government. Several federal programs over the years have either encouraged or required municipalities to operate in certain ways. For example, community development programs have encouraged cities to revitalize residential and commercial areas through the provision of program-specific funding. This is an example of programs which elicited participation by offering funding.

Other federal programs have pass-through arrangements with state governments. These programs, such as those of community action agencies (CAA), also receive funding in order to carry out their designated activities. In fact, most federal programs which affect cities directly are tied to allocation of funds.

One of the newest federal programs influencing local government is Title III of SARA, the Superfund Amendments and Reauthorization Act of 1986, which deals with hazardous materials, emergency response planning, and community right-to-know. SARA was enacted to prevent hazardous materials tragedies such as those of Bhopol, India, and Chernobyl, the USSR, from occurring in the United States. In addition, the standard contains a freedom of information provision that requires industry to divulge specific information to the public relating to chemical hazards at specific sites. This program is having a direct impact on every community and industry in the United States. It has a number of unique characteristics which differentiate it from previous federal programs.

One of the immediately recognized differences is that SARA is not tied to funding. The only funding allocated by the federal government for the implementation of this program is at the state level. This funding is intended to provide local training of first responders. All federal funds for a program which is predominantly local are designated for use by the federal Environmental Protection Agency (EPA). The only subsidy a local community may receive is in the area of required training. Even this funding, however, is minuscule and may not be available as promised. In the 1990 federal budget, the $5 million training allocation was first moved from the EPA budget to that of the Federal Emergency Management Agency (FEMA). The Office of Management and Budget then deleted the funding from the FEMA budget. As of the summer of 1988, local governments were slated to receive no support for implementing the program required by federal legislation. Thus, this new municipal responsibility for emergency planning is based on volunteerism. This expectation is in line with the Reagan administration's policy of encouraging and relying on private volunteerism to replace government subsidies. Individuals, private corporations and municipal governments are volunteering countless hours of personnel time and resources to accomplish the planning task.

Within the federal framework, SARA is designed to operate with state-level coordination. This is not a pass-through program, however. Both state and local entities have carefully defined responsibilities. There is a requirement for coordination between the two on a regular basis.

In addition to the mandated state–local coordination, SARA facilitates intergovernmental cooperation among fire departments, police departments, cities, counties, hospital districts and other local governmental entities. The comprehensive local planning requirements bring these different entities together in a cooperative enterprise in order to fulfill the federal mandate.

SARA also requires a public–private partnership in the planning process. Industries must take an active part in information assembly, response preplanning, hazard analysis and training. This is a specific program which actively links private business and local government in a cooperative undertaking.

Cities and fire departments, under the SARA Title III mandate, are now operating in new ways and new arenas. The potential impact of these new partnerships in other activities and areas of operation is not known. However, increased voluntary intergovernmental cooperation and public–private partnerships as a result of positive outcomes of the SARA experience are a distinct possibility. Federal legislation may prove the impetus for a new spirit of inter-governmental cooperation.

SARA TITLE III

Title III of SARA was signed into law by President Ronald Reagan on October 17, 1986. Also known as the "Emergency Planning and Community Right to Know Act," Sara revises and expands the authority established under the Comprehensive Environmental Response, Compensation and Liability Act of (CERCLA) 1980. Although enacted as part of SARA, the right-to-know and emergency planning sections are separate from Title I and Title II.

The purpose of SARA Title III is threefold: to (1) provide information on site-specific hazardous chemicals to communities and their residents, (2) initiate emergency planning and notification activities at the local community level which would protect the public in the event of a release of a hazardous chemical into the environment, and (3) provide training for all first responders who may become involved in a hazardous materials incident.

SARA Title III, promulgated by the EPA, establishes clearly defined linkage between two federal agencies concerned with hazardous materials: the Occupational Safety and Health Administration (OSHA) and the EPA. The EPA is primarily concerned with the release of hazardous chemicals into the environment. Such a release may have either a short-term or a long-term impact on the community, depending upon the chemical involved and the amount released. OSHA also administers programs directed at the safe handling of hazardous materials.

OSHA's hazardous materials program focuses on worker safety on the job—specifically, chemical awareness and personal protection. The first portion of OSHA's Hazard Communication Standard became effective in 1985 for employers in the Standard Industrial Classification (SIC) Codes 20 through 39. This classification identifies employers in the manufacturing sector only; all other SIC classes are excluded. Employers are required to analyze each chemical in the workplace in order to determine if it is hazardous. The question most commonly used to make this evaluation is: Will the chemical cause physical harm when in contact with human beings or harm to the environment when accidentally released?

Hazardous chemicals are organized by hazard classification such as (1) flammable, (2) toxic, (3) combustible, (4) carcinogen, (5) Other Regulated Materials ORM, (6) corrosive and (7) oxidizers. Appropriate hazardous warning labels and placards must be placed on all containers and a master list of identified materials prepared. The source document for this process is the material safety data sheet (MSDS), which contains specific information about each chemical. The information on the form is grouped into sections which provide (1) the specific name of the chemical, (2) emergency information about the manufacturer or distributor, (3) reactivity data, (4) physical data, (5) emergency handling procedures and (6) firefighting methods and extinguishing agents. The final step in the process is the training of all employees who are exposed or may become exposed to hazardous chemicals. This process must be structured so that employees are informed about the hazards of chemical exposure, taught the proper methods by which to recognize a release of the material, and trained to protect themselves against exposure.

As of late 1988, OSHA Hazard Communication coverage was expanded to include employers in all SIC codes. This action preempts local ordinances directed at worker or community right to know. It means that SARA applies to all businesses in the United States that have reportable chemicals under either EPA or OSHA. As a result, all businesses need to be not only aware of SARA requirements but thoroughly involved in compliance activities.

SARA Title III and the OSHA Hazard Communication Standard both require the assembly and transmittal of information on specific chemical hazards. Even though the fundamental goals of these agencies may differ, the issue of safe handling of hazardous materials in the United States is now at the forefront. SARA will expand the focus on hazardous chemicals and affect the policy-making process at the local government level. To understand these new municipal responsibilities, we must examine the intent of the policy and try to determine whether implementation will achieve it.

IMPLEMENTATION OF SARA

The implementation of SARA requires the cooperation of state and local agencies in addition to numerous private organizations. Step one of the process is the establishment of a State Emergency Response Commission (SERC). Members appointed to the commission by the governor of each state represent a cross section of the groups, organizations and individuals concerned with environmental issues. This includes state government agencies, law enforcement officials, disaster planners, elected representatives, fire service officials, industrial users, civic groups and environmental activists. The SERC is responsible for implementation and continued operation of the SARA program for the state. Policy issues such as (1) establishing planning districts, (2) determining a filing fee structure, (3) defining training guidelines, (4) monitoring local planning efforts and (5) evaluating emergency plan exercises are addressed by SERC.

Step two of the process is the formation of local emergency planning committees (LEPC). Local government officials submit to the SERC the names and qualifications of those persons considered most suitable to participate in the local planning process. Each committee includes elected state and local officials; police, fire, and public health officials; environmental advocates; hospital and transportation officials; representatives of facilities subject to emergency planning requirements; community groups; and the media. The function of each LEPC is to develop an effective plan of action that will be utilized if a hazardous material is released in the local community planning area.

The basic plan includes information pertaining to emergency notification systems, evacuation routes, emergency response agency preplans, local resources for handling special or unusual problems, facility site-specific data and contingency planning documents, and a hazard evaluation of each facility using or manufacturing one of EPA's designated extremely hazardous materials. A model planning document, the "Hazardous Materials Emergency Planning Guide" (NRT-1), has been issued by the National Response Team to assist the LEPCs in developing local emergency response plans. The guide is a product of the cooperation of the 14 federal agencies that constitute the National Response Team. It provides guidance for hazardous materials emergency planning and presents a federal consensus upon which future guidance, technical assistance and training will be based. A second planning guide, "Site Specific Technical Guidance for Hazards Analysis: Emergency Planning for Extremely Hazardous Substances," has been issued by EPA, FEMA, and the Department of Transportation (DOT).

Site-specific chemical information is provided to the LEPC through a series of reports completed by the chemical user. The reporting requirements of SARA call for an annual statement from each facility identifying all hazardous substances present. Only those chemicals identified by OSHA or appearing on the EPA's list of extremely hazardous substances must be reported. The EPA has established minimum reporting guidelines for specific chemicals for the years 1988 and 1989. These "threshold planning limits" apply only to the presence of any hazardous chemical that was present in quantities of 10,000 pounds or more during the previous

12 months. It has been proposed that beginning in 1990, the threshold limits will be reduced to 500 pounds. These limits apply to many of the OSHA-identified chemicals but not to the majority of the EPA's extremely hazardous substances. Another significant difference between the EPA and OSHA reporting requirements is the hazard classification of chemicals. OSHA recognized approximately 23 hazard classes; however, EPA succumbed to industry pressure and compressed the classes to 5. They are (1) acute, (2) chronic, (3) fire, (4) reactive and (5) sudden release of pressure. This action helped to ease the reporting burden of industry and simplified the hazard analysis task of the LEPCs.

IMPACT OF SARA

The primary impact of SARA is on emergency preparedness. Local communities are now ready to respond to accidental releases of hazardous materials. Emergency response plans were submitted to the SERC for review and concurrence by October 17, 1988. The individual SERCs identified a state agency as the review entity. For example, in Ohio the Emergency Management Agency (OEMA) reviews all plans. The review is annual component of the planning process. In addition, the planning process requires the collection and retention of data on hazardous chemicals. Local government officials and private citizens will have access to the site-specific hazard information through a data base operated by the SERC. This provides an increased level of awareness for those citizens residing or working near a hazardous materials user facility.

Secondary impacts go beyond the immediate policy intent of SARA. The implementation process involves the cooperation of many intergovernmental agencies. Emergency response planning policy has often focused on the responsibilities of separate departments. This resulted in uncoordinated emergency responses which often failed to produce the desired results. The new emergency response plan under Title III requires the coordination of all intergovernmental agency activities. Each agency preplan is to become an annex to the LEPC's master plan. The successful outcome of future emergency response activities will reflect these efforts.

Another impact of this new municipal responsibility is the beginning of a new era of volunteerism. Not only are individuals volunteering, but also municipal governments, private organizations and private businesses. The lack of funding has prompted this donation of personnel time and support resources. The October 17, 1988, deadline for emergency response plans could only be met by strong local government leadership and diligent volunteer effort.

Because hazardous materials are such a critical and timely issue and their potential impact is so great, citizens and governments are joining together in preventive activities. The intent of the legislation is to address a real and growing need and a potential threat to life, safety and the environment. All of the participants in the process share the concerns addressed by the legislation. Therefore, they participate in a spirit of cooperation rather than coercion. This effort could spawn a new period of intergovernmental cooperation.

The implementation of SARA is a massive national effort involving hundreds of thousand of dedicated individuals. For example, in Ohio, over 3,100 citizens in 87 planning districts are volunteering their time to enhance the safety of the community in which hazardous materials are used. This undertaking may become a model for future cooperative programs involving issues that cross the traditional service boundaries of local governments.

COMPLIANCE DATES

The implementation of SARA is taking place on a rather strict and tight time schedule. The following are the target dates for state and local governments (references are to sections of SARA Title 3).

April 17, 1987: State governors appoint members of the SERC (Sec. 301). This date was established as the official start of the state implementation efforts. Had the governors not appointed the appropriate members to the SERC at this time, they themselves would have been required to fulfill the requirements of SARA Title III.

May 17, 1987: Facilities subject to Section 302 on emergency planning notification require-

ments must notify the SERC of the presence of any extremely hazardous materials. This requirement applies to any facility where an extremely hazardous substance is present in an amount in excess of its threshold planning quantity. This is a one-time reporting requirement as of May 17 or within 60 days after a facility becomes subject to Section 302. This reporting provided the SERC with an indication of the amount of data that was likely to arrive under the second-stage reporting requirements. This information was also passed on to the LEPCs so that they could begin their data bases, begin to orient their emergency response plans, and prepare for incoming data.

July 17, 1987: SERC designates planning districts (Sec. 301). Each SERC was required to identify the geographic area for which one comprehensive response plan would be developed. These areas vary from state to state; some are coterminous with county boundaries, others correspond to existing planning regions, and some are separate planning districts based on urban–rural distinctions.

August 17, 1987: SERC appoints members of the LEPC (Sec. 301). The LEPC is the coordinating entity charged with developing the local emergency response plan. All members of the LEPC are residents of the planning district. Each is a recognized expert and a representative of concerned parties or organizations directly affected by the federal requirements.

September 17, 1988: Fixed-site facilities must notify LEPCs of the selection and identification of facility representatives (Sec. 303). Each facility storing on its premises materials identified as hazardous according to the SARA or OSHA hazardous materials lists must identify a representative to work with the LEPC and the fire department. This representative will be the facility liaison in preparing the emergency response plan for the facility. This individual coordinates the activates and plans of the facility with those of the community emergency coordinator. He or she not only transmits specific information about the facility to the LEPC but also reports back to the managers of the facility. This ensures that the facility's management and employees are aware of their responsibilities in emergency situations. The facility is also then prepared to cooperate in the event of a hazardous release. (See Chap. 4.)

October 17, 1987: Facilities submit MSDSs or a list of MSDS chemicals to the SERC, the LEPC, and local fire departments (Sec. 311). Facilities are responsible for preparing and submitting MSDSs for each hazardous chemical stored on site in excess of threshold levels. In lieu of an MSDS for each chemical, the facilities may submit a list of the chemicals by hazard classification. The information must be submitted to the SERC, the LEPC, and all local fire departments in the facility's jurisdiction. This is a one-time reporting requirement. However, any new information concerning the presence of new chemicals must be reported within 3 months.

March 1, 1988: Facilities must submit their initial Hazardous Chemical Inventory forms to the SERC, the LEPC, and local fire departments (Sec. 312). These inventory report forms indicate the type and amount of chemicals on site at a given time. Although the design of the report forms may vary from one state to another, they must all contain the same information about the hazardous chemicals. The information includes the CAS Registry number, specific chemical name, the form in which the chemical is present (e.g., components, mixutre, pure and solid, liquid or gas), and the hazard category. Tier II reporting requirements include the location and amount of chemicals stored as well. These inventory report forms provide the LEPC and the SERC with the information necessary to develop a viable emergency response plan. This is an annual report beginning March 1, 1988.

July 1, 1988: Facilities must submit initial Toxic Chemical Release forms to the EPA and designated state representatives (Sec. 313). Each facility must report the routine or accidental release of any of the 300 designated toxic substances manufactured, processed or otherwise used in quantities exceeding the threshold quantity established. This provides additional information on toxic releases into the environment which occurred during the previous year. Many of these releases would not be covered by the standard community right-to-know laws and represent a set of new information not previously available. These reports must be submitted to the EPA and to a designated state official or agency annually beginning July 1, 1988.

Table 1.1 Comparison of Notification and Reporting Requirements Under Sara Title III

	§302 EMERGENCY PLANNING NOTIFICATION	§304 EMERGENCY RELEASE NOTIFICATION	§311 MSDA REPORTS	§312 INVENTORY FORMS	§313 TOXIC CHEMICAL RELEASE FORMS
SUBSTANCES COVERED	Extremely hazardous substances	—Extremely hazardous substances —CERCLA hazardous substances	Hazardous chemicals under OSHA's Hazard Communication Standard (with limited exceptions)	Hazardous chemicals under OSHA's Hazard Communication Standard (with limited exceptions)	Toxic chemicals
REGULATED FACILITIES	—Any facility where an extremely hazardous substance is present in an amount in excess of its threshold planning quantity —Facilities designated by the governor or SERC	Any facility where there is a release of a reportable quantity of one of the above substances which extends beyond the facility's boundaries	Any facility which is required to prepare or have available an MSDS for a hazardous chemical under OSHA's Hazard Communication Standard	Any facility which is required to prepare or have available an MSDS for a hazardous chemical under OSHA's Hazard Communication Standard	Any facility which —has 10 or more full—time employees; and —manufactured, processed or otherwise used a toxic chemical in excess of its threshold amount in the preceding year
NOTIFICATION OR REPORTING REQUIREMENTS	Notification that facility is subject to Subtitle A	—Telephone notice of emergency release —Written follow-up notice	—Submittal of an MSDS for each hazardous chemical or a list of hazardous chemicals —Submittal of updates with new information	—Submittal of Tier I information on form —If requested or in lieu of Tier I submittal, submittal of Tier II information	Submittal of form regarding releases of toxic chemicals which occurred as a result of normal business operations in the preceding year
FREQUENCY OF NOTIFICATION OR REPORT	Once, by 5/17/87 or within 60 days after a facility becomes subject to # 302	Immediate notice for each covered release with written follow-up as soon as practical	—Once, by 10/17/87 or within 3 months of becoming subject to OSHA Hazard Communication Standard for new chemical —For updates, 3 months after discovering new information	Annually, beginning 3/1/88	Annually, beginning 7/1/88
AGENCY OR PERSON TO CONTACT	—SERC for 5/17/87 notifications —In addition, for subsequent notifications	—Community emergency coordinator —SERC —National REsponse Center for CERCLA hazardous substances	—SERC —LEPC —Fire department	—SERC —LEPC —Fire department	—EPA administrator —State official designated by governor

October 17, 1988: LEPCs must complete their emergency response plans and submit them to the SERC and other designated state agencies (Sec. 303). The completed local emergency response plan must be submitted to the SERC. Often the SERC or the governor has designated another state agency to review the local plans for concurrence with the overall state emergency response and disaster plans. In these instances, the plans must be submitted to that agency as well. At this point the plans are expected to be complete, requiring only minor revisions or additions.

Once these plans are complete, each local planning district must ensure that they work. This involves the simulation of a hazardous chemical incident at a facility in the local planning area. It provides each participant in the emergency response plan with the opportunity to role play an actual emergency condition. The exercise is evaluated by state and local officials.

Once these plans are completed, SARA's oversight does not end. The law calls for continuous reporting of changes in the presence of hazardous materials. As the materials change, the emergency plans must be revised to account for the differences. For this reason, it is vital to know the requirements and importance of the compliance dates. Although the dates may be past, private industry, state governments, and local governments must still comply with the requirements and adapt their information banks and emergency response plans to ensure that they are current.

SUMMARY NOTIFICATION AND REPORTING REQUIREMENTS

Table 1.1 provides a summary of the reporting requirements under SARA Title III according to the individual sections of the law. The type of facility and the substances covered under each section are specified. The type of notification or reporting that must be done and the recipient of the information are identified. The table also presents the date and frequency of reporting under each section. This overview can serve as a guide for facility compliance. Specific information on the content of each type of report can be found in the chapters dealing with hazardous materials.

SARA will be in effect for a long time, and an understanding of the policy is vital to the fulfillment of the law. Title III is an EPA standard which defines a section of the environment called the "community." As such, it will have significant impact upon other sectors of our society. In particular, private industry must amend its operations in order to comply with the requirements of SARA. Local governments, particularly fire departments, are taking on new responsibilities in their daily operations Hopefully, these new methods of operation will succeed in achieving the goal of the law: a cleaner and safer living environment and work setting.

Chapter 2

IMPACT OF LEGISLATION

COST

Any new legislation is subject to questions concerning its impact. Certainly, SARA has costs associated with implementation, since a considerable amount of reporting must be done. Costs are incurred not only by the people hired to do the collection, verification and reporting of data but also by all those who must provide such information. There is also an opportunity cost, that is, the cost incurred by devoting time to provide Title III information—time that would otherwise be used in working for the company to produce income.

There are other costs to society that involve the people who must receive the information from regulated facilities and process it in accordance with the law. Each local fire department must provide personnel to receive, use and store the information. Training must be provided to those firefighters who may be emergency responders to an incident at any regulated facility. Preplanning must be done to ensure the safety of emergency responders, workers and visitors (vendors, customers, and other invitees of the company) at the facility at which the incident has occurred, as well as that of the people, environment and exposures surrounding that facility.

Costs are also incurred by every LEPC as it makes arrangements to carry out all of its tasks. It must receive information from all regulated facilities in its jurisdiction, and store and retrieve such information to carry out its primary function of emergency planning. Most members of every LEPC are volunteers, but computer and clerical help must be provided, and it is not free. Many county disaster service agencies, fire departments, police departments and sheriff's departments are now carrying the burden by giving personnel time to do extra duties for the LEPCs, often donating computer and clerical help. These organizations cannot be expected to carry these costs much longer.

The SERCs will have a monumental job in receiving information on hazardous chemicals from the entire state and ensuring that this information is stored, used and distributed in the proper manner. In addition, SERCs must approve the emergency response plans of all LEPCs in the state, and may have to act on all requests under community right-to-know laws.

All of these tasks cost a considerable amount of money, and this is the first impact of the legislation. Title III provides very little money on a nationwide basis and none for local activities. Each state will consider legislation that will raise money to pay for all Title III activities, and some states are thinking about a reporting fee based on the number of hazardous chemicals reported. All of these costs, borne by each regulated facility, will certainly be passed on to the ultimate consumer in the form of increased prices for goods and services. This naturally affects the company's ability to do business. Some companies are more capable of absorbing extra costs than others; this will put some enterprises at an economic disadvantage, and may ultimately cost jobs to the community in which the regulated facility is located. This, in turn, will reduce the amount of taxes paid in a community, in addition to lowering the income and the subsequent disposable income of community inhabitants. This could magnify the problems of local businesses, which, in turn, could further reduce the taxes paid to local government.

However gloomy this scenario seems, it is constantly repeated with every law passed, and we still seem to survive, simply because the effects are usually nationwide. However, all firms face international competition, and foreign businesses are not subjected to the regulations facing American businesses. The economic impact may be greater than estimated by the EPA!

SOCIAL IMPACT

Congress intended the major impact of SARA Title III to be on society as a whole, supporting the populist theory that people have a right to know about the presence of chemicals in their community, what to do in case of an accidental release, and how to protect themselves from the chemical if exposed. The perception of the public generally has been that business is overly secretive about what chemicals it uses, maintaining that any secret can be discovered by reverse engineering. If this is true, they feel, then businesses can be more open and honest with the communities in which they exist, especially when questioned about the chemicals present.

Title III will make available to the public all the information needed to know how businesses manufacture, handle, store or use hazardous chemicals. This knowledge has to benefit society as a whole, because society will be better informed about a subject that has concerned them for some time.

As the public becomes involved with LEPCs and is invited to participate in safety exercises with regulated facilities, as stated below, their perception of secretive businesses and poor handling of hazardous chemicals will improve.

IMPACT ON BUSINESS

Another public perception is that business does not pay enough attention to chemical releases both inside and outside the facility, calling forth as proof the necessity to enact regulations and laws like the OSHA Hazard Communication Standard (employee right-to-know) and Title III of SARA (community right-to-know). Coupled with the publicity surrounding Bhopal and numerous industrial accidents involving chemicals in the United States, these perceptions gain widespread credence.

If the situation is handled properly, with open and honest cooperation between businesses and the communities in which they operate, the social impact will be very beneficial. The barriers between business and people, real or perceived, can be broken down rather quickly by actions taken by regulated facilities to inform and protect people living near by. Meetings held by company personnel with citizens to explain what goes on inside the facility, what chemicals are used and what their hazards are will go a long way to foster good will.

Emergency plans which include drills involving neighbors will train and inform them on what to do and how to protect themselves in a chemical emergency, and tours and meetings inside the facility will remove many fears. Companies that use hazardous chemicals and take great pains to promote safety should reap public relations benefits by showing the community how hard they work to protect employees, visitors, neighbors, property and the environment. Companies that use hazardous chemicals and do not promote chemical safety inside and outside the facility must begin to do so immediately, because they will certainly not survive the lawsuits against them for not complying with the law. The benefits to the company by complying with the OSHA standard and Title III were pointed out in Chapter 1. It has always made good economic and social sense to cooperate with employees and neighbors in the protection of their health and welfare. Now there are laws to require it, and laggard businesses will be forced to comply and to enjoy the aforementioned benefits. In short, noncompliance is foolish.

Cooperation with the local LEPC is a rapid way to develop good public relations with the community, since many of the members of the LEPC will be influential community members.

Cooperation with the fire department is good common sense, but previous relationships between business in general and fire services have shown a remarkable lack of this quality. The industrialist, for some reason, has always feared the fire inspector. Perhaps he felt that the fire department would shut him down for certain safety violations. If so, this shows how wrong the businessman can be. Of course, if the owner/operator knew of safety violations, it was encumbent upon him to correct them, certainly at some cost. If he was not aware of them, he had an opportunity to receive a *free* safety inspection, and a list of *what* to correct and how to do so. Unless conditions within the facility presented a clear and present danger to human life or health, it is doubtful that the inspector would shut the operation down. However, if such conditions *did* exist, it certainly deserved to be shut down.

Usually the owner/operator simply does not understand the function of the fire inspector and the concerns of the fire department. One usually fears what one doesn't understand. It is imperative that the fire department make itself and its operations and concerns known to businessmen, and that businessmen reciprocate.

The fire inspector doesn't want to learn any trade secrets. What he wants is to ensure that the facility conforms to the local fire code, which is concerned with human safety and health inside any facility, industrial, commercial or public. He is also concerned with the safety of emergency responders to an incident in the plant. He wants to make sure that firefighters know how to rescue persons, fight fires, or handle other emergencies in the safest and quickest manner. The only way he can do this is to perform a complete inspection of the facility. At the end of such an inspection, he will provide the owner/operator with a list of infractions (if any) and suggest how they can be corrected.

The impact on businesses will be far more beneficial than anyone intended. This law, like the OSHA Hazard Communication Standard, is *good* for business, because it forces businesses into relationships that are good for them. Many businesses have been cooperating with the public, their employees, and the fire service for a long time, but the majority have not. Title III will change that situation.

IMPACT ON THE LOCAL FIRE DEPARTMENT

Fire services across the country have been mixed in their reviews of Title III. One chief has called it a "Godsend," while others have used very different descriptive terms. Many fire departments have adopted a wait-and-see attitude, while others have taken steps to try to cope with problems. However, the authors firmly believe that SARA is very good for the fire service.

It is understood that a tremendous amount of work will have to be done as the required information is sent in by regulated facilities; it is further understood that the vast majority of fire departments feel that they do not have the capability to deal with it. Furthermore, the cost (mentioned above) to each fire department may be substantial. However, the benefits to the fire services far outweigh the costs, and the seemingly impossible task of assimilating the chemical information sent to them is not really that great, even if the department does not have computers available. A systematic approach to the gathering of chemical information is provided in Chapter 6 as Exhibits 1 and 2 and Appendix D. This approach will not severely tax the capabilities of even the smallest fire department, paid or volunteer.

The ultimate benefit to local fire departments is that eventually they will be told of every hazardous chemical present in the covered facility, where and in what container is it stored, how much is usually present, and what the major hazards are for each chemical. This provides the fire service with the long-sought information needed to protect themselves when responding to an incident at the covered facility.

They will now know for what chemicals to prepare themselves and can provide the proper education, training and equipment needed to handle these chemicals safely. This will be true for the entire department, not just the hazardous materials response team, if one exists. The department will have available detailed descriptions of all chemicals, including their physical and chemical properties, physical and chemical hazards, how to recognize them when they are released, how they behave in a release, how they behave in a fire, how to respond to both fire and nonfire situations, and the manner in which responders may protect themselves while handling the incident.

In other words, fire departments will now have all the information they need to respond *safely* to a hazardous materials incident. That information must be used promptly and properly to provide the education and training needed by everyone who might become an emergency responder. The chief of the fire department can now be forewarned of the presence of certain hazardous chemicals, and it is his responsibility to see that his people are properly educated, trained and equipped to handle incidents at the reporting facility.

This represents a radical change from the past, when the local fore department usually had no idea of what chemicals were present at a particular facility. Even if they did have this information, they usually had no idea of how to handle the situation safely. There were many injuries and deaths due to this lack of information and the subsequent lack of education, training and equipment. This is the other major goal of Title III: to make sure that vital chemical information is provided to the fire service. The sharing of this vital information is the manner in which Congress intended the fire service to be protected.

Title III is good for the fire service, but positive action will be required by each local fire department to take advantage of the law.

POSSIBLE FUTURE CHANGES IN LEGISLATION

Definite threshold reporting levels have been set for particular hazardous chemicals; the yearly changes mandated by the current law are listed in Chapter 2. However, nothing is permanent. There may be future changes in the chemicals covered, their reporting levels and the methods of reporting. Special interest groups may lobby to have their constituencies treated in a different manner from what the law currently mandates. Title III has already been expanded to cover businesses not in the manufacturing sector, and more changes will certainly come.

In enacting enabling legislation that the state legislatures feel is necessary in carrying out compliance with Title III, many states may modify some required activities, but this must be done within the framework of the federal law. Lawsuits surely will be filed as different covered entities test the parts of the law that they feel are unfair to them, or have been incorrectly interpreted and/or enforced by the LEPC or SERC. Any change will have some impact on some portion of the three groups mentioned above, namely, society, business, and the fire service. It is not possible to predict what future Congresses or other legislative bodies will do in the area of regulation of chemicals and the information concerning them, but it is safe to assume that regulation will not lessen.

It is also safe to assume that if current legislation does not produce the desired results, more stringent regulation will result. It is absolutely imperative that cooperation exist among the three above-mentioned entities for Title III to achieve what its sponsors intended. This law has been written to ensure uniform regulation across the country and to avoid the hodgepodge of local right-to-know laws that were passed after the Hazard Communication Standard was enacted. A variety of laws regulating one company in several geographic areas of the country could cripple to that company, and any like it with multiple U.S. locations.

As Title III promotes understanding and goodwill among regulated businesses, the communities that surround them, and the fire departments that serve them, the problems should ease. As other regulations now in existence correct other problems of disposal of hazardous wastes (entirely separate and different types of material from hazardous chemicals), the last generators of hazardous wastes that remain unregulated will fall under new laws that are certain to appear. This last bastion of environmental pollution is the individual household, which, because of its vast political power through the individual vote, has escaped all consideration of regulation. It is currently unknown how much damage is done to our environment by the waste generated by millions of households, but it could easily be more damaging than what has been done by industry.

If this premise is true, why has such damage to the environment not been evident up to now? The answer is simple. Industrial pollution tends to concentrate in certain areas where heavy industry itself is located. The areas where materials were dumped prior to regulation were generally close to the company dump site, and any damage done would show up rapidly (in a few years or up to 20 years) because of the concentration of dumped materials. After regulations were passed to controll where hazardous wastes could be dumped, special landfill sites were selected to receive these wastes. The landfills were constructed in such a manner as to prevent the leaching out or other escape of the hazardous wastes dumped there. It took longer (and will continue to take longer) for the damage from these sites to appear.

In the case of household waste, there are more sites available to receive such garbage, and the wastes themselves, taken as a whole, are far less hazardous than industrial wastes. Consequently, very little, if any, attention has been paid to the content of household waste. Hazardous substances are certainly discarded by every household, and it will simply take longer for this damage to become evident. At the first indication of such damage, legislation *will* be introduced to regulate it. Human beings, particularly in the industrialized countries, are continuing to foul their own nests. The really disturbing problem is that the developing nations have learned nothing about our history of environmental pollution and are therefore doomed to repeat it.

Chapter 3

REGULATED HAZARDOUS MATERIALS

Regulation of chemicals in the United States consists of a fragmented and disjointed assortment of laws, rules, standards and governmental agencies established to enforce them. There is also a great deal of confusion surrounding the difference between hazardous chemicals, hazardous materials, hazardous substances and hazardous wastes. This confusion is increased by even newer laws giving agencies which formerly controlled hazardous wastes additional regulatory responsibilities for hazardous chemicals, extremely hazardous substances and toxic substances.

It is not the purpose of this chapter to try to cover every regulation and governmental agency empowered to act in the field of hazardous materials, substances and wastes. Rather, the focus is on those aspects of current (as of this writing) regulations concerning employee and community right-to-know, with emphasis on the latter. It is also not the intention of the authors to attempt to cover the myriad state and local right-to-know laws that have been enacted in the last few years. They will be mentioned briefly in this chapter, but serious readers should inquire in their own locales about the existence of such a law and its effect on them.

Basically, the discussion of the regulation of hazardous chemicals in this chapter concerns principally the EPA and, briefly, OSHA. The chronolgy of the basic regulations covered in this book, SARA and the OSHA Hazard Communication Standard, appear in Chapter 2. This chapter focuses on what chemicals are regulated by these two laws, with a brief discussion of the original law to tie everything together (mentioned immediately below).

TOXIC SUBSTANCE CONTROL ACT

The Toxic Substance Control Act (TSCA) (15 USC 2601 *et seq.*, Public Law 94-469 [Oct. 11, 1976], Stat. 2027) was enacted to require the testing of potentially toxic chemicals in order to determine their capability of harming humans upon exposure. It also empowered the EPA to stop, or at least control, the manufacture of such chemicals based on the results of that testing. TSCA addressed all the hazards of all chemicals created before its enactment, as well as the synthesis and production of new substances. It required the creation of a list that included every "chemical substance and mixture" in existence.

TSCA was the first major attempt to control all chemical substances. There were other laws covering certain chemicals, such as pesticides, regulated under the Federal Insecticide, Fungicide and Rodenticide Act (FIFRA); food, food additives, drugs or cosmetics regulated by the Food and Drug Administration (FDA) and the Federal Food, Drug and Cosmetic Act (FFDCA); and tobacco and tobacco products controlled by the Bureau of Alcohol, Tobacco and Firearms.

Chemical substances were defined by TSCA as "any organic or inorganic substance of a particular molecular identity, including any combination of such substances occurring in whole or part as a result of a chemical reaction or occurring in nature, and any chemical element or uncombined radical." The EPA has control over these chemical substances in other areas, especially when a substance ends up as a "waste," but TSCA was intended to be the legislation that, once and for all, would gather all chemicals into a list and determine whether they were hazardous or not. It caused a great deal of anguish in American industry when it was first proposed and then again when it was enacted. However, industry survived and a giant step was taken in the effort to deal with the chemical problem in the United States.

This problem was recognized by all levels of the population, being characterized in books that brought the message home to everyone. However, at that time, the major problems were not generally believed to endanger workers exposed to chemicals in the workplace, but rather to affect the population at large when these chemicals were accidentally or deliberately released into the environment. Although it is not the purpose of this book to discuss all the regulations surrounding the issue of hazardous chemicals, the following regulations are mentioned as precursors to the current law. Indeed, the pattern of chemical regulation in the United States shows that each new regulation is built on a previous one. This condition is the major factor contributing to the confusion that exists today.

1. Section 311 of the Clean Water Act was created with the Federal Water Pollution Control Amendments of 1972 (P.L. 92-500). It was enacted in response to oil well blowouts and oil spills that occurred in the 1960s.

2. Section 7003 of the Resource Conservation and Recovery Act (RCRA) (1976 and subsequent amendments of 1980) established procedures by which lawsuits could be filed to force the cleanup of hazardous waste dump sites.

3. The Comprehensive Environmental Response, Compensation and Liability Act of 1980 (CERCLA) was the result of public furor over the health hazards presented by abandoned hazardous waste dumps. Title II of CERCLA set up the original Superfund.

These three regulations all deal with hazardous wastes and are mentioned only because they are of historical significance in the development of current employee and community right-to-know laws, which deal with hazardous chemicals, extremely hazardous chemicals and toxic substances, rather than hazardous wastes. Anyone who has dealt with hazardous chemicals in his or her company is familiar with these regulations. This is especially true of RCRA, the landmark legislation which attempts to solve the hazardous waste problem. RCRA and CERCLA are the most important laws in the war on hazardous chemicals.

OSHA HAZARD COMMUNICATION STANDARD

OSHA has been charged with the responsibility of creating far-reaching regulations to protect workers from injury in the workplace. In recent years, this effort has expanded beyond protection from dangerous work rules and injury-producing machines and tools to include exposure to hazardous chemicals in the workplace. During its public hearings held for comments about the proposal to create a Hazard Communication Standard, OSHA considered extending the regulations to create a community right-to-know law, but decided that its mission was to provide a mechanism to protect only exposed employees. Legislation to give people outside a covered facility the right to gain information concerning chemicals used inside that facility would have to be left to subsequent legislation (which turned out to be SARA).

After a few unsuccessful attempts to issue a satisfactory standard (over several few years), on November 25, 1983, OSHA published in the Federal Register its Hazard Communication Standard (HCS or Standard) final rule. This regulation, also known as the "Employee Right-to-Know Law," is basically concerned with the exposure of workers to hazardous chemicals in the workplace.

By November 25, 1985, all manufacturers, importers and distributors of hazardous chemicals had to label the containers they shipped listing the ingredients and hazards of the material in the containers, and provide MSDSs to all downstream users, handlers and storers of these chemicals.

By May 25, 1986, all employers in the manufacturing sector (businesses that had SIC codes 20 to 39) and certain other businesses had to be in compliance with all the regulations of the

Standard. (Note: On August 24, 1987, the Standard was extended to cover all employers with employees exposed to hazardous chemicals in the workplaces. MSDSs had to be provided with the next shipment after September 23, 1987, and all employers had to be in compliance with the Standard by May 23, 1988.)

Under the regulations set forth by the HCS, an employer must:

1. Develop a written hazard communication plan and make it available to employees.
2. Ensure that the proper labels and/or warnings appear on all containers of hazardous chemicals.
3. Develop and make available to all exposed employees a list that includes all hazardous chemicals known to be present in the workplace.
4. Obtain or develop an MSDS for each hazardous chemical in the workplace and make it available to all exposed workers.
5. Train and inform all exposed employees so that they will be aware of the physical and health hazards of each hazardous chemical to which they will be exposed, how to protect themselves during exposure, and how to recognize and react to an accidental release of the material.

There are a few exceptions to these rules, including somewhat less stringent requirements for laboratory workers.

Each manufacturer or importer had to determine the hazards of the chemicals they manufactured or imported; these were broken down into 23 physical and health hazards. If a substance possessed any of these properties, it was by definition a hazardous chemical and therefore had to have an MSDS listing certain properties and hazards in a loosely specified form. In any event, if, after testing, it was determined that the chemical did not fall into any of these 23 categories, but was listed in certain other references, the Standard said that it too was hazardous by definition.

The Standard recognized four references as establishing that certain chemicals are hazardous. Any materials listed in these references were also, by definition, hazardous chemicals. Those sources are:

1. 29 CFR Part 1910, Subpart Z, Toxic and Hazardous Substances.
2. *Threshold Limit Values for Chemical Substances and Physical Agents in the Work Environment,* American Conference of Governmental Industrial Hygienists (ACGIH), latest edition.
3. *National Toxicology Report (NTP) Annual Report on Carcinogens,* latest edition.
4. International Agency for Research on Cancer (IARC), Monographs on the Evaluation of Carcinogenic Risk of Chemicals to Humans.

A great deal of frustration has arisen over the way hazardous chemicals are defined by the Standard, since most people feel more comfortable if they have a list of chemicals to which they can refer, and the Standard provides no such list. In addition, chemicals that were never considered hazardous because they do not enter easily into chemical reactions or are not harmful to humans by contact with the skin are now considered a dust hazard (particularly inorganic, noncombustible, nontoxic dusts that can enter the respiratory system). Many manufacturers felt that it was easier to provide MSDSs on everything they made than to sort through the list of chemicals used at their facility in order to determine whether or not an MSDS was really necessary for each substance. In this way, materials that were nonhazardous ended up with accompanying MSDSs, which, according to some persons, made them hazardous by definition. This would have implications later under certain reporting requirements of SARA.

The heart and soul of the OSHA Hazard Communication Standard is the warning, informing and training of employees who are exposed to hazardous chemicals, with the MSDS as the main source of warnings and information. Labels and other forms of warning, including the list of hazardous chemicals, supplement the MSDS, and this information, together with training on how to use it, must be presented to the employee. All of this is part of the required written hazard communication program, which is the company's mission statement in reference to employees' right to know.

TITLE III OF SARA

SARA was enacted on October 17, 1986. It is made up of three sections or titles, only one of which will be discussed here. It is referred to simply as "Title III" or the "Community Right-to-Know Law." Its various sections on implementation, reporting and emergency planning are covered in other chapters. This chapter focuses on the chemicals regulated by the law. A combined list of the various chemicals covered by the different sections of the law is presented in Appendix C.

A. Extremely Hazardous Substances and the CERCLA Section 103(a) List

On November 17, 1986, the EPA published in the Federal Register the list of Extremely Hazardous Substances as an interim rule and published the final rule on April 22, 1987, containing 406 substances. This list determines whether or not a company becomes a "covered facility" under Section 302 of SARA. Any company that has any of these materials present in excess of their threshold planning quantity must have reported to the SERC by May 17, 1987, the fact that one or more of these materials were present. At that time, it was not necessary to disclose which material or how much of each were present; listed as a "covered facility" was enough.

This list is a "living" list, which means that additions to or subtractions from it may be made at any time. These changes are published in the Federal Register as they are made.

Section 304 calls for emergency notification of releases of any material on the list of Extremely Hazardous Substances (a Section 302(a) chemical) and specifies three methods of notification, depending upon the type of chemical released. The types of releases are as follows:

1. A Section 302(a) chemical is one that requires notification under Section 103(a) of CERCLA.
2. A Section 302(a) chemical is not subject to notification requirements of Section 103(a) of CERCLA.
3. The chemical is not a Section 302(a) chemical but does require a CERCLA notification under Section 103(a) of CERCLA

This is the portion of the law that regulates the CERCLA hazardous substances under SARA.

B. Toxic Substances

The third list of hazardous chemicals regulated by SARA (the first two being the SARA Section 302(a) list and the CERCLA Section 103(a) list) is called "Specific Toxic Chemical Listings." It is regulated under Section 313 concerning releases of such material from the facility.

C. OSHA-Defined Hazardous Chemicals

On October 17, 1987, all facilities subject to the Occupational Health and Safety Act of 1970 and all amendments (including the above-mentioned Hazard Communication Standard) had to submit MSDSs, or a list of chemicals for which an MSDS was required, to the SERC, the LEPC, and the local fire department with jurisdiction over the facility. This means that SARA regulates all substances that are characterized by the Standard as hazardous (having one or more of 23 physical and/or health hazards), as well as those listed in the four references mentioned earlier.

Since the Standard covers so many health and physical hazards, the list of substances qualifying under the regulation does not exist in any one place. Even if such a list existed, any new substances created by manufacturers using chemical reactions or simply mixing substances together would be added to the list. This is so because TSCA and the Standard provide for testing and "hazard determination," respectively. It would be rare, indeed, if a new substance did not qualify for one or both of these lists and was subsequently covered by SARA. The only exceptions, besides truly nonhazardous substances, would be materials covered under FIFRA or other federal statutes strictly regulating those materials, which, coincidentally, require stricter reporting than under SARA.

DEPARTMENT OF TRANSPORTATION

The U.S. Department of Transportation (DOT) regulates certain substances in transportation, having published a Hazardous Materials Table in the Federal Register on May 22, 1980. DOT should be consulted for any updated versions of the list. The purpose of this regulation is to promote safety in the transportation of chemicals through the use of a placarding and label warning system, proper notification through shipping papers, and the establishment of particular hazard classes. In addition, the regulation specifies certain materials that are so hazardous that they may not be shipped by common carrier.

The DOT list has nothing to do with SARA and indeed, includes devices and articles in addition to specific chemicals, solutions and mixtures. It is mentioned here because it is often included in lists of regulated hazardous substances covered by state and local right-to-know laws. However, it is safe to say that all chemicals considered hazardous by DOT are covered by OSHA and subsequently by SARA, because many of the same parameters of hazard classification are used by OSHA and DOT.

STATE AND LOCAL RIGHT-TO-KNOW LAWS

While OSHA was holding public hearings in anticipation of developing its Hazard Communication Standard, there was considerable feeling throughout the country that OSHA was dragging its feet in moving toward a tough employee right-to-know law. Basically, the labor movement, the original force behind right-to-know laws, was worried that the major chemical companies would try to dilute the beneficial effect that a strong federal standard would have on what was perceived as a major cause of occupational disease: exposure of workers to hazardous chemicals. Workers felt that if this occurred, the federal government would be able to say that it had done what it could to solve the perceived problem, and the chemical industry could continue with business as usual, allegedly causing harm to anyone who was exposed to their products.

The labor movement totally misread the chemical industry's position on the safety of anyone who came in contact with chemicals in the workplace, or anywhere else for that matter. In fact, chemical manufacturers were (and still are) just as concerned for the safety of their customers' employees as they were for their own employees—and their concern about their own employees was and still is considerable. During the public hearings held by OSHA to gather comments on the proposed Hazard Communication Standard, every major producer of chemicals spoke in favor of a strong federal standard protecting employees who were and would be exposed to chemicals in the workplace.

The rationale was simple. The major U.S. chemical companies work very hard to maintain an outstanding safety record in their own operations, and their efforts have been very successful. The vast majority of exposures to these hazardous chemicals occur downstream, in the plants of the processors who buy chemicals from the major (and sometimes minor) chemical manufacturers and use those chemicals as raw materials to make their their own products. If injuries and illnesses affected the workers exposed to such chemicals, there might be a stigma attached to the suppliers, regardless of their own safety record. If safety while using chemicals could be extended to all individuals using (and therefore exposed to) those chemicals, both the chemical manufacturing and processing industries would be safer, and the public interest would be advanced.

The question of liability also had to be considered by the chemical industry. If a buyer of a chemical was totally unaware of the hazards of exposure to that chemical, any liability for injury to himself or to an exposed employee might be attached to the manufacturer. However, if a method could be developed to transmit safety information to the employee, and if a program of training and teaching about the hazards of the chemical and safety measures to use were also mandated by law, the responsibility for providing that information would be transferred to the employer (buyer of the chemical), removing the manufacturer from a great deal of liability exposure.

But the movement for a stronger right-to-know law was already in progress. Activists all over the country began to lobby lawmakers on the state and local levels to enact laws specific to their jurisdictions. The argument against a multitude of different regulations failed in many political subdivisions, and city councilmen and state legislatures produced their own versions of protection for workers in the workplace. Some legislatures went further and included community right-to-know provisions in their laws. At one point, the flurry of regulation activity was such that legislators were passing ordinances covering their communities that contained the name of the community from which they had obtained a copy of the law.

Currently, at least 23 states have enacted right-to-know laws in some form; an unknown number of cities and other political subdivisions have also promulgated their own right-to-know regulations. This creates an extremely confusing situation, with many businesses totally unaware of their obligations under any or all of these laws. However, it is becoming increasingly clear, through litigation, that the federal OSHA Standard is paramount in any conflict with state or local laws. If doubt exists as to what substances are covered by SARA, this Standard is the regulation to which SARA refers in establishing the hazardous chemicals covered (in addition to Sections III. A. and III. B. discussed above). Again, in any particular state or other political subdivision, one must check to see if laws *in addition* to SARA are in effect. compliance with federal regulations does not *always* ensure compliance with state or local regulations.

Chapter 4

HOW INDUSTRY SHOULD COMPLY WITH SARA

THE FACILITY COORDINATOR

Compliance with SARA involves more than the mandatory reporting activities, although that is all that most people feel must be done to satisfy the requirements of the law. Built into the law is an implication of cooperation, sharing of information, and sharing of tasks in the name of the community. The law requires that a Facility Coordinator be named by the regulated facility (this had to be done by September 17, 1987) to participate in the emergency planning process. This is probably the most important function that the company can perform after reporting the presence of its hazardous chemicals.

By October 17, 1988, the LEPC must have prepared an emergency plan covering the geographical area that it represents. This plan, at a minimum, must identify all regulated facilities within the LEPC's planning district, the routes likely to be used for the transportation of extremely hazardous substances, and the presence of other facilities that contribute to additional risk (e.g., utilities like the gas company) or are subjected to additional risk (e.g., hospitals, nursing homes, schools).

The formulation of such an emergency plan is not easy. The responsibility for its eventual completion and success falls ultimately on the LEPC, but probably the most important support role is played by the Facility Coordinator. This person's job is to develop emergency plans for his or her own facility and coordinate them with the district's emergency plan. In reality, after the LEPC plans such tasks as transportation, housing, feeding and caring for evacuees plans which probably already exist as part of an overall disaster plan for natural calamities), the most important task is that of the Facility Coordinator.

It is the Facility Coordinator's job to emphasize the hazards of the chemicals manufactured, stored or used at the facility and to set up procedures by which the community (populated area) around the facility will be notified and evacuated, if necessary, in case of a release of a substance that could cause them harm. He or she must provide this information to the LEPC because, for the most part, the LEPC consists of individuals who have no special expertise in the understanding of chemicals, the potential harm of particular chemicals, or how to protect against that harm. If the LEPC does include people who have some chemical expertise, they will need all the planning help they can get from the Facility Coordinator to complete the plan.

Most companies will select their Safety Manager, or their OSHA or EPA Compliance Officer, to act as their Facility Coordinator. This is satisfactory as long as this person has the requisite chemical knowledge to determine how a chemical substance may be released, what its dispersal pattern will be under all conditions, and what kind of harm it will cause to people, property, systems (such as highways, drinking water supplies, telephone service and other utilities) and the environment. Company politics may control who is named as Facility Coordinator (It may be considered a very prestigious job and given to someone important, or it may be deemed a nuisance and assigned to the lowest-ranking person.), and this could ultimately produce disastrous results. The duties of the Facility Coordinator are very important to the safety of the community as a whole, since any chemical emergency at the facility will have a profound effect on those immediately nearby, and will spread to the entire community as the LEPC emergency plan goes into effect.

This message is clear. The Facility Coordinator for any facility should be chosen on the basis of his or her understanding of the chemicals at the facility, including the following:

1. The chemical processes (and/or storage procedures) used
2. The properties of the chemicals themselves
3. The behavior of those chemicals under all conditions of release, such as:
   a. Physical form of the chemical as released
   b. Weather condition (current and forecast) under which it was released
   c. Geographical area of impact
   d. Probable harm that will be caused
   e. Any unusual reactions to be expected (will the substance react differently than other chemicals that are similar to it?)
   f. Any special education, training and/or equipment needed by first responders
4. How much of each chemical may be present at particular times
5. Any other information that might be pertinent to a specific chemical

The Facility Coordinator must have the authority within his or her own company to undertake any and all tasks related to working with the LEPC. This person should have the power to make certain decisions during emergencies, some of which may not be in the best financial interest of the company but are necessary to protect the safety of its employees and of the community. For example, the facility may be operating a process that is extremely costly to start up and that, once running, would cause a great financial loss if shut down. If a chemical emergency occurred that would be exacerbated by the continued operation of the process, and it became clear that there was some probability of harm to the community if this process continued, the Facility Coordinator should have the power to shut it down. This may be the most difficult duty the Coordinator may ever have to perform, and it takes great courage for a company to invest this power in one person.

The Facility Coordinator must have the ability to deal with the variety of people of diverse backgrounds found in any given LEPC. This includes not only the above-mentioned people who have no knowledge of chemicals and how they may react when released, but also political appointees who may use the appointment to the LEPC for their own gain. There may also be many well-intentioned people appointed to the LEPC who have no other responsibilities and who use committee and subcommittee meetings to further their social lives. There will also be members of the LEPC from special interest groups (as mandated by SARA), whose attitude toward a chemical manufacturer or a user or storer of chemicals may not necessarily be friendly. This person may be extremely suspicious of the Facility Coordinator, thinking that the Coordinator may be trying to hide something rather than cooperating in the planning process with the other members of the LEPC.

Thus, the Facility Coordinator's job is extremely difficult. It is of paramount importance to overcome all the obstacles created by company politics and the politics of the LEPC, and to do the best kind of emergency planning for his or her company and the community. The Coordinator must start with well-documented inventory records and records of chemical shipments into and out of the facility; storage procedures used while the chemicals are on the premises; the way the materials are handled from the time they arrive and go into (and out of) storage; and the processes employed when the chemicals are utilized within the facility. The Coordinator must be familiar with all the chemical and physical properties of each substance used, since these will determine their behavior when released.

The Facility Coordinator must be familiar with the containers used to ship materials into and out of the facility, as well as the containers used to store or handle them while on site. He or she must know the signs of stress on each type of container, as well as the method by which the container will breech (open) under such stress. It is obvious that a paper bag of powdered material has different stress characteristics than a metal cylinder containing a gas under pressure, and certainly the materials in these two containers will disperse differently when released. The Coordinator must be aware that not all paper bags are the same, just as not all cylinders containing pressurized gas are the same. He or she must also be aware that some pressurized gases are merely compressed, whereas others are stored as liquids. This means that the containers are radically different, as will be the consequence of simple (or catastrophic) failure of the two types of tanks.

The Facility Coordinator should be an expert in the storage of chemicals, knowing how the safety codes (safety rules) that prevail in his or her area demand that certain hazardous substances be stored (or not stored). He or she must ensure that these safety rules are enforced in his facility.

The Facility Coordinator must be able to keep up with an ever-changing inventory and with the appearance of chemicals that are new to the facility. It is necessary to cooperate closely with the person in charge of the OSHA Hazard Communication Standard at the facility, and to have constant access to MSDSs, the list of hazardous chemicals present in the workplace, and other information. In many cases, the Facility Coordinator may also be the person in charge of hazard communication; this will ease and speed the flow of information.

Once the Facility Coordinator knows what materials are present, how they are stored and/or handled and/or used, and what their chemical and physical properties are, he or she must incorporate this information into a meaningful emergency plan for the facility. The plan must not only work for the facility, but must be able to be incorporated into the LEPC's community emergency plan.

The Facility Coordinator must be willing to share this information with the planners of the LEPC. His or her company has the right to maintain it secrets, but it is imperative that the information shared be as accurate and complete as is necessary to allow smooth functioning of all emergency procedures if a major release occurs. An emergency of this sort is no time for owners of the facility to be concerned about secret information becoming available to competitors.

A chemical release could result from a fire somewhere in the facility, or it may be a natural occurrence, such as an earthquake, hurricane, flood, or some other force of nature. The Facility Coordinator can learn from the Disaster Services Agency (or its local equivalent) what steps must be followed, since this work probably has already been done the the local Disaster Services Coordinator. He or she may also request that the facility be included in a mock disaster drill; the experience gained from practicing emergency procedures will be invaluable should an actual release ever happen.

The Facility Coordinator must share all chemical information, including container types and locations, and the probable movement of the material in all kinds of releases, terrain, and weather and wind conditions. This person should coordinate his and the facility's activities in an emergency with the fire department and other first responders and emergency personnel. He or she must coordinate the use of any special equipment that the facility may possess to help mitigate the incident. The facility might also consider donating special equipment to the local fire department, in support of a Hazardous Materials Response Team, or regular firefighting equipment, which might free up some of the department's budget for equipment of their own choosing. The facility might also consider lending some of their personnel to help train first responders in the specific chemical danger they might face.

The Facility Coordinator must also provide information to the LEPC concerning the manner in which hazardous chemicals are shipped into and out of regulated facilities, including the routes taken and the type of carrier used. Hazardous chemicals are shipped not only by truck and rail, but also by pipeline. It is important for the LEPC to know this so that the information can be incorporated into its community emergency plan.

The Facility Coordinator must also work closely with people who live near his facility and provide them with the information (and training) that they will need in case of an emergency involving hazardous chemicals. They can be involved in fire drills and mock releases, so that they will have the experience to react properly in case of a real emergency. The facility *must* become a good neighbor in every sense of the word.

HOW TO CLASSIFY HAZARDOUS MATERIALS FOR SECTION 312 REPORTING

The deadline for reporting under Section 312 was March 1, 1988. At that time, facilities subject to Section 312 reporting, that is, every facility that contained, at any given time, 10,000 pounds or more of a hazardous chemical (as defined by the five categories listed below) or 500 pounds (or the threshold planning quantity, whichever is lower) or more of an extremely hazardous substance (as listed in the Federal Register on April 22, 1987, beginning at page 13397) had to report the presence of such chemicals. This report had to be submitted to the SERC, the LEPC, and the local fire department with jurisdiction over the facility.

This information was to be reported as "Tier I" information, which is defined as general information on the amount and location of hazardous chemicals by category, or "Tier II" information, which consists of more detailed information on individual chemicals. The authors recommend that each regulated facility bypass the Tier I stage and provide Tier II information, which may (and probably will) be requested by any or all of the agencies to which the report must be sent.

You may, of course, report under Tier I, but it is to your economic advantage to have the Tier II information in your possession. The economic advantages include the fact that you will have much better knowledge of the hazardous chemicals in your facility, where they are and how they are stored. You may be able to streamline your inventory (and purchasing) procedures to the point where you will be able to save money on purchasing the proper "economic quantity," getting a lower unit price on the material because of the increased volume purchased, purchasing (and therefore receiving and handling) the material less often, and not losing valuable production time because you are out of a necessary raw material. And since you will probably be asked to provide Tier II information anyway, it will save money to do it the first time and avoid having to repeat much of the work.

Gathering Tier II information will also allow you to stay in compliance with the OSHA Hazard Communication Standard. It is possible to fall out of compliance with the Standard in the following ways:

1. Bringing in new chemicals and failing to add them to the Hazardous Chemicals List
2. Failing to provide new and/or revised MSDSs for employees
3. Failing to train and inform employees about the hazards of the new chemicals if they possess different hazards and appearances than chemicals for which the employees were previously trained
4. Failing to train and inform new employees of the hazards of current chemicals to which they will be exposed

Of course, avoiding an OSHA fine for noncompliance is an economic advantage.

Compiling Tier II information will highlight any storage problems you may have, such as storing oxidizers next materials that burn. Correct storage and handling procedures make for a safer plant, a possible lowering of insurance premiums, and uninterrupted operation due to the prevention of fires and other chemical accidents. It simply makes good sense to bypass the Tier I reporting and provide complete Tier II information. However, if the agencies in your locale to which you must report insist on Tier I reporting, you should do so from the Tier II forms that you can fill out and keep for yourself. The economic advantage of this is that one or more of the agencies will probably come back and ask for Tier II information on one or more chemicals (which they will need for emergency planning), and you will not have to reconstruct the information or the report.

The following information is the form of reporting as stated in Title III. The authors recognize that some states have modified the forms that were published by EPA; in that event, you will be given those forms and instructions on how to complete them.

Chemical Identification

Tier II information must include the following:

1. The Chemical Abstract Services (CAS) registry number (which is specific to each chemical). This must be done for every chemical stored either as a pure material or as a component of a mixture. If there is no CAS number for the mixture listed, it may be left blank.
2. The specific chemical name. If a mixture is listed and it has a specific name, provide it.
3. Whether the substance is present as a pure material or as a mixture.
4. The physical state (gas, liquid or solid) in which the gas is stored. If the same substance is stored in more than one physical state, they must all be reported.

Maximum and Average Amounts Present

Title III calls for the reporting of the maximum amount of the chemical present at any given time, plus the average amount present, and includes the following directions on how to calculate these numbers:

1. Units to be used are pounds. For the maximum amount of each hazardous chemical, *estimate* the greatest amount present at the facility at any time during the reporting period and use the code given below as "reporting ranges."
   a. If the material is a gas or liquid, the volume should be multiplied by its appropriate density factor. For example, toluene weighs about 7.2 pounds per gallon. If you have 6,500 gallons of toluene present, you would record it as 46,800 (7.2 times 6,500) pounds.
2. If the hazardous chemical is present in a mixture, you may report the entire mixture or just that weight of the mixture represented by the chemical. For example, if you have 25,500 pounds of a mixture that is made up of 40% of a hazardous chemical and 60% of a nonhazardous chemical, you could either report all of the 25,500 pounds and give the name of the substance, or you could multiply 0.4 by 25,500 and report 10,200 pounds of the hazardous chemical present, checking the mixture option in the appropriate column.
3. For the average daily amount, you may add up all the actual daily amounts present for the year and divide by 365, or you may use any other method that will give the accurate amount that would have been present daily, on average. Use the code given in the following "reporting ranges."

Reporting Ranges

RANGE VALUE	WEIGHT RANGE IN POUNDS	
	FROM:	TO:
00	0	99
01	100	999
02	1,000	9,999
03	10,000	99,999
04	100,000	999,999
05	1,000,000	9,999,999
06	10,000,000	49,999,999
07	50,000,000	99,999,999
08	100,000,000	499,999,999
09	500,000,000	999,999,999
10	1 billion	>1 billion

Chemical and Physical Hazards

The EPA has tried to simplify the reporting process required under Section 312 by reducing the definition of a hazardous chemical from having 1 or more of 23 different physical and chemical properties, as used by the Hazard Communication Standard to describe a hazardous chemical, to five categories. These categories are as follows:

1. *Acute (Immediate) Health Hazard:* This includes all highly toxic, toxic, corrosive, sensitizing, irritating and other hazardous chemicals which will damage or produce an adverse effect on a target organ, as defined in 29 CFR 1910.1200, which manifests itself within a short period of time after a one-time exposure to the substance.
2. *Chronic Health Hazard:* This includes carcinogens and other chemicals which can cause damage or have an adverse effect on a target organ, as defined in 29 CFR 1910.1200, which manifests itself after a long period of time during or following repeated exposures to the substance.
3. *Fire Hazards:* This includes flammable and combustible liquids and solids, pyrophorics (air-reactive materials which burst into flame upon contact with air) and oxidizers, as defined in 29 CFR 1910.1200.
4. *Reactive Hazards:* This includes unstable reactive substances, organic peroxides and water-reactive substances, as defined in 29 CFR 1910.1200.
5. *Sudden Release of Pressure Hazards:* This includes explosives and compressed gases as defined in 29 CFR 1910.1200.

Some chemicals may possess more than one hazard, and they should all be noted in the proper column. For example, hydrogen cyanide is a Class A poison gas that may be shipped dissolved in water as hydrocyanic acid. However, if it is stored as a compressed gas, it will have to be classified as *both* an Acute Health Hazard and a Sudden Release of Pressure. And since hydrogen cyanide is also a flammable gas, that hazard must also be indicated. Benzene, a flammable liquid that is also carcinogenic, must be listed under Chronic Health Hazard and Fire Hazard. Other chemicals may be listed under only one classification. The information you need will most often be found on the MSDS provided by the manufacturer of the material, in the Health Hazard section and in the Fire Hazard section.

There may be times when you are not sure if you have listed all the hazards of a particular substance. Reread the MSDS and perhaps consult one or more reference books on hazardous chemicals. When in doubt as to what hazard to list, act in a conservative manner and list all the hazards indicated in your search. For example, you may be trying to decide how to list a particular proprietary solvent you have purchased, and the MSDS indicates that, in addition to being a combustible liquid (flash point above 100°F), it will produce a mild irritation of the skin after repeated exposure. It is easy to decide to check the Fire Hazard column, but do you include the second hazard, which may not seem to be life-threatening? The conservative approach would dictate that you include this hazard under the Chronic Health Hazard column. This may bring protests from those who claim that a mild irritation after repeated exposure to the liquid does not make a substance hazardous, and they may be right. However, it does meet the definition of an irritant given in Appendix A of the Final Rule of the OSHA Hazard Communication Standard as expanded on August 24, 1987, and listed in the Federal Register of that date on page 31884. Whether or not the actual test was performed on an albino rabbit can be determined by further research.

In summarizing what is necessary to properly classify hazardous chemicals, the following should be followed in using an MSDS to determine hazards:

1. Check the Health Hazard section for terms like"corrosive," "irritating," "sensitizing," "toxin," "toxic," "extremely toxic," "moderately toxic," "poison" or "Poison A" or "B". Look for phrases like "Get medical attention immediately . . . if ingested, inhaled, or in contact with eyes or skin." Other warning statements include "do not come in contact with materials or vapors." Any statements similar to these that indicate immediate harm to anyone exposed means that the material is an Acute Health Hazard.
2. Again checking the Health Hazard section, look for terms like "carcinogen," or any statement indicating damage to the body or organs after repeated or prolonged exposure or

exposures over a long period of time. These indicate that a material is a Chronic Health Hazard.

3. Check the Fire and Explosion Hazard section of the MSDS. If there are any indications that the product will burn, list it in the Fire Hazard column. Look for flash points, ignition (or autoignition) temperatures, flammable (or explosive) ranges, and extinguishing agents and procedures. If any information is given in any of these categories, the material is a Fire Hazard.

4. Check the Reactivity Data section or look for any statement on reactivity. Look for words like "reactive," "unstable," "polymerizes," "decomposes," "monomer," "organic peroxide," "water-reactive" (or "reacts with water") and "air-reactive" (or "reacts in air or oxygen"). Check the Special Handling Information and Special Precaution sections and look for terms like "keep away from moisture," "keep air from reaching material," or "decomposes on exposure to." All of these statements (and others) indicate a Reactive Hazard.

5. Check the Fire and Explosion Hazard, Reactivity Data, Special Handling and Special Precaution sections. Look for terms like "explodes," "explosive," "explosion," "under pressure," "gas," "compressed gas," "pressurized gas," "liquefied gas," or "gas under pressure." Also, check the Physical Data section to see if the material is listed as a gas. All of these points (plus others) indicate that the material has a Sudden Release of Pressure Hazard.

In addition to the use of the MSDS to determine how to classify the hazards of chemicals, there are several reference books and other sources that should be used. These are listed in Appendix D.

Location

For each chemical listed on the facility's Tier II Emergency and Hazardous Chemical Inventory form, the location of each chemical listed at this location should be identified as follows:

1. You may prepare either a site plan or facility map with site coordinates indicated for all buildings, lots, areas and so on throughout the facility or a list of site coordinates which correspond to these entities. In either case, designate locations with abbreviations of three letters or less. You must check the appropriate box to indicate whether you are submitting a site plan or a list of site coordinates.

2. In the "Site Location" column, enter the proper abbreviations corresponding to the location.

3. In the "Storage Code" column, refer to the "Storage Types" and "Temperature and Pressure Conditions" tables given as follows:

   a. Storage Types

CODE	TYPE OF STORAGE
A	Aboveground tank
B	Belowground tank
C	Tank inside building
D	Steel drum
E	Plastic or nonmetallic drum
F	Can
G	Carboy
H	Silo
I	Fiber drum
J	Bag
K	Box
L	Cylinder

Code	Type of Storage
M	Glass bottles or jugs
N	Plastic bottles or jugs
O	Tote bin
P	Tank wagon
Q	Rail car
R	Other

b. Temperature and Pressure Conditions

Code	Storage Conditions
	(Pressure)
1	Ambient pressure
2	Greater than ambient pressure
3	Less than ambient pressure
	(Temperature)
4	Ambient temperature
5	Greater than ambient temperature
6	Less than ambient temperature
7	Cryogenic conditions

The authors feel that it is easier for the Facility Coordinator, the LEPC, and the local fire department if you prepare the site plan or facility map. With that in mind, the following suggestions are made:

1. Prepare and provide a facility map for recording all buildings or tanks which contain the listed hazardous chemical. The code used will be "B" for building and "T" for tank, and will be numbered 1 through 9 (or higher), preceding by 0, as in B04, B12 and T09. If a tank is stored aboveground, it will be marked "A"; if belowground, "B."
2. Rooms in buildings recorded on the map will be lettered.
3. The floor on which the chemical is stored must be recorded as "1" for the first floor, "2" for the second, and so on.

If some of these suggested forms of reporting differ from the forms provided by your SERC, those forms will contain instructions on how to provide the necessary information. Much of the information given here will be standard in all jurisdictions, with some modifications in the location and container reporting.

Confidential Location Information

Title III allows confidential location information to be withheld from public disclosure. It does this providing a separate "Confidential Location Information Sheet" which should be used if the disclosure of the location of the hazardous chemical will compromise a company secret. Instead of being given on the Tier II "Emergency and Hazardous Chemical Inventory," location information should be provided on the separate "Confidential" form. It should be noted that claimed trade secrets do not allow the facility to withhold location information; however, a separate file is kept so that this information will be not released to the public as required by Title III.

Trade Secrets

Trade secret claims may be made for certain substances in connection with information required to be reported under Sections 303, 311, 312 and 313. If the owner/operator of a regulated facility wishes to claim a trade secret, he may withhold the specific chemical identity of a hazardous chemical, an extremely substance or a toxic substance, provided that he does the following:

1. Claims that the information is a trade secret.
2. Includes in his submittal the reasons for supporting the trade secret claim.
3. Forwards a copy of the submittal to the Administrator of the EPA providing the actual information claimed to be the trade secret.

For the owner/operator to be able to substantiate his claim, he must demonstrate that the information has not been provided to anyone other than:

1. A member of the LEPC
2. An employee of any governmental entity
3. Any employee of the claimant
4. Any person bound by a secrecy agreement

All releases of the substance claimed to be covered by a trade secret are regulated under Section 304 (notification of release). No claim of trade secrecy exempts any substance from section 304 reporting.

Whenever information is requested by any health professional, doctor or nurse who needs to have such information, it must be provided immediately, all claims of trade secrecy notwithstanding. Actually, anyone may petition the EPA Administrator for disclosure of the specific chemical identity of any extremely hazardous substance, toxic substance or hazardous chemical. The Administrator will review such petitions and make a judgment on whether the claim of trade secrecy is valid or not. Whichever side loses, a court appeal can be made.

In the event of a request from any person concerning the adverse effects of a substance whose specific chemical identity is withheld on the basis of trade secrecy, the SERC must provide such information to the petitioner without disclosing the chemical identity.

In emergency situations, the trade secret provisions of Title III are similar to those of the OSHA Hazard Communication Standard. If a treating physician or nurse has determined that a medical emergency exists because of exposure to a substance, and the specific chemical identity of the substance will aid in the emergency or first-aid diagnosis and treatment, the owner/ operator *must immediately provide to such persons making the request a copy of the MSDS, an inventory form, or a toxic chemical release form, whichever will provide the specific chemical identity of the substance.* The owner/operator may request a written confidentiality agreement and a written statement of need from the requesting physician or nurse, but may not demand that this be provided first. In other words, in case of a medical emergency declared by a doctor or nurse, the owner/operator cannot insist on receiving these documents before he provides the requested information. He must provide such forms or MSDS's first; later, after the emergency, he can demand that these documents be executed.

If no medical emergency exists, the specific chemical identity must still be provided to a health professional. However, in this case, the owner/operator *must first be given a written request for the information, a signed statement of need and a signed confidentiality agreement.*

SECTION 313 REPORTING

The focus of this rule is the toxic chemical release provision of Section 313 of Title III, which requires the completion of "Toxic Chemical Release Forms" for each toxic chemical on the list in Committee Print Number 99-169 of the Senate Committee on Environment and Public Works, titled "Toxic Chemicals Subject to Section 313 of the Emergency Planning and Community Right-to-Know Act of 1986" (including any revisions). This list, current as of the time of publication on February 16, 1988 is in the Federal Register (53 FR 4500) and is included in the Chemical List in Appendix C. EPA Form R, the "Toxic Chemical Release Inventory Reporting Form," and instructions for filling out Form R are also provided in Appendix D.

In general, every owner/operator of every regulated facility must take an inventory of all the chemicals manufactured, imported, processed or used at that facility and report the quantities of toxic chemicals present during the previous year. The inventory must include the total amount of these chemicals, including toxic chemicals that appear as pure chemicals, ingredients in mixtures and trade name products, and those present as impurities in other chemicals. There is a minimal concentration limitation, but it is the responsibility of the owner/operator to make sure that the inventory of toxic chemicals is complete. There are certain exemptions relating to stand-alone facilities that support a manufacturing process and to some laboratories within a covered facility.

The inventory of toxic chemicals present during the preceding year must be prepared not only by reviewing purchasing records and other methods by which chemicals enter the physical inventory of a covered facility, but by other methods as well. The Final Rule requires that each owner/operator of a covered facility review the operation for "chemical manufacturing." This review will determine if other chemicals are manufactured as by-products or impurities in other chemicals and, as such, might not show up in a normal inventory. It also allows the chemical being manufactured to be included in that inventory if it is a toxic chemical.

Regulated facilities include any facility which has 10 or more full-time employees, is in SIC Codes 20 through 39 (in effect on January 1, 1987), and manufactured, processed or otherwise used a toxic chemical in excess of its threshold planning quantity for the preceding year. The report or notification must have been made on July 1, 1988, for 1987 and must be made on each succeeding July 1 for the preceding year. It must be sent to the EPA Administrator and to an official or officials designated by the governor of each state.

The SIC code of the facility refers to its primary code. If the facility is made up of multiple establishments, its regulation is based on a comparison of "the value of products shipped and/or produced at [SIC] 20 through 39 establishments versus non-20 through establishments in that facility" as stated in Federal Register, Tuseday, February 16, 1988, page 4052, III A(3). If the volume for the SIC Code 20 through 39 establishments is greater than for non-20 through 39 establishments, the facility is regulated. If all the establishments are in the 20 through 39 categories, the facility is regulated. The facility is also regulated if any establishment within it manufactured, imported, processed or otherwise used a toxic chemical in excess of its threshold quantity.

The thresholds provided by the law are as follows:

1. For manufacturing or processing as defined:
    1987: 75,000 pounds
    1988: 50,000 pounds
    1989 and thereafter: 25,000 pounds
2. For toxic chemicals otherwise used, the threshold is 10,000 per year for all years.

"Manufacture" has been defined by the Final Rule as "to produce, prepare, import or compound a toxic chemical. Manufacture also applies to a toxic chemical that is produced coincidentally during the manufacture, processing, use, or disposal of another chemical or mixture of chemicals, including a toxic chemical that is separated from that other chemical or mixture of chemicals as a by-product, and a toxic chemical that remains in that other chemical or mixture as an impurity."

The term "process" means "the preparation of a toxic chemical, after its manufacture, for distribution in commerce—

1. in the same form or physical state as, or in a different form or physical state from, that in which it was received by the person so preparing such chemical, or
2. as part of an article containing the toxic chemical. Process also applies to the processing of a toxic chemical contained in a mixture or trade name product."

The term "use" or "otherwise use" means "any use of a toxic chemical that is not covered by the terms 'manufacture' or 'process' and includes the use of a toxic chemical contained in a mixture or trade name product. Relabeling or redistributing a container of a toxic chemical where no repackaging of the toxic chemical occurs does not constitute use or processing of the toxic chemical."

The Final Rule of February 16, 1988, allows exemptions for auxiliary facilities such as laboratories and warehouses that are classified as SIC Code 20 through 39 establishments because they support other manufacturing establishments. The exemption is for stand-alone operations, that is, for the warehouse or laboratory that exists in facilities separate from the manufacturing operation. The laboratory is exempt if manufacturing, processing or use of chemicals in the laboratory is under the supervision of a technically qualifed individual. Stand-alone warehouses are exempt from this rule if no manufacturing, processing (including repackaging) or use of a covered toxic chemical occurs.

Within a covered facility, a laboratory will not have to be reviewed for chemical manufacturing, processing or use, provided that its operation does not conduct specialty chemical production or pilot plant activities. The Final Rule also provides that "if a toxic chemical is removed from such a laboratory for further processing or use in the facility, the facility must factor such amounts into threshold determinations and release reporting."

Mixtures and trade name products imported, processed or used at a facility must be evaluated for the presence of toxic chemicals unless they are present in the amount of less than 1% [or 0.1% in the case of a carcinogen, as defined in 29 CFR 1910.1200(d) (4)]. This last exemption is the minimal limitation.

Articles are exempted from the reporting requirements if they fit the following description: "a manufactured item: (i) which is formed to a specific shape or design during manufacture, (ii) which has end use functions dependent in whole or in part upon its shape or design during end use; and (iii) which does not release a toxic chemical under normal conditions of processing or use of that item at the facility."

Form R is in four parts; Parts I and II are the same for each chemical. They may be photocopied and provided with Parts III and IV, which must be filled out for each chemical. Form R and instructions for its completion are provided in Appendix D.

HOW TO USE THE LAW TO YOUR BENEFIT

Too often, business owners dislike new regulations because they seem to impede their ability to do business and because the costs of compliance put them at a competitive disadvantage in the marketplace. These are very real perceptions of the situation by both the business and public sectors. As stated in Chapter 2, there are definite costs related to regulation, and they may be substantial. However, in many cases, regulation is a result of failure to communicate what procedures were carried out in the past to forego the need for regulation. Additionally, there have been too many instances where businesses have not taken the proper steps to protect their employees and the surrounding community and environment. Usually these problems arise because no one really knows the properties and hazards of the materials that are present, and therefore the consequences of an accidental release.

However, since the regulations exist, complaining about them does no good, and noncompliance is not only illegal but dangerous to all involved, including the community. Also, taking a more positive view, it is sensible to look for the benefits of the regulations and take advantage of them.

Title III offers many economic benefits to all parties involved. Many times these benefits are evident, sometimes they are not, and in some cases it a little study is needed to make a case for financial benefits. The biggest example of this is the effort that each regulated facility must make to fulfill the reporting requirements. This effort will highlight the facility's greatest shortcomings involving hazardous chemicals. As stated here and elsewhere, very few enterprises know the extent of their hazardous chemicals problem, and even fewer care. This is not due to a sinister plot to deliberately keep this information from the employees or the community. The fact is that most employees (including executives) have problems of their own in the normal performance of their jobs, and they would rather have someone else handle these mysterious things called "chemicals." This attitude pervades most companies, and the job of doing whatever the regulations require usually falls to a person in the Safety Department, who knows very little about chemicals, or to a chemist in the laboratory, who knows very little about safety. And, since "we have been in business for a long time and have never had a chemical problem [usually not a correct statement], so we must be doing everything right," there is no good reason to change.

The truth is that there have probably been many problems with chemicals, but they have not been serious enough to kill anyone (as far as is known). Worse, practices in the plant, including storage, handling and use, are probably conducive to the occurrence of a very serious accident. Title III requires an actual study of what materials are being used in the facility, other than from a purchasing and inventory point of view. Someone must now look at these materials and decide under what conditions a release of a hazardous chemical may occur and what the consequences might be. The law requires communication with an outside agency (the LEPC) and with the community regarding these chemicals. The Facility Coordinator cannot help but learn more about these chemicals and make changes that have been costing the company money in the past.

At the very least, the facility will become safer because of the establishment and enforcement proper storage and handling procedures. (This is not to say that it isn't being done now in many instances, but great improvements can be made in the vast majority of covered facilities.) The direct result of this can be lowered insurance premiums.

Another result may be the realization that fire detection and protection systems are inadequate (or nonexistent) and should be installed. Although this carries an added cost of its own, reduced losses from fires will again lower insurance premiums.

Cooperation with the community and the LEPC will inform the community of what materials are present, and participation in safety drills and other activities will increase community awareness and decrease damage to the community, thereby eliminating legal claims for damages. An informed community that is trained to protect itself will less likely be damaged, and forewarning may also preclude claims of ignorance concerning potential damage.

Total cooperation with the fire service will allow it to become better informed, and with proper education, training and equipment, the fire department will be better able to mitigate any incidents at the covered facility. Indeed, some of the liability for damages might be transferrable to the fire department if it failed to act in accordance with the information provided.

Sharing of information with the community will establish better public relations, and this will have economic benefits when the company wants to expand or engage in some other activity that might have brought protests in earlier times. Many plans have been changed or dropped entirely because of misunderstanding and misinformation possessed by the neighbors of the facility. In fact, many companies have had to incur relocation expenses just to overcome complaints from neighbors. Eliminating this problem may be the biggest economic benefit of all.

Nothing more need be added here concerning the economic benefits of a more smoothly run enterprise because of information gathered through compliance with Title III. Once chemical information is gathered within the company and is correlated with the proper safety information, many existing problems (not previously recognized as having to do with the properties or safe handling of a chemical) can be eliminated.

It is not coincidence that the facilities covered by Title III are, in most cases, those covered by the OSHA Hazard Communication Standard. The economic benefits gained by having a work force that understands the hazards of working with hazardous chemicals cannot be denied. The effect of these two laws, if full compliance is achieved, will have a large positive impact on the company's financial condition.

Chapter 5

INDUSTRIAL FIRST RESPONDER TRAINING

Businesses are under no obligation to provide a "Hazardous Materials Response Team" or "Spill Response Team" within their operations. In case of a spill or other accidental release, evacuation of the area or building may be ordered, and the fire department or other emergency responders may be called to handle the situation. However, if a business does decide to have its own personnel respond to minor spills and releases, then it must adequately educate, train and equip them to handle the incident safely.

Before a call for volunteers for the team is made, the company must take the most important step in the entire procedure: getting a commitment for the team from top management. The company, if it chooses to set up an emergency response team, must do everything in its power to prepare those volunteers to carry out their duties as safely as possible. This means a commitment to provide the best education, the best training, and the best equipment possible.

Once the commitment is made by upper management, there must be no wavering. If management decides that the team is too costly, the team should be disbanded rather than an attempt made to equip and run it economically. There are no shortcuts to proper education and training, and cutting corners on equipment can literally be fatal to one or more team members and perhaps to others both inside and outside the facility.

Once the decision has been made to organize a team, recruitment of members can begin. The group should be made up of volunteers who understand the possible danger of the work. Potential members should realize that they must earn their place on the team by successfully completing the formal education and training portions of the program. No one should be coerced, however gently, to volunteer for this duty.

During the formal recruitment period, it should be made clear to all potential applicants that there will be work involved in the education and training programs, and that the company will do everything in its power to see that members are properly educated, trained and equipped to handle certain well-defined incidents.

If any employees are volunteer firefighters, they will almost certainly be the first to volunteer. These people are extremely valuable because they have already demonstrated their willingness to get involved in dangerous situations, and they are somewhat used to formal training. Volunteer firefighters should not have the preconceived notion of training that some career firefighters get from their departments. Another value of having volunteer firefighters as employees is that their firefighting experience will tend to make them leaders of the group that has volunteered for training.

The emergency group may be called a "Hazardous Materials Response Team (HMRT)" "Hazardous Incident Response Team (HIRT)," "Emergency Response Team (ERT)," or simply a "Spill Team." Other names may be chosen, but it *is* important to have a name so that the members can identify with the group and work to build a real team concept. It is important for each member to realize that his or her life, as well as the lives of others inside (and outside) the facility, depend upon the actions of every other member of the team.

HOW TO DETERMINE WHETHER A MINOR INCIDENT HAS OCCURRED

Before the team is assembled and education and training begin, the goals of the team must be laid out carefully, clearly and concisely. The most important goal is to decide to what sorts of incidents the team will respond. Most facilities train their teams to handle minor incidents, while a few have a full-time fire department capable of handling all but catastrophic situations within the facility. The level of response to which the team should be trained can be determined by studying each hazardous material used, stored, manufactured or handled at the facility and determining the following for each chemical present:

1. What are the physical and chemical properties of this material?
   a. How will it look or smell when released?
   b. Will it move when released (flow, rise, evaporate)?
   c. Is it flammable, combustible, corrosive, an oxidizing agent, toxic, unstable, explosive, air- or water-reactive under pressure?
2. How will this chemical act when released?
   a. What are the possible locations of the release?
   b. What is the physical form of the material when released?
   c. What is its natural physical form?
3. What will be affected by this release?
   a. People (inside and outside the facility)
   b. The facility itself
   c. The environment
   d. Community systems (drinking water, telephones, highways, hospitals, etc.)
4. With what other chemical(s) or material(s) will this chemical react violently?
5. What special procedures are called for by the MSDS?

Once these questions are answered for each chemical and the information is collated and digested, the decision can be made concerning the level of response required to handle minor incidents, and the education, training and equipment requirements can be determined. In other words, once all the possibilities of releases have been studied, it should become clear what response goals will be required in each situation. Once that happens, education, training and equipment needs can be designed to achieve those goals safely.

When a release occurs, the following questions must be answered:

1. What has been released?
   a. What are the hazards of this material?
   b. Has the team been trained to handle this material safely?
2. Where has the release occurred?
3. What types of release has occurred?
4. How much material has been released?
   a. Has the team been trained to handle this quantity safely?
   b. Can this quantity be contained safely by the team if enough members are present?
   c. Are the proper tools and equipment available to handle this quantity?
   d. Are any other factors present that might change the way the material might react (weather, enclosures, fire)?
5. How much time has elapsed between release of the material and arrival of the team?
6. Are any other chemicals involved?
   a. What reactions may be expected if other chemicals are present with which the released chemical may react?
7. What special procedures are necessary to handle this situation safely?
   a. Evacuation (facility and/or surrounding community)
   b. Withdrawal
   c. Call for outside help (local fire department, the manufacturer of the chemical, Chemtrec, etc.)

One must be careful not to fall into the trap of using the term "relative" in reference to the size of an incident. Certainly, a 5,000-gallon spill of a particular substance is a "relatively" small incident compared to a spill of 50,000 or 500,000 gallons, but even a 55-gallon spill of an extremely toxic material might be considered a major incident no matter where it happened. One must determine the absolute size of the incident, above which no effort will be made to mitigate the incident. This can be done by determining:

1. What resources and tools the team will have at its disposal
2. How long the incident has been going on
3. The amount of material released, broken down into hazard classes
4. The concentration of the material released
5. The hazards presented by the material

Resources and tools include education, training and equipment. The amount of resources provided to the team depends on how thoroughly the company wants it to be involved in handling in-house releases. If the company decides to have the team prepared to handle fully all small releases, it will have to determine the upper limit of such releases and define "prepared" as properly educated, trained and equipped.

The interval between the start of the incident and the arrival of the team is important to know if the substance is volatile. Volatility of the substance will determine how much has evaporated into the atmosphere. Its vapor density will indicate where it may have moved and therefore where the danger exists. If the vapors are flammable, toxic, corrosive, or present some other hazard, the time that has elapsed since the release will dictate whether or not the team should try to intervene or call for evacuation.

After all the above questions have been answered, company management can define a small or minor incident. In general, such an incident will be defined as the amount of a specific chemical or mixture of chemicals that, when released in any particular situation, can be contained and cleaned up with no danger to the response team, other employees and visitors, and the surrounding community. It must be clear that the amount and circumstances of each chemical release will determine whether or not it can be handled safely. The team could probably handle a spill of 50 pounds of a solid oxidizing agent onto a clean, dry floor, but might choose to evacuate the facility and the surrounding neighborhood if 50 pounds of sodium cyanide were spilled into an open container of sulfuric acid (which, will generate tremendous amounts of hydrogen cyanide gas).

WHEN TO CALL FOR HELP

The problem of defining minor incidents before their occurrence can be solved by setting up a matrix consisting of the material released versus the conditions of release. There must be an upper limit of the spillage above which no intervention by the team will take place. But there will never be a substitution for the decision to be made by a well-educated and well-trained head of the team. This person will not always know how much material has been released, or the answers to many of the above questions, but he *will* have to make a quick decision on whether to intervene or call for help from an outside emergency response unit. For this team leader, the decision will be based on the risk presented to his team, to other people inside the facility and to the surrounding community. After the size-up, his decision on whether to call for help will be based on his estimation of the probable harm that will occur if he doesn't intervene and waits for outside help to arrive. If the team cannot handle the situation safely and no immediate danger to human life exists (that is, evacuation can be accomplished quickly and safely), the call for help should be made. Under no circumstances should the company (or the team leader) put the team members in danger, and the team must clearly understand that a call for help is not a sign of weakness or an admission of defeat. It is also not a surrendering of company secrets. It is simply common sense to call for help when needed.

The local fire department, to which the call will usually be made, will want to be contacted as soon as possible. Too often a company fire brigade or emergency response team will not recognize that the situation is too dangerous for them to handle and will foolishly attempt to deal with it on their own. When the call for help *is* made, the emergency response personnel often arrive to find a situation that is already out of control. If the team leader puts aside the idea of handling a situation that is clearly bigger than any for what the team was trained and equipped, he will get the help that the facility needs to prevent major or catastrophic damage. Not even the biggest and best-equipped fire department can save a facility after the problem gets out of control. The last five determinations listed above will quickly tell the team leader when to call for help.

PROPER EDUCATION

The Education Must Be Formal

This does not mean that it must take place in a traditional classroom. But it *must* be at a level that will produce the kind of information the students need, and it *must* be presented in a formal, professional manner. This means education at a higher level than high school. That does not mean that it must be very difficult, but it must be presented in a manner that tells the student that this material is important and must be learned.

Formal education means several things. The student must realize that the education is required of the every prospective team member, and all team members should receive the same level of education so that they will all be speaking the same language in an emergency situation.

The student must want to be in the program and must know, understand and accept the fact that this education is necessary. In this situation, it is absolutely necessary to explain to the prospective team member what he must go through *before* education begins. There are some people who refuse to place themselves in a formal education situation. It is not good practice to place such an employee in an embarrassing position. Let such employees know that you want them on the team, but that you will understand if they refuse.

The material must be presented in a formal manner, that its, with goals in mind, a plan to follow, and the materials with which to teach.

Lectures are crucial to the educational process. Audiovisual aids may be used to augment the lecture, but the lecturer is the key. Many education programs are built around videotapes or slide/audiotape presentations, but this is not good enough in this situation. Audiovisual aids should be used to reinforce certain points and to present examples when demonstrations are too dangerous. The lecturer should be the focal point for several reasons. He sets up a crucial dialogue, encourages questions, and customizes the presentation to specialized individual needs. The lecturer also establishes credibility and becomes a resource for the spill team. This means that the lecturer must be knowledgeable and have the complete confidence of the team. He may be a company employee or an outside person; the important thing is that he be competent in the field.

The Education Must Be Challenging

The education cannot be provided in the traditional way it is presented to emergency responders such as firefighters, although this situation is beginning to change. The chemical nature of the hazardous material must be presented on the most basic level. Information must be provided that will allow the student to answer the following questions:

1. What can be expected if contact with the hazardous material is made?
2. What will happen to the immediately surrounding area in this case?
3. What will happen if the team intervenes (the answer to this question should tell the student that the best way to handle a hazardous materials incident may be to not intervene)?
4. Is there a chemical, rather than physical, way to handle this incident?
5. What chemical and physical properties of the released material are important?
6. Is it possible to protect the team against the hazards of the materials involved?
7. How can the team tell if there is another chemical or material with which the released chemical will react?

All of the above questions can be answered with a very basic knowledge of chemistry, and experience has shown that this can be successfully taught to students of all educational backgrounds, even those who failed their high school chemistry course. The one major attitude a student must bring to this educational process is the motivation to learn. That motivation can be supplied by the company in many ways, but it must be based on the employee's desire to be on the emergency team.

The Education Must Be Certifiable

Finally, in this formal educational setting, students must be tested often, that is, quizzed or examined at *every* class meeting. Regular testing ensures regular studying, and the knowledge that a student must get a certain grade to qualify for the team will be added motivation. There is so much material to cover and digest that regular and frequent testing allows the material to be broken down into manageable amounts.

The company's management may decide that passing grades are not good enough to make the team. Should the team be made up of average achievers? If employees are told that they will have to work to make the team, they will. If there is no motivation, the team may get itself into more trouble than it can handle. Don't necessarily settle for those who just make it through. The higher the standards for making the team, the harder potential members will work to succeed. The harder they work, the higher the quality of the team.

EQUIPMENT

The topic of equipment is as controversial as any that may be encountered. Everyone seems to be an expert on the subject, and there is very little agreement as to what is required for a spill team, other than some kind of totally encapsulating suit, nonsparking tools, and recovery drums. However, for a spill team in a facility where a known group of chemicals is used (no matter how many), the equipment needs will have already been spelled out. Every manufacturer, importer and distributor is required to provide users of chemicals with an MSDS, which includes required information on special protective equipment. By following each MSDS, a company can make sure that it is providing its spill team with the right protective gear and tools.

As for special equipment and tools, a decision must be made on what the team is expected to accomplish. What will be its goal? Is it to be an expert on all the chemical and physical properties of all the hazardous materials in the plant? Will its duty be to respond to all hazardous materials incidents in the plant, or only certain ones? Is it to be a complete hazardous materials resource, handling prevention, the incident *and* clean-up? Will the team have life-rescue duties?

Only after the goals and mission of the team have been determine can one decide what equipment is needed. This decision must be made part of the strategic planning for the company. Whatever equipment is chosen, it must be stored conveniently and transported quickly to the incident site. Special vans and/or trailers may be used for storage transport of the equipment, protective clothing and tools.

If the team is to get involved in all incidents, then the proper protective clothing must be provided. Again, the MSDS will indicate what is needed and what materials are impervious to the chemical. If this information is not readily available, the manufacturer can provide it. The totally encapsulating suit is essential when any contact with the released material will be life- or health-threatening. There is no material that will withstand exposure to all chemicals, and, therefore, more than one type of suit (made from different materials) may be required. The total number of encapsulating suits required will depend on the company's philosophy; at a minimum, four suits of *each material* are necessary; five are considered adequate, and six are best. This is so because any situation dangerous enough to require totally encapsulating suits will require that two men work together at all times, with two others providing emergency backup to effect a rescue if the first two get into trouble and cannot escape without help. The extra suit can be used if one is damaged. If six suits are available, two can be worn by the men entering the "hot" zone, two by the relief team (so that the teams can switch off when their air supply is low) and two by the emergency backup team.

When the decision to buy encapsulating suits is made, demand the best in workmanship and quality and expect to pay for it. The composition of the suit is critical, and time should be spent examining all materials before a decision is made. Check chemical resistance charts to see which material is best for which chemicals; then select the two (at least) different materials that will protect against the widest range of chemicals in your facility. Only one material may be needed if it protects against all chemicals present in the facility (present and future).

Make sure that the suits are airtight from the outside (as well as the inside), and be sure that they can handle positive-pressure self-contained breathing apparatus (SCBA) *and* umbilical-fed air (umbilical-fed air is air that is fed from an air compressor by an air line to the total encapsulating suit worn by the emergency responder. The air line stays connected supplying fresh air, all through the incident). (The umbilical arrangement can get a team member in trouble, since there is no limit to the air supply and the person may stay in the environment too long.) The faceplate material should be resistant to the same chemicals as the suit, but this is not always possible. Gloves and boots should also be of the same material as the suit, and in some cases they may be attached to the suit.

It is not well known, but the totally encapsulating suit can kill as easily as save a life. The person may not be able to get out of some suits and will need outside help, especially when the SCBA air supply is depleted. The way seams are constructed, and the manner in which the zippers are covered, may make it impossible for the person inside the suit to extricate himself if his air supply has expired or some other event has made it imperative to get out of the suit. The same problems can keep another member in another suit from extricating this person because of the gloves he is wearing and the danger to him if he removes them. Training procedures should therefore include methods of emergency removal of a person from a totally encapsulating suit, with minimal danger to both parties.

Beware of using disposable suits alone. Most response teams use them *over* an expensive totally encapsulating suit to save wear and tear and the need for decontamination, which is the way they were designed to be used. In many cases the disposable suits, worn as the only form of protection, are *not* better than nothing. If disposable suits are used this way (which they should not), they should be used only in cases where exposure will be to very weak or dilute materials, for short periods of time, and where the danger from contacting the material is minimal. These suits tear very easily and offer little (if any) protection from most hazardous materials.

Other equipment to be considered (some of which is provided in kits made up to handle specific chemicals) includes nonsparking tools, canvas and plastic tarps, portable collection tanks to catch spills and overflows, recovery or overpack drums, plastic sheeting and film (thinner than other sheeting, to be used in the decontamination area and to create walkways), plastic and metal tubs and buckets, a pump with fittings and hoses to transfer liquids which should have resistant fittings, tank and drum sealing and plugging kits, including plumbing supplies, gas and vapor testing equipment, sorbents, neutralizers, plugging and diking equipment, pop-rivit tool and supplies, tapes, patching equipment, o-rings, gaskets, washers, rubber sheets, wood plugs, glue, various types of equipment to test pH, fire extinguishers, lights (hand-held, spot, etc.), grounding and bonding cables, plywood sheets, decontamination kits, brooms and assorted brushes, first-aid kits, hard hats, eye wash, ear plugs, a portable shower and a good reference library. This list is certainly not all-inclusive, but it should be used as a guide for a basic inventory of safety equipment on which to build for specific chemicals and hazards.

TRAINING

The subject of training is just as controversial as the equipment and education requirements, if not more so. Fire departments have been following standard operating procedures in training firefighters for decades, exchanging ideas and honing their training programs to fit their needs. They are now having difficulty changing some of those procedures to train their people properly to handle hazardous materials incidents, simply because of the differences in the type of response necessary for fires as opposed to hazardous materials incidents. Private businesses should have none of these preconceived notions, and should be able to design the proper training programs themselves.

Training for handling hazardous materials incidents is relatively difficult because, after the first run-through, it is boring, uncomfortable, hard work. Once again, the purpose for forming the spill team comes into focus. For what sorts of incidents should the team to be ready? Certainly these will be only small incidents. But will they be spills or accidental releases from the equipment used in a particular process, or in moving the material to the process, or at the loading/unloading area, or somewhere (or everywhere) else in the facility?

Will the team have to respond to transportation accidents involving material being shipped to or from the facility? Will they be called upon by the local fire department to handle incidents away from the facility, whether such incidents involve the company's raw material or finished product or some other material for which the team may not be prepared?

As a practical matter, the company should first concentrate on training the team to handle the hazardous materials that are used, handled, or stored, and any that are manufactured on site. They should probably be prepared to handle incidents both inside and outside the facility in order to prevent any hazardous material from leaving the property, especially through a sewer or waterway. There are limited procedures that can be used for an air discharge, but seldom will those actions be effective unless the discharge continues over a long period of time.

How to Start

First, everyone who has volunteered to be on the team must get into shape and stay there. Even those volunteers who think they are in good shape will soon find out that it takes an entirely different sort of conditioning to be able to handle the tasks that must be done inside a totally encapsulating suit. Potential team members may become tired while getting into and out of the suit, and having to practice walking or climbing or both, some distance to the source of the simulated incident will quickly wear them out.

Second, everyone must become totally familiar with the suits. There is no substitute for practicing the acts of getting into and out of (donning and doffing) these suits. Each potential team member must get to know the idiosyncracies of each type of suits provided, because the design of every suit is different. Each person will have to get to know the best way *in* and *out* of each type of suit. Each person will need practice in helping another person into and out of the suit, since they will always be working on the "buddy system." Each team member's life may depend on being helped to zip and unzip the suit. Each person must practice helping another team member to unsuit *his or her suit*.

Third, each potential team member must practice doing everything that will have to be done while in the suit, before the suit is donned, using *all* the tools that will have to be used during the incident. In other words, each person will have to learn how to crawl over railroad cars and tank trucks, and through piping and plumbing, turning valves and patching or plugging holes, in regular work clothing. This will familiarize the volunteers with the tasks that must be done during the incident and get them used to climbing and crawling in strange surroundings. The same practice should be followed in operations on the ground. All persons should walk around and climb over drums and machinery to patch leaks or get samples and use all of the tools they will use in an actual incident.

A few words of warning should be given about totally encapsulating suits. A small percentage of the population has claustrophobia, and the majority of these persons may not be aware of their problem. However, if a potential member of the emergency response team is affected, this problem will show up clearly once he dons a suit. This experience could be traumatic to a volunteer who consider himself fearless, and a public display of the problem should be avoided. This can be accomplished, in addition to saving the effort of education and training, by having all volunteers try on a suit at the beginning of the program in the privacy of a screening interview. In this manner, an otherwise eligible member of the team will be saved the embarrassment of failure and may even be valuable in some other function that will not require donning the suit.

Fourth, the incident scenarios likely to be encountered may now be set up. Every chemical present in the facility will fall into a particular hazard class, the members of this class reacting in a similar manner under similar conditions. Thus, training exercises will not have to be designed for *every chemical* present, but only for certain groups. However, if there is a great preponderance of one chemical used, for example, if sulfuric acid makes up 75% of the volume of chemicals present, training exercises specifically for sulfuric acid should be designed and run through.

It must be said here that all incidents must be simulated. That is, the exercise should be designed using an inert, safe material rather than practicing on the real thing. There are machines and devices that produce simulated, safe smoke, and these should be used in exercises where gas leaks must be stopped. Water should be used in situations where any hazardous liquids must be simulated, and sand or clay substituted for solid hazardous materials.

Fifth, after these exercises have been done repeatedly, they must be done again, also repeatedly, with team members wearing the totally encapsulating suits. While all the above tasks are being repeated, communication between the partners should be attempted. Communicating without radio contact will be difficult, if not impossible. Team members must establish a system of hand signals to make up for this lack of communication, which could be extremely dangerous or even fatal. The use of grease pen and whiteboards, or chalk and chalkboard, or even pencil and paper should be considered to aid communication. Of course, if radio communication can be provided, it should be.

Sixth, after all the above procedures have been done so well that each team member can do them automatically, they should be done still again, this time with simulated smoke, rain (and/or snow) and total darkness (as in a maze). After all, conditions probably will not be perfect when the incident occurs, and members of the team should become used to operating under adverse conditions.

Only after everyone has successfully completed the above training (including anything the facility's management wants to add to supplement the suggested training program) can they be considered fully trained. Only after the formal education process, total familiarization with the proper tools and equipment, and, finally, proper training, is the team ready for its duties.

TRAINING UPDATES

Once the team is ready, having finished its education and training program, the training must be updated. The fact that the team has had its formal education and has completed training doesn't mean that the learning process is complete. There will always be new tools and techniques to be learned, and therefore training must be updated and repeated. Promotions, transfers and other factors will create vacancies on the team (remember to include vacation time when determining the size of the team), and members will have to be replaced. Also, new threats will appear (new chemicals, processes, equipment and other dangers will constantly crop up), so education and training must be repeated and expanded on at least an annual basis. In any event, retraining is necessary because people tend to forget information and procedures unless they are repeated regularly.

However, waiting for an annual update could be very dangerous if a hazardous new chemical is introduced into the workplace before the retraining begins and the team is not trained to handle it. These situations must be handled as they arise, and the team must be educated and trained well before the new chemical's introduction into the facility. Any new equipment needed to handle the new material must also be incorporated into the training process immediately. Constant vigilance by management will keep any surprises from threatening the safety of the facility and all persons inside and outside.

Chapter 6

FIRE DEPARTMENT AND FIRST RESPONDER TRAINING REQUIREMENTS

Training is a fundamental element in the SARA Title III program. Section 305 of the law stipulates that "officials of the United States Government carrying out existing training programs for emergency training are authorized to specifically provide training and education programs for Federal, state and local personnel in hazard mitigation and emergency preparedness. Such programs shall provide special emphasis for such training and education with respect to hazardous chemicals." This training is to be made available to all first responders. First responders include police, security professionals, emergency medical personnel, utility and municipal service employees, government officials, industrial management, media personnel, industrial response teams and dispatchers. In addition, advanced training to mitigate a chemical spill must be provided to all hazardous materials response teams, both public and private.

Since fire departments throughout the United States are the primary agencies responsible for the delivery of emergency services, it seems only logical that the fire service should expand its system to include hazardous materials. However, before this can be successfully achieved, fire executives must reevaluate their current training process in terms of its *producing the desired results*.

In order for any training to be truly effective, the managers of the training program must have a clear, concise and comprehensive understanding of its purpose. Fire executives must know in advance the information they want their personnel to have, the skills they need to learn, and how the knowledge will be utilized on the job. Without this understanding before the implementation of a training program, the likelihood of the training's being appropriate is severely diminished.

The success of any training program should be measured by the resultant performance of the trainees. This criterion must apply to all emergency fire service personnel who respond to hazardous materials ("hazmat") incidents. The mitigation of such an incident should directly correlate with the pre-emergency training program.

Fire department hazmat training programs vary from state to state. Some states require that all firefighters attend a basic training program covering the fundamental elements of hazardous materials containment. These programs are specifically designed for first responders, and emphasize the recognition and identification of potential hazardous material spills, as well as the initial actions a first responder should take to control the situation until additional help can be summoned. The goal of this program is to train the emergency responder to recognize a dangerous situation and react appropriately. Often this type of training does not measure the retained knowledge or learned skill levels of the participants, but instead provides only a certificate of attendance.

Other states provide training programs that focus only on members of an organized hazardous materials response team. (Other states provide both levels of training, requiring persons to attend the program most suitable for their individual assignments.) In this case, the training focuses more on the actual handling and containment of spilled chemicals. Specialized tools and equipment designed specifically for this purpose are introduced to those who attend. Countless hours are devoted to learning the skills necessary to operate this equipment. These courses are designed to prepare the attendees to respond to an incident and contain the hazardous material released. They are of vital importance in preplanning for an emergency response.

QUALITY TRAINING PROGRAMS

A major concern is that much of the training being provided is generic and not community focused. Often no attempt is made to determine (1) what chemicals are present in the community or even at a specific site, (2) what is the probability of a release of those chemicals, (3) what tools and specialized equipment will be required to contain the material, (4) what reference materials will be required to identify the material and determine the necessary actions to be taken, and (5) what additional community resources will be needed to control the situation. Without this type of site-specific information, it is impossible for a hazmat response team to preplan the specific actions that must be taken in an incident. Thus, generic training is of limited applied value.

Another concern with this type of training is the lack of attention given to the classification of hazardous chemicals. Traditionally, the fire service has been called upon to control a number of hazardous conditions involving flammable and combustible liquids and gases. Most fire service executives will readily state that their department has trained for and is prepared to handle this type of emergency.

Too often, hazardous material training programs devote many instructional hours to flammable liquid hazards and ignore or gloss over the many other hazards a response team may be called upon to control. This type of training is popular because it is fun and entertaining. It often elicits enthusiastic comments such as "Boy! We really fought some hot fires" or "You should have seen the attack we made on that burning tanker!" Yes, this training is important and should be included in a hazmat program. This approach is good in that it builds enthusiasm for the training program. It also gives non-fire-department hazmat responders an idea of what to expect from flammable liquids. However, the primary focus must include other hazards such as corrosives, compressed gases, unstable (reactive) or water-reactive materials, explosives, irritants, oxidizers, and others that are not as well understood by emergency response personnel.

HOW TO DEVELOP A TRAINING PROGRAM

The training program must be well organized, documented and measurable. For emergency training to serve those for whom it is intended, the trainer must first establish learning/ educational goals which clearly state the purpose of the training. Some educators prefer to combine the program goals with a "program rationale." The purpose of this rationale is to provide background information concerning the need for such a program. It should contain an overview of current federal and state legislation on the training topic, the status of other programs in the development process, and a suggested target audience for the training. A list of the references used to prepare the rationale should also be included.

The next step is to develop a series of general goal statements that can be applied to each segment of the training program. They may be either generic or specific and technical, depending upon the level of sophistication desired. Each goal statement may contain several measurable objectives (statements) that can be utilized to accomplish the stated goals. The objectives should focus on student performance levels and clearly identify the skills to be learned or the knowledge retained. The following are examples of general goal statements:

1. The student will analyze community emergency evacuation procedures pertaining to the release of hazardous materials.
2. The student will develop an understanding of the potential fire and personal safety hazards associated with chemical accidents.

3. The student will become aware of the importance of site-specific chemical inventory reporting, pre-emergency response planning, facility inspections and emergency plan exercises.

Once the general goals and their corresponding objectives have been established, the next step is to organize the proposed training into an outline of workable modules or sections. This can be accomplished by developing a simple outline highlighting the primary points to cover. Each module should be designed to address the training goals previously established and contain information relevant to the subject. The outline should contain primary headings for each major section and short descriptions of the material to be covered in each. The following is an example of a program outline:

    I. Introduction to Hazardous Materials
       A. What are hazardous materials?
          1. OSHA definition
          2. SARA definition
          3. DOT definition
          4. Other definitions
       B. Regulations pertaining to hazardous material
          1. Transportation
          2. Fixed facilities
   II. Classification of Hazardous Materials
       A. Properties of hazardous materials
          1. Flammable liquids
          2. Oxidizing agents
          3. Corrosives
          4. Toxics
          5. Reactives
          6. Combustible liquids
          7. Compressed gases
          8. Others
       B. Health and physical hazards
          1. Acute short-term exposure
          2. Chronic long-term exposure
          3. Methods to use for personal protection
  III. Hazardous Materials First Responder Awareness
       A. Methods used to identify a release
       B. Procedures for identifying the material
       C. Actions to be taken to report a release
       D. Evacuation procedures
       E. How to protect yourself

Once this phase has been completed, the next step is to develop a lesson plan that encompasses all of the necessary information included in the organizational outline. It must, however, be flexible enough to permit alterations and/or additions to the instructional or technical information as necessary. This facilitates adaptation of the training to specific local areas or facilities. The lesson plan must be well documented to ensure (1) uniformity in the sequence of presentation, (2) that the same information is presented in each training session, and (3) that future training sessions will include the same information and will utilize the same instructional techniques. To be organized, the instructor's first step is to develop a teaching outline. This document should contain all of the major skills or information to be presented.

Student objectives must also be included to facilitate the measurement process once the training is completed. For example:

Performance Objectives: The student will be able to identify the following terms and explain the relevance of each:

Flash point
Vapor density
Upper flammable limit
Lower flammable limit
Water solubility

Once these objectives have been defined, the next step is to develop a lesson plan, using the outline to guide the process. Include in the plan (1) clearly stated goals for the specific lesson, (2) student performance objectives for achieving the goals, (3) instructional materials necessary to conduct training, and (4) reference material that will be used as foundation material. Lesson plans that are well documented in writing will serve as an instructional guide for the trainer.

This approach will ensure training and information continuity within the emergency response agency and among other emergency responders.

One important point to remember: The use of "war stories" in formalized emergency training is acceptable only to emphasize a specific aspect or stress the importance of a particular skill. Unless a connection is made between the story and the instruction point, the class becomes a "story time" in which the attendees remember stories but have no idea why they were important. How often have you attended a training session and become bored or disinterested because the instructor told *too many* stories? Students do learn from the experiences of their instructors; however, outstanding instruction does not rely upon such stories as the foundation of the instructional process.

Good instruction is based upon validated information presented in a professional manner, using recognized instructional techniques. Focused organization and lesson plan documentation will prevent overuse of this questionable teaching technique. "Dog and pony shows" should be reserved for circus entertainment—not hazardous materials response training!

Measurement, the most important component of any emergency training program, is often overlooked. How do we know what knowledge and skills the student has learned? Many programs fail to provide a test to measure the results of a structured training course. Instead, the student is awarded only a certificate of attendance indicating that he or she sat through the scheduled training. The only value of this document is that it proves that the student did in fact attend the training program. Many fire and hazardous materials executives are becoming concerned with this approach and are beginning to ask some very pointed questions. Did the student learn the information presented? Did the student learn the necessary skills required to perform a variety of tasks? Can the student perform at the desired level of emergency response? Only the student can answer these questions if no test is administered to measure the level of retention and skill mastery. Tests should be administered often during the course. When a course is taught over a period of several weeks, a test should be given at the beginning of each class after the initial week. This will motivate the student to review the previously covered material in preparation for the test. It also puts the students on notice that a standard has been established for the class and they are expected to meet it.

How can emergency response managers effectively manage a hazardous materials spill if they don't know the information and skills retention level of the responders involved? The answer is: They can't. Without knowledge and skills testing, the manager will not know whether the response team is prepared until they respond to an incident. That is a dangerous time to discover that the training was inadequate. Therefore, all training programs must contain a test to (1) measure knowledge retention, (2) validate course content, (3) measure skill mastery, and (4) provide an attendance record.

This test provides both the student and the emergency manager with a recognized level of hazardous materials training accomplishment. It also reduces the potential liability concern of many managers, which often stems from the utilization of untrained or undertrained personnel.

OSHA AND EPA TRAINING REQUIREMENTS

Using safe handling of hazardous materials as the primary focal point, both OSHA and the EPA have mandated strong training programs. Although the purpose of each standard is hazmat safety, the emphasis on specific training requirements and target audiences varies with the intent of the standard. The following is a comparative analysis of each standard.

The *OSHA Hazard Communication Standard* took effect in May 1986. It required employers in SIC codes 20–39 to develop and implement an employee information and training program. It states:

> Employers shall provide employees with information and training on hazardous chemicals in their work area at the time of their initial assignment, and whenever a new hazard is introduced into their work area. (OSHA 1910.1200 (h).)

The information portion of the program requires that employees be informed of (1) the Hazards Communication Standard, (2) any operations within the facility or the work area in which hazardous chemicals are present, (3) the location and availability of the written hazard communication program, (4) the location of the list identifying all hazardous chemicals in the facility, along with their corresponding hazard, and (5) the location of the MSDS for each chemical.

The training section is more applied and involves skill development in certain aspects of hazard recognition. This requires several specific areas of training. Employees must be trained in the methods and operations that may be used to detect the presence or release of a hazardous material. This involves knowing the visual appearance or distinctive odor of the chemical when released or of the operation of monitoring devices which may be used. Employees must also be trained in the physical and health hazards of the chemicals in the work area so that they will know exactly what risks they are facing on their daily job. In many cases, chemicals are grouped by health hazard or physical hazard classification to reduce the redundancy of employee training in each and every chemical.

Another component of the required training covers the measures employees can take to protect themselves from the hazards. These measures may include the use of personal protective equipment (e.g., safety glasses, gloves, vapor or particulate respirators, aprons, boots, SCBA apparatus), emergency evacuation procedures, audible alarm systems, safe means of egress and appropriate work practices. The hazard communication program developed by the employer must be explained in detail. In addition, employees must be trained to recognize the standard labeling system in use at the facility and how to read and interpret an MSDS.

A variety of programs and systems have been used by industry to deliver the required information and training programs. These range from short, professionally created videotapes to slide presentations with accompanying audiotapes and films. In most cases the employee, upon completion of the program, is not challenged by a test; thus, it is uncertain whether the material presented was understood or retained.

One of the most comprehensive OSHA training programs was developed by Industrial Hazards Data Inc. (IHD), of Massillon, Ohio. The IHD program provides each trainee with a partial outline, which must be completed by the employee during the training sessions. This compels the employee to pay attention and absorb the information presented. Thus, the audial presentation is reinforced by the visual outline and activity on the part of the learner. In this way, three primary learning techniques are utilized in one program, facilitating broader audience impact. At the conclusion of the IHD training program, a test is administered to each employee. This test is graded, and the grade is returned to the employer for permanent retention in the employee's file. The test can be used as proof of compliance complied with the OSHA Hazard Communication Standard requirements, as it objectively documents successful employee training. As such, it can provide evidence in legal cases centering on employee right-to-know.

As indicated at the beginning of this chapter, the *EPA SARA Title III* standard requires training of first responders and advanced training of those who deal with the containment and mitigation of a release. A first responder is generally defined as one who is called to or discovers the release of a hazardous chemical. According to the National Fire Protection Association's proposed standard, NFPA 472, entitled "Professional Competence of Responders to Hazardous Materials Incidents—1988 Edition," first responders are divided into two levels of competency. The first level called the "First Responder Awareness Level," deals with the awareness level and states that these persons should be trained to act in a safe manner when confronted with a hazardous materials incident. This includes: (1) understanding what hazardous materials are and the risks associated with them, (2) understanding the potential outcome of an emergency created by a hazardous materials release, (3) having the ability to identify the hazardous material and to determine the basic hazard and response information, and, finally (4) understanding the role of the first responder at a hazardous materials incident and identifying the local contingency plan for such an incident.

The second level is referred to as the "First Responder Operational Level." This level requires advanced competency in areas such as basic chemistry terms; hazardous materials control, containment and confinement; decontamination procedures; and resource and planning skills. Due to the vagueness of the SARA standard in determining who is classified as a first responder, the Ohio SERC Training Subcommittee held a number of strategy meetings during the summer of 1987. During these meetings, the subcommittee developed several alternative definitions. They then carefully evaluated the appropriateness of each alternative. Finally, they identified and defined the target audiences for different levels of training.

The following definitions of training levels are those adopted by the Ohio SERC. Level 1 is called "Terminology" and involves the adoption of a basic glossary of hazardous materials terms. Terminology varies from state to state and from area to area. Due to the potential magnitude of a hazardous materials incident extending beyond the boundaries of a LEPC, the Ohio SERC Training Subcommittee felt that standardization at least across this heavily populated state was necessary. Level 2 is called "Preplanning." It involves the collection of data for regulated facilities, including hazardous chemical presence, water supplies, utilities, identification of the Facility Coordinator, and emergency plan preparation. Level 3, called "Recognition," is described as identifying potential hazardous materials releases and risks. This correlates closely with the NFPA 472 First Responder Awareness Level. Level 4 is called "Mitigation Procedures," which involves containment, stabilization, rescue, reporting procedures and personal protective equipment. This level, commonly referred to as the "hazardous materials response team level," is comparable to the NFPA 472 First Responder Operational Level. Level 5 is called "Response Management" and addresses the issues of planned management and exercise. It also includes resource identification, evacuation procedures, incident clean-up, fiscal responsibility and legal matters. Once the five levels of training were defined, the target audience groups were established.

The target audience was broken down into 13 categories: cleanup contractors, dispatchers, emergency medical service, environmental protection agency (both U.S. and state), fire service, government officials, health agencies, industrial emergency teams, law enforcement, media personnel, industrial management, private security personnel and utility companies. Each category was evaluated as to the level of training it needed, and this determination was then adopted as the training standard required in the state of Ohio. The chart on the next page details the categories and the associated levels of appropriate training.

This system enables all participants in the process to know the type of training they need, as well as the level of training they can expect other participants to have. This facilitates communication and achievement of the goal of emergency response preparedness.

The *OSHA Hazardous Waste Operations and Emergency Response Final Rule* effective March 6, 1990 requires training for employees engaged in hazardous waste operations at uncontrolled hazardous waste sites. The level of training depends upon the specific work assignments of each employee. The standard also addresses off site emergency response and identifies employees such as Hazmat teams, fire fighters, police officers, emergency medical

Training Needs

AUDIENCE	TRAINING LEVEL				
	I	2	3	4	5
Cleanup contractors	x		x	x	a
Dispatchers	x	a	x		
Emergency medical service	x	x	x	a	a
State environmental protection agency	x	x	x	x	a
Fire service	x	x	x	x	a
Government officials	x		x	x	x
Health agencies	x				x
Industrial emergency response teams	x	x	x	x	a
Law enforcement	x	x	x	a	a
Media	x				x
Industrial management	x	x			x
Private security personnel	x	x	x	a	a
Utility companies	x		x		

x = mandatory; a = if appropriate.

personnel and industrial fire brigades. Training level for this group are based on the duties, responsibilities and functions performed by each member of an emergency response organization.

FIRE DEPARTMENT CONCERNS

Pre-Emergency Planning

The process of pre-emergency planning has plagued the fire service for years. Although many fire executives are committed to the concept of pre-emergency planning, the actual process has not been satisfactory for many reasons. Some fire officers simply like to wait until the emergency is in progress before making the decisions necessary to control it. These individuals have never learned how to preplan, and their unfamiliarity with the process makes them hesitant to undertake it. Not having the tools necessary to develop a preplan often prevents one from being created.

While most professionals prefer not to operate by this "seat of the pants" method, many have little choice, since the availability of capable personnel to initiate a preplanning effort is limited. Not only are the necessary skills sometimes absent, but the time is sometimes unavailable even when the capabilities are present. Budgetary restrictions have caused some fire chiefs to reevaluate their departments' priorities. In doing so, they have chosen to pursue more visible activities more aggressively. Planning is a tedious process, with little reward for those involved. Even when planning does pay off, those who were active in the process are often not the persons recognized when the plan is put into effect. In addition, if the plan is never used, its value goes unrecognized by the public. As a result, fire executives focus more on equipment acquisition and providing emergency medical services than on planning. Therefore, planning becomes a low-priority task subordinate to the more traditional response/suppression type of activity.

Another problem is information, training and education. Research and experience have proven the best strategies to use in various emergency situations. However, often this information is not readily available to local fire department. When this happens, emergency managers are hampered in their efforts to plan for an emergency incident.

Experts refer to this process as "technology transfer." It is the method whereby technical information is passed on to the practitioner in the field by the researcher or technician in the laboratory. In recent years, a number of organizations have begun to address the problem, including the National Fire Protection Association, the University of Maryland, the Society of Fire Protection Engineers, the University of Akron, Worcester Polytechnic Institute, Oklahoma State University, the United States Fire Academy and the Fire Research Center at the National Bureau of Standards. Each organization is committed to transferring new and redefined information pertaining to fire and hazardous materials to the fire service. In this way, the critical information required to develop a viable pre-emergency plan is becoming available.

The United States Fire Administration has started a special process of technology transfer by broadcasting a series of monthly ''teleconferences'' featuring relevant topics of interest to emergency services. These outstanding teleconference programs are valuable not only for the public sector but for private companies as well. Much of the information presented focuses on correct methods of handling an emergency situation, regardless of whether the responders are members of a municipal department or a private industrial response team.

These and other sources of information and planning resources can be used to organize a workable pre-emergency plan. A pre-emergency plan does not have to be an onerous undertaking. Any fire department can develop one. The key is to know how. The following is an example of how to do a pre-emergency plan for hazardous materials.

A preplan should, first of all, be site specific and include all of the available chemical information a facility is capable of providing. The most convenient method of organizing chemical data is to review the inventory reporting form that is required under SARA Section 312. This form should contain the CAS Registry Number, the specific chemical name, a description of its form, and indicate one or more of the five hazard categories to which the chemical belongs. The inventory form will also identify the facility by name, address, and county of location. In most cases, the name of the Facility Coordinator will also be included.

The best method for organizing the information into a preresponse data file is to utilize Exhibit 1, the Chemical File Form, and Exhibit 2, the Facility Location File Form.

Exhibit 1 Chemical File Form

Chemical Name:
Common Synonyms:
CAS#:   NFPA 704 Hazard Rating: UN/NA#:
DOT Hazard Class: STCC#:
Description and Hazards:

Common Containers:
Delivery By:
Special Equipment Needed:
Neutralizing Agents:
Personal Protection Equipment:
First Aid:
Release Mitigation Techniques (Fire and Nonfire)

PLANTS OR OTHER LOCATIONS WHERE THIS MATERIAL MAY BE FOUND

Location	Average Volume	Running Total
1.		
2.		
3.		
4.		
5.		

Source: Form developed by Industrial Hazards Data, Inc. Massillon, Ohio.

Exhibit 2 Facility Location File Form

Facility Name: Fire Dept. Preplan Code#:_____
Address:
Type of Business:
Access Route:
Emergency Telephone Number(s):
Manager's Name:
Business Telephone Numbers:
Facility Coordinator:
Facility Coordinator's Office and Home Phone Numbers:
Alternate Coordinator:
Alternate Coordinator's Phone Numbers:
On-Site Response Capabilities and Equipment:
　　　_____ First Responder Team
　　　_____ Cleanup Equipment—Type _____
　　　_____ Automatic Suppression System—Type _____
　　　_____ Automatic Alarm Systems—Type _____

CHEMICAL	VOLUME	CONTAINER TYPE(S)	LOCATION(S)
1.			
2.			
3.			
4.			
5.			

Source: Form developed by Industrial Hazards Data, Inc., Massillon, Ohio.

The Chemical File and Facility Location Forms

The top portion of the Chemical File Form contains the information required to make basic response decisions. The middle portion of the form provides information which can be found by reviewing the MSDS. Since many of the facilities submit only the inventory list forms and not the MSDSs, the fire executive may need to request the MSDSs from the facility in order to have the information necessary to do the preplan analysis. The information on the lower portion of the form is referred to in SARA as "Tier II information" and must be requested by the LEPC or the fire executive. As indicated in the discussion of chemicals and chemical inventories elsewhere in this volume, an easy method of identifying plant location is through the use of a number code system.

Once the Chemical File Form has been completed, the information can be assembled on the Facility Location File Form. The prudent fire executive will complete this form in the presence of the Facility Coordinator to ensure its accuracy. This enhances communication and understanding between the Facility Coordinator and the fire executive.

The dialogue associated with this exercise will generate the answers to the following key questions:

1. Does the facility have an emergency response team?
2. At what level has the response team been trained?
3. What hazardous materials containment and cleanup equipment is maintained at the facility?
4. What procedures have been established for notifying the local fire department, the LEPC, and the SERC of a spill?
5. Have facility evacuation procedures been established and exercised?

6. What communication link is available other than public telephone service to communicate between the local emergency response people and facility management (e.g., two-way radios, cellular phones)?
7. Is a facility site plan documented and available?
8. What spill, leak or fire detection and suppression equipment is installed in the facility?

Once these questions have been answered, the answers must be documented. Written documentation informs both parties of the exact information shared and enables the transfer of the information from one individual to another in case of a change in personnel.

Once these questions have been answered, the fire executive is ready to formulate the response plan. Chief Alan Brunacini of the Phoenix, Arizona, Fire Department wrote a book titled *Fire Command,* published by NFPA in 1985. Much of this book focuses on the planning process and the development of standard operating procedures. Although Brunacini's work emphasizes fire emergency situations, much of the information can be applied to a hazardous materials incident and can be used as a model for fire executives beginning the preplanning process.

The actual planned response to any situation is determined by the personnel and the equipment of the local fire department. However, there are a number of things every fire officer should consider when developing a local or department plan. *Standard operating procedures* should describe a standard course of action to be taken by the department. They should be written and applied to all emergency situations. Many departments have experienced insurmountable *communications* problems at the scene of a hazardous materials emergency. It is important to know how many emergency frequencies are available in your district and whether any of these frequencies are common among emergency response agencies such as law enforcement, emergency medical service (EMS), and the fire department. If they are not, immediate steps should be taken to establish a single channel that all units can use.

The EMS response system must be centrally coordinated and assigned a zone. This effectively controls the response to areas of need and eliminates acting on false alarms, and duplication of runs. A *controlled access corridor* should be established in the preplan so that all responding personnel are aware of where the entry and exit corridors are. This eliminates the possibility of mutual response units (fire departments from adjacent communities which agree to aid in incident mitigation when requested) entering extremely hazardous areas without the proper protective gear.

One person should be identified to designate *evacuation shelters* if this action becomes necessary. Often this individual is not a municipal responder but a manager in a peripheral response agency such as the Red Cross or the local disaster service. An *emergency notification list* should be current and available to all senior fire executives. This list contains the names and phone numbers of members of various supporting agencies needed to mitigate the incident, as well as the major public officials in charge of the jurisdiction, whether it be the mayor, city manager, county commissioners or governor.

These individuals, as the elected representatives and highest-ranking public officials, have as their primary duty service to their constituents. They also have the legal authority to declare a disaster and to take the steps necessary to ensure that appropriate mitigation activities take place. It is vital that these public officials be contacted early and that they be present in the command post during the incident. These individuals are not there to take charge of the mitigation procedures, but they are responsible for other interactive situations that may arise. For example, should testing of materials be required, these officials have the authority to order them. These officials are also the best contacts with state and federal agencies, should additional assistance become necessary.

Lockbox

One tool in the emergency response process that is receiving a lot of attention and support is the emergency response lockbox. The lockbox is simply a locked unit which can sustain inclement weather conditions. It is installed outside on the facility site, usually near the main entrance.

The lockbox may be attached to a building or to a surrounding fence. It is permanently attached and secured.

The lockbox should contain the following:

1. A current list of key facility personnel knowledgeable about safety procedures for on-site materials, complete with the telephone numbers of such personnel in the event of an incident after normal hours of facility operation.
2. Current emergency and hazardous chemical inventory forms, per Section 312 of SARA, and a binder containing the MSDSs required under Section 311 of SARA. (If there are too many MSDSs to be kept in the repository container, the information in the container must identify the location of the on-site MSDS.)
3. The facility site plan, including:
   a. The location of storage and usage areas of hazardous materials, with a building floor plan
   b. The local of emergency fire suppression and spill cleanup equipment
   c. A diagram of the complete sewer system and water system with hydrants
   d. A copy of the local municipal fire department preplan
   e. Any other information deemed necessary by the fire executive.

The lockbox should be controlled by the Facility Coordinator to ensure the updating of information. It should be keyed to allow both the facility management and the fire response unit to have independent access. Some consideration has been given to extending this shared lockbox system to contiguous mutual support emergency response departments and agencies, should they be called upon to serve as the first response unit.

The presence of a lockboxes supposedly ensures that, should there be an incident on site, the response units have all of the necessary information immediately at hand. This ensures that appropriate suppression and mitigation procedures will be followed.

However, this on-site information is *never to substitute for a preplan*. It is to be used only as a reference source. Should a department not become familiar with the facilities in its district, anticipating the use of the lockbox information, critical problems may easily arise due to, among other things, the complexity of the information. It is impossible for anyone to learn how to quickly read and comprehend an MSDS under the stress of an emergency situation. Likewise, selecting from among alternative access routes according to a building floor plan needs careful deliberation prior to an incident. The material in the lockbox can be used only as backup reference material.

Another possibility in working with lockboxes must be recognized. The information may not be usable. The contents may have been removed to be updated on the day of the incident, or the box itself may be in a contaminated area, preventing access. Even if a box in a contaminated area could be accessed, the information inside it could not be used because of contamination of the materials. This is why it is imperative that the lockbox be used as a backup reference source, not a crutch.

These concerns can be dealt with in a comprehensive training program. In fact, not only the fire department needs to consider these issues, but the other participants in the process as well. This encourages understanding among the participants as they share their information and concerns. The sharing of a concern is often all that is necessary to alleviate it. Thus, information and training are the crucial elements of a successful emergency response plan.

Chapter 7

THE STATE EMERGENCY RESPONSE COMMISSION

INTRODUCTION

Under the U.S. system of government, the executive branch is charged with the implementation of the laws passed by the legislature. The governor, as chief executive of the state, is given the responsibility of executing or implementing SARA at the state level. This is to be done via the appointment of the SERC. Should the governor fail to appoint the commission within the time limit set by the law, the governor must personally operate as the commission.

This requirement clearly designates where the responsibility for the effort at the state level rests. The governor is given a great deal of discretion in appointment, but appointments must be made. This requirement also enables each state to adapt the implementation procedures to its own situation. This provides the necessary balance between conforming to a national minimum standard and adjusting to local differences.

The governor of each state, as noted above, is charged with appointing the SERC. The governor has the option of appointing a new commission or designating one or more existing organizations as the SERC. In order to use an existing organization(s), it (they) must deal with emergency response and must be appointed or sponsored by the state. This provision allows those states with preexisting emergency response commissions operating under a different name and directive to simply incorporate the Title III requirements into existing planning efforts. This avoids duplication of effort and ensures compatibility of plans. It is vital that statewide planning efforts complement rather than duplicate each other within the state. As a result, when a new commission is appointed, membership is a crucial issue.

MEMBERSHIP

The law states that the governor is to appoint persons "who have technical expertise in the emergency response field" (SARA Title III, Sec. 301.a.) There are no other qualifications specifically designated in the law. The term "technical expert" can mean many things. Generally it refers to someone who has advanced knowledge or training about specialized equipment or scientific areas. In this case, it does include individuals such as these, but it includes other "experts" as well, due to the type of information and awareness that is necessary to complete the tasks assigned the committee.

The most traditional types of technical experts that should be represented on the SERC are those familiar with hazardous materials. Representatives in this category could come from a variety of sources. What is important is that they be (1) well versed in the properties of the designated hazardous chemicals; (2) acquainted with the regulations concerning the use, transportation, and storage of hazardous materials; and (3) willing to share their expertise in a useful fashion with the other members of the SERC. This last criterion is vital for every member of the SERC and of the LEPCs, as information is useless if it not made available and used. In this effort, it is vital that persons with training in hazardous materials be available on the SERC.

One source of hazardous materials experts is private industry, a segment that deserves representation in its own right.

Private industry, which is given a number of new and very specific responsibilities, needs to be represented on the SERC. It is important for the members of the SERC to learn how industry deals with hazardous materials, what the general understanding of the requirements are, and how various alternative approaches for fulfilling the requirements would affect industry in general, as well as specific types of businesses. Industry will be very interested in the activities of the SERC and should be quite willing to provide representation, as it is the primary user of hazardous materials.

As the legislation deals with emergency response, experts in this area should also be on the SERC. Emergency response involves those who answer the call for aid should a spill occur. The obvious responders include the fire service, police or public safety department and emergency medical personnel. Each of these professions should be represented on the SERC. They know what is required in given circumstances, what is feasible, and what is not feasible. Due to the specialized nature of hazardous chemicals and the rigors of preplanning, representatives of these fields need to be familiar with both the organization and operation of the professions and the specifics of technical equipment and training. As a result, the SERC may need more than one representative from these areas, especially the fire service.

Fire departments are generally the first responders in a hazardous materials incident. The legislation has direct impact on their operation and future responsibilities. The SERC needs to be in close communication with local fire departments in order to keep in mind the impact that their decisions have on the departments, the hazardous materials response units, the equipment requirements, and the personnel and training requirements. The manner in which the legislation is implemented at the state level can have a major impact on budgets and daily operations of local fire departments. The SERC must be constantly aware of the status of local progress and of potential side effects certain types of requirements may produce. In addition, the activities and response of the fire service must be closely coordinated with the other participants in this process.

Another segment of society which is aware of the potential impact of a hazardous materials spill is the environmentalists. Environmental protection interest groups have a keen interest in Title III, and many are following it closely. They are also often aware of the location of hazardous chemicals and of violations in their use. Their representatives serve two purposes: (1) they can inform the SERC of the primary concerns in the state, and (2) they can inform their members of the activities and efforts undertaken by the SERC to deal with these issues. Information exchange is crucial in this process. This effort should be as open as possible.

In addition to the environmental interest groups, any state environmental protection agency should be represented on the SERC. Obviously, a hazardous materials spill would affect the environment, especially if it were near water, which could carry the material a great distance. The environmental protection agency can provide a great deal of information on topography, environmental sensitivities and secondary impact potentials. They can also provide existing regional plans for controlling water pollution and other such problems, plans which may be useful in dealing with or preparing the local response plans. Their representative on the SERC would, therefore, be the logical contact person for the LEPC should they latler require such information.

Just as the state environmental protection agency can provide useful information, other state agencies which provide various state and regional planning activities could be valuable additions to the SERC. Two such agencies which are particularly appropriate, given the materials involved in their areas of operation, are the agriculture department (pesticides) and the utilities department (fuels).

Technical expertise includes the areas of planning, training and education. Agencies involved in preplanning such as state disaster services, of which hazardous materials preplanning is a logical component, need to be involved in order to avoid duplication of effort and to facilitate merging of the new plans with those already in existence. Given the training requirements of

SARA, a representative of the educational community familiar with professional training would be a great asset to the SERC.

This cross section of representatives ensures that the segments of the state community most directly affected by Title III requirements have a voice in implementing the law at the state level. It must be remembered that the purpose of this committee is to enable the implementation of the law in the most efficient and effective manner possible. The letter and intent of the law must be met. There is no room for negotiation of level of compliance, and the time for lobbying for revision of requirements has passed. The SERC is charged with implementing a law that has clearly stated requirements and a deadline that leaves little time for inaction. This must be a cooperative effort if the maximum benefit is to be gained by all concerned.

REPRESENTATION

Representation on any committee is a two-way street. Individual members bring to the committee concerns, problems, specific information and the progress of the group they represent. In addition, these members are expected to share the decisions and activities of the committee with the group they represent. One of the most crucial components of this process is communication. It doesn't matter what action the SERC takes if no one knows about it. The members of the SERC are expected to share the progress made with the members of their representative organizations, with their supervisors, with the general public, and with anyone else who would like to or needs to know what is happening with the implementation of Title III in their state. Comments and concerns from these groups then need to be conveyed to the SERC in the form of constructive feedback. It may happen that some initial plans of procedure must be amended. That is preferable to implementing a flawed plan which either would not work or whose negative consequences would outweigh the positive.

The SERC is attempting to implement the law in a way which maximizes the positions of all concerned. It is recognized that each participant will have to take on new roles and expend resources to implement the law. However, it is not expected that any participant will be so taxed by the requirements that he or she is unable to comply. Industry- or business-specific characteristics that would result in certain requirements causing severe difficulties may exist, however, and need to be discussed so that they can be taken into consideration. These are the kinds of feedback that representatives need to bring to the SERC as the process unfolds. The exchange of information and ideas is central to this undertaking.

Another crucial aspect of representation is that it enables the integration of existing information, plans and other efforts, thus reducing duplication of activities. SARA is not intended to replace or duplicate existing emergency response plans. It is designed to ensure that there is a response plan specifically geared hazardous materials in fixed facilities with a certain minimum set of criteria. This plan can become an addendum to or expansion of an existing plan if that is appropriate. It is not meant to override existing plans, but rather to supplement them and ensure a common minimum standard.

In order for this to take place, the SERC members must first be aware of the information and plans available through their respective groups or agencies and must then make this known to the SERC. If this is not done by the SERC members, then representation on the committee is immaterial. It doesn't matter who sits on the committee if there is no dialogue and sharing of information.

At the state level, the sharing of information involves a greater degree of responsiveness in terms of the area covered and the numbers and locations of people who need to get the information. Getting the information means not only receiving periodic and timely reports concerning the activities and decisions of the SERC, but also being able to ask questions and get quick and correct answers. The members of the SERC must be accessible to members of the LEPCs and other persons directly affected by their activities.

In addition, the SERC must be open and responsive to information on how its decisions are affecting those whom the laws addresses. The SERC is the decision-making body which decides how the federal law will be implemented within the state. As such, it needs to make informed decisions. This can occur only when it is open to information from outside sources. When the SERC makes a decision, it should want as well as expect a response from the community and its members on how the decision will affect them. This does not mean that each time a decision is made, the SERC must reconsider and change. It does mean that the SERC may need to reconsider a decision on the basis of more information. The decision can stand, but the SERC will know more completely what the impact of that decision is. This leads to more informed and responsive decision making.

CRITIQUE VERSUS CRITICISM

The SERC should not only want but actively seek critiques of its activities. A critique of the SERC is a careful analysis of the positive and negative aspects of its decisions and activities. Too often criticism is offered in lieu of a critique. Criticism is seldom useful unless it is accompanied by suggestions for alternatives and improvements. All public entities received criticism; that is part of the normal operation. A critique, unfortunately, is not that common. Yet is a useful tool for assessing the impact of programs, policies and decisions.

One of the things the SERC should do is to try to convert a criticism into a critique. Generally, criticism is based on specific reasons; however, those reasons are seldom clearly expressed. If the SERC encouraged expression of the reasons, and of the positive as well as the negative impacts of and reactions to a process or decision, it could diffuse some criticism and change it into helpful feedback. This would enable the SERC to make more informed decisions and to plan for diffusion, as much as possible, of the negative impacts of the decisions.

RESPONSIBILITIES OF THE SERC

The primary responsibilities of the SERC are set forth in Public Law 99-499 and in subsequent "Rules and Regulations" in the Federal Register. In fulfilling these responsibilities, it is expected that the SERC will perform whatever activities and make whatever decisions and/or provisions are necessary. Thus, even though the regulations do not specifically mention the creation of subcommittees, for example, this is a logical activity in fulfilling the SERC's responsibilities. Thus, although these responsibilities may seem to be narrow and limited, they are, in fact, important and complex.

Since the SERC is the coordinating and implementing entity at the state level, it has the authority to take whatever actions are necessary to see that compliance with the law takes place within the state. When a commission or agency must carry out a federal legal requirement, it also, by default, receives the authority necessary to make certain that this is done. Thus, the SERC can, within reason, mandate activities designed to implement the federal requirements of Title III.

Establishment of Emergency Planning Districts

The first responsibility of the SERC is the establishment of emergency planning districts within the state by July 1987.

> Not later than nine months after the date of the enactment of this title, the State emergency response commission shall designate emergency planning districts in order to facilitate preparation and implementation of emergency plans. Where appropriate, the State emergency response commission may designate existing political subdivisions or multijurisdictional planning organizations as such districts. (Public Law 99-499, Oct. 17, 1986. Title III, Subtitle A, Sec. 301 (b))

The establishment of local planning districts ensures that the information and plans are available to and appropriate for those who will serve as first responders in any hazardous materials incident. The designation of these sites is assigned to the SERC in order to maximize adaptation of the federal program to local situations. Although the information, reporting, training and planning requirements are universal, the EPA has tried to allow latitude for specific local characteristics which may facilitate easier and more rapid compliance. It is felt that the state has a better understanding of the current situation in local areas than the federal government, even through its regional office. Thus, the states can take into consideration the existing situation when establishing the local emergency planning districts.

The SERC has the option of designating "existing political subdivisions or multijurisdictional planning organizations" as the local planning districts. States with comprehensive planning mechanisms, especially for disaster planning, in place can simply dovetail the SARA Title III requirements into existing planning structures. This avoids duplication of effort and facilitates the integration of SARA planning requirements with other comprehensive planning activities. An example of such a multijurisdictional planning entity is the Regional Councils of Governments, which coordinate a variety of comprehensive planning efforts within a specified regional boundary. Examples of such local planning district designations include California, which designated six preexistent districts for other planning needs, and Idaho, where the six districts correspond to transportation districts ranging in size from 5 to 11 counties.

The SERC can also choose to designate existing political subdivisions as the planning districts, even if there are no current comprehensive disaster plans at that level. This choice is logical in that it utilizes accepted preestablished boundaries which are recognized as legal entities and jurisdictions within which planning activities take place and legal requirements are enforced. An example of such political subdivisions would be counties. Indeed, some states have identified counties as the smallest planning unit because (1) they are well established and easily identifiable to the public, (2) in most cases, the primary responders to a hazardous materials incident would come from within the county, (3) the area encompassed is reasonable in terms of response time and secondary aid planning, and (4) there is a precedent for coordination between counties at the state level.

Arizona, Nevada, Ohio, Arkansas and Oklahoma are among those states that have designated counties as the local emergency planning districts. Many of these states, although based on the county division, allow special exceptions to account for special local circumstances. Ohio allowed counties to join together into one planning district if they so desired, and two counties, Montgomery and Green, in the Dayton area, did. In Washington, cities were allowed to form their own planning committees, and as of November 1987, 30 had done so. A list of the emergency response commissioners as of April 1988 and the nature of the local emergency planning districts designated by the SERC is provided in Appendix E.

The rationale for designating local areas as the primary planning sites is that, in addition to being most practical for first responders, it facilitates public input into the planning process and encourages the representation of multiple interests in the planning process. In particular, those individuals and groups supporting the community-right-to-know requirements, which is one of the driving forces behind SARA, have a chance to become involved in the planning process at the local level. This philosophy is also present in the approval of the membership on the LEPC, as will be discussed later. At this point, however, this recognition is important in relation to the designation of the local emergency planning districts. A number of states have designated the entire state as the local emergency planning district. The EPA has approved this in some instances, but there is a major debate as to whether it violates the intent of the law by restricting local public participation and site-specific considerations. The outcome of this debate is not certain at this time. However, if the final interpretation is that statewide planning districts do not meet the intent of the law, those states operating in such a fashion will be faced with the need to redo their planning, a duplication of effort which everyone would prefer to avoid.

Establishment of Local Emergency Planning Committees

Each local planning district is to have its own LEPC. The SERC is responsible for appointing the members of the LEPC. However, the SERC seldom actually chooses local members. Generally, the SERC instructs a local individual or entity, such as the county government, to identify and nominate members for the LEPC. These individuals are then approved through formal appointment by the SERC. This appointment authority is assigned to the SERC to ensure central coordination of activities and adherence to the federally mandated representation requirements.

SARA requires that each LEPC contain, at a minimum, "representatives from each of the following groups or organizations: elected State and local officials; law enforcement, civil defense, firefighting, first aid, health, local environmental, hospital, and transportation personnel; broadcast and print media; community groups; and owners and operators of facilities subject to the requirements of this subtitle" (Public Law 99-499, Oct. 17, 1986. Title III, Subtitle A, Sec. 301 (c)). The reasons for identifying these groups as the ones with mandatory representation will be discussed in the following chapter. At this point, it is enough to state that there is a reason for each group to be present and that the SERC must ensure that it is represented on each LEPC.

Having one central authority responsible for all LEPC appointments in the state also ensures that the same interpretation of group membership is used within the state. This eliminates some of the confusion and debate over the representation requirements established by SARA Title III.

Revision of LEPC Membership or Local Planning District Designation

Since the SERC has the responsibility for designating the planning districts and for appointing members to the LEPCs, it has the option of amending those designations and/or appointments as well. Thus, if the SERC decides later in the planning process that the amount of overlap and coordination needed between two or more planning districts requires them to work together to create one plan, the planning districts can be condensed into one. Conversely, a district which demonstrates two different operational considerations on the basis of geography, population or industry dispersion may petition for separation. The SERC can then choose to accept this petition and create two planning districts from the one.

These illustrate the two basic ways in which planning district boundaries may be changed. The SERC, upon review of the situation, may decide on its own to change the designation, or individuals or groups may petition for reconsideration. When a group or individual does present a reasoned, formal petition for consideration and offers documented evidence to substantiate its case, the SERC must consider it. The SERC does not have to grant the petition, but it does need to consider it formally and provide a formal response to the petitioners.

This response is especially important in regard to petitions concerning representation on a LEPC. The SERC can amend the membership of a LEPC as necessary during the planning process. Given the intent of the law to ensure broad representation on these groups, community members or members of other designated groups who feel that they are not being adequately represented may petition to modify the local membership. As part of the SERC's responsibility in appointing members is to ensure appropriate representation, such petitions should receive high priority and serious consideration. Again, the SERC does not have to modify the membership, but it does need to respond seriously to the petition.

Coordination of Information and Response to Public Requests for Information

The State emergency response commission shall establish procedures for receiving and processing requests from the public for information under section 324, including tier II information under section 312. Such procedures shall include the designation of an official to serve as coordinator for information. (Public Law 99-499, Oct. 17, 1988. Title III, Subtitle A, Sec. 301 (a))

In choosing the official to serve as coordinator for information, the SERC needs to be cognizant of the type and amount of work this may entail. Generally, the individual named is chosen because of his or her official position. For example, the information officer for the state

EPA would be a logical choice, as the infrastructure for handling inquiries is already in place. The purpose of selecting an information coordinator is that the public, including the LEPCs, has one authoritative source for information they need or want. This precludes the problem getting different information, depending on which official is called. With one information source designated, the same information is given in response to all similar requests.

As mentioned earlier, it is vital that the SERC maintain good communication with the LEPCs. The LEPCs need to be kept up-to-date on the various decisions, debates or discussions being held by the SERC. The LEPCs may have important information that the SERC needs to consider as it makes its decisions. The LEPCs, however, will not know what information is needed, or when, unless they know what topics are being considered. It is not enough for the SERC to disperse decisions that are made; it also needs to be in constant communication with the LEPCs and other entities involved in this program. It is recommended that the minutes of each SERC meeting be distributed to each LEPC in a timely fashion. It would be helpful to circulate meeting agendas as well.

The role of the SERC in receiving and processing requests from the public for information under Sections 324 and 312 is more complex than it initially seems. The community right-to-know intent of SARA enables members of the public to find out what types of hazardous materials are stored in their community and what plans are in place to deal with a potential emergency situation. Thus, Section 324 provides that

(e)ach emergency response plan, material safety data sheet, list described in section 311(a)(2), inventory form, toxic, chemical release form and followup emergency notice shall be made available to the general public, consistent with section 322, during normal working hours at the location or locations designated by the . . . State emergency response commission, or local emergency planning committee, as appropriate. Upon request by an owner or operator of a facility subject to the requirements of section 312, the State emergency response commission and the appropriate local emergency planning committee shall withhold from disclosure under this section the location of any specific chemical required by section 312(d)(2) to be contained in an inventory form as tier II information. (Public Law 99-499, Oct. 17, 1986. Title III, Sec. 324 (a))

Although the LEPC is also charged with making information available to the public, since the SERC is charged with "establishing procedures for receiving and processing requests for information from the public" as well as providing information, it must take the lead in this activity.

Initial consideration of Title III indicates that specific information on all hazardous chemicals is to be made available to the public across the board. Closer examination shows that this is not true. The first set of hazardous materials information which can be withheld by industry consists of those elements classified as trade secrets. (See Public Law 99-499, Sec. 322, for specific details on trade secrets.) The EPA determines whether a petition for classification as a trade secret is acceptable. If so, the industry information is *not* accessible to the public. In addition, on information sheets, generally MSDSs, given to the emergency planning committees, the specific chemical identity may be withheld, although the generic class or category of the substance involved must be reported.

Section 312 (d) (2) discusses in detail the Tier II information which is to be provided on the MSDSs. Subpart (F) of that section states that the inventory form shall provide "an indication of whether the owner elects to withhold location information of a specific hazardous chemical from disclosure to the public under section 324." Thus, the facility owner can elect not to make certain location information on certain chemicals available to the public. The reason for allowing this withholding of location information is the concern about possible attacks on the facility for the purpose of releasing or stealing a hazardous chemical. This is possible in a terrorist situation aimed at destruction or blackmail or both. Thus, a community resident living across the street from a facility who wishes to know whether a given chemical is located in the building may not be able to get that information.

Section 312 (e) (3) deals with the availability of information to the public. Subpart (A) says, in part, "(a)ny . . . request shall be in writing and shall be with respect to a specific facility." Thus, neither the SERC nor the LEPC is obligated to respond to telephone calls asking about a facility. Nor must they respond to requests about the general presence of toxic or hazardous materials in the community. The purpose of the law is to provide serious people who have a personal interest in knowing what hazards are present in their community a means of getting this information. Its purpose is not to provide public support for irate crank calls and activities or for enterprising businessmen.

One SERC received a request from a chemical manufacturing and sales firm. This company wanted a list, including the contact person and address, of every facility in the state which reported having certain chemicals on site. Attached to this request was a list of almost 100 chemicals. Since the request was not for information on a specific facility, the SERC did not reply. Nor should it. The law was intended to provide public information, not help identify targets for sales calls.

The law does require the SERC and the LEPC to provide Tier II information on a specific facility in its possession upon request. If the information is not in its possession, the LEPC and/or the SERC must ask the facility owner or operator to supply it, and will then provide it to the person making the request. In addition, if an individual requests Tier II information on a chemical which is stored in quantities of less than 10,000 pounds at the facility, the need for the information must be specified. Thus, the public may be able to get certain information on chemicals for quantities less than the threshold amounts established. The law further states that in instances of such requests, the "State emergency response commission or the local emergency planning committee *may* . . . request the facility owner or operator for the Tier II information on behalf of the person making the request" (Public Law 99-499, Oct. 17, 1986. Tittle III, Sec. 312 (e) (3) (C)).

This is where discretion on the part of the SERC and the LEPC again comes into play. The reason for requiring a need for such information is that the determination of a reasonable request can be made. When the SERC or LEPC does request information on chemicals below the threshold amounts, the facility must comply. The SERC or LEPC must then pass the information on to the person making the request. Determinations of reasonable request should be made on the basis of the spirit of the law. If an individual or community group has a real interest in or need for the information, then the spirit of the law would support gathering it and passing it on. The SERC must not only make these determinations, but must establish a procedure for considering and processing all requests for information.

The vital need for the early establishment of a procedure to process and respond to information requests is supported not only by the intent of the law to provide information to the public in a timely manner, but also by the letter of the law. Section 312 (e) (3) (D) requires the SERC or the LEPC to respond to a request for Tier II information within 45 days after the date of receipt. Thus, a mechanism for response must be in place.

The law does not discuss funding for the public dispersal of information. However, it is obvious that responses to public requests for information could be costly. As a result, it may be necessary to charge small fees for the processing of required information. These fees must be reasonable so as not to be prohibitive to the general public. A fee that was set too high for the average individual to afford would be considered a violation of the intent of the law, as it would bar access to public information. Reasonable, moderate fees, especially if there were a process in place to allow for a petition to waive fees by an individual with cause, would, however, be a logical component of the processing procedures. It would also facilitate record keeping of the numbers and types of requests received over time for future evaluation of the success and merit of the community right-to-know component of SARA.

Thus, the coordination of public information dispersal is a potentially heavy responsibility for the SERC. Although requests for information will also go to the LEPCs (as will be discussed in the next chapter), the final arbiter of requests will be the SERC. If a serious request to the LEPC is not satisfactorily resolved, it is relatively certain that the citizen will take the request and his or her dissatisfaction forward to the SERC. Therefore, it is vital that the mechanism for dealing with these requests and problems be in place before requests arrive.

Receiving Reports on the Presence of Toxic and Hazardous Substances

The SERC receives copies of all reports on the presence of toxic and hazardous substances. These facility reports go to three entities: the SERC, the LEPC, and the local fire department. Each of them needs an information compilation and processing system appropriate to its own needs. It is important that these systems be compatible, however, so that the three components of the emergency planning process can communicate effectively with one another.

Once again, it is natural for the SERC to take the lead in this endeavor. The local fire departments especially will need help in establishing the capability and procedures for massive information processing. They must also have a quick means of access to the state in the event of a hazardous incident. When the degree of interaction and cooperation necessary for quick, effective communication is so complex, and the location of the components is as physically spread out as it is in many states, it is logical and necessary to have one component coordinate the process. Since the SERC is given the responsibility for appointing the LEPCs and their districts, it is logical that it take the lead in establishing the communication system.

Thus, being responsible for receiving information means much more than simply boxing up sheafs of paper. Although the law does not specifically state that the SERC is to be responsible for information processing, except for the aforementioned public requests, it is logical to operate with the knowledge that the law intended the SERC to be more than a simple storehouse for information.

By linking into a statewide information system, local fire departments can have immediate access to expert information concerning a specific chemical in a hazardous material release. The SERC can provide a uniform information processing system that will enable fire departments and LEPCs to communicate easily with each other, facilitating appropriate backup in an emergency situation. Additionally, since the information coming to the SERC is also being given to the LEPCs and local fire departments, the SERC will know what is and is not being provided. If there is a systemic reason for not receiving information, the SERC may be in a better position to resolve the issue at the state level.

Designation of Additional Facilities to be Covered

Facilities automatically covered under Title III are those which have on site an extremely hazardous substance in quantities in excess of its threshold quantity. In addition, however, the law states:

> For purposes of emergency planning, a Governor or a State emergency response commission may designate additional facilities which shall be subject to the requirements of this subtitle, if such designation is made after public notice and opportunity for comment. The Governor or State emergency response commission shall notify the facility concerned of any facility designation under this paragraph. (Public Law 99-499, Oct. 17, 1986. Sec. 302 (b) (2))

This section deals with the designation of additional facilities rather than the specific characteristics of facilities to be so designated. Basically the procedure is in conformity with public information and response laws which require individuals, groups, corporations or any other entities which would be affected by an addition to the law to be allowed to present their case for amending or not establishing the ruling. The governor or the SERC, whichever was the designating entity, would have to provide timely public notice and an opportunity for comment, which generally means well-advertised public hearings.

This provision of the law is designed to account for individual circumstances which may arise. For example, a facility that is known to use hazardous substances but is careful to always have an amount just under the threshold limit on site at any one time may seek to avoid the letter of the law by violating the intent. In this instance, the SERC could designate that facility as covered. Likewise, if a state-specific or region-specific industry uses, in large amounts, a hazardous substance that is not on the published list of covered substances, facilities with that substance on site can be designated as subject to the requirements of Title III. Once a facility is so designated, it must be notified by the SERC that it must now comply.

Review of the Local Emergency Response Plans

Once the LEPC has completed its emergency response plan, it must submit a copy to the SERC: "The [SERC] shall review the plan and make recommendations to the committee on revisions of the plan that may be necessary to ensure coordination of such plan with emergency response plans of other emergency planning districts. To the maximum extent practicable, such review *shall not delay implementation* of such plan" (Public Law 99-499, Oct. 17, 1986. Title III, Sec. 303 (e)). This does not necessarily mean that the members of the SERC will actually review each plan. It does mean, however, that the SERC is responsible for ensuring that each plan is carefully reviewed. The SERC must designate an entity to be charged with complete and accurate review of all emergency response plans submitted.

The primary purpose of the review is to ensure that the plans are coordinated with other existing state emergency response plans and with those of adjoining or superimposed LEPCs. This is crucial when the facilities in question are located on district borders or when a city is a separate planning district within a county or regional district. In these instances, the response to an emergency situation may well involve more than one planning district, and there must be a mechanism to insure coordination.

Note that the law says that the SERC shall make *recommendations* to the committee concerning revisions. The SERC is not responsible for enforcing the plan. LEPCs are expected to respond to suggestions and recommendations, as they are motivated to have the best and most appropriate plan in place. The SERC should spend its time and effort seeing that the LEPCs have the information necessary to draw up these plans and guidance on their content and structure, rather than worrying about noncompliance by LEPCs. The SERC is not meant to be an enforcement entity, even though, as the next section explains, it may choose to assume that role.

If possible, the SERC or its designated agent should provide whatever additional aid it can to the LEPCs in the creation of the emergency response plan. The National Response Team has published the *Hazardous Materials Emergency Planning Guide* (better known as the *NRT-1*) to aid the LPCs. This document will be discussed in more detail in Chapter 7. Additional supplements to this directive are encouraged and would be most helpful. For example, in Ohio, the State Disaster Services Agency has been designated as the reviewer of emergency response plans. This agency has produced a *Hazardous Materials Cross Reference* which lists the various planning elements it expects to find in each local hazardous materials emergency Response Plan. It also provides a section for reference to the local plan to facilitate review and comparison. This lets the LEPCs know in detail what their plan is expected to contain.

Commencement of Civil Action Against a Facility for Failure to Comply

Subpart (1) (B) of Title III states that "(a)ny State emergency response commission or local emergency planning committee may commence a civil action against an owner or operator of a facility for failure to provide information under section 303(d) or for failure to submit tier II information under section 312(e)(1)." Thus, although not conceived as an enforcement entity, the SERC may take civil action to force a facility to comply if, after a reasonable effort, it fails to do so.

Should the SERC or LEPC decide to file a civil action suit against a facility, it must first give 60 days' notice of intent to the state governor and to the federal EPA. This ensures that the facility in question is not under an administrative order to civil action by the EPA to enforce the requirement or to impose a penalty. It also serves to give the facility final notice. Such action is expected to be undertaken only after repeated attempts to get the facility to comply have failed.

The SERC and/or the LEPC must demonstrate that the facility had been reasonably and repeatedly approached, had been informed of the legal requirements, and had refused to cooperate. Although ignorance of the law is no excuse, it is reasonable to ask for documentation that the SERC had informed the facility of compliance requirements and requested cooperation in a reasonable fashion.

Steadfast and absolute refusal to comply is not expected. There may be facilities which, for one reason or another, are late in complying or which report only partial information. If this occurs, the LEPC and SERC will contact them for additional information. If the facility is unreasonably late or fails to provide the comprehensive information required, the SERC or LEPC can then undertake a civil action.

The law provides that in cases such as this, the courts may award the costs of litigation to the prevailing party. This means that if the SERC wins, its court costs are paid by the facility sued. If the SERC does not win, however, it must pay the facility's court costs. For this reason as well as because of the time involved, the civil suit, while not to be disregarded, should be an action of last resort. It also underscores the necessity of building a solid record of attempts at nonjudicial reconciliation of the problem.

THE SERC AND TRAINING

Although not specifically listed as a responsibility of the SERC, coordination of mandated training within the state is a logical duty. SARA and the OSHA Hazards Communications Act require training in hazardous materials response for all first responders. Title III states that existing federal programs for emergency training are authorized to provide the requisite training. This refers to courses such as those prepared by the National Fire Academy of the Federal Emergency Management Agency (FEMA), which already exist. These courses are to be made available to first responders and other eligible state and local personnel. Rather than having the LEPCs contact FEMA directly for a course which only the members of an individual LEPC may attend, it is better to have a coordinated system of providing training and, if possible, access to training across the state.

Such coordination would enable integration of the courses available from different federal programs, diminish duplication of information, and facilitate the coverage of all types of information that are necessary and available. It is possible that some new courses may need to be prepared. This, however, is not specifically addressed in the law.

The law does refer to the appropriation of $5 million per year for 4 years, 1987–1990, to support programs "designed to improve emergency planning, preparedness, mitigation, response, and recovery capabilities." Although $5 million seems like a lot of money, dividing that amount by 50 states and then by the number of LEPCs within a state quickly demonstrates that funding at the local level is nominal. These funds are not designed to pay for all of the local training costs which may be incurred. They are targeted for programs to enhance and facilitate the availability of training. Thus, the state, through the SERC, once again needs to take the lead in coordinating training efforts to ensure the quality and availability of training.

It must be noted that all first responders are to be trained. This includes not only professional or paid firefighters, but also volunteer firefighters, law officers, medical personnel, security professionals and government officials. This is an expansive training program designed to complement the planning process which encompasses more individuals than the traditionally narrowly defined emergency personnel.

The training likewise has a broader definition. It should include more than a simple rundown of the characteristics and effects of a few of the more common chemicals in one or two hazard classifications. It must encompass, at a minimum, recognition of the placarding systems, methods of cross-classification and chemical identification, characteristics of the five major hazard classifications, response techniques for the different classifications, communication procedures in the event of a release, notification requirements, how to read an MSDS, emergency medical treatment for different types of hazards and evacuation procedures. As a result, it is probably necessary to expand and/or adapt existing training programs.

The SERC has an obligation to the citizens of the state to monitor the type of training received and the persons trained. In the event of a hazardous material release, no emergency response plan will make a difference if those responding have not received appropriate training.

ORGANIZATION OF THE SERC

The law does not provide guidelines for the organization and operation of the SERC. Its responsibilities and duties lead to some obvious organizational preferences, however. There must be a chair, either appointed by the governor or elected by the members of the commission. The same is true for a vice-chair. The primary functions of these individuals are to call and chair meetings. These functions may seem obvious, but a committee without a chair seldom meets. The traditional position of secretary may or may not be necessary. It is expected that staff support will be available to take minutes and prepare them for distribution. If it seems necessary to have someone verify the minutes before they are distributed, this could be done either by the chair, vice-chair or secretary, as the commission prefers. The need for the position of treasurer is likewise negotiable, depending on the funding provisions for the commission and its discretion over available funds.

The size of the commission and the variety of tasks it faces do indicate the need for subcommittees. It is difficult for a very large group to work on detailed assignments. Subcommittees can investigate and track a single issue more thoroughly. The number of tasks to be performed also supports the creation of subcommittees so that work on these tasks can proceed simultaneously. It is simply not possible for everyone to give the same amount of time and attention to each task.

The subcommittees should maintain a broad representation, while at the same time calling upon the expertise of some of the members of the commission. For example, a logical subcommittee would be one dealing with training. Obviously, members of the SERC with a background in education and training should be on this committee. It is also wise to have representatives of those groups which are to receive training on the committee as well. This provides expert knowledge with important responsive information on the impact of alternatives considered. Other logical subcommittees include information and data coordination, finance/funding and public information. Obviously, the subcommittees designated by the SERC should be appropriate to the state in question. The need for subcommittees is universal, however, given the representation and task requirements.

THE SERC: A SUMMARY

The SERC is the leading entity in the implementation of SARA at the state level. As such, it has a vital role in the process. Many of its responsibilities are the cornerstones for successful implementation of the policy. The membership of the SERC is crucial, as it mirrors the intent of the legislation in opening government to the people. The broad representation on the SERC facilitates the communication that is so crucial to the enactment of this program. Those who are appointed and who agree to serve must be willing to take their part seriously and consider the good of the program, as well as the specific interests of the constituencies they represent.

A good and active SERC can make the difference between a successful, comprehensive emergency response plan which spans the state, as well as focusing on local levels, and late, half-hearted and half-completed plans which would serve no use in a hazardous materials release incident.

Chapter 8

THE LOCAL EMERGENCY RESPONSE COMMITTEE

Each local emergency planning district designated by the SERC has its own LEPC. The members of the LEPC are appointed to by the SERC under Section 301 (c). It is this committee which has responsibility for implementation of the law at the local level.

Several aspects of the LEPCs and their operation deserve detailed attention. One of the keys to successfully carrying out the intent of the law is the effective operation of the local committees. In the final analysis, the product of their labors will determine the success or failure of SARA.

It must be remembered that the two purposes of SARA are emergency planning and facilitating community right-to-know. It is at the local level that emergency planning is most crucial because it is there that the emergency response to a hazardous chemical release must take place. An emergency plan that is comprehensive and appropriate for the local situation is the visible outcome of this massive nationwide effort. It is hoped that the success of the program will never be tested, for the truest test lies in the evaluation of a response to a hazardous materials incident. Undoubtedly, and unfortunately, such tests will occur. Until they do, the best measure of success will be the degree of readiness of emergency first responders and responders at the local level.

MEMBERSHIP

Although the specific membership of the LEPC will vary by locality, SARA does require representation from certain areas of the community. The law states:

> Each committee shall include, at a minimum, representatives from each of the following groups or organizations: elected State and local officials; law enforcement, civil defense, firefighting, first aid, health, local environmental, hospital, and transportation personnel; broadcast and print media; community groups; and owners and operators of facilities subject to the requirements of this subtitle. (Public Law 99-499, Section 301 (c))

There is a reason for requiring representation from each of these groups. Each group brings a specific contribution to the LEPC.

The *elected state and local officials,* or their designated and empowered representatives, bring legitimate authority to the committee. These individuals have been elected by the citizens of the community to lead them. They are the legitimate leaders of the community. As a result, they have the authority to take action and to enforce decisions made. Without this authority, the decisions and actions of the LEPC could not be enforced and the work accomplished.

Recognizing this unique attribute of elected governments, the NRT-1 points out four other reasons that the participation of the local governments is so vital: (1) The major responsibilities for protecting public health and safety rest with government agencies. (2) Although not always clearly defined, one of the functional responsibilities of local government is to mediate and resolve the sometimes competing interests of different interest groups in a manner that is in the best interest of the community as a whole. (3) Local governments have the resources and authorization to gather the necessary planning data. (4) Local and state governments have the legislative authority to raise funds for equipment and personnel required for an emergency response (*NRT-1*, p. 14) For these reasons, active support from the executive and legislative branches is essential to successful planning. It is imperative that the local and state government representatives on the LEPC have the authority necessary to make decisions concerning emergency planning which will be supported and carried out.

Those governmental entities specifically cited in the law each bring a separate area of expertise and responsibility to the planning process. *Law enforcement* personnel are often first responders in emergency situations, as they often discover hazardous material releases on routine patrols. In addition, should a major release occur, the responsibility of evacuating and securing an area rests with the law enforcement officials. They need to be involved in the planning process in order to have input concerning the most effective reporting, evacuation and communication systems which would facilitate their jobs. They must also be aware of the procedures adopted by the LEPC so that they can effectively coordinate their activities with others.

The *civil defense, disaster services, or emergency management* local agency representatives need to be involved for a couple of reasons. First, they need to be certain that the response plan coordinates with other plans already in place. Knowing what is already available may facilitate the completion and increase the likely success of the plan. Using preexisting mechanisms is also a beneficial use of resources that avoids duplication of effort and of other more tangible resources. The participation of civil defense or disaster services enables the LEPC not only to obtain copies of existing plans, but also to gain an understanding of these plans from individuals familiar with their purpose as well as their content.

The second benefit of having the civil defense or disaster services represented on the LEPC is that they will be familiar with procedures in the event of an incident. This will enable them to respond with needed resources in a more timely and appropriate fashion. This cooperation and prior understanding are key goals of the entire SARA program.

Local fire departments must be included on the LEPC. Usually the hazardous materials response teams are special units of these departments. In addition, the fire department takes the most active and direct role in containing a spill and/or suppressing any reaction that may occur following an accidental release. The fire department is not only a first responder unit but also a primary responder. The preplanning has most direct impact on the fire department, as its personnel must know what types of hazardous materials are present in their district. This determines the type of equipment and suppression supplies necessary. Obviously, different hazardous materials require different suppression mechanisms. A water-reactive chemical, for example, requires a different strategy. The use of the standard traditional water supply would be disastrous.

The presence of fire department representatives allows two things. It enables the fire department to provide a realistic picture of its capabilities and resources to the LEPC. It also gives the fire department an understanding of the types of incidents to which it may need to respond in the future. This facilitates long-range planning in the areas of equipment acquisition, personnel hiring and training. The departments can better focus its resources on predicted potential situations rather than on the unknown.

The presence of *first aid, health and hospital* representatives brings an added dimension to the planning process. The agencies previously mentioned are all involved in the activities geared to immediate response to and suppression of a hazardous materials release. The health and first aid agencies deal with the impact of the release, both immediately and possibly for some time after the situation. First aid providers may include ambulance companies, EMS units of fire departments (in which case representation could be dual for one member of the LEPC), hospital emergency rooms and others. The health care providers include primarily hospitals and public health departments which will be counted on to treat victims of accidental releases. These responses may be either large in scale or confined to one or two individuals present when the release occurred.

Their presence on the planning committee and their designated responsibilities in the plan should cover both of these eventualities. All health provider organizations should have a plan for emergency care of large numbers of individuals in the event of a disaster, whether related to hazardous materials or not. Most health care organizations do, in fact, have such emergency disaster plans in effect. These agencies need to expand these plans to include the special types of care that may be necessary should a hazardous materials release occur. Again, their presence on the LEPC enables the emergency response plan to be dovetailed with existing agency plans and allows the health organizations to interface effectively with other responders in an emergency situation. Valuable information is thus exchanged.

First aid responders may or may not be the same as the health care providers. In either case, a key element in their participation is the ability to plan for the special type of first aid that may be necessary for a given release. This information can be shared with facilities planning to create an on-site response team. Members of this team could benefit from special training geared directly to dealing with the effects of the chemicals on site. In addition, off-site first aid responders (EMS) would know what type of aid would be required for any specific facility in the area.

Local and state environmental agencies are responsible for the preservation of the environment. As such, they have information on the current condition of the environment and the potential impacts of various hazardous materials. Their presence on the committee brings this knowledge to the local level. In addition, they can be ready to assist a local area in the event of a release.

Local transportation agency personnel are important, as they may be called upon to aid in evacuation procedures or in the activities necessary to secure an area. Mass transit is seen as an effective tool in evacuation procedures. It enables the quick movement of people away from the disaster scene, often without using public highways, as in the case of the San Francisco BART system. This would eliminate the problems associated with traffic jams, which could impede the arrival of emergency responders to the site.

State highway agencies are responsible for monitoring and planning for accidental releases during the transportation of hazardous materials. As materials are often transported to and from fixed facilities, it is logical for these organizations to work together to prevent duplication of effort and to share scarce resources.

In many states, the battle over territory and power associated with control and responsibility has won out over logical cooperation to maximize resources, reduce duplication of effort and resource acquisition, and truly comprehensive emergency response planning. The types of information required under the DOT hazardous materials planning requirements are similar if not identical to those required under SARA. The difference lies in whether the materials are in transport or in fixed facilities. The materials in fixed facilities had to have been transported there, however, and if they leave, they are transported elsewhere. In addition, the hazard associated with a specific chemical is the same regardless of its location. A flammable material is flammable in a fixed facility or in a truck or railroad tank car.

The establishment of statewide data bases to compile hazardous materials information could be designed to accommodate both transportation and fixed-facility information. The difficulty lies not in the capability of either technology or humans. Nor does it lie in the level of resources available. Instead, it lies in the petty battles for power through control of information. And the losers who pay for this are the citizens of the state, who have a less comprehensive response plan in place and whose taxes pay for the same service twice. Hopefully, the presence of these representatives on the LEPC can help to bridge this barrier and begin to build, instead, a spirit of cooperation for mutual benefit.

The foregoing are the governmental representatives who need to be present on the LEPCs. Each one brings a piece of the total information necessary to build a comprehensive response plan. In addition, each is expected to play a role in the response to an accidental hazardous materials release. Thus, these persons take back to their agency the information needed to prepare for such an eventuality. Other nongovernmental entities need to be represented on the LEPCs as well.

The broadcast and print media are an important part not only of the emergency response process but also of the planning process. In the event of a hazardous material release, the broadcast media are generally the primary sources of communication with the public. Residents of an affected area can be warned of the incident by the media, which then broadcast instructions on the procedures to be followed. This communication is vital in an emergency situation. The channels of communication need to be specified in advance. Individuals to be contacted must be identified, accessible, and have the authority to act quickly. The information to be broadcast must also be precise and accurate. Thus, it must be prepared in advance. Because of this crucial role, the media must participate in the planning process.

During the planning process and prior to emergency incidents, the print media, as well as the broadcast media, can provide a vital function in preparing the public to act quickly if needed. Stories and editorials about the planning process and the procedures to follow in the event if an incident can help inform the citizens and prepare them to act quickly and without panic in an emergency.

Another vital service the media can perform during the planning stage is that of soliciting and securing cooperation from private industry. Often facilities are unaware of the importance of their participation in the process. In addition, they do not realize that the timeliness of their response with the requisite information is not only legally enforceable but necessary to plan for an emergency response. Although newspaper editors may feel that stories about the planning process are not newsworthy, if they continue to uphold their mandate of informing the public, they will publish at least some of them.

One of the ways the LEPC may be able to access the newspapers is through the editorial pages. Contacting the editorial editor may result in an article concerning the importance of the process and the necessity of cooperation from private industry. Often industry leaders do not clearly understand the specific requirements or importance of SARA. An editorial pointing out their responsibilities and the consequences of meeting or not meeting them, will encourage more active participation on their part.

Community groups include residents near facilities storing or using hazardous chemicals on their premises, neighborhood organizations, civic groups, community activist groups, and possibly local environmental groups. The requirement for citizen participation rests on a number of justifications. First, participatory democracy prescribes the involvement of citizens in all levels and aspects of government rather than simply voting in elections. Second, the right-to-know component of the law is aimed at informing citizens, and participation is one way to ensure that the information is readily accessible. Third, the citizens can voice their concerns about the process and the presence of hazardous materials. At the same time, they can begin to understand the safety procedures already in place to protect them from an accidental release.

The owners and operators of facilities subject to the requirements of Title III must participate in the planning process. A major portion of the preplan is site specific. As a result, detailed information on the facility is necessary. In addition, it is logical to assume that in the event of a release, facility personnel will be on site and may well be the ones who report the incident. They therefore need to know the proper procedures to follow and who to contact. The same holds true in reverse. In order to have an effective response plan, the emergency responders must be familiar with the facility's layout and the location of various hazardous materials. In the event of a release, they need to know the identity and location of the facility contact person, how to gain access to the facility, the location of various hazards, and the location and operation of any on-site suppression systems. Due to the great importance of the Facility Coordinator or representative, their role is examined in greater detail in Chapters 4 and 9.

These are the mandatory representatives on the LEPC. They cover the groups or agencies which will be directly involved in responding to a hazardous materials release. As such, their input during the planning process is invaluable. They, in turn, must be kept informed about the response plan and their part in the activities which will take place. Contact persons and emergency procedures must be agreed upon and made known to all concerned. Any changes which take place over time must also be communicated to all participants. (This function of the committee will be discussed later.) Although the above-named entities are the only ones whose participation is required, membership is not restricted to these groups.

Communities with unique individual characteristics may want or need to include others on the LEPC. For example, a planning district which is primarily agricultural may wish to include a representative from *a local agricultural agency* which could share information on pesticide and fertilizer problems, as well as dangers that may exist from silo explosions or other such sources. Other planning districts include or lie next to Indian reservations and should include representatives of the *Indian tribe*. Districts located near the sea coast or Great Lakes may want participation by the *Coast Guard* in order to plan for responses to offshore and river and stream spills.

Local environmental groups were instrumental in getting the law passed in the first place. As a result, they have a vested interest in its successful implementation. Their concern lies with the immediate and long-term effects of the release of hazardous materials on the environment. They are a fount of expertise and can bring to the LEPC very real concerns. Their concerns lead to a follow-through of planning for post-incident activities. Not only the immediate response to an incident, but also the following clean-up and monitoring of its impact, are crucial. Communities with these active groups present should certainly include them on their LEPC.

Volunteer organizations which are active in a community, such as the Red Cross, may also wish to participate. Districts with a great deal of cross-border activity or with facilities located on or near the district border may wish to include *representatives from adjoining planning districts* in order to coordinate response plans and provide for mutual support operations. In areas with labor-intensive industries, it may be helpful to include *labor union representatives* or *workers in local facilities*. This would facilitate worker cooperation and information dissemination.

Other agencies or groups that could be included in the process, depending on the specific characteristics of the local planning district, include *public works and planning departments, legal counsel, the local business community, schools or school districts* (especially if located near a fixed facility), *state representatives, and a federal agency representative*.

The key element in deciding on appropriate membership is to ensure (1) that any source of information necessary for the plan can be gathered from the members and (2) that all elements of the community which need to be involved or informed in an emergency situation are reached. In order to do this, some understanding of the nature of the community must be present as members are selected.

One other item must be recognized. It is not necessary that each of the agencies represented have a member on the LEPC. It is possible for one individual to represent more than one agency or organization, as long as they all agree. Thus, a representative from the local hospital who also serves as a Red Cross volunteer could represent both groups as long as the hospital, the Red Cross, the individual and the LEPC agree.

Although the LEPC members are appointed by the SERC, it is logical to have local input into the appointment process. In fact, if the SERC intends to do a good job in appointing the right people to local committees, it will be careful to discuss the selection with some local authorities. The link between the SERC and the LEPCs must be firm and ongoing. In order for this process to work, there must be mutual support and continuous open communication.

ORGANIZING THE LEPC

The LEPC is responsible for organizing itself in terms of selecting a chair and establishing rules by which the committee shall function (Public Law 99-499 Section 301 (c)). The chair is the only officer specifically mentioned; however, at a minimum, it is advisable to select a vice-chair and a secretary/recorder as well. The vice-chair would run the meetings in the event of the chair's absence. The secretary/recorder would be responsible for seeing that minutes of the meetings and other progress reports were compiled and available in an orderly fashion. This record of proceedings and decisions is very important in a public planning process.

The selection of committee officers is important. The NRT-1 points out five specific factors which are important in selecting a team leader: (1) The individual must be respected by the groups represented on the committee and in the community. (2) The chair must be able to commit time and resources to the process. (3) There should be a history of good working relationships with the agencies, organizations and facilities involved. (4) The chair must have good interpersonal and management skills that facilitate communication and completion of responsibilities. (5) The chair may benefit from having existing responsibilities and/or interests relating to emergency planning, incident prevention and/or emergency response. These characteristics, especially (1), (2) and (4), are important for the other officers as well. They facilitate an effective and efficient operation (*NRT-1*, 1987, p. 15).

Generally, the traditional election of officers by the majority vote of committee members is the best method. Prior to that election, however, it is paramount that the duties of the office, as well as the characteristics described above, be understood by all. This is for two reasons. Obviously, the first is that the person elected as well as those voting need to be certain of what the position entails so that everyone knows that the job will be done by the person elected. The other reason for this clear understanding is that since the chair's job is to see to it that the deadline is met and projects are completed as needed, the members must be receptive to the tasks assigned and must accept the leadership of the person elected chair.

The LEPC must designate one other individual: the coordinator for the information gathered. It must be remembered that one of the two reasons for SARA and the two responsibilities of the LEPC deal with public access to information under the right-to-know provisions. Thus, as discussed in the next section, the LEPC must process and respond to requests for information. This individual may be called the "public information officer," "community liaison," "information officer," or any other appropriate name. It is important, however, that the identity of the individual be made known to (1) the SERC, (2) the members of the LEPC and their represented agencies, and (3) to the community and the public at large. Good communication skills are an absolute requirement for the individual in this position. This individual will have most direct contact with people external to the committee and the process.

For all members, attendance at LEPC meetings is vital. Too often members take their appointment lightly and do not participate in the process. Three things happen in these cases. First, they are not informed of the progress being made. Second, they do not share their expertise with the committee, and the benefit of their membership is lost. Third, their absence may cripple the functioning of the committee, as it prevents the existence of a quorum.

ESTABLISHMENT OF LEPC PROCEDURES

Given its responsibilities, the LEPC needs to be certain to have the necessary and appropriate procedures in place. The LEPC must establish, first of all, basic operational procedures. The regulations specify:

> [The LEPC] shall appoint a chairperson and shall establish rules by which the committee shall function. Such rules shall include provisions for public notification of committee activities, public meetings to discuss the emergency plan, public comments, response to such comments by the committee, and distribution of the emergency plan. The local emergency planning committee shall establish procedures for receiving and processing requests from the public for information under section 324, including tier II information under section 312. (Public Law 99-499, Sec. 301 (c))

The rules specified here deal primarily with public access, input and information. Any federal program contains requirements for citizen information and participation. During the social movements of the 1960s one of the permanent outcomes was the advent of "sunshine laws," which dictate that the citizens are entitled to have access to and participate in government planning and decision making. As a major component of SARA Title III is community right-to-know, these requirements are doubly important in this process.

One frequent complaint about open meeting laws is that no citizens ever show up. That is not the point; the point is that they could if they wanted to do so. The purpose of these requirements is to provide access, not to force actions. Often the ability to attend or gather information is enough. Knowing that it is available is reassuring to people, as they believe that information is hidden because it is damaging. Therefore, if the information is available, the chemicals and other materials stored must not be immediate hazards.

Procedures should be set up at the beginning of the planning process to ensure that these basic public information requirements are met. *Prescheduled, standard meeting times* facilitate advance public notification and access. The LEPC should set a standard time for committee meetings. This schedule can be published in its entirety as a public service announcement in the newspaper, on radio and on TV. Areas with a public service channel on a cable network can and should announce the meetings on that channel. This will accomplish two things: (1) The committee members will know well in advance when they are to meet and can plan their personal and professional agendas accordingly. (2) Citizens can plan to attend meetings if they are interested.

The general requirement is that any *public meeting* be announced three separate times. Public meetings for the express purpose of reviewing the progress to date and soliciting public input should be held at least three times during the process. The first public meeting should be held immediately following the appointment of the committee, selection of officers and adoption of rules of procedure. This meeting should be devoted to sharing this information and soliciting concerns and ideas from the public. In addition, any questions from the public should be noted. If answers cannot be supplied at the meeting, the LEPC must respond later in the planning process.

In fact, soliciting public input does not mean simply taking notes. Federal legislation and procedure requires that committees, including the *LEPC, respond to any and all citizen input*. Thus, if at the suggestion of a citizen attending a public meeting a specific situation is dealt with in the plan, the minutes of the meeting and/or the plan should reflect the source of the concern. Likewise, the minutes should reflect not only the comments from citizens but also the committee's response to them. This does not mean that the LEPC must do everything that the citizens request. The LEPC can say no as long as a reason is given. Response does not mean acquiescence; it means thoughtful consideration and reply. Flippant answers or a brush-off are not only inappropriate, they violate the requirements of the law.

The second public meeting should be held approximately two-thirds of the way through the planning process. It encourages input from citizens and provides a forum in which to share progress to date and provide responses to previous citizen input. The third public meeting should be held after the response plan has been completed and before it is submitted to the SERC. This review is basically a presentation of accomplishment, and serves to inform the public of decisions made and provisions for response. It also informs them about the permanent location of copies of the plan for their detailed review.

Once the local emergency response plan has been completed and reviewed by the SERC and any other designated state agency, *the plan must be distributed* throughout the community. Every entity that may some day participate in a hazardous materials release must have a copy of the preplan. This includes each responding agency, each covered facility and the general public. The preplan must reach the appropriate agencies and organizations in order for them to incorporate the information into their emergency plans and procedures. Any entity affected by the response must be given a copy of the plan, regardless of whether it was directly represented on the LEPC or not. This ensures that such entities are informed of their responsibilities prior to any incident which may occur.

The *public* must have *access to the emergency plan and to the other information* on the presence of hazardous materials submitted. This is the essence of right-to-know. As such, there must be a central information gathering and storage point which is reasonably accessible to the public. There can and should be different access provisions for the emergency plan and the site-specific hazardous material information. The emergency plan should be accessible in a couple of places. A primary one that should be used is the reserve section of the public library. This would enable any citizen to gain access in a timely and reasonable manner.

As specified in Section 324, the site-specific information, which must be reported under Sections 311 and 312, must also be available to the public. The LEPC must establish procedures for responding to public requests for this information. Information can be made available to the public in a variety of ways. The LEPC may provide copies of the information to the requestor. They may provide information over the phone. They may respond only to written requests. They may require the citizen to come to the storage site to look up the information. The procedure adopted will vary according to the characteristics of the local area. Whatever the procedure is, it must be established early and clearly. Deviations from the procedure are not recommended, as they tend to set a precedent. What is vital is that the procedure be reasonable and workable.

Timely access means that the information must be available to the average citizen who works 40 hours a week. As such, there must be provisions for access after hours or during lunch periods. The LEPC does not need to set special staff hours to provide such access. It can simply state, for example, that "Upon written request providing a two-week advance notice, arrangements will be made for the viewing of hazardous materials data during other than regular working hours." Then an arrangement can be made to ensure access.

The position of coordinator of information is vital not only because of the responsibility of enabling public access, but also because of the need to gather and arrange the information in a logical format. Although plans are currently underway to computerize the hazardous materials information, few if any systems will be in place during the initial planning phases. As a result, the LEPCs will be working with information sheets rather than data bases. Thus, organization is vital as the information is included in the plan and stored to provide access to the LEPC and public. The coordinator is also the individual to whom public requests for information will be directed. He or she needs to be accessible and easily identifiable in the community.

In addition to the required procedures, it is recommended that the LEPC adopt other standard committee operating procedures. Whether the LEPC wishes to operate under *Robert's Rules of Order* or under self-designed rules of procedure, the rules must be set, adopted and followed. Specifically, the rules must set procedures for (1) establishing a quorum, (2) voting privileges, (3) deadlines for completion and (4) subcommittee or task force operation.

This is a good point at which to cite a few things that are necessary for the effective and efficient operation of the LEPC. Committee members must be conscientious about attending meetings. Members have been chosen so that they can be available to share their expertise. If a member is absent, the entire committee and the planning process lose the benefit of that person's expertise. In addition, that member and the group or agency she or he represents lose their voice in the process. A final problem that occurs in some planning committees when absenteeism is high is that the meetings do not have a quorum and cannot complete any official business. This hampers the entire process. For this reason, members must agree to attend and participate. Committees may also want to consider as a rule something to the effect that after three "prenotified and unexcused absences" or six "prenotified and excused absences" the member's agency will be asked to appoint a new representative. Hopefully, this will encourage participation and discourage absenteeism.

TRAINING FOR LEPCS

LEPCs need training, too. Their training should be of two types: (1) operational training, which deals with the issues described above, and (2) training in how to prepare an emergency response plan. The first type of training does not need to be lengthy, but it should include, at a minimum, information on how to organize, how to establish procedures, how to hold meetings, and how to keep records. The training covering the preparation of the emergency response plan must be much more detailed and technical.

The entire planning process and each of its component steps (see Chapter 9) should be explained in detail. In addition, the LEPC needs to be trained in such technical areas as hazards identification and community risk analysis. These procedures are not terribly difficult, but they must be performed appropriately in order to be of value. This type of training should be available to the LEPCs at the beginning of the process. Unfortunately, such training was not available for most LEPCs at the outset. As this is the case, the LEPCs should take the training as soon as it is available. The LEPCs will be responsible for annual updates of the emergency response plan, and as they review and update the original plan, they can use the information provided. *It is never too late to train the LEPC in hazard identification and community risk analysis.*

COMMITTEE SUPPORT STAFF

It is obvious that given the duties of the LEPC, a support staff is not only helpful but necessary. There are three primary ways in which this staffing can be provided. A "lead agency," often the one whose representative is elected chair, assigns employees to provide staff support. This is helpful and can work well. A difficulty arises when the lead agency does not have the resources, including staff time, to spare. An added difficulty may occur if the lead agency is in a situation similar to that of Disaster Services, which is forbidden to use any funds on the Title III EPA planning process. Again, this is a situation where the battle over turf take precedent over responsible, comprehensive activities, necessitating the duplication of resources and hampering the combining of existing plans with the one being developed.

Another alternative is to hire contractors or consultants to perform certain designated tasks. These consultants should have an established background in working in the area for which they are engaged. They may be experts in group processing or planning rather than risk analysis. "Expertise" does not always refer to scientific or technical data. It means that the individuals have the talents and abilities needed to get the job done. If a consultant is hired, however, it is paramount that the duties be made crystal clear. It must also be remembered that hiring the consultant does not release the LEPC from the responsibility of ensuring that the plan is finished on time and is truly comprehensive.

The main difficulty with the two previous suggestions is that they require expenditure of funds. In the case of hiring consultants, these funds must be on hand and in the possession of and under the discretion of the LEPC. Unfortunately, as mentioned in Chapter 1, there is no federal funding for the planning process. Therefore, the funds must be raised either locally or by the state. This is not highly probable early in the planning process, although it may be more feasible in later years as the LEPC works on the annual plan updates.

Thus, the LEPC will probably need to complete most of its duties and staff tasks itself. In order to do so, it would be helpful to establish a number of task forces which are assigned specific duties. Although the core membership of any LEPC task force should consist of committee members, nonmembers can be asked to participate in order to provide needed expertise. This method of operation distributes the workload among committee members and enables them to secure aid from outside the committee. This is the most frequent mode of operation for unfunded public planning committees.

A task force or subcommittee should be organized as a smaller version of the committee, with a chair and a recorder. The composition of the task force should be based on its purpose and function. A task force dealing with public information, for example, should include a representative from the media, while one dealing with communication coordination would need representatives from the fire and police departments, as well as from any central dispatching unit that may exist.

Task forces may also be asked to perform portions of the overall hazards analysis, reviews of existing plans, or even the writing of assigned portions of the emergency response plan. This would distribute the workload and allow greater attention to detail. If this process is to work, however, there must be a detailed outline and a comprehensive understanding of what the plan is to be, what each component entails, and how they all fit together. Communication must be clear and ongoing. Parts of the plan build upon one another, and the timing of the completion of various tasks is critical so that the process is not slowed. For this reason, many LEPCs may not wish to use the task force in the actual plan preparation, but rather to reserve it for special information gathering or projects.

RELATIONSHIP WITH THE SERC

The SERC is responsible for compliance at the state level, as well as at the local level through the activities of the LEPCs. As such, the SERC should take the lead in securing the resources, including funding, necessary to carry out the requirements of the law. The LEPCs need to let the SERC know of their concerns and problems as they arise. They cannot afford to sit back and complain among themselves when they are incapable of solving the problem. The SERC, although not the final solution, can play an important role in dealing with the daily frustrations and drawbacks of the local planning process.

Communication between the SERC and the LEPCs must be ongoing and formal as well as informal. Minutes of each SERC meeting should be distributed to each LEPC in a timely manner. This enables the LEPCs to maintain a current understanding of events relating to the SARA planning process. They should also be informed of decisions and recommendations made by the SERC which will have a direct impact on their operation.

The LEPCs should also receive agendas of the upcoming SERC meetings. This will enable them to express concerns and opinions about items to be considered in upcoming meetings. This exchange of information aids both parties in completing their jobs successfully. The SERC has a better idea of how plans are progressing, and the LEPCs understand the parameters under which they must operate.

The expertise of the SERC should also be available to the LEPCs on a need basis. For example, if a given LEPC has a specific problem in planning for potential releases near or into a waterway, but has no member who is familiar with responses of this type, they could call upon a member of the SERC with expertise in the field to either provide answers or to put them in touch with someone who could aid the LEPC. This is not a case of the SERC doing the work of the LEPC; the SERC simply offers the support and aid necessary to accomplish the task successfully.

ISSUES CONCERNING THE LEPCS

A number of issues come up repeatedly in discussions concerning LEPCs. These issues are the result of the specifics of the law and the way in which the planning process is designed to operate. It may not be possible to provide definite solutions here, but at least the issues can be dealt with, analyzed and planned for.

The members of the LEPC are basically *volunteers*. They receive no compensation for their time. Hopefully, these members of the agencies represented will receive time off from work in order to attend meetings, but that is all they are likely to get. For many representatives, missing time in the office will not mean a reduction in workload. Instead, the committee member may somehow have to make up the time missed during the meeting. Hopefully, the agency will realize the importance of membership on the LEPC and will make arrangements. Even so, however, the entire SARA Title III program, as stated in Chapter 1, is a massive volunteer effort.

The primary impetus behind the volunteer nature of the planning process is that there is *no federal funding* available. The main burden of implementation falls on the states and local planning districts. Fire departments and private industry are also responsible for specific activities for which there is no federal funding. The only federal monies available for local entities are reserved for training.

These funds, $5 million, were available in fiscal year 1987. When divided among the 50 states on an equal per state basis (which is not how they were, in fact, distributed), this came to an average of $100,000 per state. States have approximately 25 planning districts each, ranging from one—the entire state—to 254, one for each county in Texas. This means that a LEPC would receive an average of $4,000 for training all first responders and fire department personnel in its district. This is obviously a minuscule amount of support. As a result, what some states did with the funding was to support "Train the Trainer" programs, which produced a cadre of qualified trainers upon whom the LEPCs and fire departments could call. (Programs of this type are described in Chapter 5.)

The federal funds earmarked for training, again $5 million, appeared in the 1988 EPA budget for SARA as well. However, during the budgetary process, it was decided that since FEMA conducts most of the emergency management training, it should have the funds for training, and the monies were transferred. During the transfer, however, the Office of Budget and Management (OMB) removed them completely. Following state agency outcry, the funding was restored. However, there is no guarantee the funding will extend past 1990. Thus, major funding for training costs was left to state and local governments.

In addition, the funding available for the implementation of SARA Title III is woefully inadequate. In order to establish the statewide data base required under the law, to provide local fire departments with the equipment necessary to access the data base, to provide the training mandated, and to administer the program, the states must generate revenue. Initially, the states used a variety of means for securing funds, including general revenue appropriations, redirecting existing emergency agency funds, annual registration fees for regulated facilities, user fees for processing chemical reporting forms, filing fees for regulated facilities, temporary personnel transfers from existing state funded programs, MSDS filing fees, Tier I and Tier II filing fees, toxic chemical annual release filing fees, supplemental state funding bills, legislation establishing a contingency fund for hazardous materials referred to as a "trust fund" and administered by the SERC, surcharges on hazardous waste sites, exposure fees based on the amount of dangerous chemicals at a facility and on the number of containers and the location of containers, and penalty fees for late reporting of information. Some states are simply incorporating the operation of SARA Title III into existing agency budgets. How long this will remain a possibility, given the amount of work involved, is uncertain. It is clear that the initial establishment of the comprehensive data base and training programs, which are to be ongoing and updated annually, will cost a great deal, in many cases more than estimated.

There are a number of opinions as to who should provide funding for this program, including the claim that federal funding should be required for federal programs. This position, however, is untenable because the funding *will not* be coming from that source. The federal government's argument is that these are local programs designed to ensure local safety, and the only role of the federal government is to ensure uniformity of standards and compatibility of information. As such, SARA Title III is, in practice, a local program and should be supported by state and local funding. The arguments for industry fees as a source of funding center on the fact that they are the users of the hazardous materials for which the planning must take place. As such, they cause the potential danger and should pay for the emergency planning on the basis of how great their potential threat to community safety might be. How to measure this threat, whether by numbers of chemicals, types of chemicals, amount of chemicals, releases, or some other measure, is open to interpretation. This argument is supplemented by the public sector's belief that industry can afford the program, whereas the public sector, much of it practicing cutback management, cannot. The final argument is that the fees are nominal, mostly under $50 per filing, and will not constitute a burden on industry. When combined, these arguments provide enough support in a number of states to place the revenue-generating burden on industry.

It must be remembered that these are not really one time filing fees because annual updating is mandated by SARA. *SARA is a permanent program.* It requires ongoing collection and analysis of data. It also requires and annual updating of the emergency response plan (see Chapter 9). As such, the LEPC, as the entity in charge of and responsible for the emergency preplan, is a permanent committee. Memberships may change, and probably should, but the LEPC will live on.

Due to its permanence, the LEPC may want to consider a system for rotating memberships or asking agencies to replace representatives on a periodic basis. It is best to have such an established system in place to ensure what is termed "institutional memory." That is, the committee needs members who are familiar with the decisions made and the procedures followed the previous year in order to explain the rationale, provide continuity and prevent duplication of effort. As the membership is appointed by the SERC, any such procedure will have to be instituted in cooperation with the commission.

It must be remembered that the LEPC is a planning committee, not an *enforcement agency*. It does not have the power to force local industries to comply with the reporting requirements. The local fire departments do not have this authority either unless it has been specifically allocated to them by state legislation (an action which, for numerous reasons, is not recommended). The state agency in charge of SARA, usually the state environmental agency, and the SERC share enforcement authority. If the LEPC and the fire department fail to gain cooperation, they should report the offenders to the appropriate state authority. This should take place only after a reasonable effort has been made to secure voluntary cooperation. Generally, three written notifications and one telephone call are considered reasonable. The LEPC has much to do in preparing the emergency plan. It should not waste its resources taking on duties for which it is not responsible.

The LEPC is the key actor in the entire emergency response planning process. Unless it operates well and performs its tasks, the entire emergency preparedness program will come to naught. There is a lot of work involved, but the payoff in terms of preventing or reducing the impact of hazardous materials releases is worth the effort.

Chapter 9

PREPARING THE EMERGENCY RESPONSE PLAN

Preparing and updating the emergency response plan is the heart of SARA Title III. It is this activity toward which everything else is directed. A good response plan will not only enable a quick and appropriate reponse to an emergency situation, but can also help to prevent accidental releases. In the process of preparing the plan, many potential threats to safety will be identified by industry, the fire service and the community. Action can then be taken to avert a potentially hazardous situation. For this reasion, the planning process, regardless of whether it is ever used, has significant value.

The key players in this process were identified in the preceding chapter. There are a few participants, however, who will receive extra attention in this section due to either their unique characteristics or their special role in the process.

THE FACILITY COORDINATOR

SARA Title III is often perceived as another intrusion of government in private business. In fact, SARA is giving industry the opportunity to improve its operating procedures and safety programs. Not only does this reduce the impact of accidental releases and the associated liability, but it increases the level of safety in the plant operation. Too often the incentives for working on SARA and OSHA are that (1) it is required by law and (2) if it is not done, the industry will be fined, sued and held liable. These are both very negative incentives; should they be the driving forces behind the effort, the result will probably be a negative program. This is sad because industry is missing an important opportunity.

Whenever there is an accidental release of hazardous material, especially if accompanied by a fire or explosion, industry loses money—a lot of money. Therefore, a primary beneficiary of a program that facilitates rapid containment and mitigation of an incident, and indirectly reduces the likelihood of an incident, is industry. Industry stands to benefit most from proper implementation of Title III.

In addition, industry can benefit indirectly from the planning process. Part of the planning process is the hazards analysis, which includes risk analysis and vulnerability analysis. When a facility conducts this study as part of the planning process, it will be possible to identify procedures and storage patterns which will lessen the risk level, making the working environment safer. Making such changes provides justification for lower insurance rates and increases employee safety. A business that cares enough about its employees to change methods of operation in order to increase their safety gains employee loyalty and dedication. This translates into better employee production and work habits. Approached correctly, this planning process could prove to be a boon to businesses—but only to those who seek to take advantage of the opportunity to improve their performance.

The Facility Coordinator is the primary link between the LEPC and the facility. In order to complete the plan, specific information concerning the types of chemicals, their quantity and their location must be provided. While this indicates to some that a chemist or other technical person should be the coordinator, this is not necessarily so. The Facility Coordinator needs to have access to this information, but it is more important to be able to communicate well with the LEPC and facility managers, to understand the planning process, than it is to be able to explain the properties of every chemical present. (The question of chemicals covered by trade secrecy will be covered later. But it is pertinent to note that it is the Facility Coordinator who will communicate the necessary information about the protected materials to the LEPC for incorporation in the plan.) This is a planning process, and when specific chemical information is needed, the Facility Coordinator can get it. In the day-to-day operations, that will not be a primary qualification.

The Facility Coordinator is a two-way conduit. The industry represented will receive its primary information from this individual. Therefore, it is crucial that he or she have a good understanding of the process in order to inform and update management on the progress being made. Management will be very interested in the outcome of the plan, as it may have a direct impact on operations. A Facility Coordinator who does not communicate with management is doing only half the job.

In addition, it is logical to incorporate any facility site response plan into the overall emergency response plan. Information of this type must come from the Facility Coordinator. If the facility does not have a response team, it may be wise to discuss its feasibility. Although the facility may decide not to have an on-site response team, it is important that this be the result of an informed decision, not oversight. The interface of such a team with the local fire department and other hazardous materials response units is mandatory. This is true even if the only contact is notification of a release totally contained on site. Thus, reference to this on-site response team must be included in the local emergency response plan, as this team or its director will be facility contact persons.

If a facility does not have a response team, it will be necessary to identify other contact persons, such as security professionals, who may serve as initial contact persons or provide the reports involved. Obviously, each facility will designate someone as the official liaison in case of an incident; however, there may be others who first recognize and report an incident and who may be key to gaining immediate access to the facility. Once these persons are identified in the plan, the facility needs to inform and train the appropriate on-site personnel in their roles and responsibilities. Again, the Facility Coordinator is the logical person to take the lead role in this endeavor.

As mentioned previously, SARA is an ongoing program. In addition to providing annual plan updates, industry will notify appropriate agencies and local fire departments whenever there is a change in the types, amount or location of chemicals in the facility. This ensures an ongoing dialogue with various community agencies and groups. This dialogue can and should extend beyond the specific requirements of the law to deal with other shared issues such as transportation difficulties. This planning experience can be used to increase and improve the facility's dialogue with the community. This dialogue may involve one other member in the planning process or a group of them. In either case, there will be an established communication channel and a level of trust upon which to base discussions and deal with additional issues.

As a result of this continued interaction in what can be developed as a partnership, the public is likely to have increased confidence in local industry, knowing that they do care about the protection of their lives, health, homes and the environment. This can serve as a strong public relations program that does more to enhance the credibility and acceptance of an industry than a sophisticated, expensive advertising campaign.

The Facility Coordinator is a vital participant in this process. The selection of the coordinator by industry is crucial, as the wrong person will not give industry what it needs or the LEPC what it needs. Simply meeting the letter of the law will not enhance the process, the plan or the industry. Information flow is critical, and the information must be well given and well received. That is the most important role of the Facility Coordinator.

CONTENTS OF THE EMERGENCY RESPONSE PLAN

The *Hazardous Materials Emergency Planning Guide (NRT-1)* prepared by the National Response Team provides the best guide to the preparation of the preplan. It outlines the contents and specifies the order in which the necessary information should appear. This planning document is being updated and will continue to be the recommended primary source of information for the LEPC. As such, it will not be paraphrased here. Instead, the principal components which seem to present the greatest difficulty to the LEPCs will be explored and a narrative overview of the process provided.

Throughout this discussion, the fundamental purpose and use of the emergency response plan must be kept in mind. This document is to be used to ensure emergency response preparedness in the event of a hazardous material release. It must be usable, understandable and available, as well as accurate. Thus, each piece of information gathered and processed has a place in the final product. Nothing is gathered simply out of interest or curiosity.

In order to facilitate the use of the document, it is helpful to place a glossary or definition of terms used frequently in the document at the beginning. This and the table of contents are two seemingly minor components that can greatly enhance the utilization of the plan.

PREPARING THE HAZARDS ANALYSIS

The reporting requirements of hazardous materials at fixed facilities are detailed elsewhere. The processing and use of the information is the topic of concern here. The primary use of chemical information is in the preparation of the hazards analysis, which is part of the emergency response plan. The hazards analysis is used, first, to priortize the facilites in order of preparedness preplanning needs. Before discussing the methods of hazards analysis, it is important to gain a clear understanding of what it is, how it is used and why it is important. There are several non-technical decisions that must be made concerning the preparation of the hazards analysis as planning progresses. In order to make the correct decisions, the LEPC must have a clear understanding of the use and importance of the information which can be generated. That will be clarified once a firm understanding of hazards analysis is established.

A hazards analysis consists of three components: hazards identification, vulnerability analysis and risk analysis. The *hazards identification* provides information on facility and transportation situations that have the potential for causing injury to life or damage to property and the environment. *Vulnerability analysis* identifies the susceptibility of life, property and the environment to injury or damage should a hazardous materials release occur. *Risk analysis* assesses the probability of damage or injury to life, property and the environment due to a hazardous materials release. These three studies are conducted in stages in order to produce a hazards analysis.

The nature of the hazards analysis should be determined by the local situation. The analysis can range from a cursory review of the local situation to a highly complex, mathematically based formula utilizing probability analysis, historical precedent, and scientific research. It is unlikely that most communities will go to this extreme. In fact, the *NRT-1* addresses this issue:

> As important as knowing how to perform a hazards analysis is deciding how detailed an analysis to conduct. While a complete analysis of all hazards would be informative, it may not be feasible or practical given resource and time constraints. The value of a limited hazards analysis should not be underestimated. Often the examination of only major hazards is necessary, and these may be studied without undertaking an elaborate risk analysis. Thus, deciding what is really needed and what can be afforded is an important early step in the hazards analysis process. In fact, the screening of hazards and setting analysis priorities is an essential task of the planning team. (*NRT-1,* 1987, p. 21.)

The decision on how detailed an analysis to perform is, as stated, a local one. There are a few things which should be considered in making this decision, however. These include the number of facilities in the community, the population density of the area, the amount and type of information available, the response capabilities of local emergency responders, the participation of private industry, the sophistication of the planning committee members, the number and types of hazards identified and the resources available to be used in the planning process. The LEPC should remember that since SARA is an ongoing program, the hazards analysis can be refined in the future. If it is not possible to do everything at once the first time, more can be done in subsequent years as the plan is updated. It is more important to have a good start than a poor finish.

The first phase of the hazard analysis is the *screening process*. It involves the screening of facilities, using assumptions for a credible worst-case scenario, and enables the setting of priorities. This sets the stage for the reevaluation of facilities by priorities, which involves more in-depth hazards analysis and response planning. The three steps of the analysis are used to obtain and organize the initial basic information. At this stage, the hazard identification determines:

Where hazardous materials are found in the community
What types of hazards are present
How much of the hazardous substances exist

The vulnerability analysis identifies:

The population type and density in the area surrounding the location of the hazardous substances
The geography of the area
The atmospherics and seasonal variations of the area
The number and type of access routes to the site

The risk analysis incorporates:

The emergency response plans currently in place
The prior record of the facility
The facility's response to and participation in the process

This information allows the LEPC to identify areas susceptible to a hazardous materials release and to examine the vulnerability of the surrounding areas. On the basis of this information, the LEPC can establish planning priorities.

In order to establish priorities, there must be some means of weighing the vulnerability and risk factors. An ordinal scale which simply ranks the hazards relative to one another is acceptable at this stage. This involves simply ranking the risk level and the vulnerability level as high, medium or low. Facilities with high vulnerability rankings and high risk factors would be considered top priority, those with high risk and medium vulnerability or medium risk and high vulnerability would be given second priority, and so on.

Some questions are likely to arise concerning the vulnerability and risk rankings, and obviously no facility likes to be designated as a high risk. However, as the amount of risk is directly correlated with the amount of information known about the facility and the cooperation given by the facility to the process, this first screening stage, designed to prioritize the planning process, may well provide an incentive to increase the response of reluctant facility management. The high ranking of a facility due to lack of information is *not* a back-door, underhanded attempt to enforce participation. In planning for emergency situations, accurate and complete information reduces the risk and increases the ability to plan. Thus, denial of information by the facility puts the community at greater risk should a release occur. Once facilities recognize this, they are more willing to cooperate in the process.

The amount of vulnerability is directly related to the composition of the community immediately surrounding the facility. A densely populated area is more vulnerable than a more sparsely populated area; hospitals, nursing homes and other group homes are more vulnerable than single-family residences; and so on. In a way, it is easier to determine the initial vulnerability ranking than the risk level because vulnerability deals with the impact should a release occur, which is fixed on the basis of the community characteristics and natural phenomena, whereas the risk analysis deals with the probability of a release occurring.

The *FEMA Hazardous Materials Contingency Planning Course Module 4: Conducting a Hazard/Vulnerability Analysis for Hazardous Materials* provides good information on how to collect information and make decisions on vulnerability and risk analysis. It makes clear that during the screening phase the planning committee must work with the worst-case scenario. It assumes a total release of a hazardous material and considers the total impact. Once the priority is established through the first phase of hazards analysis, the second phase begins.

The second phase involves the *reevaluation* of the facilities by priority. Remember, in the first draft of the SARA emergency response plan, it may not be possible to deal in detail with every facility in the community. Therefore, it is necessary to deal first with those that present the greatest potential hazard. These facilities are identified in the screening process. Now the LEPC needs to undertake further analysis of the potential hazards of the priority facilities by following the steps of hazards analysis in greater detail. This process is repeated for each facility until all of the facilities in the planning district are covered. Thus, the LEPC may wish to establish a set of objectives for including a certain proportion of the facilities in each annual update until all facilities are covered by comprehensive hazards analysis and a preplan.

As mentioned, the second phase of the hazards analysis is more detailed. As such, it is worthwhile to discuss its specific contents, even though some of its components are repetitive. The hazards analysis again has the three components of hazards identification, vulnerability analysis, and risk analysis.

The *hazards identification* gathers information on a given chemical. For each hazardous chemical, it is necessary to secure the name of the chemical, its CAS number, its physical and chemical properties, the average quantity in which it is present, the potential hazards of the chemical in the event of a release, the specific location of the chemical, the storage conditions in which it is kept, the manufacturing conditions in which it is used (if applicable), and the local transportation modes in terms of route and method of transport. This information can be gathered from a variety of sources. Although the most logical and helpful one is the required Title III report forms, should these not be available, other sources can be used and these sources can also be used as a validation double-check mechanism. The facility representative or coordinator is a prime source for this information. Facility inspectors such as insurance adjustors and fire inspectors can provide information on the safety conditions within the plant. Other federal agencies such as DOT and the Department of Commerce have information on facilities, as do a number of state agencies such as the state EPA. Existing disaster plans or other regional plans such as those required under the Clean Water Act may contain valuable information about a specific facility and the area surrounding it. For example, the information concerning watersheds in the Clean Water Act's comprehensive regional plans indicates the potential impact of vulnerability should a release enter the groundwater system.

Although transportation of hazardous chemicals is regulated primarily by DOT, SARA Title III does cover transportation of chemicals to and from fixed facilities. Thus, local transportation corridors should be covered in the response plan. Transportation information can be obtained from shipping papers, DOT reports, and the Facility Coordinator. This information should include, at a minimum, the type of chemical, the route taken to the facility, the quantity shipped at a time and the frequency of shipment.

The *vulnerability analysis* identifies the zone of impact should a release occur and describes what inhabits the area. Vulnerability zones are calculated for each chemical, and their specific boundaries are affected by factors such as wind direction. In fact, one of the things that must be taken into consideration as the response plan is developed is that there may have to be seasonal variations in the planned response. For example, in some communities the wind is primarily northwestern during the summer but northern during the winter. Thus, the area of impact will differ greatly according to the season. As temperature also influences the dispersion of a chemical, that factor may need to be considered as well. Atmospheric conditions are not simply an afterthought. They can have a great impact on the aftermath of a release, and should the wind shift and an area not be evacuated, the results could be devastating.

Vulnerability zones are either concentric for fixed facilities or corridors for transportation routes. To calculate the vulnerability zone, it is necessary to look at the quantity of chemical stored and the probable rate of release in order to determine how great an area would be affected. The worst-case scenario tends to assume total release within 10 minutes. Two or more levels of vulnerability zones may be established for each chemical. For example, the primary vulnerability zone is one requiring evacuation, whereas the secondary zone requires confinement of residents to their homes. Once these zones have been established, they should be plotted on a map. The plan should then address the actions to be taken in those zones in the event of a release. These actions will depend, in large measure, on the inhabitants of the zones. Hospitals and other facilities housing numerous individuals who require aid in transport need a different evacuation plan than residents of single-family homes or rural areas. In addition, it is necessary to describe the environment that may be affected and the impact on sensitive natural areas and endangered species.

The *risk analysis* at this point expands to incorporate a more realistic estimate of the likelihood of occurrence and its severity. Once the plan is being developed for a specific facility, the LEPC should work closely with the Facility Coordinator to gather more detailed information. The Facility Coordinator can share information concerning safety mechanisms in place within the facility which would moderate the impact of a potential release, alarm systems which decrease response time, safety features of storage mechanisms such as release valves, and the presence of any on-site response teams or equipment. In addition, information on the safety record of certain types of storage equipment and processing methods, as well as the history of accidents associated with specific chemicals, can be factored into the risk analysis. This additional information not only increases the base on which to determine the probability of a release, it also supports more informed response planning as the nature of the potential release becomes better understood. Once the site-specific or facility-specific hazards analysis is complete, the response segment of the plan can be developed. It is necessary for this section to be very detailed because the planners must know exactly to what they are responding.

THE PLANNED EMERGENCY RESPONSE

The next component of the plan is a detailed description of the response itself. A response plan should be developed for each facility, with appropriate adaptations based on the chemical released. For example, should chemical A be released, the command post location and access corridor may be the same as for chemical B, but the evacuation procedures or vulnerability zone may differ, as may the response requirements in terms of equipment and protective clothing. In order to standardize the responses so they they are more easily learned, it is best to keep as many of the response procedures as possible the same. However, this must be done without compromising safety due to differing threats.

As the response plan is developed, the LEPC must conduct a *community response capability analysis* which identifies the different response agencies, their equipment, the number of personnel and the training of personnel. This analysis should also state their location and their anticipated response times to an incident alarm. This community response capability can be very enlightening, as it may reveal severe shortages or duplications of capability and equipment. One of the positive by-products of this process is that local communities can better coordinate their equipment purchasing and training programs to match their unmet needs.

Response capability includes agencies other than those relied upon to mitigate the incident. It includes volunteer organizations such as the Red Cross, medical treatment facilities such as hospitals, and special medical treatment units such as toxic centers or burn units. It should consider the presence of agencies such as disaster services or emergency management and environmental information entities including environmental groups as well as state environmental agencies. Public law enforcement agencies play an important role in emergency management, and the coordination of multiple jurisdictions needs to be done prior to an emergency incident. In fact, coordination among all involved agencies must be established prior to an incident. That is the central purpose of the preplan. All battles over turf and areas of responsibility must be settled prior to an emergency. There is no time for petty bickering once an incident occurs. The planning process is the negotiation period. Once the plan is adopted, its procedures must be adhered to by all concerned until or unless it is formally changed.

Another important component of this community response analysis is the identification of technical support resources whose services may become necessary in the event of a release. For example, chemical analysis laboratories may be needed in order to analyze the exact nature of the material released, especially if it is a combination. Transportation or communication consultants may be needed in the event of damage to roads, bridges or rail systems, or public utilities. Alternative communication facilities may be needed quickly, and it is important to know who to contact. The public utilities are a good source for aid in this endeavor, but the private enterprises should not be overlooked. The provision of a bank of cellular phones could prove invaluable in an emergency incident. These expert resources must be identified ahead of time, and the names and telephone numbers of contact persons must be kept up to date. This is true for all emergency response personnel participating in any capacity.

Once the hazards analysis and the community response capability assessment are complete, the emergency response plan can be developed, matching the best response capability with the worst-case hazardous materials release. This, then, is the core of the planning process. It requires the gathering of information necessary to make informed decisions. The *NRT-1* provides a sample outline of a hazardous materials emergency plan which has become the standard for review, with one exception. A number of states have added a section on training due to its importance in the process. The outline is presented here, with the added training component.

SAMPLE OUTLINE OF A HAZARDOUS MATERIALS EMERGENCY PLAN*

  A. Introduction
    1. Incident Information Summary
    2. Promulgation Document
    3. Legal Authority and Responsibility for Responding
    4. Table of Contents
    5. Abbreviations and Definitions
    6. Assumptions/Planning Factors
    7. Concept of Operations
      a. Governing Principles
      b. Organizational Roles and Responsibilities
      c. Relationship to Other Plans
    8. Instructions on Plan Use
      a. Purpose
      b. Plan Distribution
    9. Record of Amendments
  B. Emergency Assistance Telephone Roster
  C. Training Activities
    1. Fire Department Training
    2. First Responder Training
    3. Simulated Hazardous Incident Exercise

---

* Source: *NRT-1 Hazardous Materials Emergency Planning Guide,* Washington D.C.: National Response Team, 1987, pp. 37–38.

D. Response functions
   1. Initial Notification of Response Agencies
   2. Direction and Control
   3. Communications (Among Responders)
   4. Warning Systems and Emergency Public Notification
   5. Public Information/Community Relations
   6. Resource Management
   7. Health and Medical Services
   8. Response Personnel Safety
   9. Personal Protection of Citizens
      a. Indoor Protection
      b. Evacuation Procedures
      c. Other Public Protection Strategies
   10. Fire and Rescue
   11. Law Enforcement
   12. Ongoing Incident Assessment
   13. Human Services
   14. Public Works
   15. Others
E. Containment and Cleanup
   1. Techniques for Spill Containment and Clean-up
   2. Resources for Cleanup and Disposal
F. Documentation and Investigative Follow-up
G. Procedures for Testing and Updating Plan
   1. Testing the Plan
   2. Updating the Plan
H. Hazards Analysis (Summary)
I. References
   1. Laboratory, Consultant, and Other Technical Support Resources
   2. Technical Library

Specifics governing the contents of each of these sections can be found in *NRT-1*, which should be in the possession of anyone seriously interested in SARA Title III. They will not be detailed here.

LEGAL CONSIDERATIONS

Although it is not required by SARA, it would be helpful to deal with the legal responsibilities and liabilities of various participants in the planning process. Due to the method of implementation, the SARA planning process is governed by federal, state and possibly even local laws. As such, the defined responsibilities can become rather confusing at times. In addition, they change to some extent based on state legislation to enact SARA and on local community right-to-know laws. Providing this information in the emergency response plan would be very helpful.

For example, Hamilton County, Ohio, has as its Appendix 1 to the emergency response plan a section titled *"Laws, Ordinances, Statutory Provisions,"* which covers primarily state and federal laws. It clarifies greatly the amount and type of discretion and the location of responsibility in what has become too often a litigious society. This appendix is not intended to be the final legal statement on a given situation, but merely an illustration of the type of information that would be helpful to a LEPC and to emergency managers facing a potential emergency situation. The federal laws cited are, or course, applicable to all emergency response districts.

In terms of liability, one thing is certain: SARA describes actions required by most of the participants in a hazardous materials release situation. Failure to perform this action or to provide the information mandated places liability directly on the offending party. This does not mean that participants are totally liable for errors of judgment. For example, if a release occurs and the vulnerability zone is larger than planned, and more people than anticipated need to be evacuated, the LEPC is not automatically at fault. However, the failure to have an evacuation procedure as part of the emergency plan when it was known that evacuation would be needed in the event of a release is a direct and deliberate shirking of defined responsibility. A review of the pertinent laws applying to emergency response and to emergency response planning would be very helpful.

The hazardous materials emergency response plan developed under SARA requirements may be a stand-alone plan or it may be created as an appendix to an existing comprehensive emergency response plan. In either case, it must be reviewed by the SERC or another designated entity in order to ensure compliance. In Ohio, as in most other states, the SERC is working with another agency, in this case the Emergency Management Agency, to establish review guidelines and criteria. This review process is important to the LEPC as well as to the statewide requirement for comprehensive planning.

REVIEWING THE PLAN

Section 303 (e) of Title III requires that the written emergency response plans be sent to the SERC or its designated representative to be evaluated for content. The plans must be reviewed against a set of guidelines which serve as evaluation criteria. This ensures that all plans contain the required information as outlined in the *NRT-1*. Making certain that all plans have the required content ensures uniformity and consistency of plans and confirms that the LEPCs have planned and addressed all information vital to effective public and environmental protection when responding to hazardous materials incidents. Section 303 (g) of Title III states that the regional response team, where appropriate, may review the response plans at the request of the LEPC. This ensures regional compatibility and consistency among local district plans. The LEPC, according to Section 303 (a), is responsible for reviewing its plan at least once a year, or more frequently if necessary due to local changes, to make certain that the plan remains accurate and timely.

The emergency response plan, as mentioned previously, may be a stand-alone plan or it may be an appendix to an existing emergency response plan. If it is an appendix, both the Standard Emergency Operations Plan and the SARA Title III Hazardous Materials Appendix must be submitted for review. This enables an evaluation of the total content of the plan. The SERC may add to the information requested by *NRT-1* should it enhance the local planning effort. The chart below details the entire review process.

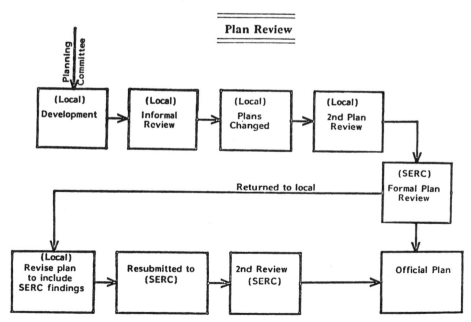

The Ohio SERC Planning Sub-Committee developed a plan cross reference based on a comparison of the National Response Team requirements and a FEMA criteria document. The cross reference requires the LEPCs to make certain that all necessary information is in the plan. The LEPC must fill out the cross reference and submit it with the plan for review. The cross reference identifies the various pieces of information that must be contained in the plan, and the LEPC must identify the location of those pieces in the cross reference. The cross reference is used as evaluation criterion. This provides a standard by which to evaluate the different local plans.

As soon as the plan is complete, it should be sent to the SERC for review, as any revisions or additions must be completed prior to the original deadline established by SARA Title III. The review by the SERC should not take more than 60 days to complete.

SARA Title III states:

The [State Emergency Response] Commission shall review the plan and make recommendations to the committee on revisions of the plan that may be necessary to ensure coordination of such plan with emergency response plans of other emergency planning districts. (Public Law 99-499, Oct. 17, 1986. Title III, Sec. 303 (e))

Its use of the word "recommendations" has led some to interpret this as meaning that the LEPC does not have to follow the revisions requested. This interpretation is inappropriate for any portion of the plan which fails to coordinate with the plans of other emergency planning districts to the detriment and threat to the safety of people and the environment. Several states are considering legislation which makes this clear. The interpretation of allowed noncompliance would effectively negate the impact of the law and destroy its intent. Coordination is necessary in order to have maximum use of resources and to provide a comprehensive response plan for the entire state built on the local level. The review at the state level ensures such compatibility and comprehensiveness.

EXERCISING THE PLAN

Once the plan has been completed, it is not placed on a shelf to accumulate dust. It forms the basis for training of local emergency responders. The law states, "Each emergency plan shall include . . . Methods and schedules for exercising the emergency plan" (Public Law 99-499, Sec. 303 (c) (9)). This means that a hazardous materials release simulation drill or exercise must be performed involving the various responders in the community. This is done for two reasons. The first is to have it serve as a training exercise in which the information gathered is put to use. The second purpose of the exercise is to provide an evaluation of the plan.

Only through implementation can the plan's precision and suitability to the local area be established. A plan is implemented in one of two ways: as an actual response to an emergency situation or as a simulation exercise. The latter is preferable as an evaluation and training mechanism. During the exercise, unforeseen and unplanned-for difficulties are likely to arise. Following the exercise, the plan should be reviewed and amended in order to solidify the preparation and to remedy the deficiencies identified.

The exercise is also useful in determining whether the training received by the first responders, and the fire department in particular, has been effective. The number of hours of training received is not as important as its content and effectiveness. If the training has been inappropriate or has failed to address specifics required by the local situation, the deficiencies will be manifested during the exercise. At this point, it is incumbent on the LEPC, the fire department and other relevant agencies to correct them. The plan review and update should incorporate the changes, and any new additions to training should be documented.

The planning process is a continuing effort. The emergency response plan is a document that is never completed. As the community changes, the hazards change, the resources change, and the laws change; the plan, therefore, will have to change as well. The goal of SARA Title III is to ensure emergency response preparedness and capability at the local level. This can only be accomplished with a current plan of action. That is why the legislation calls for annual reporting, review and update.

This constant review and update will do more than maintain the timely character of the document. It will also guarantee familiarity with the specifications on the part of emergency response personnel and their affiliates who have key roles in preventing as well as responding to and mitigating hazardous materials incidents. In this way, SARA will have fulfilled its intent.

Chapter 10

CURRENT AND FUTURE CONCERNS WITH SARA: WHERE ARE WE GOING?

There are some major concerns about the future of SARA Title III. Some of them deal with basic operational problems at either the state or the national level. Many of these problems are typical of any new program and will disappear with time as people become familiar with the operations and responsibilities of the law. More importantly, however, several of the concerns can only be addressed by legislative change.

SARA is working because all 50 states have now established SERCs. The membership on these commissions varies widely, from states with a few select state agencies to states such as Ohio, New Hampshire, Texas, Oregon, Kentucky, Louisiana, Maryland, Kansas, Florida, Connecticut, California and Idaho, which include not only state agency representatives but a variety of special interest groups. These states have made massive efforts to address the intent as well as the letter of the law. They have a genuine concern for the people of their state and the environment of the nation. Both are vital resources and assets that can never be replaced should they be damaged or destroyed.

According to the EPA, approximately 80% of the LEPCs forecasted to be in existence were operating as of February 1988. That is quite a record, considering the initial gloomy evaluations which claimed that the dates were unrealistic and that people would not work on such a plan. The EPA stood by its requirements and refused to delay the implementation deadlines, and once again the communities and citizens of America rallied to a worthwhile cause.

Recognizing both the need for the legislation and the fact of its existence, the states reacted quickly and fulfilled their obligations. That, perhaps, is the key to the success of the legislation. It is very clear on the requirements of each entity and the date by which those requirements must be fulfilled. There is no excuse for shirking responsibility due to lack of information or misinterpretation of the law.

Not only did the public sector react promptly. The Chemical Manufacturers Association, Community Awareness and Emergency Response (CAER) program, led the way in informing member industries of the requirements of SARA. They let them know what was coming and helped train the members of industry in establishing worker safety and public information programs. Large industries are well aware of the reporting requirements and, on the whole, are responding favorably and working well with the LEPCs.

Some small and medium-sized industries are not as cooperative, whether due to lack of understanding, limited resources or a mistaken belief that the law doesn't apply to them. As of February 1988, only about 50% of such facilities had reported the presence of chemicals and designated coordinators to participate in the planning process. They are now coming into line, however, and once the deadlines for reporting arrive and civil fine enforcement is in place, they will respond even more quickly. One positive note is that although the fines are providing an extra incentive to comply, the main reason for industry cooperation appears to be a genuine understanding of the need to be prepared should an accidental release occur. Industry has come to recognize and accept the need for worker, community and environmental safety.

A concern that will need to be addressed in the future is the need for information gathering and preplanning for all facilities housing hazardous materials. A fire in Alliance, Ohio, in the spring of 1988, which involved hazardous materials took place in a warehouse, and the response would have been no different and the emergency responders no better prepared had it occurred on October 18, 1988. The company utilizing the hazardous materials was located in an adjacent community and therefore had reported the chemicals to that jurisdiction. The fire department and other government agencies of the municipality in which the warehouse was located had not received any information. This question of to whom multi-site companies must report as well as the debate concerning exactly which facilities are covered will be discussed more widely in the future. This topic of expanded inclusion will be discussed widely in the coming years until a definite decision is made.

Agricultural exemptions are another area of concern, as runoffs from farms containing pesticides are entering both the groundwater and aquifer water reservoirs used to supply the drinking water for cities and towns across America. Currently, farmers are exempt, but the facilities manufacturing and transporting pesticides and fertilizers that contain hazardous chemicals are not. This must be made clear, and the debate over reporting requirements from farmers is not yet over.

Although the federal legislation does not preempt local or state right-to-know laws, except to require that they meet the federal minimum standard, there is some fear that SARA may be used to roll back progress made at the local level over the past years. Some states are considering legislation that would have the federal regulations preempt local and state ordinances. In many cases, this would result in a reduction of reporting requirements and community preparedness. Moves such as this would effectively set back the progress made in emergency reponse planning and community right-to-know efforts. Communities that led the way in this area would, in effect, be punished for being progressive. The federal legislation, as stated, is to be the minimum common standard, not—ever or in any sense—the maximum allowable standard.

Problems with the information data bases may arise, and the need for coordination and consolidation of information will become more evident. The problems are associated with different data bases being established because of the power associated with control of information and turf. It will become increasingly apparent that access to transportation information is needed by SARA emergency response planners, and fixed-facility information will be helpful to DOT emergency responders. Somehow these information needs will have to be met.

Another area of information sharing and compatibility requirements is that between states. Communities situated on the border of two or more states, or astride the border of states, need to have access to a single compatible data base. This naturally implies that the most logical way to proceed is to have a national standard for state data base construction and access. Until that standard is in place, border cities may have to contend with two different information sources and reporting systems. This defeats the basic intent of emergency preparedness, as it hampers the response in a real emergency.

The reporting of actual releases of extremely hazardous materials has also been very low. While this is largely due to purposeful nonreporting, much of the problem also stems from lack of knowledge and confusion over requirements and chemical lists. The establishment of one master chemical list detailing the different reporting requirements for each would be a big help.

Even where facilities report locally as well as to the state, most LEPCs and first responders are initially overwhelmed by the paperwork. Until a uniform computerized information storage and retrieval system is established, this will continue to cause problems. The development of such a system has been left to the states, and this initially seems a logical extension of state's rights and local adaptation. However, the realization that shared information is needed across state lines should begin to make communities and states a bit uncomfortable. Not only is there no uniform reporting procedure and data sharing among federal hazardous materials regulating programs, there is no current provision for uniform reporting among states within a federal program.

This means that, at some future date, one nationwide system will probably be adopted and will necessitate the adaptation of data sets in the states. This may also occur on a smaller scale across states as the SERCs begin to adopt standard procedures for all LEPCs. The inconvenience of standardizing information files is worth the convenience, efficiency and increased safety it will provide.

This standardization will be accompanied by the development of data processing capabilities at the local level. Each LEPC will need some type of computer facility to enable the accessing of local data and state information as needed in an emergency. This requires careful planning and the participation of computer-literate personnel who understand how the equipment will be used. The purchase of some unnecessary and inadequate equipment is almost a certainty. This can be minimized, however, through careful, objective consideration of data and information processing and transfer needs.

Some emergency responders, most notably fire departments, are initially overwhelmed by the amount of information and, rather than processing it systematically as most other agencies are doing, are trying to find alternative means of complying. These alternative means are chosen specifically to avoid the processing of data and the required detailed preplan for the response to a facility emergency. One of the more visible methods is an attempt to rely on the lockbox as an alternative to preplanning. As discussed earlier, the lockbox is designed to *supplement,* not *replace,* preplanning. Attempts to avoid the requirements of the law are, in fact, violations of the law. While it is true that the law will require increased activity on the part of first responders, it is also true that the time is better spent complying with the law than trying to avoid it.

For many people involved in the process, SARA Title III often seems to be two separate programs: community right-to-know and emergency response planning. In truth, these are two sides of the same coin. The intent of both is to provide for a safer community. Better integration of the understanding of these two sections of the law would be helpful. In addition, the integration of the information segments of these two sections would avoid duplication of effort, as the reporting of chemicals is required for both sections. It is the use of and access to the information that are somewhat different. Once it is understood that these are integrated programs, their enactment is certain to become more efficient.

One of the most difficult areas of implementation for SARA is the lack of training of LEPCs. Training in recognition of and response to hazardous materials is available from many sources. However, training on how to prepare a response plan or how to do community analysis is not. FEMA, as noted earlier, has a "Hazardous Materials Contingency Planning Course" that is available but not widely offered. Basic training in organizing a committee, running a committee and preparing a plan is sorely needed. The elimination of this particular weakness in the implementation of the program would greatly strengthen SARA. It would lead immediately to better and more accurate local activities.

SARA Title III will exist for a long time. There will be changes over time. The chemical lists will continue to change, and the uses of the data will become more complex and preventive in nature. The types of facilities covered are certain to expand as more accidental releases from non-reporting facilities occur. Consolidated information and data sets will become a reality. As this unification across the United States takes place, another major trend will develop.

International steps will be taken to cooperate and coordinate the regulation of hazardous materials. Hazardous materials are no longer a local problem, as their effect may have international secondary as well as primary impact. In addition, U.S. companies are discovering that they cannot simply move their facilities to other nations and thereby avoid responsibility. Increasingly, developing nations are searching for ways to deal with hazardous materials and worker and community safety.

In October 1988, for example, the International Conference on Ergonomics, Occupational Safety, Health, and the Environment was sponsored by the Chinese Metals Society and the Australian Darling Downs Institute in Beijing, China. One of the papers presented was entitled "Working with Hazardous Materials: A Chance to Do It Right" (presented by David Hoover and Nancy Grant). This paper grew out of the writing of this book and integrated the various components of existing laws and programs into one comprehensive program for dealing with hazardous materials. Although the enactment of such a program, especially on an international basis, lies far in the future, the very selection of the paper for presentation demonstrates the importance developing nations place on planning hazardous materials programs and legislation. Eventually such a comprehensive program will be in place. And SARA Title III will be a major cornerstone.

PART II

HAZARDOUS MATERIALS

Chapter 11

OVERVIEW OF HAZARDOUS MATERIALS

HAZARDOUS MATERIALS DEFINED

Hazardous materials have been defined in many ways, depending on the person issuing the definition and the audience for whom it is intended. DOT states that a hazardous material is any substance that could cause a transportation problem if released. OSHA has defined a hazardous chemical as any substance with certain physical hazards, such as being a flammable or combustible liquid, a compressed gas, an explosive, an oxidizer, an organic peroxide, or being pyrophoric, unstable (reactive) or water-reactive. In addition, OSHA has said that a substance is hazardous if it poses a health hazard, such as being carcinogenic, a toxic or highly toxic agent, a reproductive toxin, hepatoxin, nephrotoxin, neurotoxin, hematopoietic system toxin, corrosive, irritant, a sensitizer or an agent that can damage the eyes, lungs, skin and mucous membranes.

There are probably dozens of other definitions that try to provide a clear description, but they are either too long and complicated or they omit large classes of hazardous materials. The simplest definition of a hazardous material that these authors have ever heard is ''any substance that is released from its container or process and has the capability of causing harm to life, property, systems or the environment.''

Regardless of how hazardous materials are defined, the intent of SARA Title III is to classify and regulate them so that their manufacture, use, storage and transportation will not cause harm to people, animals, plants, property, the systems our society uses to function in an orderly manner or the environment.

HAZARDOUS MATERIALS AND HAZARDOUS WASTES

There is no doubt that hazardous wastes would fit most definitions of hazardous materials, but the two types are defined and regulated differently. A hazardous waste is defined as follows.

a solid waste, or combination of solid wastes, which because of its quantity, concentration, or physical, chemical, or infectious characteristics may—

(A) cause of significantly contribute to an increase in mortality or an increase in serious irreversible, or incapacitating reversible, illness; or

(B) pose a substantial present or potential hazard to human health or the environment when improperly treated, stored, transported or disposed of, or otherwise managed.

The definition of solid waste includes the statement ''and other discarded material, including solid, liquid, semisolid, or contained gaseous material'' [40CFR261.2(c)(1)]. Therefore, hazardous wastes can be solids, liquids, or gases.

The EPA lists four basic characteristics of hazardous wastes: ignitability, corrosivity, reactivity, and toxicity. The EPA also defines hazardous wastes which include the above characteristics as substances being discarded, recycled, or inherently waste-like, and excludes all common wastes that are inherently nonhazardous.

Confusion arises whenever the terms "hazardous materials" and "hazardous wastes" are used. Although some hazardous materials and some hazardous wastes have exactly the same hazards, there are basic differences. Hazardous materials are usually considered pure substances or uncontaminated mixtures that are designed to perform a certain task, and, when used in industry, are the raw materials used in a manufacturer's process or in the process or normal business of some other organization. Hazardous wastes, on the other hand, are usually the end result of a process, and are the materials created or used and contaminated, or left over after the process is complete, to be discarded or recycled.

An example of the difference can be shown using a degreasing operation in a metal treatment facility. Trichloroethylene is a solvent commonly used to remove grease and oil from the surface of metals before processing. As it is manufactured, transported, stored and finally used by a company, it is classified as a hazardous material because of its chemical and physical properties. During its use, it becomes contaminated with the materials it dissolves, and after a certain level of contamination, it loses its efficiency as a solvent. At this point, it is discarded (in the proper fashion, of course) and is now classified as a hazardous waste. Of course, it is not exactly the same material that it was before use. As it was received by the buyer, it was probably certified to have a certain purity. After use, it contained a considerable amount of dissolved grease and other organic materials. It also contained much suspended solids and was darker in color. But it may still be called trichloroethylene on the paperwork accompanying the "waste."

SARA, and specifically Title III, deals with hazardous materials or hazardous chemicals (synonymous with hazardous materials) rather than hazardous wastes. The confusion arises partly because the original Superfund law (CERCLA) was concerned with hazardous wastes and partly because hazardous materials don't get the same publicity as hazardous wastes. This section, and the appendixes that follow, deal with the hazardous materials and hazardous chemicals as regulated by SARA. They will usually be grouped under the term "hazardous materials."

CLASSIFICATION OF HAZARDOUS MATERIALS

There are many different ways of classifying hazardous materials; none of them are entirely satisfactory. A certain chemical or mixture may have more than one hazard, and the question which arises is: In what group should it be included? The answer appears to be that a chemical or substance shall be placed in all classifications in which it is hazardous. For example, a corrosive (as classified by DOT), such as chlorine, will also be included in such classifications as poison, oxidizer, irritant and compressed gas, since chlorine has all the hazards of these hazard classes. To make such classification easier, the following definitions of the various hazard classes are provided, including a list of other hazards that may be possessed by the listed hazardous materials.

FLAMMABLE AND COMBUSTIBLE LIQUIDS

A *flammable liquid* is defined as a liquid with a flash point below 100°F (liquids don't burn, but some produce vapors that do). A *combustible liquid* is a liquid whose flash point is 100°F or higher. It is important to know if a liquid is classified as flammable or combustible, since this is a key to its safe handling. Knowing the definitions of the properties of these liquids will aid in understanding the hazards.

FLASH POINT

Flash point is defined as the minimum temperature at which the liquid produces vapors sufficient to form an ignitable mixture with air near the surface of the liquid or the container. Flash point is the most important property of any liquid that produces vapors that burn, since it is only at this temperature that enough fuel will be mixed with the air to allow ignition to occur. It is important to know that not all of the liquid must be raised to its flash point to produce sufficient vapors to burn. *Any* amount of the liquid, once raised to this temperature, will produce the needed fuel for combustion.

Some texts on the chemistry and physics of fire mention a *fire point,* which technically is the temperature at which self-sustained combustion will occur. However, in the real world, where most accidents happen, fire point is not important. If enough vapors have been produced to ignite (i.e., the flash point has been reached), an ignition source will produce an *explosion* rather than the gentle "flash" that is achieved in the laboratory flash point determination. This is almost always followed by a fire, which is due to the energy released by the explosion, causing nearby combustibles to reach their ignition temperatures (defined below).

IGNITABLE MIXTURE

An *ignitable mixture* is defined as the ratio of gas or vapor (or fumes or dust) in air within the flammable range. *Flammable range* is defined as the area between the upper and lower flammable (or explosive) limits. The *upper flammable limit* is the maximum ratio of gas or vapor in air above which ignition will not occur. Any mixture of gas or vapor in air above the upper flammable limit is said to be "too rich." The *lower flammable limit* is the minimum ratio of gas or vapor in air below which ignition will not occur. Any mixture of gas or vapor in air below the lower flammable limit is said to be "too lean." Any mixture of gas or vapor in air outside of these flammable limits, sometimes referred to as *explosive limits,* will not ignite.

IGNITION TEMPERATURE

If the vapors of a flammable or combustible liquid are within these flammable limits, ignition will still not occur until the *ignition temperature* of the fuel has been reached. Ignition temperature (or *ignition point*) is defined as the minimum temperature to which the fuel must be raised before it will ignite. *Any* source of energy may raise the temperature of a fuel to its ignition point. The ignition source need not be an open flame impinging on the liquid or within the gas or vapor. It may be a spark caused by friction, static electricity discharge or electrical arcing. It may be the radiant heat from another heat source (such as flames from some distance), an uninsulated steam line or the heat released from a chemical reaction. The only prerequisite of the energy source is that the fuel must absorb enough of the energy to be heated to its ignition temperature.

BOILING POINT

An important property of any liquid is its boiling point. This is especially important with flammable and combustible liquids because it is at the boiling point of the liquid that the maximum amount of vapors will be generated. *Boiling point* is defined as the exact temperature at which the vapor pressure of a liquid just equals atmospheric pressure (or the pressure above the liquid, as in the case of liquids under pressures higher than 1 atm). It may be a difficult concept to grasp, but boiling point is *pressure dependent* rather than temperature dependent. We always think of a liquid as boiling at a specific temperature, but in reality, it will boil at a different temperature if the pressure above it is different.

Another difficult concept to visualize is that gases also have boiling points. At temperatures above their boiling point (that is, when their vapor pressure is greater than atmospheric pressure), they will exist in the gaseous state. But if they are cooled to their boiling point or below, their vapor pressure will drop below that of the pressure surrounding them, and they will condense into a liquid. In practical terms, the simplest way to liquify a gas is to lower it below its boiling point. As you can imagine, the boiling points of most gases are below 0°F (a notable exception is butane, whose boiling point is 31°F). The concept of a substance boiling at temperatures below (and many are considerably below) 0°F is difficult to grasp.

VAPOR DENSITY

Another important property of liquids (and gases) is *vapor density,* which is defined as the relative density of the vapors or gas (with no air present) as compared to that of clean, dry air. Arbitrarily, the vapor density of pure, dry air at sea level is set at 1.0. The importance of knowing the vapor density of a gas or of the vapors of a liquid is that this property will indicate if the gas or vapor will rise or fall in air, as well as the relative speed at which it will disperse (spread so far apart in air that its hazard disappears). Any vapor or gas having a vapor density of less than 1.0 will rise in air, and the smaller the number, the faster it will rise and disperse. If the vapor density is greater than 1.0, it will fall in air to the low spots on the ground and will actually flow along the ground, following its contours like a liquid (indeed, gases and vapors are *fluids,* just as liquids are). The higher the vapor density, the longer the vapors will "hang together" as they move and the longer they will take to disperse.

Knowing the vapor density of a substance allows one to predict the pattern of movement of such vapors, which, in turn, will indicate where the danger from this material will be. Vapors with high densities (1.5 or higher) also tend to gather in low spots or confined areas protected from dispersing breezes, and present very hazardous conditions depending upon the hazards of the material itself. Vapor densities are usually calculated at a temperature near room temperature, so that if a gas or vapor is very cold or very hot, it will react differently than expected. For example, a gas or vapor with a vapor density of 0.6 is expected to rise and disperse rapidly under normal conditions. However, if it is very cold (as in the case of a gas being generated by the boiling of a liquified gas), it may not rise very rapidly, or may even sink to the ground until it begins to warm up. By contrast, a gas or vapor with a vapor density of 2.0, which is expected to sink to the ground or to low spots in an occupancy, may rise in air if heated enough and not begin to sink until it begins to cool. This is due to the fact that when a gas is cooled, it becomes more dense than it is at room temperature, and when it is heated, it becomes less dense.

There is a very simple way of calculating the vapor density of a gas or vapor if no reference book is handy. To do this, one must know the molecular formula for the gas or liquid and the atomic weights of the atoms in the molecule to determine the molecular weight. Once the total molecular weight of the substance is known, it is divided by 29, which is the *average* molecular weight of air (since air is a *mixture* of molecules, 29 represents the weighted average of the molecular weight of all the gases present in air). For example, the molecular formula for propane is C_3H_8, and the atomic weights for carbon and hydrogen are 12 and 1, respectively. Therefore, the molecular weight of propane is $3 \times 12 + 8 \times 1$, or 44; $44 \div 29 = 1.517$. Most reference books list the vapor density of propane as 1.5, so the system is accurate. Ammonia's molecular formula is NH_3. Nitrogen's atomic weight is 14; therefore, the molecular weight of ammonia is 17 $(14 + 3 \times 1)$; $17 \div 29 = 0.586$. This means that ammonia is lighter than air (whose vapor density is 1.0) and will therefore rise and disperse fairly rapidly unless it is significantly colder than ambient temperature.

WATER SOLUBILITY

Whether or not a flammable or combustible liquid dissolves in water will play an important role in the control of that liquid. *Water solubility* is the ability of the liquid to dissolve in or mix with water. Some texts list a substance as being *miscible* with water in all proportions. The two terms are sometimes used interchangeably. If a material does dissolve in water, like ethyl alcohol, the resulting *solution* will have a lower flash point than the pure material, because the molecules of the flammable or combustible liquid are spread farther apart by the water molecules, and fewer of them will escape the solution and form a mixture with the air at the same temperature.

SPECIFIC GRAVITY

If a liquid is not soluble in water, it will separate and stratify according to its *specific gravity,* which is defined as the ratio of the weight of a material compared to the weight of an equal *volume* of water. The specific gravity of pure water is 1.0. Any material (liquid or solid) that is not soluble in water, having a specific gravity of less than 1.0, will float on the water. Any material with a specific gravity greater than 1.0 will sink to the bottom of the water. Most flammable liquids have a specific gravity of less than 1.0 and a vapor density greater than 1.0. However, many classes of these liquids are soluble in water.

CROSS-HAZARDS OF FLAMMABLE LIQUIDS

Although the major hazard of flammable liquids is the flammability itself, many flammable and combustible liquids have other hazards, which may trap and injure or kill the unwary person who protects against fire only. Some flammable liquids, like methyl alcohol and ethyl amine, are also toxic, and exposure to the vapors or liquid is extremely hazardous. Other liquids, like dimethyl ether and diethyl ether, are anesthetic, and the vapors may overcome a person without respiratory protection. Still other liquids, like tetrahydrofuran and ethers, may form explosive organic peroxides upon exposure to air. Ethylene oxide will burn inside its own container (with no air present), and the vapors of the flammable and combustible halogenated hydrocarbons will attack the liver and kidneys of humans who have prolonged unprotected exposure to the vapors. Acrylonitrile and styrene will *polymerize* (to polymerize means that the chemical in question—a tiny molecule known as a monomer—will react with itself to form a "giant" molecule called a polymer). This chemical reaction which liberates large quantities of heat is called polymerization. Polymerization may occur violently if not properly stabilized, and this uncontrolled polymerization may be so violent that it resembles an explosion. These are but a few examples of the additional hazards possessed by many flammable or combustible liquids. There are many other multiple-hazard liquids, and each should be identified and handled in accordance with these additional hazards.

GASES

Because liquids evaporate, and the product of that evaporation is a vapor, there is usually some confusion between gases and vapors. There are three natural states of matter: gas, liquid, and solid. A *natural state* is the physical existence of the material at room temperature. Water's natural state is liquid, propane's natural state is gas, and iron's natural state is solid. All three of these materials may exist in other states. Any liquid, like water, when it evaporates, produces a *vapor,* not a gas. When *liquified* propane evaporates, technically it produces a gas, although we often refer to it as "propane vapors." The two terms are sometimes used interchangeably. As long as the natural state of the material is known, no misunderstanding should occur. The difference may seem like hair splitting, but to control hazardous materials, it is important to know the natural state of a substance, so that it will be known in what form the material will exist when it is released.

Gases are defined as fluids having a vapor pressure higher than 40 pounds per square inch (psi) at 100°F, while *liquids* are defined as fluids having a vapor pressure of not more than 40 psi at 100°F. Both materials, then, are fluids and will follow similar flowing patterns. The major difference is the *rate of evaporation,* which is proportional to the *vapor pressure* of the material. Vapor pressure is defined as the pressure exerted on the sides of a closed container by the molecules of the gas at equilibrium. Since gases, by definition, have higher vapor pressures than liquids, they will produce more material as they evaporate. This means that more material is being mixed with the air, bringing with it its inherent hazards.

Gases are molecules in constant motion, and gases have no shape. They will expand to fill the container in which they exist. Gases are always shipped and stored in one of two conditions: either as a pressurized gas (a gas in a container at pressures higher than 14.7 psi of atmospheric pressure) and still in the gaseous state, or as a liquefied gas. This is done for reasons of economy: more gas can be stored in a container under pressure or liquefied than not. Propane, for example, if liquified, has 270 times the volume stored in a container if it is not liquified.

Liquification of gases may be done in one of three ways: pressurizing the gas, cooling it, or a combination of both. To liquify by cooling alone, the temperature of the gas must be lowered to its boiling point. It can then be kept in the liquid state by keeping it under pressure. Insulation may or may not be needed, depending upon how low its boiling point is. Butane, the gas used in clear plastic cigarette lighters, has a boiling point of 31°F; therefore, very little pressure is required to keep it in the liquid state. On the other hand, cryogenic gases, which have boiling points below −150°F, are kept in very well-insulated containers, and the liquids are so cold that there is very little pressure above them.

Containers

The hazardous property of all gases is that they are always stored under pressure (with the exception of the cryogenic gases, of which there are only about a dozen). This can be a major hazard any time the pressure inside the container nears, reaches or exceeds the design strength specification of the container in which it is held. Containers which hold *compressed gases,* which are defined as either pressurized or liquified gases, usually have pressure relief devices (one exception will be mentioned), which are safety devices that function to keep the pressure within the container from rising to a dangerous level. Increased pressure within the vessel that rises to its design strength causes the container to fail catastrophically (that is, explode), releasing parts of the tank as shrapnel or projectiles, together with its contents. These devices work in two ways, both to relieve the pressure. In the first case, pressure is relieved by the action of a valve that opens and closes; in the second case, all the gas is allowed to escape from the container.

The most common, the spring-loaded valve, is set to operate when the internal pressure rises to a certain level, usually at one-fourth of the design strength of the container. When the pressure reaches this point, the spring is elongated and the valve opens, allowing gas to escape to the atmosphere. When enough gas has vented to reduce the internal pressure below the strength of the spring, the spring pulls the valve back into a sealed position, effectively closing the container. This continues until whatever is causing the internal pressure to rise is eliminated or the container is cooled enough to offset the rise in pressure caused by the increased heat.

Both the frangible disc and the fusible plug, once activated, will allow the total contents of the container to escape. The frangible (burstible) disc will blow out when the pressure within the container rises to a specified level, and the fusible (meltable) plug will melt away when the temperature reaches a specified level.

Additional Hazards of Gases

In addition to pressure (the main hazard), there are several other hazards associated with gases. The most common pressurized gas is natural gas, and its additional hazard is that it is flammable. All flammable gases, when mixed with the air in the proper proportions (that is, within the flammable range), will explode when an ignition source capable of raising a small portion of the gas to its ignition temperature ignites the gas. If the source of the gas is still present after the explosion, the gas will burn as it is being generated and/or released. Any other combustible matter nearby will probably burn, and the container itself (or other containers nearby), if still intact and containing significant amounts of the gas, will be subject to explosion by rising internal pressure. This will cause the formation of shrapnel and the release of more flammable gas.

A brief explanation is proper here concerning the use of the word ''flammable'' or ''combustible'' in conjunction with liquids and gases. When used in conjuction with a liquid, these terms refer to the flash point of the liquid (see the definitions above). There is no such reference to gases, since gases in the gaseous form are ready to burn (some references will show flash points for liquified gases). Therefore, gases are usually referred to as being ''flammable,'' although the term ''combustible'' is sometimes used. There is no difference in the burning characteristics of the gas, regardless of the term used.

Another possible hazard of a gas is that it may be an oxidizer. The most common such gas is oxygen; flourine and chlorine are also oxidizers.

There are gases that are corrosive, like fluorine and chlorine, as well as materials known as the "halogen acid gases," such as hydrogen fluroide, hydrogen chloride, hydrogen bromide and hydrogen iodide.

Some gases are toxic. The toxicity ranges from that of gases that are dangerous over a prolonged exposure period, to that of poison A gases, which can kill after a few breaths; hydrogen cyanide is an example of the latter. The toxicity of gases is an important property to know; this information, like all the above hazards is present on the MSDS, which is available to all exposed employees.

Some gases are unstable. This means that under certain circumstances, a violent reaction such as an explosion or a sudden, violent release of heat may occur. Acetylene is an example of an unstable gas that will detonate if shocked when under pressure higher then 15 psi. Vinyl chloride is another unstable gas that will react violently when certain conditions occur. Vinyl chloride is a monomer which will polymerize violently if heat and pressure are applied outside of a polymerization reactor.

The final hazard of some compressed gases is a unique, violent reaction called a "BLEVE" (an acronym for Boiling Liquid, Expanding Vapor Explosion). The gases that are usually subject to BLEVE are the easily liquifiable, flammable gases. The BLEVE usually occurs when fire causes direct flame impingement on the vapor space of a large container (stationary tank, truck tanker, railroad tank car, etc.) containing a liquified, flammable gas. This flame impingement causes a weakening of the metal fabric of the container, which, when combined with the rapid pressure rise inside the container caused by conducted heat, results in a catastrophic disintegration of the container. This releases the liquified gas within the container to the atmosphere, resulting in a rapid conversion of the liquid to gas (the gas was stored inside the container under pressure at temperatures considerably above its boiling point), which is ignited by the impinging flame, resulting in a tremendous explosion and a devastating fireball. This propensity to BLEVE is not listed on the MSDS, but there will always be a warning to protect containers of gas from exposure to heat.

Cryogenic Gases

Some gases are not easily liquifiable, since their boiling points are very low. When a gas has a boiling point of −150°F or lower, it is arbitrarily called a "cryogenic gas" or, more simply, a "cryogen." To be liquified, these gases must be cooled to or below their boiling points. These gases are liquified for the same reason as the easily liquifiable gases: economy. So much more of these materials can be stored in the liquid form than in the compressed form that a considerable amount of money is saved in transportation and storage by liquifying them.

Cryogenic gases may have any of the above hazards. They also have two more hazards with which emergency responders and users of the materials must contend: extreme cold and a very high liquid-to-vapor ratio. The extreme coldness is self-evident, but many users are surprised at the expansion ratio of these gases when allowed to vaporize. The extreme examples are liquid xenon, which produces 560 volumes of gas for each volume of liquid and liquid neon, which produces 1,445 volumes of gas for each volume of liquid. Liquid oxygen (LOX), the most common cryogenic gas, expands at a ratio of 857 to 1. The dangers of the extremely low temperatures will be listed on the MSDS, but the expansion ratios probably will not. These ratios can be found by reading the manufacturer's specification literature for each product.

Safety personnel at each facility must familiarize themselves not only with the properties and hazards of cryogenics, but also with their storage and handling techniques, which are unique.

FLAMMABLE SOLIDS

Flammable solids are a very confusing set of hazardous materials simply because of their label. DOT requires many of these materials to carry a "Flammable Solid" placard when they do not actually burn. In at least one case, calcium carbide, the solid itself will not burn. However, if water contacts the material, acetylene gas, which *is* highly flammable, is generated. An additional placard, "Dangerous When Wet," may also accompany such a material. However, when the "Flammable Solid" warning is used, the handler must be aware that special hazards are present.

Many solid materials will burn and are quite hazardous, apart from those known as "ordinary combustibles" (paper and paper products, wood and wood products, plastics, cloth, etc.). Some of these materials are exotic chemicals like N-methyl-N'-nitro-N-nitrosoguanidine, and some are as common as aluminum. In fact, all metals (with the exception of some precious metals) will burn, and all of them will explode if reduced to a fine powder. Sodium and potassium are metals that will react violently when in contact with water. Carbon, sulfur and phosphorus are nonmetallic elements that will burn (phosphorus is pyrophoric, to be defined later).

Anything organic will burn, and if any organic material is reduced to a powder, an explosion is possible. There are many explosions in grain elevators every year, and each one seems to come as a surprise to someone. The MSDS must be read carefully, especially the sections on fire and explosion hazards, to determine if a solid material being used by the facility will burn or react violently in some other manner.

OXIDIZERS

Oxidizers, or *oxidizing agents,* are materials that contain oxygen and will give it up readily or will otherwise support combustion. The first implication of this definition is that these materials represent the second leg of the "fire triangle" (fuel, an oxidizer and energy, when brought together in the proper proportions, will *produce* a fire). This means that atmospheric oxygen (the most common oxidizer) need not be present to produce a fire hazard. The second implication is that these materials should never be stored next to anything that will burn. The third implication is that these materials should never be subjected to heat or other forms of energy, since this will cause them to release their oxidizing power. In some cases (ammonium compounds and organic oxidizing agents), not only will the oxygen be released and be available to support a fire, but the other portion of the compound may be combustible, thus providing the fuel for the fire.

The MSDS must be consulted to determine the relative ease with which the substance will give up its oxygen and with what materials the oxidizer is incompatible. The materials listed as imcompatible must always be isolated from the oxidizer; this, of course, has implications for transportation and storage. The standard rule for storage is that oxidizing agents must never be stored near combustible materials, and they must be protected from heat, shock and contamination.

Oxidizers come in many forms and have uses other than acting as the oxidizing agent in a chemical reaction. That is, the material may have a principal use that indicates nothing about its oxidizing potential, and yet this may be its major hazard.

A prime example is ammonium nitrate. This white, water-soluble salt's principal use is as a fertilizer, and yet it is a very efficient oxidizer. Not only will ammonium nitrate yield its oxygen readily when heated, it will also burn, and on occasion will detonate with tragic results. In Galveston Harbor, in 1947, at Texas City, Texas, a small fire broke out in the hold of a ship. It eventually spread to and involved a large amount of ammonium nitrate, which began to burn. Some time later, the ammonium, nitrate detonated, killing nearly 500 people, including 27 members of the Texas City Fire Department.

Lead chromate, when reduced to a powder, is used as a pigment in paints, plastics and coatings and is not considered an oxidizing agent under normal circumstances. However, when mixed with powdered aluminum, lead chromate can release its oxygen, causing a violent explosion of the mixture.

Ethylene oxide, a colorless gas that is shipped and stored as a liquid, has many important industrial uses. However, its molecular structure will allow the oxygen to be released, supporting the combustion of any material that will burn, including itself.

The message is clear. Examine the MSDS to determine if oxygen is present in the chemical makeup of the substance in question. If its principal use is as an oxidizing agent, this hazard will be listed prominently. However, if the principal use of the substance is something else, the incompatibility section of the MSDS must be consulted. If warnings are present there that the material in question is incompatible with organic materials, reducing agents, or anything combustible or flammable, it is probably an oxidizer. If the incompatability section lists chemicals with which you are unfamiliar, they should be identified in terms of *their* hazards. These materials may be strong reducing agents, which in turn might indicate the oxidizing danger of the substance in question.

Also, check the storage section of the MSDS. If it indicates that the material should be kept separate from any materials that burn (it may say "Keep away from all organic materials" or "Keep away from all fuels" or "Keep away from all combustibles" or some similar warning), chances are that it is an oxidizing agent.

Additional Hazards

Oxidizers may have other hazards in addition to the support of combustion. Some oxidizing agents may be combustible, such as ammonium nitrate, ethylene oxide, and all organic peroxides. As stated above, an additional hazard of ammonium nitrate is that it will detonate.

Some oxidizers will decompose violently; this hazard characterizes the peroxides, both organic and inorganic. All peroxides must be transported, stored and handled very carefully. The transportation and storage of organic peroxides is carefully regulated, and any deviation from the safety instructions provided by the manufacturer in the MSDS or other technical data must be prohibited. State and national fire codes contain sections on the storage and handling of oxidizing agents, with special sections dedicated to organic peroxides. Inorganic peroxides are different in their chemistry, and their reactions may be different from those of organic peroxides, but in many cases they are just as dangerous. As a group, the peroxides may be the most hazardous class of chemicals used by industry in the United States.

Some oxidizers are very reactive. Again, the organic peroxides are the main group of materials in this hazard class. Indeed, it is their reactivity in specialized chemical reactions that make them so valuable to industry. Reactivity indicates that the chemical reaction can get out of control, and that the chemical may even get out of its container in one manner or another. In either case, the results of an out-of-control reactive material is the release of energy (heat from the reaction sufficient to start a fire or shock in the form of an explosion) or of products of the reaction that might be toxic, corrosive, flammable or in some other way harmful to people, the environment, property or vital societal systems.

Some oxidizing agents are unstable. This instability may result in a violent explosion or the release of a dangerous product with properties stated above. Highly concentrated hydrogen peroxide is an example of an oxidizer that becomes very unstable if it is heated or contaminated.

Oxidizing agents may also be corrosive and/or toxic. Many of the organic peroxides are either corrosive or toxic or both, and hydrogen peroxide is very corrosive. The halogens—fluorine, chlorine, bromine and iodine—are all corrosive and toxic.

CORROSIVES

A *corrosive* is defined as any material that will attack and destroy, by chemical action, any living tissue with which it comes in contact. This definition can be extended to include the attack and destruction of any mineral, metal or other substance with which it comes in contact.

Corrosives contain many classes of chemicals, the most familiar of which are the acids. Fortunately, the names of these materials almost always include the word "acid." Among the more familiar ones are sulfuric acid, nitric acid, hydrochloric acid, and perchloric acid. These acids are inorganic, or mineral, acids. They are called "strong" acids because they ionize almost completely in water. They are the more reactive of the two types of acids, and therefore they are the more corrosive. Generally speaking, the more concentrated an acid is, the more corrosive it is.

Some acids may be more than 100% concentrated. That is, the water solution of the acid may contain more acid than it can normally hold. In this case, the acid is said to be "fuming." Oleum (fuming sulfuric acid) and red- and white-fuming nitric acids are examples of fuming acids.

The organic acids are often called "weak" acids because they ionize very little. However, in high concentrations, they may be very corrosive to living tissue and other materials. The term "concentration," which refers to the amount of the acid dissolved in water, is often confused with the term "strong" or "weak." All highly concentrated acids are corrosive and dangerous, regardless of their strength. Organic acids include acetic acid, formic acid, picric acid, acrylic acid and methacrylic acid.

All acids must be handled carefully and stored safely. They must never be allowed to become contaminated, and they must be prevented from mixing with other chemicals.

Additional Hazards

In addition to being corrosive, acids may possess other hazards. For instance, nitric acid is very corrosive, but its major hazard may be that it is a powerful oxidizer.

Some acids are water reactive. That is, when they are in contact with water, a violent reaction will take place. Sulfuric acid is a prime example of a water-reactive acid.

Some acids will burn, and a few will detonate. All the organic acids will burn (all organic materials burn). Picric acid is an example of an explosive acid.

Some acids will polymerize. That is, the relatively small molecules of some organic acids, like acrylic acid and methacrylic acid (monomers), will react with themselves to form "giant" molecules called "polymers." The polymerization reaction is very exothermic (heat releasing) and, in an uncontrolled state, can turn into an explosion.

Some acids are toxic. Hydrocyanic acid is a solution of hydrogen cyanide in water. Needless to say, this acid is deadly.

Many of the inorganic acids, when in contact with metals, will liberate the extremely flammable hydrogen gas. There may be other reaction products, some flammable, some toxic, and some corrosive, when these inorganic acids contact other materials.

Other Corrosives

Acids are not the only chemicals classed as corrosive. A class of materials called "bases" are the chemical opposites of inorganic acids, and many are just as corrosive as the strong acids. Sodium and potassium hydroxides ("caustic soda" and "caustic potash," respectively, are synonyms for these materials) are very powerful corrosives when dissolved in water. They are particularly damaging to human tissue, as they dissolve in the moisture on such tissue.

The halogens—fluorine, chlorine, bromine and iodine—are extremely corrosive to human tissue, in addition to being oxidizers and toxic. Fluorine and chlorine are gases, while bromine is a fuming liquid and iodine is a solid that sublimes (converts from a solid directly to a gas, bypassing the liquid state).

Hydrogen fluoride, hydrogen chloride, hydrogen bromide and hydrogen iodide, collectively known as the "halogen acid gases," are extremely corrosive when they contact human tissue. They will dissolve in the moisture on the skin (or anywhere else, for that matter) to form hydrofluoric, hydrochloric, hydrobromic, and hydrohydriodic acids, respectively. These are all strong acids.

Hydrogen peroxide and many other peroxides have corrosiveness as one of their additional hazards (they are oxidizers).

The chlorines of many metals, particularly the metals known as the "transition elements," and the chlorides of nonmetals are all corrosive to the degree that they must be considered hazardous in addition to their other hazards.

WATER-REACTIVE MATERIALS

As the name implies, this group of chemicals will produce a reaction with water, sometimes violent, and usually includes a hazardous by-product. These reactions usually fall into one or more of five different types of reactions: violent reactions, such as spattering or exploding; the evolution of dangerous gases (flammable, corrosive or toxic); the generation of heat; the ignition of combustibles; and the acceleration of the rate of combustion.

The alkali metals (lithium, sodium, potassium, and, more rarely, cesium and rubidium) all react in water to liberate highly flammable hydrogen gas, plus enough heat energy to ignite the hydrogen, and leave behind a caustic (corrosive) solution.

The alkaline earth metals, particularly magnesium, react in a much more violent manner under special conditions. When small pieces (high surface area) of magnesium are wetted with water, a sudden shock can cause the metal to detonate. A slower reaction will liberate hydrogen gas. Other alkaline earth metals are beryllium, calcium, strontium and barium.

The hydrides are ionic compounds of a metal or metals with hydrogen. When water contacts a metallic hydride, hydrogen gas is liberated and a caustic solution is left behind.

The carbides are ionic combinations of carbon and a metal. Not all the carbides are water-reactive, but those that are liberate highly flammable gases. A prime example is calcium carbide, which liberates acetylene. Beryllium carbide and aluminum carbide liberate methane, while magnesium carbide liberates propyne. Silver carbide has been known to detonate even before it contacts water.

The phosphides are ionic compounds of phosphorus and a metal. Contact with water by a phosphide such as aluminum phosphide generally yields the very toxic gas phosphine.

Nitrides are ionic compounds of nitrogen and a metal. Contact with water by a nitride such as magnesium nitride yields ammonia gas and leaves a caustic solution behind.

When metallic (inorganic) peroxides contact water, the result is the liberation of heat and the release of oxygen. The heat may be great enough to ignite combustibles, whose combustion will be vigorously supported by the liberated oxygen.

The chlorides of the Group III metals, the transition metals, and nonmetals such as aluminum chloride, titanium tetrachloride, and sulfur monochloride, all release hydrogen chloride when contacted by water.

Sulfuric acid and calcium oxide are examples of materials that generate tremendous quantities of heat when they come in contact with water.

Additional Hazards

It should be obvious that each class of hazardous materials has hazards other than the one that placed them in a particular hazard category. An examination of the above materials reveals hazards that include toxicity, corrosiveness, oxidizing power and flammability.

AIR-REACTIVE MATERIALS

Air-reactive materials are also known as pyrophoric materials. *Pyrophoric* means that the material will begin to react as soon as it comes in contact with air. It is actually reacting with the oxygen in the oxygen in the air. Some reference sources state that when the alkali metals, and even the alkaline earth metals, are reduced to very fine powders, they become pyrophoric. This is arguable, since it is probably the moisture in the air with which the metallic powders are reacting, rather than the oxygen.

The most common pyrophoric material is elemental phosphorus. When it comes in contact with air, it begins to burn with a bright light, releasing a tremendous amount of heat. The combustion product is phosphorus pentoxide.

The chemicals known as the "organo-metallic compounds" are pyrophoric. These materials have names that usually include an organic radical and one or more metals. Included in this group are tetraethyl lead, nickel carbonyl, chlorodiethyl aluminum, diethyl cadmium, dimethyl zinc, triethyl aluminum, trimethyl aluminum, triisobutyl aluminum and trimethyl aluminum ethereate.

Dimethyl arsine is a non-organo-metallic compound that is pyrophoric.

These materials all possess other hazards, but these are far overpowered by their reactions in air.

TOXIC MATERIALS

The toxicity of a material is often misunderstood and is very difficult to define. The ability of a chemical substance to produce injury once it reaches a susceptible site in or near the body can be considered a definition of a toxic substance, but there are many other definitions of toxicity that will cause different materials to be rated differently as far as this hazard is concerned.

There is a strong difference between the materials that are recognized as and called *poisons* and those that have some degree of toxicity. In industry, as well as anywhere else, care must be taken when a person is exposed to a material that possesses any degree of toxicity. It is not the intent of the authors to discuss each toxic material or each toxic hazard, but rather to introduce the topic of toxicity and allow readers to classify the materials with which they are concerned.

Not only are there many ways of defining toxicity, there are also many ways of measuring it.

The lethal concentration (LC_{50}) is a measure of toxicity that is used to determine the toxicity of gases, vapors, fumes and dusts in air. It is defined as a lethal concentration of gases, vapors, fumes or dusts in air to which animals have been exposed for a specified time and that kills half of the animals during the observation period. The animals are usually secured in a container. The gases, vapors, fumes and dusts are then introduced into the atmosphere (in a specified ratio of parts per million by volume of air) breathed by the animals for a specified amount of time. The exposed animals are then observed for a specified observation period, during which a count of fatalities is kept. The LC_{50} is that lethal concentration that kills half the animals during the observation period.

The lethal dosage (LD_{50}) is a measure of the toxicity of a material that is defined as the lethal dose, expressed in milligrams of toxin per kilogram of body weight (mg/kg) of the laboratory animals exposed, that kills half of the animals in an observation period after exposure. A number of white mice, or other selected animals, are fed or injected with a dosage of the material under examination. The amount administered is different for each animal because of differences in body size. However, each animal is fed or injected with an amount that is proportionately equal, based on each animal's weight. The animals are then observed for a period of time, usually 2 weeks. If more than half of the animals die during the observation period (which, or course, may be some other length of time), the experiment is repeated with a smaller dosage (conversely, if less than half die, the dosage is increased). The objective is to establish, as precisely as possible, the amount of the material that will kill exactly half of the animals during the observation period. This is then reported as the LD_{50}.

The *threshold limit value (TLV-TWA)* is defined as the upper limit of a toxic material to which an average person in average health may be exposed to repeatedly on a day-to-day basis with no adverse effects. These limits are expressed in milligrams per cubic meter (mg/m^3) for gases or vapors in air and in micrograms per cubic meter ($\mu g/m^3$) for fumes and mists in air. These standards are set and revised annually by the American Conference of Governmental Industrial Hygienists (ACGIH) for concentrations of airborne substances in workroom air. They are time-weighted averages (TWA) based on conditions which it is believed that workers may be repeatedly exposed to during their normal work week with no ill effects. The values are *not* intended to serve as definitive lines between safe and dangerous concentrations, but rather as guides in the control of health hazards.

The *maximum allowable concentration (MAK)* is an easier measure to understand than the TLV-TWA. Whereas the TLV is a time-weighted average of concentration over a workday and work week, the MAK sets the absolute maximum exposure at any one given time. Like TLV, it is usually expressed in parts per million (ppm).

There are many other measures of toxicity, but the first three mentioned above are the major ones listed by most references. Others include *short-term exposure limits (STEL), effective concentration (EC_{50}), incapacitation concentration (IC_{50}), immediately dangerous to life and health (IDLH),* and *Permissible Exposure Limit (PEL)*. More measures will be developed as researchers try to define the effects for which they are looking. It is important to realize that the vast majority of chemicals have some degree of toxicity, but that they will be found classified under some other hazard for which the danger of exposure is greater.

Toxic materials may be classified in many ways. The only attempt made here will be to classify them with regard to general reactions within the body rather than at specific sites with specific reactions.

Irritants are corrosive materials which attack the mucous membrane surfaces of the body. These materials are classified as irritants by definition, but if they are encountered in very high concentrations, they will produce death rather than just irritation.

Water-soluble irritants are very soluble in water, and therefore will dissolve in the first moisture they meet, usually in the eyes, mouth, nose and upper respiratory tract, so it is in these areas of the body that they will be most dangerous. These irritants include the halogen acid gases (hydrogen chloride [HCl], hydrogen fluoride [HF], hydrogen bromide [HBr], hydrogen iodide [HI]), sulfer dioxide (SO_2) and ammonia, (NH_3).

Sulfur dioxide forms sulfurous acid the same way the halogen acids are formed. Hence, its irritating properties are similar, if less severe.

Ammonia forms a caustic (basic) solution when dissolved in water, converting to ammonium hydroxide (NH_4OH). Ammonia is a very pungent gas that, like the others, will force the individual to seek fresh air if encountered.

Although the above-named materials are irritants as far as toxicologists are concerned, DOT considers them all nonflammable gases, and that is how they are placarded when transported. The major "fooler," however, is ammonia, which will burn within a flammable range of 16 to 25% in air.

The moderately soluble irritants do not dissolve in water as rapidly or as easily as the materials described above, so their effects are felt further along the respiratory tract, that is, the upper respiratory tract and the lungs. They include the halogens (fluorine, chlorine, the fumes of bromine and the vapor of iodine), ozone (O_3), phosphorus trichloride (PCl_3), and phosphorus pentachloride (PCl_5). These materials are all corrosive, and irritate sensitive areas in small amounts, but cause severe damage and even death in high concentrations.

The slightly water-soluble irritants bypass all the moist areas that the first two groups of irritants attach and instead damage the lungs, attacking the alveoli and destroying them by chemical action. In small quantities, these irritants will not do great damage, but in high concentrations they will be fatal, usually by delayed effects. In the case of the nitrogen oxides (NO_x), the delay ranges from 4 to 48 hours. The oxides of nitrogen are nitrous oxide (N_2O), nitric oxide (NO), nitrogen dioxide (NO_2), nitrogen trioxide (N_2O_3), dinitrogen tetroxide (N_2O_4), and dinitrogen pentoxide (N_2O_5). Of these, nitrous oxide is a nonirritating gas, sometimes used as an anesthetic (laughing gas). The other material sometimes classified as an irritant in this class is phosgene ($COCl_2$). DOT considers phosgene a class A poison.

Another mild irritant that is slightly soluble in water is trichloroethylene (C_2HCl_3). Its vapor is extremely dense (vapor density = 4.53), which makes it very dangerous in close quarters, where it displaces air and causes death either by asphyxiation or by its own action.

Asphyxiants are gases that interfere with the oxidation processes in the body. Simple asphyxiants are materials that are not toxic in their own right but that kill by diluting or replacing the oxygen in the air needed for breathing. The most common simple asphyxiant is carbon dioxide (CO_2), an inert gas produced in great quantities as a product of oxidation (combustion) of carbon-based materials. Although carbon dioxide is considered a very mild toxic material, when it does cause death, it usually does so by acting as a simple asphyxiant.

Another simple asphyxiant is nitrogen, another relatively inert gas. The nitrogen molecule (N_2) has almost the same molecular weight as air and therefore will not disperse quickly.

Hydrogen (dangerous as a simple asphyxiant only in airtight rooms or containers because it is so light that it rises in air and disperses rapidly) is another simple asphyxiant, but it has an added hazard. Hydrogen is one of the most flammable and hottest-burning gases known. Therefore, care must be taken not only to prevent it from diluting oxygen but also to protect individuals from its explosion and fire hazards.

The noble gases (helium, neon, argon, krypton, and xenon) are all simple asphyxiants simply because of their inertness.

The saturated hydrocarbons are another group of simple asphyxiants. These gases, methane (and, or course, natural gas), ethane, propane and butane are all nontoxic, but they are flammable. Methane and natural gas are lighter than air, but ethane, propane and butane are heavier than air. The vapors of the liquid alkanes will also be nontoxic.

Blood asphyxiants are materials that combine with the red blood cells and render them incapable of combining with oxygen and thereby carrying it to the cells of the body. The normal process after breathing is the formation of a compound in the red blood cell called "oxyhemoglobin." This weak compound carries oxygen to the cells, where it is "dumped," and carbon dioxide is picked up and brought back to the lungs for disposal. Anything that interferes with this process by preventing the formation of oxyhemoglobin is a blood asphyxiant. By far the most common blood asphyxiant is carbon monoxide, the deadly gas formed in all fires involving carbon-based combustibles.

Two other blood asphyxiants are aniline ($C_6H_5NH_2$) and nitrobenzene ($C_6H_5NO_2$). Both are toxic by inhalation, ingestion and absorption.

Tissue asphyxiants are materials that are carried by the red blood cells to the cells of the body, given up to those cells in exchange for the carbon dioxide held by the cells, and render the body cells incapable of accepting oxygen from the red blood cells. Unlike carbon monoxide, which attaches itself to the red blood cell so tightly that it will not let go and renders that cell incapable of picking up oxygen, the tissue asphyxiant allows itself to be "dumped" to the receiving body cell just like oxygen. But upon acceptance of this material from the red blood cell, the body cell itself is poisoned so that it can no longer accept oxygen. By far the most common tissue asphyxiant is hydrogen cyanide (HCN). When hydrogen cyanide dissolves in water, it becomes hydrocyanic acid, or prussic acid. Both the acid and the gas have the smell of bitter almonds, and the gas is colorless.

Respiratory paralyzers are materials that, upon entering the body, short-circuit the respiratory nervous system. The most common respiratory paralyzer is hydrogen sulfide (H_2S), a flammable, colorless gas with an overpowering smell of rotten eggs.

Another respiratory paralyzer is carbon disulfide (CS_2), also called "carbon bisulfide." It is a clear, colorless liquid with the very disagreeable odor of rotten cabbage. It has a flash point of $-22°F$ and a remarkably low ignition temperature of $212°F$. With a tolerance of only 10 ppm, it is very toxic.

Other respiratory paralyzers include materials that have an anesthetic or narcotic effect on the body. They include acetylene (C_2H_2), a highly flammable and unstable gas; ethylene (C_2H_4), another flammable gas that is a very popular monomer and has many uses; diethyl ether ($C_2H_5)_2O$, a popular anesthetic that is very flammable; acetone (($CH_3)_2CO$), a flammable solvent; and ethyl alcohol (C_2H_5OH), a flammable liquid that is the alcohol in alcoholic drinks.

A material is a systemic poison if it interferes with any vital bodily processes. We classify the following types of systemic poisons by the vital organ whose function is disrupted.

The most common systemic poison that disrupts the function of the liver and kidneys is arsenic.

The heavy metals such as lead, cadmium and mercury are also systemic poisons that attack the liver and kidneys. These metals are very common and therefore have many uses. Lead compounds were used as paint pigments and gasoline additives for many years. Cadmium pigments are still very popular. Mercury compounds are not as common, but much mercury is discarded in many metal reduction operations and has become a major water pollutant.

A third group of systemic poisons include all the halogenated hydrocarbons. This is a very large group of hazardous materials, although many manufacturers will take exception, claiming that their materials are not hazardous. However, a great body of research shows conclusively that after enough exposure to halogenated hydrocarbons, liver and kidney problems will develop.

The most common hazardous material that attacks the bone marrow is benzene (C_6H_6).

Other materials that are suspected of being attackers of bone marrow are toluene ($C_6H_5CH_3$), xylene ($C_6H_4(CH_3)_2$), and naphthalene ($C_{10}H_8$). Toluene and xylene are very popular solvents that have replaced benzene, and naphthalene is a white crystalline solid that sublimes.

By far the most common systemic poison that attacks the muscles is strychnine ($C_{21}H_{22}N_2O_2$). It is a white powder with a bitter taste.

The largest group of poisons that interfere with vital nerve impulses are the organic phosphates, which are commonly used in pesticides. It is not possible to list all the nerve impulses with which they interfere, but in high enough dosages death will be quite unpleasant.

Carbon disulfide, a material discussed earlier as a respiratory paralyzer, will also affect other nerves besides those of the respiratory system.

Methyl alcohol (CH_3OH), also known as "methanol," is a very common material that interferes with vital nerve impulses, being specific in its attack on the optic nerve.

DOT classifies toxic materials in a different manner. Poison A is a classification that includes extremely dangerous poisons, those substances that are poisonous gases or liquids of such nature that a very small amount of the gas, or vapor of the liquid, mixed with air is dangerous to life.

Poison B is a classification that includes less dangerous poisons, substances, liquids, or solids (including pastes and semisolids), other than Class A or irritating materials, which are known to be so toxic to humans as to constitute a health hazard during transportation or which, in the absence of adequate data on human toxicity, are presumed to be toxic to humans.

Irritating materials are liquids or solid substances which, upon contact with fire or when exposed to air, give off dangerous or intensely irritating fumes, but excluding Class A poisonous materials.

More exotic chemicals produce many other toxic effects. These include materials classified as neurotoxins (primarily affects the nervous system), hemototoxins (primarily affects the blood system), nephrotoxins (produce kidney damage), hepatotoxins (produce liver damage), and agents which cause damage to the reproductive system, lungs, eyes and skin.

APPENDIX A

PUBLIC LAW 99-499:
SUPERFUND AMENDMENTS AND REAUTHORIZATION ACT
OF 1986:
TITLE III—EMERGENCY PLANNING AND
COMMUNITY RIGHT-TO-KNOW

Public Law 99-499
99th Congress

An Act

To extend and amend the Comprehensive Environmental Response, Compensation, and Liability Act of 1980, and for other purposes.

Oct. 17, 1986
[H.R. 2005]

Hazardous materials.
Environmental protection.
42 USC 9601 note.

SECTION 1. SHORT TITLE AND TABLE OF CONTENTS.

This Act may be cited as the "Superfund Amendments and Reauthorization Act of 1986".

TABLE OF CONTENTS

---

*Note: The printed text of Public Law 99-499 is a reprint of the hand enrollment, signed by the President on October 17, 1986.

100 STAT. 1614   PUBLIC LAW 99-499—OCT. 17, 1986

Emergency
Planning and
Community
Right-To-Know
Act of 1986.
42 USC 11001
note.

TITLE III—EMERGENCY PLANNING AND COMMUNITY RIGHT-TO-KNOW

SEC. 300. SHORT TITLE; TABLE OF CONTENTS.

(a) SHORT TITLE.—This title may be cited as the "Emergency Planning and Community Right-To-Know Act of 1986".

(b) TABLE OF CONTENTS.—The table of contents of this title is as follows:

Subtitle A—Emergency Planning and Notification

SEC. 301. ESTABLISHMENT OF STATE COMMISSIONS, PLANNING DISTRICTS, AND LOCAL COMMITTEES.   42 USC 11001.

(a) ESTABLISHMENT OF STATE EMERGENCY RESPONSE COMMISSIONS.—Not later than six months after the date of the enactment of this title, the Governor of each State shall appoint a State emergency response commission. The Governor may designate as the State emergency response commission one or more existing emergency response organizations that are State-sponsored or appointed. The Governor shall, to the extent practicable, appoint persons to the State emergency response commission who have technical expertise in the emergency response field. The State emergency response commission shall appoint local emergency planning committees under subsection (c) and shall supervise and coordinate the activities of such committees. The State emergency response commission shall establish procedures for receiving and processing requests from the public for information under section 324, including tier II information under section 312. Such procedures shall include the designation of an official to serve as coordinator for information. If the Governor of any State does not designate a State emergency response commission within such period, the Governor shall operate as the State emergency response commission until the Governor makes such designation.

(b) ESTABLISHMENT OF EMERGENCY PLANNING DISTRICTS.—Not later than nine months after the date of the enactment of this title, the State emergency response commission shall designate emergency planning districts in order to facilitate preparation and implementation of emergency plans. Where appropriate, the State emergency response commission may designate existing political subdivisions or multijurisdictional planning organizations as such districts. In emergency planning areas that involve more than one State, the State emergency response commissions of all potentially affected States may designate emergency planning districts and local emergency planning committees by agreement. In making such designation, the State emergency response commission shall indicate which facilities subject to the requirements of this subtitle are within such emergency planning district.

(c) ESTABLISHMENT OF LOCAL EMERGENCY PLANNING COMMITTEES.—Not later than 30 days after designation of emergency planning districts or 10 months after the date of the enactment of this title, whichever is earlier, the State emergency response commission shall appoint members of a local emergency planning committee for each emergency planning district. Each committee shall include, at a minimum, representatives from each of the following groups or organizations: elected State and local officials; law enforcement, civil defense, firefighting, first aid, health, local environmental, hospital, and transportation personnel; broadcast and print media; community groups; and owners and operators of facilities subject to the requirements of this subtitle. Such committee shall appoint a chairperson and shall establish rules by which the committee shall function. Such rules shall include provisions for public notification of committee activities, public meetings to discuss the emergency plan, public comments, response to such comments by the committee, and distribution of the emergency plan. The local emergency planning committee shall establish procedures for receiving and processing requests from the public for information under section 324, including tier II information under section 312. Such procedures shall include the designation of an official to serve as coordinator for information.

(d) REVISIONS.—A State emergency response commission may revise its designations and appointments under subsections (b) and (c) as it deems appropriate. Interested persons may petition the State emergency response commission to modify the membership of a local emergency planning committee.

42 USC 11002.

SEC. 302. SUBSTANCES AND FACILITIES COVERED AND NOTIFICATION.

(a) SUBSTANCES COVERED.—

(1) IN GENERAL.—A substance is subject to the requirements of this subtitle if the substance is on the list published under paragraph (2).

(2) LIST OF EXTREMELY HAZARDOUS SUBSTANCES.—Within 30 days after the date of the enactment of this title, the Administrator shall publish a list of extremely hazardous substances. The list shall be the same as the list of substances published in November 1985 by the Administrator in Appendix A of the "Chemical Emergency Preparedness Program Interim Guidance".

Regulations.

(3) THRESHOLDS.—(A) At the time the list referred to in paragraph (2) is published the Administrator shall—

(i) publish an interim final regulation establishing a threshold planning quantity for each substance on the list, taking into account the criteria described in paragraph (4), and

(ii) initiate a rulemaking in order to publish final regulations establishing a threshold planning quantity for each substance on the list.

(B) The threshold planning quantities may, at the Administrator's discretion, be based on classes of chemicals or categories of facilities.

(C) If the Administrator fails to publish an interim final regulation establishing a threshold planning quantity for a substance within 30 days after the date of the enactment of this title, the threshold planning quantity for the substance shall be 2 pounds until such time as the Administrator publishes regulations establishing a threshold for the substance.

(4) REVISIONS.—The Administrator may revise the list and thresholds under paragraphs (2) and (3) from time to time. Any revisions to the list shall take into account the toxicity, reactivity, volatility, dispersability, combustability, or flammability of a substance. For purposes of the preceding sentence, the term

"toxicity" shall include any short- or long-term health effect which may result from a short-term exposure to the substance.

(b) FACILITIES COVERED.—(1) Except as provided in section 304, a facility is subject to the requirements of this subtitle if a substance on the list referred to in subsection (a) is present at the facility in an amount in excess of the threshold planning quantity established for such substance.

(2) For purposes of emergency planning, a Governor or a State emergency response commission may designate additional facilities which shall be subject to the requirements of this subtitle, if such designation is made after public notice and opportunity for comment. The Governor or State emergency response commission shall notify the facility concerned of any facility designation under this paragraph.

(c) EMERGENCY PLANNING NOTIFICATION.—Not later than seven months after the date of the enactment of this title, the owner or operator of each facility subject to the requirements of this subtitle by reason of subsection (b)(1) shall notify the State emergency response commission for the State in which such facility is located that such facility is subject to the requirements of this subtitle. Thereafter, if a substance on the list of extremely hazardous substances referred to in subsection (a) first becomes present at such facility in excess of the threshold planning quantity established for such substance, or if there is a revision of such list and the facility has present a substance on the revised list in excess of the threshold planning quantity established for such substance, the owner or operator of the facility shall notify the State emergency response commission and the local emergency planning committee within 60 days after such acquisition or revision that such facility is subject to the requirements of this subtitle.

(d) NOTIFICATION OF ADMINISTRATOR.—The State emergency response commission shall notify the Administrator of facilities subject to the requirements of this subtitle by notifying the Administrator of—

(1) each notification received from a facility under subsection (c), and

(2) each facility designated by the Governor or State emergency response commission under subsection (b)(2).

SEC. 303. COMPREHENSIVE EMERGENCY RESPONSE PLANS.

42 USC 11003.

(a) PLAN REQUIRED.—Each local emergency planning committee shall complete preparation of an emergency plan in accordance with this section not later than two years after the date of the enactment of this title. The committee shall review such plan once a year, or more frequently as changed circumstances in the community or at any facility may require.

(b) RESOURCES.—Each local emergency planning committee shall evaluate the need for resources necessary to develop, implement, and exercise the emergency plan, and shall make recommendations with respect to additional resources that may be required and the means for providing such additional resources.

(c) PLAN PROVISIONS.—Each emergency plan shall include (but is not limited to) each of the following:

(1) Identification of facilities subject to the requirements of this subtitle that are within the emergency planning district, identification of routes likely to be used for the transportation of substances on the list of extremely hazardous substances

referred to in section 302(a), and identification of additional facilities contributing or subjected to additional risk due to their proximity to facilities subject to the requirements of this subtitle, such as hospitals or natural gas facilities.

(2) Methods and procedures to be followed by facility owners and operators and local emergency and medical personnel to respond to any release of such substances.

(3) Designation of a community emergency coordinator and facility emergency coordinators, who shall make determinations necessary to implement the plan.

(4) Procedures providing reliable, effective, and timely notification by the facility emergency coordinators and the community emergency coordinator to persons designated in the emergency plan, and to the public, that a release has occurred (consistent with the emergency notification requirements of section 304).

(5) Methods for determining the occurrence of a release, and the area or population likely to be affected by such release.

(6) A description of emergency equipment and facilities in the community and at each facility in the community subject to the requirements of this subtitle, and an identification of the persons responsible for such equipment and facilities.

(7) Evacuation plans, including provisions for a precautionary evacuation and alternative traffic routes.

(8) Training programs, including schedules for training of local emergency response and medical personnel.

(9) Methods and schedules for exercising the emergency plan.

(d) PROVIDING OF INFORMATION.—For each facility subject to the requirements of this subtitle:

(1) Within 30 days after establishment of a local emergency planning committee for the emergency planning district in which such facility is located, or within 11 months after the date of the enactment of this title, whichever is earlier, the owner or operator of the facility shall notify the emergency planning committee (or the Governor if there is no committee) of a facility representative who will participate in the emergency planning process as a facility emergency coordinator.

(2) The owner or operator of the facility shall promptly inform the emergency planning committee of any relevant changes occurring at such facility as such changes occur or are expected to occur.

(3) Upon request from the emergency planning committee, the owner or operator of the facility shall promptly provide information to such committee necessary for developing and implementing the emergency plan.

(e) REVIEW BY THE STATE EMERGENCY RESPONSE COMMISSION.—After completion of an emergency plan under subsection (a) for an emergency planning district, the local emergency planning committee shall submit a copy of the plan to the State emergency response commission of each State in which such district is located. The commission shall review the plan and make recommendations to the committee on revisions of the plan that may be necessary to ensure coordination of such plan with emergency response plans of other emergency planning districts. To the maximum extent practicable, such review shall not delay implementation of such plan.

(f) GUIDANCE DOCUMENTS.—The national response team, as established pursuant to the National Contingency Plan as established under section 105 of the Comprehensive Environmental Response, Compensation, and Liability Act of 1980 (42 U.S.C. 9601 et seq.), shall publish guidance documents for preparation and implementation of emergency plans. Such documents shall be published not later than five months after the date of the enactment of this title.

42 USC 9605.

(g) REVIEW OF PLANS BY REGIONAL RESPONSE TEAMS.—The regional response teams, as established pursuant to the National Contingency Plan as established under section 105 of the Comprehensive Environmental Response, Compensation, and Liability Act of 1980 (42 U.S.C. 9601 et seq.), may review and comment upon an emergency plan or other issues related to preparation, implementation, or exercise of such a plan upon request of a local emergency planning committee. Such review shall not delay implementation of the plan.

42 USC 9605.

SEC. 304. EMERGENCY NOTIFICATION.

42 USC 11004.

(a) TYPES OF RELEASES.—

(1) 302(a) SUBSTANCE WHICH REQUIRES CERCLA NOTICE.—If a release of an extremely hazardous substance referred to in section 302(a) occurs from a facility at which a hazardous chemical is produced, used, or stored, and such release requires a notification under section 103(a) of the Comprehensive Environmental Response, Compensation, and Liability Act of 1980 (hereafter in this section referred to as "CERCLA") (42 U.S.C. 9601 et seq.), the owner or operator of the facility shall immediately provide notice as described in subsection (b).

Ante, p. 1730.

42 USC 9603.

(2) OTHER 302(a) SUBSTANCE.—If a release of an extremely hazardous substance referred to in section 302(a) occurs from a facility at which a hazardous chemical is produced, used, or stored, and such release is not subject to the notification requirements under section 103(a) of CERCLA, the owner or operator of the facility shall immediately provide notice as described in subsection (b), but only if the release—

(A) is not a federally permitted release as defined in section 101(10) of CERCLA,

(B) is in an amount in excess of a quantity which the Administrator has determined (by regulation) requires notice, and

(C) occurs in a manner which would require notification under section 103(a) of CERCLA.

Unless and until superseded by regulations establishing a quantity for an extremely hazardous substance described in this paragraph, a quantity of 1 pound shall be deemed that quantity the release of which requires notice as described in subsection (b).

(3) NON-302(a) SUBSTANCE WHICH REQUIRES CERCLA NOTICE.—If a release of a substance which is not on the list referred to in section 302(a) occurs at a facility at which a hazardous chemical is produced, used, or stored, and such release requires notification under section 103(a) of CERCLA, the owner or operator shall provide notice as follows:

(A) If the substance is one for which a reportable quantity has been established under section 102(a) of CERCLA, the owner or operator shall provide notice as described in subsection (b).

Ante, p. 1617.

(B) If the substance is one for which a reportable quantity has not been established under section 102(a) of CERCLA—

(i) Until April 30, 1988, the owner or operator shall provide, for releases of one pound or more of the substance, the same notice to the community emergency coordinator for the local emergency planning committee, at the same time and in the same form, as notice is provided to the National Response Center under section 103(a) of CERCLA.

42 USC 9603.

(ii) On and after April 30, 1988, the owner or operator shall provide, for releases of one pound or more of the substance, the notice as described in subsection (b).

(4) EXEMPTED RELEASES.—This section does not apply to any release which results in exposure to persons solely within the site or sites on which a facility is located.

(b) NOTIFICATION.—

(1) RECIPIENTS OF NOTICE.—Notice required under subsection (a) shall be given immediately after the release by the owner or operator of a facility (by such means as telephone, radio, or in person) to the community emergency coordinator for the local emergency planning committees, if established pursuant to section 301(c), for any area likely to be affected by the release and to the State emergency planning commission of any State likely to be affected by the release. With respect to transportation of a substance subject to the requirements of this section, or storage incident to such transportation, the notice requirements of this section with respect to a release shall be satisfied by dialing 911 or, in the absence of a 911 emergency telephone number, calling the operator.

Ante, p. 1729.

(2) CONTENTS.—Notice required under subsection (a) shall include each of the following (to the extent known at the time of the notice and so long as no delay in responding to the emergency results):

(A) The chemical name or identity of any substance involved in the release.

(B) An indication of whether the substance is on the list referred to in section 302(a).

(C) An estimate of the quantity of any such substance that was released into the environment.

(D) The time and duration of the release.

(E) The medium or media into which the release occurred.

(F) Any known or anticipated acute or chronic health risks associated with the emergency and, where appropriate, advice regarding medical attention necessary for exposed individuals.

(G) Proper precautions to take as a result of the release, including evacuation (unless such information is readily available to the community emergency coordinator pursuant to the emergency plan).

(H) The name and telephone number of the person or persons to be contacted for further information.

(c) FOLLOWUP EMERGENCY NOTICE.—As soon as practicable after a release which requires notice under subsection (a), such owner or operator shall provide a written followup emergency notice (or notices, as more information becomes available) setting forth and updating the information required under subsection (b), and including additional information with respect to—

(1) actions taken to respond to and contain the release,

PUBLIC LAW 99-499—OCT. 17, 1986   100 STAT. 1735

(2) any known or anticipated acute or chronic health risks associated with the release, and

(3) where appropriate, advice regarding medical attention necessary for exposed individuals.

(d) TRANSPORTATION EXEMPTION NOT APPLICABLE.—The exemption provided in section 327 (relating to transportation) does not apply to this section.

Post, p. 1757.

SEC. 305. EMERGENCY TRAINING AND REVIEW OF EMERGENCY SYSTEMS.

42 USC 11005.

(a) EMERGENCY TRAINING.—

(1) PROGRAMS.—Officials of the United States Government carrying out existing Federal programs for emergency training are authorized to specifically provide training and education programs for Federal, State, and local personnel in hazard mitigation, emergency preparedness, fire prevention and control, disaster response, long-term disaster recovery, national security, technological and natural hazards, and emergency processes. Such programs shall provide special emphasis for such training and education with respect to hazardous chemicals.

(2) STATE AND LOCAL PROGRAM SUPPORT.—There is authorized to be appropriated to the Federal Emergency Management Agency for each of the fiscal years 1987, 1988, 1989, and 1990, $5,000,000 for making grants to support programs of State and local governments, and to support university-sponsored programs, which are designed to improve emergency planning, preparedness, mitigation, response, and recovery capabilities. Such programs shall provide special emphasis with respect to emergencies associated with hazardous chemicals. Such grants may not exceed 80 percent of the cost of any such program. The remaining 20 percent of such costs shall be funded from non-Federal sources.

Appropriation authorization. Grants.

(3) OTHER PROGRAMS.—Nothing in this section shall affect the availability of appropriations to the Federal Emergency Management Agency for any programs carried out by such agency other than the programs referred to in paragraph (2).

(b) REVIEW OF EMERGENCY SYSTEMS.—

(1) REVIEW.—The Administrator shall initiate, not later than 30 days after the date of the enactment of this title, a review of emergency systems for monitoring, detecting, and preventing releases of extremely hazardous substances at representative domestic facilities that produce, use, or store extremely hazardous substances. The Administrator may select representative extremely hazardous substances from the substances on the list referred to in section 302(a) for the purposes of this review. The Administrator shall report interim findings to the Congress not later than seven months after such date of enactment, and issue a final report of findings and recommendations to the Congress not later than 18 months after such date of enactment. Such report shall be prepared in consultation with the States and appropriate Federal agencies.

Reports.

(2) REPORT.—The report required by this subsection shall include the Administrator's findings regarding each of the following:

(A) The status of current technological capabilities to (i) monitor, detect, and prevent, in a timely manner, significant releases of extremely hazardous substances, (ii) determine the magnitude and direction of the hazard posed by each release, (iii) identify specific substances, (iv) provide data on the specific chemical composition of such releases, and (v) determine the relative concentrations of the constituent substances.

(B) The status of public emergency alert devices or systems for providing timely and effective public warning of an accidental release of extremely hazardous substances into the environment, including releases into the atmosphere, surface water, or groundwater from facilities that produce, store, or use significant quantities of such extremely hazardous substances.

(C) The technical and economic feasibility of establishing, maintaining, and operating perimeter alert systems for detecting releases of such extremely hazardous substances into the atmosphere, surface water, or groundwater, at facilities that manufacture, use, or store significant quantities of such substances.

Reports.

(3) RECOMMENDATIONS.—The report required by this subsection shall also include the Administrator's recommendations for—

(A) initiatives to support the development of new or improved technologies or systems that would facilitate the timely monitoring, detection, and prevention of releases of extremely hazardous substances, and

(B) improving devices or systems for effectively alerting the public in a timely manner, in the event of an accidental release of such extremely hazardous substances.

Subtitle B—Reporting Requirements

42 USC 11021.

SEC. 311. MATERIAL SAFETY DATA SHEETS.

(a) BASIC REQUIREMENT.—

(1) SUBMISSION OF MSDS OR LIST.—The owner or operator of any facility which is required to prepare or have available a material safety data sheet for a hazardous chemical under the Occupational Safety and Health Act of 1970 and regulations promulgated under that Act (15 U.S.C. 651 et seq.) shall submit a material safety data sheet for each such chemical, or a list of such chemicals as described in paragraph (2), to each of the following:

29 USC 651 note.

(A) The appropriate local emergency planning committee.

(B) The State emergency response commission.

(C) The fire department with jurisdiction over the facility.

(2) CONTENTS OF LIST.—(A) The list of chemicals referred to in paragraph (1) shall include each of the following:

Regulations.

(i) A list of the hazardous chemicals for which a material safety data sheet is required under the Occupational Safety and Health Act of 1970 and regulations promulgated under that Act, grouped in categories of health and physical hazards as set forth under such Act and regulations promulgated under such Act, or in such other categories as the Administrator may prescribe under subparagraph (B).

(ii) The chemical name or the common name of each such chemical as provided on the material safety data sheet.

(iii) Any hazardous component of each such chemical as provided on the material safety data sheet.

(B) For purposes of the list under this paragraph, the Administrator may modify the categories of health and physical hazards as set forth under the Occupational Safety and Health Act of 1970 and regulations promulgated under that Act by requiring information to be reported in terms of groups of hazardous chemicals which present similar hazards in an emergency.

Reports.

29 USC 651 note.

(3) TREATMENT OF MIXTURES.—An owner or operator may meet the requirements of this section with respect to a hazardous chemical which is a mixture by doing one of the following:

(A) Submitting a material safety data sheet for, or identifying on a list, each element or compound in the mixture which is a hazardous chemical. If more than one mixture has the same element or compound, only one material safety data sheet, or one listing, of the element or compound is necessary.

(B) Submitting a material safety data sheet for, or identifying on a list, the mixture itself.

(b) THRESHOLDS.—The Administrator may establish threshold quantities for hazardous chemicals below which no facility shall be subject to the provisions of this section. The threshold quantities may, in the Administrator's discretion, be based on classes of chemicals or categories of facilities.

(c) AVAILABILITY OF MSDS ON REQUEST.—

(1) TO LOCAL EMERGENCY PLANNING COMMITTEE.—If an owner or operator of a facility submits a list of chemicals under subsection (a)(1), the owner or operator, upon request by the local emergency planning committee, shall submit the material safety data sheet for any chemical on the list to such committee.

(2) TO PUBLIC.—A local emergency planning committee, upon request by any person, shall make available a material safety data sheet to the person in accordance with section 324. If the local emergency planning committee does not have the requested material safety data sheet, the committee shall request the sheet from the facility owner or operator and then make the sheet available to the person in accordance with section 324.

(d) INITIAL SUBMISSION AND UPDATING.—(1) The initial material safety data sheet or list required under this section with respect to a hazardous chemical shall be provided before the later of—

(A) 12 months after the date of the enactment of this title, or

(B) 3 months after the owner or operator of a facility is required to prepare or have available a material safety data sheet for the chemical under the Occupational Safety and Health Act of 1970 and regulations promulgated under that Act.

29 USC 651 note.

(2) Within 3 months following discovery by an owner or operator of significant new information concerning an aspect of a hazardous chemical for which a material safety data sheet was previously submitted to the local emergency planning committee under subsection (a), a revised sheet shall be provided to such person.

(e) HAZARDOUS CHEMICAL DEFINED.—For purposes of this section, the term "hazardous chemical" has the meaning given such term by section 1910.1200(c) of title 29 of the Code of Federal Regulations, except that such term does not include the following:

(1) Any food, food additive, color additive, drug, or cosmetic regulated by the Food and Drug Administration.

100 STAT. 1738   PUBLIC LAW 99-499—OCT. 17, 1986

(2) Any substance present as a solid in any manufactured item to the extent exposure to the substance does not occur under normal conditions of use.

(3) Any substance to the extent it is used for personal, family, or household purposes, or is present in the same form and concentration as a product packaged for distribution and use by the general public.

(4) Any substance to the extent it is used in a research laboratory or a hospital or other medical facility under the direct supervision of a technically qualified individual.

(5) Any substance to the extent it is used in routine agricultural operations or is a fertilizer held for sale by a retailer to the ultimate customer.

42 USC 11022.

SEC. 312. EMERGENCY AND HAZARDOUS CHEMICAL INVENTORY FORMS.

(a) BASIC REQUIREMENT.—(1) The owner or operator of any facility which is required to prepare or have available a material safety data sheet for a hazardous chemical under the Occupational Safety and

29 USC 651 note.

Health Act of 1970 and regulations promulgated under that Act shall prepare and submit an emergency and hazardous chemical inventory form (hereafter in this title referred to as an "inventory form") to each of the following:

(A) The appropriate local emergency planning committee.

(B) The State emergency response commission.

(C) The fire department with jurisdiction over the facility.

(2) The inventory form containing tier I information (as described in subsection (d)(1)) shall be submitted on or before March 1, 1988, and annually thereafter on March 1, and shall contain data with respect to the preceding calendar year. The preceding sentence does not apply if an owner or operator provides, by the same deadline and with respect to the same calendar year, tier II information (as described in subsection (d)(2)) to the recipients described in paragraph (1).

(3) An owner or operator may meet the requirements of this section with respect to a hazardous chemical which is a mixture by doing one of the following:

(A) Providing information on the inventory form on each element or compound in the mixture which is a hazardous chemical. If more than one mixture has the same element or compound, only one listing on the inventory form for the element or compound at the facility is necessary.

(B) Providing information on the inventory form on the mixture itself.

(b) THRESHOLDS.—The Administrator may establish threshold quantities for hazardous chemicals covered by this section below which no facility shall be subject to the provisions of this section. The threshold quantities may, in the Administrator's discretion, be based on classes of chemicals or categories of facilities.

(c) HAZARDOUS CHEMICALS COVERED.—A hazardous chemical subject to the requirements of this section is any hazardous chemical for which a material safety data sheet or a listing is required under section 311.

(d) CONTENTS OF FORM.—

(1) TIER I INFORMATION.—

(A) AGGREGATE INFORMATION BY CATEGORY.—An inventory form shall provide the information described in subparagraph (B) in aggregate terms for hazardous chemicals in categories of health and physical hazards as set forth under the Occupational Safety and Health Act of 1970 and regulations promulgated under that Act.

29 USC 651 note.

(B) REQUIRED INFORMATION.—The information referred to in subparagraph (A) is the following:

(i) An estimate (in ranges) of the maximum amount of hazardous chemicals in each category present at the facility at any time during the preceding calendar year.

(ii) An estimate (in ranges) of the average daily amount of hazardous chemicals in each category present at the facility during the preceding calendar year.

(iii) The general location of hazardous chemicals in each category.

(C) MODIFICATIONS.—For purposes of reporting information under this paragraph, the Administrator may—

(i) modify the categories of health and physical hazards as set forth under the Occupational Safety and Health Act of 1970 and regulations promulgated under that Act by requiring information to be reported in terms of groups of hazardous chemicals which present similar hazards in an emergency, or

Regulations.

(ii) require reporting on individual hazardous chemicals of special concern to emergency response personnel.

(2) TIER II INFORMATION.—An inventory form shall provide the following additional information for each hazardous chemical present at the facility, but only upon request and in accordance with subsection (e):

(A) The chemical name or the common name of the chemical as provided on the material safety data sheet.

(B) An estimate (in ranges) of the maximum amount of the hazardous chemical present at the facility at any time during the preceding calendar year.

(C) An estimate (in ranges) of the average daily amount of the hazardous chemical present at the facility during the preceding calendar year.

(D) A brief description of the manner of storage of the hazardous chemical.

(E) The location at the facility of the hazardous chemical.

(F) An indication of whether the owner elects to withhold location information of a specific hazardous chemical from disclosure to the public under section 324.

(e) AVAILABILITY OF TIER II INFORMATION.—

(1) AVAILABILITY TO STATE COMMISSIONS, LOCAL COMMITTEES, AND FIRE DEPARTMENTS.—Upon request by a State emergency planning commission, a local emergency planning committee, or a fire department with jurisdiction over the facility, the owner or operator of a facility shall provide tier II information, as described in subsection (d), to the person making the request. Any such request shall be with respect to a specific facility.

(2) AVAILABILITY TO OTHER STATE AND LOCAL OFFICIALS.—A State or local official acting in his or her official capacity may have access to tier II information by submitting a request to the State emergency response commission or the local emergency planning committee. Upon receipt of a request for tier II information, the State commission or local committee shall,

pursuant to paragraph (1), request the facility owner or operator for the tier II information and make available such information to the official.

(3) AVAILABILITY TO PUBLIC.—

(A) IN GENERAL.—Any person may request a State emergency response commission or local emergency planning committee for tier II information relating to the preceding calendar year with respect to a facility. Any such request shall be in writing and shall be with respect to a specific facility.

(B) AUTOMATIC PROVISION OF INFORMATION TO PUBLIC.— Any tier II information which a State emergency response commission or local emergency planning committee has in its possession shall be made available to a person making a request under this paragraph in accordance with section 324. If the State emergency response commission or local emergency planning committee does not have the tier II information in its possession, upon a request for tier II information the State emergency response commission or local emergency planning committee shall, pursuant to paragraph (1), request the facility owner or operator for tier II information with respect to a hazardous chemical which a facility has stored in an amount in excess of 10,000 pounds present at the facility at any time during the preceding calendar year and make such information available in accordance with section 324 to the person making the request.

(C) DISCRETIONARY PROVISION OF INFORMATION TO PUBLIC.—In the case of tier II information which is not in the possession of a State emergency response commission or local emergency planning committee and which is with respect to a hazardous chemical which a facility has stored in an amount less than 10,000 pounds present at the facility at any time during the preceding calendar year, a request from a person must include the general need for the information. The State emergency response commission or local emergency planning committee may, pursuant to paragraph (1), request the facility owner or operator for the tier II information on behalf of the person making the request. Upon receipt of any information requested on behalf of such person, the State emergency response commission or local emergency planning committee shall make the information available in accordance with section 324 to the person.

(D) RESPONSE IN 45 DAYS.—A State emergency response commission or local emergency planning committee shall respond to a request for tier II information under this paragraph no later than 45 days after the date of receipt of the request.

(f) FIRE DEPARTMENT ACCESS.—Upon request to an owner or operator of a facility which files an inventory form under this section by the fire department with jurisdiction over the facility, the owner or operator of the facility shall allow the fire department to conduct an on-site inspection of the facility and shall provide to the fire department specific location information on hazardous chemicals at the facility.

(g) FORMAT OF FORMS.—The Administrator shall publish a uniform format for inventory forms within three months after the date of the enactment of this title. If the Administrator does not publish such forms, owners and operators of facilities subject to the requirements of this section shall provide the information required under this section by letter.

SEC. 313. TOXIC CHEMICAL RELEASE FORMS.

42 USC 11023.

(a) BASIC REQUIREMENT.—The owner or operator of a facility subject to the requirements of this section shall complete a toxic chemical release form as published under subsection (g) for each toxic chemical listed under subsection (c) that was manufactured, processed, or otherwise used in quantities exceeding the toxic chemical threshold quantity established by subsection (f) during the preceding calendar year at such facility. Such form shall be submitted to the Administrator and to an official or officials of the State designated by the Governor on or before July 1, 1988, and annually thereafter on July 1 and shall contain data reflecting releases during the preceding calendar year.

(b) COVERED OWNERS AND OPERATORS OF FACILITIES.—

(1) IN GENERAL.—(A) The requirements of this section shall apply to owners and operators of facilities that have 10 or more full-time employees and that are in Standard Industrial Classification Codes 20 through 39 (as in effect on July 1, 1985) and that manufactured, processed, or otherwise used a toxic chemical listed under subsection (c) in excess of the quantity of that toxic chemical established under subsection (f) during the calendar year for which a release form is required under this section.

(B) The Administrator may add or delete Standard Industrial Classification Codes for purposes of subparagraph (A), but only to the extent necessary to provide that each Standard Industrial Code to which this section applies is relevant to the purposes of this section.

(C) For purposes of this section—

(i) The term "manufacture" means to produce, prepare, import, or compound a toxic chemical.

(ii) The term "process" means the preparation of a toxic chemical, after its manufacture, for distribution in commerce—

(I) in the same form or physical state as, or in a different form or physical state from, that in which it was received by the person so preparing such chemical, or

(II) as part of an article containing the toxic chemical.

(2) DISCRETIONARY APPLICATION TO ADDITIONAL FACILITIES.—The Administrator, on his own motion or at the request of a Governor of a State (with regard to facilities located in that State), may apply the requirements of this section to the owners and operators of any particular facility that manufactures, processes, or otherwise uses a toxic chemical listed under subsection (c) if the Administrator determines that such action is warranted on the basis of toxicity of the toxic chemical, proximity to other facilities that release the toxic chemical or to population centers, the history of releases of such chemical at

such facility, or such other factors as the Administrator deems appropriate.

(c) TOXIC CHEMICALS COVERED.—The toxic chemicals subject to the requirements of this section are those chemicals on the list in Committee Print Number 99-169 of the Senate Committee on Environment and Public Works, titled "Toxic Chemicals Subject to Section 313 of the Emergency Planning and Community Right-To-Know Act of 1986" (including any revised version of the list as may be made pursuant to subsection (d) or (e)).

(d) REVISIONS BY ADMINISTRATOR.—

(1) IN GENERAL.—The Administrator may by rule add or delete a chemical from the list described in subsection (c) at any time.

(2) ADDITIONS.—A chemical may be added if the Administrator determines, in his judgment, that there is sufficient evidence to establish any one of the following:

(A) The chemical is known to cause or can reasonably be anticipated to cause significant adverse acute human health effects at concentration levels that are reasonably likely to exist beyond facility site boundaries as a result of continuous, or frequently recurring, releases.

(B) The chemical is known to cause or can reasonably be anticipated to cause in humans—

(i) cancer or teratogenic effects, or

(ii) serious or irreversible—

(I) reproductive dysfunctions,

(II) neurological disorders,

(III) heritable genetic mutations, or

(IV) other chronic health effects.

(C) The chemical is known to cause or can reasonably be anticipated to cause, because of—

(i) its toxicity,

(ii) its toxicity and persistence in the environment, or

(iii) its toxicity and tendency to bioaccumulate in the environment,

a significant adverse effect on the environment of sufficient seriousness, in the judgment of the Administrator, to warrant reporting under this section. The number of chemicals included on the list described in subsection (c) on the basis of the preceding sentence may constitute in the aggregate no more than 25 percent of the total number of chemicals on the list.

Science and technology. Research and development.

A determination under this paragraph shall be based on generally accepted scientific principles or laboratory tests, or appropriately designed and conducted epidemiological or other population studies, available to the Administrator.

(3) DELETIONS.—A chemical may be deleted if the Administrator determines there is not sufficient evidence to establish any of the criteria described in paragraph (2).

(4) EFFECTIVE DATE.—Any revision made on or after January 1 and before December 1 of any calendar year shall take effect beginning with the next calendar year. Any revision made on or after December 1 of any calendar year and before January 1 of the next calendar year shall take effect beginning with the calendar year following such next calendar year.

(e) PETITIONS.—

(1) IN GENERAL.—Any person may petition the Administrator to add or delete a chemical from the list described in subsection (c) on the basis of the criteria in subparagraph (A) or (B) of subsection (d)(2). Within 180 days after receipt of a petition, the Administrator shall take one of the following actions:

(A) Initiate a rulemaking to add or delete the chemical to the list, in accordance with subsection (d)(2) or (d)(3).

(B) Publish an explanation of why the petition is denied.

(2) GOVERNOR PETITIONS.—A State Governor may petition the Administrator to add or delete a chemical from the list described in subsection (c) on the basis of the criteria in subparagraph (A), (B), or (C) of subsection (d)(2). In the case of such a petition from a State Governor to delete a chemical, the petition shall be treated in the same manner as a petition received under paragraph (1) to delete a chemical. In the case of such a petition from a State Governor to add a chemical, the chemical will be added to the list within 180 days after receipt of the petition, unless the Administrator—

(A) initiates a rulemaking to add the chemical to the list, in accordance with subsection (d)(2), or

(B) publishes an explanation of why the Administrator believes the petition does not meet the requirements of subsection (d)(2) for adding a chemical to the list.

(f) THRESHOLD FOR REPORTING.—

(1) TOXIC CHEMICAL THRESHOLD AMOUNT.—The threshold amounts for purposes of reporting toxic chemicals under this section are as follows:

(A) With respect to a toxic chemical used at a facility, 10,000 pounds of the toxic chemical per year.

(B) With respect to a toxic chemical manufactured or processed at a facility—

(i) For the toxic chemical release form required to be submitted under this section on or before July 1, 1988, 75,000 pounds of the toxic chemical per year.

(ii) For the form required to be submitted on or before July 1, 1989, 50,000 pounds of the toxic chemical per year.

(iii) For the form required to be submitted on or before July 1, 1990, and for each form thereafter, 25,000 pounds of the toxic chemical per year.

(2) REVISIONS.—The Administrator may establish a threshold amount for a toxic chemical different from the amount established by paragraph (1). Such revised threshold shall obtain reporting on a substantial majority of total releases of the chemical at all facilities subject to the requirements of this section. The amounts established under this paragraph may, at the Administrator's discretion, be based on classes of chemicals or categories of facilities.

(g) FORM.—

(1) INFORMATION REQUIRED.—Not later than June 1, 1987, the Administrator shall publish a uniform toxic chemical release form for facilities covered by this section. If the Administrator does not publish such a form, owners and operators of facilities subject to the requirements of this section shall provide the information required under this subsection by letter postmarked on or before the date on which the form is due. Such form shall—

Public information.

(A) provide for the name and location of, and principal business activities at, the facility;

(B) include an appropriate certification, signed by a senior official with management responsibility for the person or persons completing the report, regarding the accuracy and completeness of the report; and

(C) provide for submission of each of the following items of information for each listed toxic chemical known to be present at the facility:

(i) Whether the toxic chemical at the facility is manufactured, processed, or otherwise used, and the general category or categories of use of the chemical.

(ii) An estimate of the maximum amounts (in ranges) of the toxic chemical present at the facility at any time during the preceding calendar year.

(iii) For each wastestream, the waste treatment or disposal methods employed, and an estimate of the treatment efficiency typically achieved by such methods for that wastestream.

(iv) The annual quantity of the toxic chemical entering each environmental medium.

(2) USE OF AVAILABLE DATA.—In order to provide the information required under this section, the owner or operator of a facility may use readily available data (including monitoring data) collected pursuant to other provisions of law, or, where such data are not readily available, reasonable estimates of the amounts involved. Nothing in this section requires the monitoring or measurement of the quantities, concentration, or frequency of any toxic chemical released into the environment beyond that monitoring and measurement required under other provisions of law or regulation. In order to assure consistency, the Administrator shall require that data be expressed in common units.

Public
information.

(h) USE OF RELEASE FORM.—The release forms required under this section are intended to provide information to the Federal, State, and local governments and the public, including citizens of communities surrounding covered facilities. The release form shall be available, consistent with section 324(a), to inform persons about releases of toxic chemicals to the environment; to assist governmental agencies, researchers, and other persons in the conduct of research and data gathering; to aid in the development of appropriate regulations, guidelines, and standards; and for other similar purposes.

(i) MODIFICATIONS IN REPORTING FREQUENCY.—

(1) IN GENERAL.—The Administrator may modify the frequency of submitting a report under this section, but the Administrator may not modify the frequency to be any more often than annually. A modification may apply, either nationally or in a specific geographic area, to the following:

(A) All toxic chemical release forms required under this section.

(B) A class of toxic chemicals or a category of facilities.

(C) A specific toxic chemical.

(D) A specific facility.

(2) REQUIREMENTS.—A modification may be made under paragraph (1) only if the Administrator—

PUBLIC LAW 99-499—OCT. 17, 1986   100 STAT. 1745

(A) makes a finding that the modification is consistent with the provisions of subsection (h), based on—

(i) experience from previously submitted toxic chemical release forms, and

(ii) determinations made under paragraph (3), and

(B) the finding is made by a rulemaking in accordance with section 553 of title 5, United States Code.

(3) DETERMINATIONS.—The Administrator shall make the following determinations with respect to a proposed modification before making a modification under paragraph (1):

(A) The extent to which information relating to the proposed modification provided on the toxic chemical release forms has been used by the Administrator or other agencies of the Federal Government, States, local governments, health professionals, and the public.

(B) The extent to which the information is (i) readily available to potential users from other sources, such as State reporting programs, and (ii) provided to the Administrator under another Federal law or through a State program.

(C) The extent to which the modification would impose additional and unreasonable burdens on facilities subject to the reporting requirements under this section.

(4) 5-YEAR REVIEW.—Any modification made under this subsection shall be reviewed at least once every 5 years. Such review shall examine the modification and ensure that the requirements of paragraphs (2) and (3) still justify continuation of the modification. Any change to a modification reviewed under this paragraph shall be made in accordance with this subsection.

(5) NOTIFICATION TO CONGRESS.—The Administrator shall notify Congress of an intention to initiate a rulemaking for a modification under this subsection. After such notification, the Administrator shall delay initiation of the rulemaking for at least 12 months, but no more than 24 months, after the date of such notification.

(6) JUDICIAL REVIEW.—In any judicial review of a rulemaking which establishes a modification under this subsection, a court may hold unlawful and set aside agency action, findings, and conclusions found to be unsupported by substantial evidence.

(7) APPLICABILITY.—A modification under this subsection may apply to a calendar year or other reporting period beginning no earlier than January 1, 1993.

(8) EFFECTIVE DATE.—Any modification made on or after January 1 and before December 1 of any calendar year shall take effect beginning with the next calendar year. Any modification made on or after December 1 of any calendar year and before January 1 of the next calendar year shall take effect beginning with the calendar year following such next calendar year.

(j) EPA MANAGEMENT OF DATA.—The Administrator shall establish and maintain in a computer data base a national toxic chemical inventory based on data submitted to the Administrator under this section. The Administrator shall make these data accessible by computer telecommunication and other means to any person on a cost reimbursable basis.

Communications and tele-communications.

(k) REPORT.—Not later than June 30, 1991, the Comptroller General, in consultation with the Administrator and appropriate officials in the States, shall submit to the Congress a report including each of the following:

(1) A description of the steps taken by the Administrator and the States to implement the requirements of this section, including steps taken to make information collected under this section available to and accessible by the public.

(2) A description of the extent to which the information collected under this section has been used by the Environmental Protection Agency, other Federal agencies, the States, and the public, and the purposes for which the information has been used.

(3) An identification and evaluation of options for modifications to the requirements of this section for the purpose of making information collected under this section more useful.

(l) MASS BALANCE STUDY.—

(1) IN GENERAL.—The Administrator shall arrange for a mass balance study to be carried out by the National Academy of Sciences using mass balance information collected by the Administrator under paragraph (3). The Administrator shall submit to Congress a report on such study no later than 5 years after the date of the enactment of this title.

Reports.

(2) PURPOSES.—The purposes of the study are as follows:

(A) To assess the value of mass balance analysis in determining the accuracy of information on toxic chemical releases.

(B) To assess the value of obtaining mass balance information, or portions thereof, to determine the waste reduction efficiency of different facilities, or categories of facilities, including the effectiveness of toxic chemical regulations promulgated under laws other than this title.

(C) To assess the utility of such information for evaluating toxic chemical management practices at facilities, or categories of facilities, covered by this section.

(D) To determine the implications of mass balance information collection on a national scale similar to the mass balance information collection carried out by the Administrator under paragraph (3), including implications of the use of such collection as part of a national annual quantity toxic chemical release program.

State and local governments.

(3) INFORMATION COLLECTION.—(A) The Administrator shall acquire available mass balance information from States which currently conduct (or during the 5 years after the date of enactment of this title initiate) a mass balance-oriented annual quantity toxic chemical release program. If information from such States provides an inadequate representation of industry classes and categories to carry out the purposes of the study, the Administrator also may acquire mass balance information necessary for the study from a representative number of facilities in other States.

Public information.
Classified information.

(B) Any information acquired under this section shall be available to the public, except that upon a showing satisfactory to the Administrator by any person that the information (or a particular part thereof) to which the Administrator or any officer, employee, or representative has access under this section if made public would divulge information entitled to protection under section 1905 of title 18, United States Code, such information or part shall be considered confidential in accord-

PUBLIC LAW 99-499—OCT. 17, 1986   100 STAT. 1747

ance with the purposes of that section, except that such information or part may be disclosed to other officers, employees, or authorized representatives of the United States concerned with carrying out this section.

(C) The Administrator may promulgate regulations prescribing procedures for collecting mass balance information under this paragraph.

Regulations.

(D) For purposes of collecting mass balance information under subparagraph (A), the Administrator may require the submission of information by a State or facility.

State and local governments.

(4) MASS BALANCE DEFINITION.—For purposes of this subsection, the term "mass balance" means an accumulation of the annual quantities of chemicals transported to a facility, produced at a facility, consumed at a facility, used at a facility, accumulated at a facility, released from a facility, and transported from a facility as a waste or as a commercial product or byproduct or component of a commercial product or byproduct.

Subtitle C—General Provisions

SEC. 321. RELATIONSHIP TO OTHER LAW.

(a) IN GENERAL.—Nothing in this title shall—

(1) preempt any State or local law;

(2) except as provided in subsection (b), otherwise affect any State or local law or the authority of any State or local government to adopt or enforce any State or local law, or

(3) affect or modify in any way the obligations or liabilities of any person under other Federal law.

State and local governments.
42 USC 11041.

(b) EFFECT ON MSDS REQUIREMENTS.—Any State or local law enacted after August 1, 1985, which requires the submission of a material safety data sheet from facility owners or operators shall require that the data sheet be identical in content and format to the data sheet required under subsection (a) of section 311. In addition, a State or locality may require the submission of information which is supplemental to the information required on the data sheet (including information on the location and quantity of hazardous chemicals present at the facility), through additional sheets attached to the data sheet or such other means as the State or locality considers appropriate.

SEC. 322. TRADE SECRETS.

(a) AUTHORITY TO WITHHOLD INFORMATION.—

(1) GENERAL AUTHORITY.—(A) With regard to a hazardous chemical, an extremely hazardous substance, or a toxic chemical, any person required under section 303(d)(2), 303(d)(3), 311, 312, or 313 to submit information to any other person may withhold from such submittal the specific chemical identity (including the chemical name and other specific identification), as defined in regulations prescribed by the Administrator under subsection (c), if the person complies with paragraph (2).

Classified information.
Claims.
42 USC 11042.

(B) Any person withholding the specific chemical identity shall, in the place on the submittal where the chemical identity would normally be included, include the generic class or category of the hazardous chemical, extremely hazardous substance, or toxic chemical (as the case may be).

(2) REQUIREMENTS.—(A) A person is entitled to withhold information under paragraph (1) if such person—

(i) claims that such information is a trade secret, on the basis of the factors enumerated in subsection (b),

(ii) includes in the submittal referred to in paragraph (1) an explanation of the reasons why such information is claimed to be a trade secret, based on the factors enumerated in subsection (b), including a specific description of why such factors apply, and

(iii) submits to the Administrator a copy of such submittal, and the information withheld from such submittal.

(B) In submitting to the Administrator the information required by subparagraph (A)(iii), a person withholding information under this subsection may—

(i) designate, in writing and in such manner as the Administrator may prescribe by regulation, the information which such person believes is entitled to be withheld under paragraph (1), and

(ii) submit such designated information separately from other information submitted under this subsection.

(3) LIMITATION.—The authority under this subsection to withhold information shall not apply to information which the Administrator has determined, in accordance with subsection (c), is not a trade secret.

(b) TRADE SECRET FACTORS.—No person required to provide information under this title may claim that the information is entitled to protection as a trade secret under subsection (a) unless such person shows each of the following:

(1) Such person has not disclosed the information to any other person, other than a member of a local emergency planning committee, an officer or employee of the United States or a State or local government, an employee of such person, or a person who is bound by a confidentiality agreement, and such person has taken reasonable measures to protect the confidentiality of such information and intends to continue to take such measures.

(2) The information is not required to be disclosed, or otherwise made available, to the public under any other Federal or State law.

(3) Disclosure of the information is likely to cause substantial harm to the competitive position of such person.

(4) The chemical identity is not readily discoverable through reverse engineering.

(c) TRADE SECRET REGULATIONS.—As soon as practicable after the date of enactment of this title, the Administrator shall prescribe regulations to implement this section. With respect to subsection (b)(4), such regulations shall be equivalent to comparable provisions in the Occupational Safety and Health Administration Hazard Communication Standard (29 C.F.R. 1910.1200) and any revisions of such standard prescribed by the Secretary of Labor in accordance with the final ruling of the courts of the United States in United Steelworkers of America, AFL–CIO–CLC v. Thorne G. Auchter.

(d) PETITION FOR REVIEW.—

(1) IN GENERAL.—Any person may petition the Administrator for the disclosure of the specific chemical identity of a hazardous chemical, an extremely hazardous substance, or a toxic chemical which is claimed as a trade secret under this section. The Administrator may, in the absence of a petition under this paragraph, initiate a determination, to be carried out in accord-

ance with this subsection, as to whether information withheld constitutes a trade secret.

(2) INITIAL REVIEW.—Within 30 days after the date of receipt of a petition under paragraph (1) (or upon the Administrator's initiative), the Administrator shall review the explanation filed by a trade secret claimant under subsection (a)(2) and determine whether the explanation presents assertions which, if true, are sufficient to support a finding that the specific chemical identity is a trade secret.

(3) FINDING OF SUFFICIENT ASSERTIONS.—

(A) If the Administrator determines pursuant to paragraph (2) that the explanation presents sufficient assertions to support a finding that the specific chemical identity is a trade secret, the Administrator shall notify the trade secret claimant that he has 30 days to supplement the explanation with detailed information to support the assertions.

(B) If the Administrator determines, after receipt of any supplemental supporting detailed information under subparagraph (A), that the assertions in the explanation are true and that the specific chemical identity is a trade secret, the Administrator shall so notify the petitioner and the petitioner may seek judicial review of the determination.

(C) If the Administrator determines, after receipt of any supplemental supporting detailed information under subparagraph (A), that the assertions in the explanation are not true and that the specific chemical identity is not a trade secret, the Administrator shall notify the trade secret claimant that the Administrator intends to release the specific chemical identity. The trade secret claimant has 30 days in which he may appeal the Administrator's determination under this subparagraph to the Administrator. If the Administrator does not reverse his determination under this subparagraph in such an appeal by the trade secret claimant, the trade secret claimaint may seek judicial review of the determination.

(4) FINDING OF INSUFFICIENT ASSERTIONS.—

(A) If the Administrator determines pursuant to paragraph (2) that the explanation presents insufficient assertions to support a finding that the specific chemical identity is a trade secret, the Administrator shall notify the trade secret claimant that he has 30 days to appeal the determination to the Administrator, or, upon a showing of good cause, amend the original explanation by providing supplementary assertions to support the trade secret claim.

(B) If the Administrator does not reverse his determination under subparagraph (A) after an appeal or an examination of any supplementary assertions under subparagraph (A), the Administrator shall so notify the trade secret claimant and the trade secret claimant may seek judicial review of the determination.

(C) If the Administrator reverses his determination under subparagraph (A) after an appeal or an examination of any supplementary assertions under subparagraph (A), the procedures under paragraph (3) of this subsection apply.

(e) EXCEPTION FOR INFORMATION PROVIDED TO HEALTH PROFESSIONALS.—Nothing in this section, or regulations adopted pursuant to this section, shall authorize any person to withhold information which is required to be provided to a health professional, a doctor, or a nurse in accordance with section 323.

(f) PROVIDING INFORMATION TO THE ADMINISTRATOR; AVAILABILITY TO PUBLIC.—Any information submitted to the Administrator under subsection (a)(2) or subsection (d)(3) (except a specific chemical identity) shall be available to the public, except that upon a showing satisfactory to the Administrator by any person that the information (or a particular part thereof) to which the Administrator has access under this section if made public would divulge information entitled to protection under section 1905 of title 18, United States Code, such information or part shall be considered confidential in accordance with the purposes of that section, except that such information or part may be disclosed to other officers, employees, or authorized representatives of the United States concerned with carrying out this title.

(g) INFORMATION PROVIDED TO STATE.—Upon request by a State, acting through the Governor of the State, the Administrator shall provide to the State any information obtained under subsection (a)(2) and subsection (d)(3).

Health and medical care.

(h) INFORMATION ON ADVERSE EFFECTS.—(1) In any case in which the identity of a hazardous chemical or an extremely hazardous substance is claimed as a trade secret, the Governor or State emergency response commission established under section 301 shall identify the adverse health effects associated with the hazardous chemical or extremely hazardous substance and shall assure that such information is provided to any person requesting information about such hazardous chemical or extremely hazardous substance.

(2) In any case in which the identity of a toxic chemical is claimed as a trade secret, the Administrator shall identify the adverse health and environmental effects associated with the toxic chemical and shall assure that such information is included in the computer database required by section 313(j) and is provided to any person requesting information about such toxic chemical.

(i) INFORMATION PROVIDED TO CONGRESS.—Notwithstanding any limitation contained in this section or any other provision of law, all information reported to or otherwise obtained by the Administrator (or any representative of the Administrator) under this title shall be made available to a duly authorized committee of the Congress upon written request by such a committee.

Classified information.
42 USC 11043.

SEC. 323. PROVISION OF INFORMATION TO HEALTH PROFESSIONALS, DOCTORS, AND NURSES.

(a) DIAGNOSIS OR TREATMENT BY HEALTH PROFESSIONAL.—An owner or operator of a facility which is subject to the requirements of section 311, 312, or 313 shall provide the specific chemical identity, if known, of a hazardous chemical, extremely hazardous substance, or a toxic chemical to any health professional who requests such information in writing if the health professional provides a written statement of need under this subsection and a written confidentiality agreement under subsection (d). The written statement of need shall be a statement that the health professional has a reasonable basis to suspect that—

(1) the information is needed for purposes of diagnosis or treatment of an individual,

(2) the individual or individuals being diagnosed or treated have been exposed to the chemical concerned, and

(3) knowledge of the specific chemical identity of such chemical will assist in diagnosis or treatment.

Following such a written request, the owner or operator to whom such request is made shall promptly provide the requested information to the health professional. The authority to withhold the specific chemical identity of a chemical under section 322 when such information is a trade secret shall not apply to information required to be provided under this subsection, subject to the provisions of subsection (d).

(b) MEDICAL EMERGENCY.—An owner or operator of a facility which is subject to the requirements of section 311, 312, or 313 shall provide a copy of a material safety data sheet, an inventory form, or a toxic chemical release form, including the specific chemical identity, if known, of a hazardous chemical, extremely hazardous substance, or a toxic chemical, to any treating physician or nurse who requests such information if such physician or nurse determines that—

(1) a medical emergency exists,

(2) the specific chemical identity of the chemical concerned is necessary for or will assist in emergency or first-aid diagnosis or treatment, and

(3) the individual or individuals being diagnosed or treated have been exposed to the chemical concerned.

Immediately following such a request, the owner or operator to whom such request is made shall provide the requested information to the physician or nurse. The authority to withhold the specific chemical identity of a chemical from a material safety data sheet, an inventory form, or a toxic chemical release form under section 322 when such information is a trade secret shall not apply to information required to be provided to a treating physician or nurse under this subsection. No written confidentiality agreement or statement of need shall be required as a precondition of such disclosure, but the owner or operator disclosing such information may require a written confidentiality agreement in accordance with subsection (d) and a statement setting forth the items listed in paragraphs (1) through (3) as soon as circumstances permit.

(c) PREVENTIVE MEASURES BY LOCAL HEALTH PROFESSIONALS.—

(1) PROVISION OF INFORMATION.—An owner or operator of a facility subject to the requirements of section 311, 312, or 313 shall provide the specific chemical identity, if known, of a hazardous chemical, an extremely hazardous substance, or a toxic chemical to any health professional (such as a physician, toxicologist, or epidemiologist)—

(A) who is a local government employee or a person under contract with the local government, and

(B) who requests such information in writing and provides a written statement of need under paragraph (2) and a written confidentiality agreement under subsection (d).

Following such a written request, the owner or operator to whom such request is made shall promptly provide the requested information to the local health professional. The authority to withhold the specific chemical identity of a chemical under section 322 when such information is a trade secret shall not apply to information required to be provided under this subsection, subject to the provisions of subsection (d).

(2) WRITTEN STATEMENT OF NEED.—The written statement of need shall be a statement that describes with reasonable detail one or more of the following health needs for the information:

(A) To assess exposure of persons living in a local community to the hazards of the chemical concerned.

(B) To conduct or assess sampling to determine exposure levels of various population groups.

(C) To conduct periodic medical surveillance of exposed population groups.

(D) To provide medical treatment to exposed individuals or population groups.

(E) To conduct studies to determine the health effects of exposure.

(F) To conduct studies to aid in the identification of a chemical that may reasonably be anticipated to cause an observed health effect.

(d) CONFIDENTIALITY AGREEMENT.—Any person obtaining information under subsection (a) or (c) shall, in accordance with such subsection (a) or (c), be required to agree in a written confidentiality agreement that he will not use the information for any purpose other than the health needs asserted in the statement of need, except as may otherwise be authorized by the terms of the agreement or by the person providing such information. Nothing in this subsection shall preclude the parties to a confidentiality agreement from pursuing any remedies to the extent permitted by law.

(e) REGULATIONS.—As soon as practicable after the date of the enactment of this title, the Administrator shall promulgate regulations describing criteria and parameters for the statement of need under subsection (a) and (c) and the confidentiality agreement under subsection (d).

42 USC 11044.

SEC. 324. PUBLIC AVAILABILITY OF PLANS, DATA SHEETS, FORMS, AND FOLLOWUP NOTICES.

(a) AVAILABILITY TO PUBLIC.—Each emergency response plan, material safety data sheet, list described in section 311(a)(2), inventory form, toxic chemical release form, and followup emergency notice shall be made available to the general public, consistent with section 322, during normal working hours at the location or locations designated by the Administrator, Governor, State emergency response commission, or local emergency planning committee, as appropriate. Upon request by an owner or operator of a facility subject to the requirements of section 312, the State emergency response commission and the appropriate local emergency planning committee shall withhold from disclosure under this section the location of any specific chemical required by section 312(d)(2) to be contained in an inventory form as tier II information.

(b) NOTICE OF PUBLIC AVAILABILITY.—Each local emergency planning committee shall annually publish a notice in local newspapers that the emergency response plan, material safety data sheets, and inventory forms have been submitted under this section. The notice shall state that followup emergency notices may subsequently be issued. Such notice shall announce that members of the public who wish to review any such plan, sheet, form, or followup notice may do so at the location designated under subsection (a).

SEC. 325. ENFORCEMENT.

42 USC 11045.

(a) CIVIL PENALTIES FOR EMERGENCY PLANNING.—The Administrator may order a facility owner or operator (except an owner or operator of a facility designated under section 302(b)(2)) to comply with section 302(c) and section 303(d). The United States district court for the district in which the facility is located shall have jurisdiction to enforce the order, and any person who violates or fails to obey such an order shall be liable to the United States for a civil penalty of not more than $25,000 for each day in which such violation occurs or such failure to comply continues.

(b) CIVIL, ADMINISTRATIVE, AND CRIMINAL PENALTIES FOR EMERGENCY NOTIFICATION.—

(1) CLASS I ADMINISTRATIVE PENALTY.—(A) A civil penalty of not more than $25,000 per violation may be assessed by the Administrator in the case of a violation of the requirements of section 304.

(B) No civil penalty may be assessed under this subsection unless the person accused of the violation is given notice and opportunity for a hearing with respect to the violation.

(C) In determining the amount of any penalty assessed pursuant to this subsection, the Administrator shall take into account the nature, circumstances, extent and gravity of the violation or violations and, with respect to the violator, ability to pay, any prior history of such violations, the degree of culpability, economic benefit or savings (if any) resulting from the violation, and such other matters as justice may require.

(2) CLASS II ADMINISTRATIVE PENALTY.—A civil penalty of not more than $25,000 per day for each day during which the violation continues may be assessed by the Administrator in the case of a violation of the requirements of section 304. In the case of a second or subsequent violation the amount of such penalty may be not more than $75,000 for each day during which the violation continues. Any civil penalty under this subsection shall be assessed and collected in the same manner, and subject to the same provisions, as in the case of civil penalties assessed and collected under section 16 of the Toxic Substances Control Act. In any proceeding for the assessment of a civil penalty under this subsection the Administrator may issue subpoenas for the attendance and testimony of witnesses and the production of relevant papers, books, and documents and may promulgate rules for discovery procedures.

(3) JUDICIAL ASSESSMENT.—The Administrator may bring an action in the United States District court for the appropriate district to assess and collect a penalty of not more than $25,000 per day for each day during which the violation continues in the case of a violation of the requirements of section 304. In the case of a second or subsequent violation, the amount of such penalty may be not more than $75,000 for each day during which the violation continues.

15 USC 2615.

(4) CRIMINAL PENALTIES.—Any person who knowingly and willfully fails to provide notice in accordance with section 304 shall, upon conviction, be fined not more than $25,000 or imprisoned for not more than two years, or both (or in the case of a second or subsequent conviction, shall be fined not more than $50,000 or imprisoned for not more than five years, or both).

(c) CIVIL AND ADMINISTRATIVE PENALTIES FOR REPORTING REQUIRE-MENTS.—(1) Any person (other than a governmental entity) who violates any requirement of section 312 or 313 shall be liable to the United States for a civil penalty in an amount not to exceed $25,000 for each such violation.

(2) Any person (other than a governmental entity) who violates any requirement of section 311 or 323(b), and any person who fails to furnish to the Administrator information required under section 322(a)(2) shall be liable to the United States for a civil penalty in an amount not to exceed $10,000 for each such violation.

(3) Each day a violation described in paragraph (1) or (2) continues shall, for purposes of this subsection, constitute a separate violation.

(4) The Administrator may assess any civil penalty for which a person is liable under this subsection by administrative order or may bring an action to assess and collect the penalty in the United States district court for the district in which the person from whom the penalty is sought resides or in which such person's principal place of business is located.

(d) CIVIL, ADMINISTRATIVE, AND CRIMINAL PENALTIES WITH RESPECT TO TRADE SECRETS.—

(1) CIVIL AND ADMINISTRATIVE PENALTY FOR FRIVOLOUS CLAIMS.—If the Administrator determines—

(A)(i) under section 322(d)(4) that an explanation submitted by a trade secret claimant presents insufficient assertions to support a finding that a specific chemical identity is a trade secret, or (ii) after receiving supplemental supporting detailed information under section 322(d)(3)(A), that the specific chemical identity is not a trade secret; and

(B) that the trade secret claim is frivolous,

the trade secret claimant is liable for a penalty of $25,000 per claim. The Administrator may assess the penalty by administrative order or may bring an action in the appropriate district court of the United States to assess and collect the penalty.

(2) CRIMINAL PENALTY FOR DISCLOSURE OF TRADE SECRET INFORMATION.—Any person who knowingly and willfully divulges or discloses any information entitled to protection under section 322 shall, upon conviction, be subject to a fine of not more than $20,000 or to imprisonment not to exceed one year, or both.

(e) SPECIAL ENFORCEMENT PROVISIONS FOR SECTION 323.—Whenever any facility owner or operator required to provide information under section 323 to a health professional who has requested such information fails or refuses to provide such information in accordance with such section, such health professional may bring an action in the appropriate United States district court to require such facility owner or operator to provide the information. Such court shall have jurisdiction to issue such orders and take such other action as may be necessary to enforce the requirements of section 323.

(f) PROCEDURES FOR ADMINISTRATIVE PENALTIES.—

(1) Any person against whom a civil penalty is assessed under this section may obtain review thereof in the appropriate district court of the United States by filing a notice of appeal in such court within 30 days after the date of such order and by simultaneously sending a copy of such notice by certified mail to the Administrator. The Administrator shall promptly file in such court a certified copy of the record upon which such

Records.

violation was found or such penalty imposed. If any person fails to pay an assessment of a civil penalty after it has become a final and unappealable order or after the appropriate court has entered final judgment in favor of the United States, the Administrator may request the Attorney General of the United States to institute a civil action in an appropriate district court of the United States to collect the penalty, and such court shall have jurisdiction to hear and decide any such action. In hearing such action, the court shall have authority to review the violation and the assessment of the civil penalty on the record.

(2) The Administrator may issue subpoenas for the attendance and testimony of witnesses and the production of relevant papers, books, or documents in connection with hearings under this section. In case of contumacy or refusal to obey a subpoena issued pursuant to this paragraph and served upon any person, the district court of the United States for any district in which such person is found, resides, or transacts business, upon application by the United States and after notice to such person, shall have jurisdiction to issue an order requiring such person to appear and give testimony before the administrative law judge or to appear and produce documents before the administrative law judge, or both, and any failure to obey such order of the court may be punished by such court as a contempt thereof.

SEC. 326. CIVIL ACTIONS.   42 USC 11046.

(a) AUTHORITY TO BRING CIVIL ACTIONS.—

(1) CITIZEN SUITS.—Except as provided in subsection (e), any person may commence a civil action on his own behalf against the following:

(A) An owner or operator of a facility for failure to do any of the following:

(i) Submit a followup emergency notice under section 304(c).

(ii) Submit a material safety data sheet or a list under section 311(a).

(iii) Complete and submit an inventory form under section 312(a) containing tier I information as described in section 312(d)(1) unless such requirement does not apply by reason of the second sentence of section 312(a)(2).

(iv) Complete and submit a toxic chemical release form under section 313(a).

(B) The Administrator for failure to do any of the following:

(i) Publish inventory forms under section 312(g).

(ii) Respond to a petition to add or delete a chemical under section 313(e)(1) within 180 days after receipt of the petition.

(iii) Publish a toxic chemical release form under 313(g).

(iv) Establish a computer database in accordance with section 313(j).

(v) Promulgate trade secret regulations under section 322(c).

(vi) Render a decision in response to a petition under section 322(d) within 9 months after receipt of the petition.

Public
information.
State and local
governments.

(C) The Administrator, a State Governor, or a State emergency response commission, for failure to provide a mechanism for public availability of information in accordance with section 324(a).

(D) A State Governor or a State emergency response commission for failure to respond to a request for tier II information under section 312(e)(3) within 120 days after the date of receipt of the request.

(2) STATE OR LOCAL SUITS.—

(A) Any State or local government may commence a civil action against an owner or operator of a facility for failure to do any of the following:

(i) Provide notification to the emergency response commission in the State under section 302(c).

(ii) Submit a material safety data sheet or a list under section 311(a).

(iii) Make available information requested under section 311(c).

(iv) Complete and submit an inventory form under section 312(a) containing tier I information unless such requirement does not apply by reason of the second sentence of section 312(a)(2)..

(B) Any State emergency response commission or local emergency planning committee may commence a civil action against an owner or operator of a facility for failure to provide information under section 303(d) or for failure to submit tier II information under section 312(e)(1).

(C) Any State may commence a civil action against the Administrator for failure to provide information to the State under section 322(g).

(b) VENUE.—

(1) Any action under subsection (a) against an owner or operator of a facility shall be brought in the district court for the district in which the alleged violation occurred.

District of
Columbia.

(2) Any action under subsection (a) against the Administrator may be brought in the United States District Court for the District of Columbia.

(c) RELIEF.—The district court shall have jurisdiction in actions brought under subsection (a) against an owner or operator of a facility to enforce the requirement concerned and to impose any civil penalty provided for violation of that requirement. The district court shall have jurisdiction in actions brought under subsection (a) against the Administrator to order the Administrator to perform the act or duty concerned.

(d) NOTICE.—

(1) No action may be commenced under subsection (a)(1)(A) prior to 60 days after the plaintiff has given notice of the alleged violation to the Administrator, the State in which the alleged violation occurs, and the alleged violator. Notice under this paragraph shall be given in such manner as the Administrator shall prescribe by regulation.

Regulations.

(2) No action may be commenced under subsection (a)(1)(B) or (a)(1)(C) prior to 60 days after the date on which the plaintiff gives notice to the Administrator, State Governor, or State emergency response commission (as the case may be) that the plaintiff will commence the action. Notice under this paragraph

Regulations.

PUBLIC LAW 99-499—OCT. 17, 1986   100 STAT. 1757

shall be given in such manner as the Administrator shall prescribe by regulation.

(e) LIMITATION.—No action may be commenced under subsection (a) against an owner or operator of a facility if the Administrator has commenced and is diligently pursuing an administrative order or civil action to enforce the requirement concerned or to impose a civil penalty under this Act with respect to the violation of the requirement.

(f) COSTS.—The court, in issuing any final order in any action brought pursuant to this section, may award costs of litigation (including reasonable attorney and expert witness fees) to the prevailing or the substantially prevailing party whenever the court determines such an award is appropriate. The court may, if a temporary restraining order or preliminary injunction is sought, require the filing of a bond or equivalent security in accordance with the Federal Rules of Civil Procedure.

(g) OTHER RIGHTS.—Nothing in this section shall restrict or expand any right which any person (or class of persons) may have under any Federal or State statute or common law to seek enforcement of any requirement or to seek any other relief (including relief against the Administrator or a State agency).

18 USC app.
State and local governments.

(h) INTERVENTION.—

(1) BY THE UNITED STATES.—In any action under this section the United States or the State, or both, if not a party, may intervene as a matter of right.

(2) BY PERSONS.—In any action under this section, any person may intervene as a matter of right when such person has a direct interest which is or may be adversely affected by the action and the disposition of the action may, as a practical matter, impair or impede the person's ability to protect that interest unless the Administrator or the State shows that the person's interest is adequately represented by existing parties in the action.

SEC. 327. EXEMPTION.

Natural gas.
42 USC 11047.

Except as provided in section 304, this title does not apply to the transportation, including the storage incident to such transportation, of any substance or chemical subject to the requirements of this title, including the transportation and distribution of natural gas.

SEC. 328. REGULATIONS.

42 USC 11048.

The Administrator may prescribe such regulations as may be necessary to carry out this title.

SEC. 329. DEFINITIONS.

42 USC 11049.

For purposes of this title—

(1) ADMINISTRATOR.—The term "Administrator" means the Administrator of the Environmental Protection Agency.

(2) ENVIRONMENT.—The term "environment" includes water, air, and land and the interrelationship which exists among and between water, air, and land and all living things.

(3) EXTREMELY HAZARDOUS SUBSTANCE.—The term "extremely hazardous substance" means a substance on the list described in section 302(a)(2).

(4) FACILITY.—The term "facility" means all buildings, equipment, structures, and other stationary items which are located

on a single site or on contiguous or adjacent sites and which are owned or operated by the same person (or by any person which controls, is controlled by, or under common control with, such person). For purposes of section 304, the term includes motor vehicles, rolling stock, and aircraft.

(5) HAZARDOUS CHEMICAL.—The term "hazardous chemical" has the meaning given such term by section 311(e).

(6) MATERIAL SAFETY DATA SHEET.—The term "material safety data sheet" means the sheet required to be developed under section 1910.1200(g) of title 29 of the Code of Federal Regulations, as that section may be amended from time to time.

(7) PERSON.—The term "person" means any individual, trust, firm, joint stock company, corporation (including a government corporation), partnership, association, State, municipality, commission, political subdivision of a State, or interstate body.

(8) RELEASE.—The term "release" means any spilling, leaking, pumping, pouring, emitting, emptying, discharging, injecting, escaping, leaching, dumping, or disposing into the environment (including the abandonment or discarding of barrels, containers, and other closed receptacles) of any hazardous chemical, extremely hazardous substance, or toxic chemical.

(9) STATE.—The term "State" means any State of the United States, the District of Columbia, the Commonwealth of Puerto Rico, Guam, American Samoa, the United States Virgin Islands, the Northern Mariana Islands, and any other territory or possession over which the United States has jurisdiction.

(10) TOXIC CHEMICAL.—The term "toxic chemical" means a substance on the list described in section 313(c).

42 USC 11050.   **SEC. 330. AUTHORIZATION OF APPROPRIATIONS.**

There are authorized to be appropriated for fiscal years beginning after September 30, 1986, such sums as may be necessary to carry out this title.

APPENDIX B

OCCUPATIONAL SAFETY AND HEALTH ADMINISTRATION
(OSHA)
1910.1200—HAZARD COMMUNICATION STANDARD

1910.1200—HAZARD COMMUNICATION

(a) Purpose.

(1) The purpose of this section is to ensure that the hazards of all chemicals produced or imported by chemical manufacturers or importers are evaluated, and that information concerning their hazards is transmitted to affected employers and employees within the manufacturing sector. This transmittal of information is to be accomplished by means of comprehensive hazard communication programs, which are to include container labeling and other forms of warning, material safety data sheets and employee training.

(2) This occupational safety and health standard is intended to adress comprehensively the issue of evaluating and communicating chemical hazards to employees in the manufacturing sector, and to preempt any state law pertaining to this subject. Any state which desires to assume responsibility in this area may only do so under the provisions of § 18 of the Occupational Safety and Health Act (29 U.S.C. 651 et. seq.) which deals with state jurisdiction and state plans.

(b) Scope and application.

(1) This section requires chemical manufacturers or importers to assess the hazards of chemicals which they produce or import, and all employers in SIC Codes 20 through 39 (Division D, Standard Industrial Classification Manual) to provide information to their employees about the hazardous chemicals to which they are exposed, by means of a hazard communication program, labels and other forms of warning, material safety data sheets, and information and training. In addition, this section requires distributors to transmit the required information to employers in SIC Codes 20–39.

(2) This section applies to any chemical which is known to be present in the workplace in such a manner that employees may be exposed under normal conditions of use or in a foreseeable emergency.

(3) This section applies to laboratories only as follows:

(i) Employers shall ensure that labels on incoming containers of hazardous chemicals are not removed or defaced;

(ii) Employers shall maintain any material safety data sheets that are received with incoming shipments of hazardous chemicals, and ensure that they are readily accessible to laboratory employees; and,

(iii) Employers shall ensure that laboratory employees are apprised of the hazards of the chemicals in their workplaces in accordance with paragraph (h) of this section.

(4) This section does not require labeling of the following chemicals:

(i) Any pesticide as such term is defined in the Federal Insecticide, Fungicide, and Rodenticide Act (7 U.S.C. 136 et seq.), when subject to the labeling requirements of that Act and labeling regulations issued under that Act by the Environmental Protection Agency;

(ii) Any food, food additive, color additive, drug, or cosmetic, including materials intended for use as ingredients in such products (e.g., flavors and fragrances), as such terms are defined in the Federal Food, Drug, and Cosmetic Act (21 U.S.C. 301 et seq.) and regulations issued under that Act, when they are subject to the labeling re-

STANDARDS AND INTERPRETATIONS

quirements of that Act and labeling regulations issued under that Act by the Food and Drug Administration;

(iii) Any distilled spirits (beverage alcohols), wine, or malt beverage intended for nonindustrial use, as such terms are defined in the Federal Alcohol Administration Act (27 U.S.C. 201 et seq.) and regulations issued under that Act, when subject to the labeling requirements of that Act and labeling regulations issued under that Act by the Bureau of Alcohol, Tobacco, and Firearms; and,

(iv) Any consumer product or hazardous substance as those terms are defined in the Consumer Product Safety Act (15 U.S.C. 2051 et seq.) and Federal Hazardous Substances Act (15 U.S.C. 1261 et seq.) respectively, when subject to a consumer product safety standard or labeling requirement of those acts, or regulations issued under those Acts by the Consumer Product Safety Commission.

(5) This section does not apply to:

(i) Any hazardous waste as such term is defined by the Solid Waste Disposal Act, as amended by the Resource Conservation and Recovery Act of 1976, as amended (42 U.S.C. 6901 et seq.), when subject to regulations issued under that Act by the Environmental Protection Agency;

(ii) Tobacco or tobacco products;

(iii) Wood or wood products;

(iv) Articles; and,

(v) Foods, drugs, or cosmetics intended for personal consumption by employees while in the workplace.

(c) Definitions.

"Article" means a manufactured item:

(i) Which is formed to a specific shape or design during manufacture;

(ii) which has end use function(s) dependent in whole or in part upon its shape or design during end use; and

(iii) which does not release, or otherwise result in exposure to, a hazardous chemical under normal conditions of use.

"Assistant Secretary" means the Assistant Secretary of Labor for Occupational Safety and Health, U.S. Department of Labor, or designee.

"Chemical" means any element, chemical compound or mixture of elements and/or compounds.

"Chemical manufacturer" means an employer in SIC Codes 20 through 39 with a workplace where chemical(s) are produced for use or distribution.

"Chemical name" means the scientific designation of a chemical in accordance with the nomenclature system developed by the International Union of Pure and Applied Chemistry (IUPAC) or the Chemical Abstracts Service (CAS) rules of nomenclature, or a name which will clearly identify the chemical for the purpose of conducting a hazard evaluation.

"Combustible liquid" means any liquid having a flashpoint at or above 100°F (37.8°C), but below 200°F (93.3°C), except any mixture having components with flashpoints of 200°F (93.3°C), or higher, the total volume of which make up 99 percent or more of the total volume of the mixture.

"Common name" means any designation or identification such as code name, code number, trade name, brand name or generic name used to identify a chemical other than by its chemical name.

"Compressed gas" means:

(i) A gas or mixture of gases having, in a container, an absolute pressure exceeding 40 psi at 70°F (21.1°C); or

(ii) A gas or mixture of gases having, in a container, an absolute pressure exceeding 104 psi at 130°F (54.4°C) regardless of the pressure at 70°F (21.1°C); or

(iii) A liquid having a vapor pressure exceeding 40 psi at 100°F (37.8°C) as determined by ASTM D–323–72.

STANDARDS AND INTERPRETATIONS

"Container" means any bag, barrel, bottle, box, can, cylinder, drum, reaction vessel, storage tank, or the like that contains a hazardous chemical. For purposes of this section, pipes or piping systems are not considered to be containers.

"Designated representative" means any individual or organization to whom an employee gives written authorization to exercise such employee's rights under this section. A recognized or certified collective bargaining agent shall be treated automatically as a designated representative without regard to written employee authorization.

"Director" means the Director, National Institute for Occupational Safety and Health, U.S. Department of Health and Human Services, or designee.

"Distributor" means a business, other than a chemical manufacturer or importer, which supplies hazardous chemicals to other distributors or to manufacturing purchasers.

"Employee" means a worker employed by an employer in a workplace in SIC Codes 20 through 39 who may be exposed to hazardous chemicals under normal operating conditions or foreseeable emergencies, including, but not limited to production workers, line supervisors, and repair or maintenance personnel. Office workers, ground maintenance personnel, security personnel or non-resident management are generally not included, unless their job performance routinely involves potential exposure to hazardous chemicals.

"Employer" means a person engaged in a business within SIC Codes 20 through 39 where chemicals are either used, or are produced for use or distribution.

"Explosive" means a chemical that causes a sudden, almost instantaneous release of pressure, gas, and heat when subjected to sudden shock, pressure, or high temperature.

"Exposure" or "exposed" means that an employee is subjected to a hazardous chemical in the course of employment through any route of entry (inhalation, ingeston, skin contact or absorption, etc.), and includes potential (e.g., accidental or possible) exposure.

"Flammable" means a chemical that falls into one of the following categories:

(i) "Aerosol, flammable" means an aerosol that, when tested by the method described in 16 CFR 1500.45, yields a flame projection exceeding 18 inches at full valve opening, or a flashback (a flame extending back to the valve) at any degree of valve opening;

(ii) "Gas, flammable" means:

(a) A gas that, at ambient temperature and pressure, forms a flammable mixture with air at a concentration of thirteen (13) precent by volume or less; or

(b) A gas that, at ambient temperature and pressure, forms a range of flammable mixtures with air wider than twelve (12) percent of volume, regardless of the lower limit;

(iii) "Liquid, flammable" means any liquid having a flashpoint below 100°F (37.8°C), except any mixture having components with flashpoints of 100°F (37.8°C) or higher, the total of which make up 99 percent or more of the total volume of the mixture.

(iv) "Solid, flammable" means a solid, other than a blasting agent or explosive as defined in § 1910.109(a), that is liable to cause fire through friction, absorption of moisture, spontaneous chemical change, or retained heat from manufacturing or processing, or which can be ignited readily and when ignited burns so vigorously and persistently as to create a serious hazard. A chemical shall be considered to be a flammable solid if, when tested by the method described in 16 CFR 1500.44, it ignites and burns with a self-sustained flame at a rate greater than one-tenth of an inch per second along its major axis.

"Flashpoint" means the minimum temperature at which a liquid gives off a vapor in sufficient concentration to ignite when tested as follows:

(i) Tagliabue Closed Tester (See American National Standard Method of Test for Flash Point by Tag Closed Tester, Z11.24–1979 (ASTM D 56–79)) for liquids with a viscosity

STANDARDS AND INTERPRETATIONS

of less than 45 Saybolt Universal Seconds (SUS) at 100°F (37.8°C), that do not contain suspended solids and do not have a tendency to form a surface film under test; or

(ii) Pensky-Martens Closed Tester (see American National Standard Method of test for Flash Point by Pensky-Martens Closed Tester, Z11.7–1979 (ASTM D 93–79)) for liquids with a viscosity equal to or greater than 45 SUS at 100°F (37.8°C), or that contain suspended solids, or that have a tendency to form a surface film under test; or

(iii) Setaflash Closed Tester (see American National Standard Method of Test for Flash Point by Setaflash Closed Tester (ASTM D 3278–78)).

Organic peroxides, which undergo autoaccelerating thermal decomposition, are excluded from any of the flashpoint determination methods specified above.

"Foreseeable emergency" means any potential occurrence such as, but not limited to, equipment failure, rupture of containers, or failure of control equipment which could result in an uncontrolled release of a hazardous chemical into the workplace.

"Hazard warning" means any words, pictures, symbols, or combination thereof appearing on a label or other appropriate form of warning which convey the hazards of the chemical(s) in the container(s).

"Hazardous chemical" means any chemical which is a physical hazard or a health hazard.

"Health hazard" means a chemical for which there is statistically significant evidence based on at least one study conducted in accordance with established scientific principles that acute or chronic health effects may occur in exposed employees. The term "health hazard" includes chemicals which are carcinogens, toxic or highly toxic agents, reproductive toxins, irritants, corrosives, sensitizers, hepatotoxins, nephrotoxins, neurotoxins, agents which act on hematopoietic system, and agents which damage the lungs, skin, eyes, or mucous membranes. Appendix A provides further definitions and explanations of the scope of health hazards covered by this section, and Appendix B describes the criteria to be used

to determine whether or not a chemical is to be considered hazardous for purposes of this standard.

"Identity" means any chemical or common name which is indicated on the material safety data sheet (MSDS) for the chemical. The identity used shall permit cross-references to be made among the required list of hazardous chemicals, the label and the MSDS.

"Immediate use" means that the hazardous chemical will be under the control of and used only by the person who transfers it from a labeled container and only within the work shift in which it is transferred.

"Importer" means the first business with employees within the Customs Territory of the United States which receives hazardous chemicals produced in other countries for the purpose of supplying them to distributors or manufacturing purchasers within the United States.

"Label" means any written, printed, or graphic material displayed on or affixed to containers of hazardous chemicals.

"Manufacturing purchaser" means an employer with a workplace classified in SIC Codes 20 through 39 who purchases a hazardous chemical for use within that workplace.

"Material safety data sheet (MSDS)" means written or printed material concerning a hazardous chemical which is prepared in accordance with paragraph (g) of this section.

"Mixture" means any combination of two or more chemicals if the combination is not, in whole or in part, the result of a chemical reaction.

"Organic peroxide" means an organic compound that contains the bivalent-O-O-structure and which may be considered to be a structural derivative of hydrogen peroxide where one or both of the hydrogen atoms has been replaced by an organic radical.

"Oxidizer" means a chemical other than a blasting agent or explosive as defined in § 1910.109(a), that initiates or promotes combustion in other materials thereby causing fire either of itself or through the release of oxygen or other gases.

"Physical hazard" means a chemical for which there is scientifically valid evidence that it is a combustible liquid, a compressed gas, explosive, flammable, an organic peroxide, an oxidizer, pyrophoric, unstable (reactive) or water-reactive.

"Produce" means to manufacture, process, formulate, or repackage.

"Pyrophoric" means a chemical that will ignite spontaneously in air at a temperature of 130° F (54.4° C) or below.

"Responsible party" means someone who can provide additional information on the hazardous chemical and appropriate emergency procedures, if necessary.

"Specific chemical identity" means the chemical name, Chemical Abstracts Service (CAS) Registry Number, or any other information that reveals the precise chemical designation of the substance.

"Trade secret" means any confidential formula, pattern, process, device, information or compilation of information (including chemical name or other unique chemical identifier) that is used in an employer's business, and that gives the employer an opportunity to obtain an advantage over competitors who do not know or use it.

"Unstable (reactive)" means a chemical which in the pure state, or as produced or transported, will vigorously polymerize, decompose, condense, or will become self-reactive under conditions of shocks pressure or temperature.

"Use" means to package, handle, react, or transfer.

"Water-reactive" means a chemical that reacts with water to release a gas that is either flammable or presents a health hazard.

"Work area" means a room or defined space in a workplace where hazardous chemicals are produced or used, and where employees are present.

"Workplace" means an establishment at one geographical location containing one or more work areas.

(d) Hazard determination.

(1) Chemical manufacturers and importers shall evaluate chemicals produced in their workplaces or imported by them to determine if they are hazardous. Employers are not required to evaluate chemicals unless they choose not to rely on the evaluation performed by the chemical manufacturer or importer for the chemical to satisfy this requirement.

(2) Chemical manufacturers, importers or employers evaluating chemicals shall identify and consider the availabile scientific evidence concerning such hazards. For health hazards, evidence which is statistically significant and which is based on at least one positive study conducted in accordance with established scientific principles is considered to be sufficient to establish a hazardous effect if the results of the study meet the definitions of health hazards in this section. Appendix A shall be consulted for the scope of health hazards covered, and Appendix B shall be consulted for the criteria to be followed with respect to the completeness of the evaluation, and the data to be reported.

(3) The chemical manufacturer, importer or employer evaluating chemicals shall treat the following sources as establishing that the chemicals listed in them are hazardous:

(i) CFR Part 1910, Subpart Z, Toxic and Hazardous Substances, Occupational Safety and Health Administration (OSHA); or,

(ii) *Threshold Limit Values for Chemical Substances and Physical Agents in the Work Environment*, American Conference of Governmental Industrial Hygienists (ACGIH) (latest edition).

The chemical manufacturer, importer, or employer is still responsible for evaluating the hazards associated with the chemicals in these source lists in accordance with the requirements of the standard.

(4) Chemical manufacturers, importers and employers evaluating chemicals shall treat the following sources as establishing that a chemi-

STANDARDS AND INTERPRETATIONS

cal is a carcinogen or potential carcinogen for hazard communication purposes:

(i) National Toxicology Program (NTP), *Annual Report on Carcinogens* (latest edition);

(ii) International Agency for Research on Cancer (IARC) *Monographs* (latest editions); or

(iii) 29 CFR Part 1910, Subpart Z, Toxic and Hazardous Substances, Occupational Safety and Health Administration.

Note.—The *Registry of Toxic Effects of Chemical Substances* published by the National Institute for Occupational Safety and Health indicates whether a chemical has been found by NTP or IARC to be a potential carcinogen.

(5) The chemical manufacturer, importer or employer shall determine the hazards of mixtures of chemicals as follows:

(i) If a mixture has been tested as a whole to determine its hazards, the results of such testing shall be used to determine whether the mixture is hazardous;

(ii) If a mixture has not been tested as a whole to determine whether the mixture is a health hazard, the mixture shall be assumed to present the same health hazards as do the components which comprise one percent (by weight or volume) or greater of the mixture, except that the mixture shall be assumed to present a carcinogenic hazard if it contains a component in concentrations of 0.1 percent or greater which is considered to be a carcinogen under paragraph (d)(4) of this section;

(iii) If a mixture has not been tested as a whole to determine whether the mixture is a physical hazard, the chemical manufacturer, importer, or employer may use whatever scientifically valid data is available to evaluate the physical hazard potential of the mixture; and

(iv) If the employer has evidence to indicate that a component present in the mixture in concentrations of less than one percent (or in the case of carcinogens, less than 0.1 per-

cent) could be released in concentrations which would exceed an established OSHA permissible exposure limit or ACGIH Threshold Limit Value, or could present a health hazard to employees in those concentrations, the mixture shall be assumed to present the same hazard.

(6) Chemical manufacturers, importers, or employers evaluating chemicals shall describe in writing the procedures they use to determine the hazards of the chemical they evaluate. The written procedures are to be made available, upon request, to employees, their designated representatives, the Assistant Secretary and the Director. The written description may be incorporated into the written hazard communication program required under paragraph (e) of this section.

(e) Written hazard communication program.

(1) Employers shall develop and implement a written hazard communication program for their workplaces which at least describes how the criteria specified in paragraphs (f), (g), and (h) of this section for labels and other forms of warning, material safety data sheets, and employee information and training will be met, and which also includes the following:

(i) A list of the hazardous chemicals known to be present using an identity that is referenced on the appropriate material safety data sheet (the list may be compiled for the workplace as a whole or for individual work areas);

(ii) The methods the employer will use to inform employees of the hazards of non-routine tasks (for example, the cleaning of reactor vessels), and the hazards associated with chemicals contained in unlabeled pipes in their work areas; and,

(iii) The methods the employer will use to inform any contractor employers with employees working in the employer's workplace of the hazardous chemicals their employees may be exposed to while performing their work, and any suggestions for appropriate protective measures.

(2) The employer may rely on an existing hazard communication program to comply with

these requirements, provided that it meets the criteria established in this paragraph (e).

(3) The employer shall make the written hazard communication program available, upon request, to employees, their designated representatives, the Assistant Secretary and the Director, in accordance with the requirements of 29 CFR 1910.20(e).

(f) Labels and other forms of warning.

(1) The chemical manufacturer, importer, or distributor shall ensure that each container of hazardous chemicals leaving the workplace is labeled, tagged or marked with the following information:

  (i) Identity of the hazardous chemical(s);

  (ii) Appropriate hazard warnings; and

  (iii) Name and address of the chemical manufacturer, importer, or other responsible party.

(2) Chemical manufacturers, importers, or distributors shall ensure that each container of hazardous chemicals leaving the workplace is labeled, tagged, or marked in accordance with this section in a manner which does not conflict with the requirements of the Hazardous Materials Transportation Act (18 U.S.C. 1801 et seq.) and regulations issued under that Act by the Department of Transportation.

(3) If the hazardous chemical is regulated by OSHA in a substance-specific health standard, the chemical manufacturer, importer, distributor or employer shall ensure that the labels or other forms of warning used are in accordance with the requirements of that standard.

(4) Except as provided in paragraphs (f)(5) and (f)(6) the employer shall ensure that each container of hazardous chemicals in the workplace is labeled, tagged, or marked with the following information:

  (i) Identity of the hazardous chemical(s) contained therein; and

  (ii) Appropriate hazard warnings.

(5) The employer may use signs, placards, process sheets, batch tickets, operating procedures, or other such written materials in lieu of affixing labels to individual stationary process containers, as long as the alternative method identifies the containers to which it is applicable and conveys the information required by paragraph (f)(4) of this section to be on a label. The written materials shall be readily accessible to the employees in their work area throughout each work shift.

(6) The employer is not required to label portable containers into which hazardous chemicals are transferred from labeled containers, and which are intended only for the immediate use of the employee who performs the transfer.

(7) The employer shall not remove or deface existing labels on incoming containers of hazardous chemicals, unless the container is immediately marked with the required information.

(8) The employer shall ensure that labels or other forms of warning are legible, in English, and prominently displayed on the container, or readily available in the work area throughout each work shift. Employers having employees who speak other languages may add the information in their language to the material presented, as long as the information is presented in English as well.

(9) The chemical manufacturer, importer, distributor or employer need not affix new labels to comply with this section if existing labels already convey the required information.

(g) Material safety data sheets.

(1) Chemical manufacturers and importers shall obtain or develop a material safety data sheet for each hazardous chemical they produce or import. Employers shall have a material safety data sheet for each hazardous chemical which they use.

(2) Each material safety data sheet shall be in English and shall contain at least the following information.

  (i) The identity used on the label, and, except as provided for in paragraph (f) of this section on trade secrets:

STANDARDS AND INTERPRETATIONS

(a) If the hazardous chemical is a single substance, its chemical and common name(s);

(b) If the hazardous chemical is a mixture which has been tested as a whole to determine its hazards, the chemical and common name(s) of the ingredients which contribute to these known hazards, and the common name(s) of the mixture itself; or,

(c) If the hazardous chemical is a mixture which has not been tested as a whole:

(1) The chemical and common name(s) of all ingredients which have been determined to be health hazards, and which comprise 1% or greater of the composition, except that chemicals identified as carcinogens under paragraph (d)(4) of this section shall be listed if the concentrations are 0.1% or greater; and,

(2) The chemical and common name(s) of all ingredients which have been determined to present a physical hazard when present in the mixture;

(ii) Physical and chemical characteristics of the hazardous chemical (such as vapor pressure, flash point);

(iii) The physical hazards of the hazardous chemical, including the potential for fire, explosion, and reactivity;

(iv) The health hazards of the hazardous chemical, including signs and symptoms of exposure, and any medical conditions which are generally recognized as being aggravated by exposure to the chemical;

(v) The primary route(s) of entry;

(vi) The OSHA permissible exposure limit, ACGIH Threshold Limit Value, and any other exposure limit used or recommended by the chemical manufacturer, importer, or employer preparing the material safety data sheet, where available;

(vii) Whether the hazardous chemical is listed in the National Toxicology Program

(NTP) *Annual Report on Carcinogens* (latest edition) or has been found to be a potential carcinogen in the International Agency for Research on Cancer (IARC) *Monographs* (latest editions), or by OSHA;

(viii) Any generally applicable precautions for safe handling and use which are known to the chemical manufacturer, importer or employer preparing the material safety data sheet, including appropriate hygienic practices, protective measures during repair and maintenance of contaminated equipment, and procedures for clean-up of spills and leaks;

(ix) Any generally applicable control measures which are known to the chemical manufacturer, importer or employer preparing the material safety data sheet, such as appropriate engineering controls, work practices, or personal protective equipment;

(x) Emergency and first aid procedures;

(xi) The date of preparation of the material safety data sheet or the last change to it; and,

(xii) The name, address and telephone number of the chemical manufacturer, importer, employer or other responsible party preparing or distributing the material safety data sheet, who can provide additional information on the hazardous chemical and appropriate emergency procedures, if necessary.

(3) If no relevant information is found for any given category on the material safety data sheet, the chemical manufacturer, importer or employer preparing the material safety data sheet shall mark it to indicate that no applicable information was found.

(4) Where complex mixtures have similar hazards and contents (i.e. the chemical ingredients are essentially the same, but the specific composition varies from mixture to mixture), the chemical manufacturer, importer or employer may prepare one material safety data sheet to apply to all of these similar mixtures.

(5) The chemical manufacturer, importer or employer preparing the material safety data sheet shall ensure that the information recorded accurately reflects the scientific evidence used in making the hazard determination. If the chemical manufacturer, importer or employer becomes newly aware of any significant information regarding the hazards of a chemical, or ways to protect against the hazards, this new information shall be added to the material safety data sheet within three months. If the chemical is not currently being produced or imported the chemical manufacturer or importer shall add the information to the material safety data sheet before the chemical is introduced into the workplace again.

(6) Chemical manufacturers or importers shall ensure that distributors and manufacturing purchasers of hazardous chemicals are provided an appropriate material safety data sheet with their initial shipment, and with the first shipment after a material safety data sheet is updated. The chemical manufacturer or importer shall either provide material safety data sheets with the shipped containers or send them to the manufacturing purchaser prior to or at the time of the shipment. If the material safety data sheet is not provided with the shipment, the manufacturing purchaser shall obtain one from the chemical manufacturer, importer, or distributor as soon as possible.

(7) Distributors shall ensure that material safety data sheets, and updated information, are provided to other distributors and manufacturing purchasers of hazardous chemicals.

(8) The employer shall maintain copies of the required material safety data sheets for each hazardous chemical in the workplace, and shall ensure that they are readily accessible during each work shift to employees when they are in their work area(s).

(9) Material safety data sheets may be kept in any form, including operating procedures, and may be designed to cover groups of hazardous chemicals in a work area where it may be more appropriate to address the hazards of a process rather than individual hazardous chemicals. However, the employer shall ensure that in all cases the required information is provided for each hazardous chemical, and is readily accessible during each work shift to employees when they are in their work area(s).

(10) Material safety data sheets shall also be made readily available, upon request, to designated representatives and to the Assistant Secretary, in accordance with the requirements of 29 CFR 1910.20(e). The Director shall also be given access to material safety data sheets in the same manner.

(h) Employee information and training. Employers shall provide employees with information and training on hazardous chemicals in their work area at the time of their initial assignment, and whenever a new hazard is introduced into their work area.

(1) Information. Employees shall be informed of:

(i) The requirements of this section;

(ii) Any operations in their work area where hazardous chemicals are present; and,

(iii) The location and availability of the written hazard communication program, including the required list(s) of hazardous chemicals, and material safety data sheets required by this section.

(2) Training. Employee training shall include at least:

(i) Methods and observations that may be used to detect the presence or release of a hazardous chemical in the work area (such as monitoring conducted by the employer, continuous monitoring devices, visual appearance or odor of hazardous chemicals when being released, etc.);

(ii) The physical and health hazards of the chemicals in the work area;

(iii) The measures employees can take to protect themselves from these hazards, including specific procedures the employer has implemented to protect employees from exposure to hazardous chemicals, such as appropriate work practices, emergency procedures, and personal protective equipment to be used; and,

(iv) The details of the hazard communication program developed by the employer, including an explanation of the labeling system and

STANDARDS AND INTERPRETATIONS

the material safety data sheet, and how employees can obtain and use the appropriate hazard information.

(i) Trade secrets.

(1) The chemical manufacturer, importer or employer may withhold the specific chemical identity, including the chemical name and other specific identification of a hazardous chemical, from the material safety data sheet, provided that:

(i) The claim that the information withheld is a trade secret can be supported;

(ii) Information contained in the material safety data sheet concerning the properties and effects of the hazardous chemical is disclosed;

(iii) The material safety data sheet indicates that the specific chemical identity is being withheld as a trade secret; and,

(iv) The specific chemical identity is made available to health professionals, in accordance with the applicable provisions of this paragraph.

(2) Where a treating physician or nurse determines that a medical emergency exists and the specific chemical identity of a hazardous chemical is necessary for emergency or first-aid treatment, the chemical manufacturer, importer, or employer shall immediately disclose the specific chemical identity of a trade secret chemical to that treating physician or nurse, regardless of the existence of a written statement of need or a confidentiality agreement. The chemical manufacturer, importer, or employer may require a written statement of need and confidentiality agreement, in accordance with the provisions of paragraphs (i) (3) and (4) of this section, as soon as circumstances permit.

(3) In non-emergency situations, a chemical manufacturer, importer, or employer shall, upon request, disclose a specific chemical identity, otherwise permitted to be withheld under paragraph (i)(1) of this section, to a health professional (i.e. physician, industrial hygienist, toxicologist, or epidemiologist) providing medical or other occupational health services to exposed employee(s) if:

(i) the request is in writing;

(ii) The request describes with reasonable detail one or more of the following occupational health needs for the information:

(a) To assess the hazards of the chemicals to which employees will be exposed;

(b) To conduct or assess sampling of the workplace atmosphere to determine employee exposure levels;

(c) To conduct pre-assignment or periodic medical surveillance of exposed employees;

(d) To provide medical treatment to exposed employees;

(e) To select or assess appropriate personal protective equipment for exposed employees;

(f) To design or assess engineering controls or other protective measures for exposed employees; and,

(g) To conduct studies to determine the health effects of exposure.

(iii) The request explains in detail why the disclosure of the specific chemical identity is essential and that, in lieu thereof, the disclosure of the following information would not enable the health professional to provide the occupational health services described in paragraph (ii) of this section:

(a) The properties and effects of the chemical;

(b) Measures for controlling workers' exposure to the chemical;

(c) Methods of monitoring and analyzing worker exposure to the chemical; and,

(d) Methods of diagnosing and treating harmful exposures to the chemical;

(iv) The request includes a description of the procedures to be used to maintain the confidentiality of the disclosed information; and,

(v) The health professional, and the employer or contractor of the health professional's services (i.e., downstream employer, labor organization, or individual employer), agree in a written confidentiality agreement that the health professional will not use the trade secret information for any purpose other than the health need(s) asserted and agree not to release the information under any circumstances other than to OSHA, as provided in paragraph (i)(6) of this section, except as authorized by the terms of the agreement or by the chemical manufacturer, importer, or employer.

(4) The confidentiality agreement authorized by paragraph (i)(3)(iv) of this section:

(i) May restrict the use of the information to the health purposes indicated in the written statement of need;

(ii) May provide for appropriate legal remedies in the event of a breach of the agreement, including stipulation of a reasonable pre-estimate of likely damages; and,

(iii) May not include requirements for the posting of a penalty bond.

(5) Nothing in this standard is meant to preclude the parties from pursuing non-contractual remedies to the extent permitted by law.

(6) If the health professional receiving the trade secret information decides that there is a need to disclose it to OSHA, the chemical manufacturer, importer, or employer who provided the information shall be informed by the health professional prior to, or at the same time as, such disclosure.

(7) If the chemical manufacturer, importer, or employer denies a written request for disclosure of a specific chemical identity, the denial must:

(i) Be provided to the health professional within thirty days of the request;

(ii) Be in writing;

(iii) Include evidence to support the claim that the specific chemical identity is a trade secret;

(iv) State the specific reasons why the request is being denied; and,

(v) Explain in detail how alternative information may satisfy the specific medical or occupational health need without revealing the specific chemical identity.

(8) The health professional whose request for information is denied under paragraph (i)(3) of this section may refer the request and the written denial of the request to OSHA for consideration.

(9) When a health professional refers the denial to OSHA under paragraph (i)(8) of this section, OSHA shall consider the evidence to determine if:

(i) The chemical manufacturer, importer, or employer has supported the claim that the specific chemical identity is a trade secret;

(ii) The health professional has supported the claim that there is a medical or occupational health need for the information; and,

(iii) The health professional has demonstrated adequate means to protect the confidentiality.

(10)

(i) If OSHA determines that the specific chemical identity requested under paragraph (i)(3) of this section is not a *bona fide* trade secret, or that it is a trade secret but the requesting health professional has a legitimate medical or occupational health need for the information, has executed a written confidentiality agreement, and has shown adequate means to protect the confidentiality of the information, the chemical manufacturer, importer, or employer will be subject to citation by OSHA.

(ii) If a chemical manufacturer, importer, or employer demonstrates to OSHA that the execution of a confidentiality agreement would not provide sufficient protection against the potential harm from the unau-

STANDARDS AND INTERPRETATIONS

thorized disclosure of a trade secret specific chemical identity, the Assistant Secretary may issue such orders or impose such additional limitations or conditions upon the disclosure of the requested chemical information as may be appropriate to assure that the occupational health services are provided without an undue risk of harm to the chemical manufacturer, importer, or employer.

(11) If, following the issuance of a citation and any protective orders, the chemical manufacturer, importer, or employer continues to withhold the information, the matter is referrable to the Occupational Safety and Health Review Commission for enforcement of the citation. In accordance with Commission rules, the Administrative Law Judge may review the citation and supporting documentation *in camera* or issue appropriate protective orders.

(12) Notwithstanding the existence of a trade secret claim, a chemical manufacturer, importer, or employer shall, upon request, disclose to the Assistant Secretary any information which this section requires the chemical manufacturer, importer, or employer to make available. Where there is a trade secret claim, such claim shall be made no later than at the time the information is provided to the Assistant Secretary so that suitable determinations of trade secret status can be made and the necessary protections can be implemented.

(13) Nothing in this paragraph shall be construed as requiring the disclosure under any circumstances of process or percentage of mixture information which is trade secret.

(j) Effective dates. Employers shall be in compliance with this section within the following time periods:

(1) Chemical manufacturers and importers shall label containers of hazardous chemicals leaving their workplaces, and provide material safety data sheets with initial shipments by November 25, 1985.

(2) Distributors shall be in compliance with all provisions of this section applicable to them by November 25, 1985.

(3) Employers shall be in compliance with all provisions of this section by May 25, 1986, including initial training for all current employees.

APPENDIX A TO § 1910.1200—HEALTH HAZARD DEFINITIONS (MANDATORY)

Although safety hazards related to the physical characteristics of a chemical can be objectively defined in terms of testing requirements (e.g. flammability), health hazard definitions are less precise and more subjective. Health hazards may cause measurable changes in the body—such as decreased pulmonary function. These changes are generally indicated by the occurrence of signs and symptoms in the exposed employees—such as shortness of breath, a non-measurable, subjective feeling. Employees exposed to such hazards must be apprised of both the change in body function and the signs and symptoms that may occur to signal that change.

The determination of occupational health hazards is complicated by the fact that many of the effects or signs and symptoms occur commonly in nonoccupationally exposed populations, so that effects of exposure are difficult to separate from normally occurring illnesses. Occasionally, a substance causes an effect that is rarely seen in the population at large, such as angiosarcomas caused by vinyl chloride exposure, thus making it easier to ascertain that the occupational exposure was the primary causative factor. More often, however, the effects are common, such as lung cancer. The situation is further complicated by the fact that most chemicals have not been adequately tested to determine their health hazard potential, and data do not exist to substantiate these effects.

There have been many attempts to categorize effects and to define them in various ways. Generally, the terms "acute" and "chronic" are used to delineate between effects on the basis of severity or duration. "Acute" effects usually occur rapidly as a result of short-term exposures, and are of short duration. "Chronic" effects generally occur as a result of long-term exposure, and are of long duration.

The acute effects referred to most frequently are those defined by the American National Standards Institute (ANSI) standard for Precautionary Labeling of Hazardous Industrial Chemicals (Z129.1–1982)—irritation, corrosivity, sensitization and lethal dose. Although these are important health effects, they do not adequately cover the considerable range of acute effects which may occur as a result of occupational exposure, such as, for example, narcosis.

Similarly, the term chronic effect is often used to cover only carcinogenicity, teratogenicity, and mutagenicity. These effects are obvious a concern in the workplace, but again, do not adequately cover the area of chronic effects, excluding, for example, blood dyscrasias (such as anemia), chronic bronchitis and liver atrophy.

The goal of defining precisely, in measurable terms, every possible health effect that may occur in the workplace as a result of chemical exposures cannot realistically be accomplished. This does not negate the need for employees to be informed of such effects and protected from them.

STANDARDS AND INTERPRETATIONS

Appendix B, which is also mandatory, outlines the principles and procedures of hazard assessment.

For purposes of this section, any chemicals which meet any of the following definitions, as determined by the criteria set forth in Appendix B are health hazards:

1. Carcinogen: A chemical is considered to be a carcinogen if:

(a) It has been evaluated by the International Agency for Research on Cancer (IARC), and found to be a carcinogen or potential carcinogen; or

(b) It is listed as a carcinogen or potential carcinogen in the *Annual Report on Carcinogens* published by the National Toxicology Program (NTP) (latest edition); or,

(c) It is regulated by OSHA as a carcinogen.

2. Corrosive: A chemical that causes visible destruction of, or irreversible alterations in, living tissue by chemical action at the site of contact. For example, a chemical is considered to be corrosive if, when tested on the intact skin of albino rabbits by the method described by the U.S. Department of Transportation in Appendix A to 49 CFR Part 173, it destroys or changes irreversibly the structure of the tissue at the site of contact following an exposure period of four hours. This term shall not refer to action on inanimate surfaces.

3. Highly toxic: A chemical falling within any of the following categories:

(a) A chemical that has a median lethal dose (LD_{50}) of 50 milligrams or less per kilogram of body weight when administered orally to albino rats weighing between 200 and 300 grams each.

(b) A chemical that has a median lethal dose (LD_{50}) of 200 miligrams or less per kilogram of body weight when administered by continuous contact for 24 hours (or less if death occurs within 24 hours) with the bare skin of albino rabbits weighing between two and three kilograms each.

(c) A chemical that has a median lethal concentration (LC_{50}) in air of 200 parts per million by volume or less of gas or vapor, or 2 milligrams per liter or less of mist, fume, or dust, when administered by continuous inhallation for one hour (or less if death occurs within one hour) to albino rats weighing between 200 and 300 grams each.

4. Irritant: A chemical, which is not corrosive, but which causes a reversible inflammatory effect on living tissue by chemical action at the site of contact. A chemical is a skin irritant if, when tested on the intact skin of albino rabbits by the mehtods of 16 CFR 1500.41 for four hours exposure or by other appropriate techniques, it results in an empirical score of five or more. A chemical is an eye irritant if so determined under the procedure listed in 16 CFR 1500.42 or other appropriate techniques.

5. Sensitizer: A chemical that causes a substantial proportion of exposed people or animals to develop an allergic reaction in normal tissue after repeated exposure to the chemicals.

6. Toxic: A chemical falling within any of the following categories:

(a) A chemical that has a median lethal dose (LD_{50}) of more than 50 milligrams per kilogram but not more than 500 milligrams per kilogram of body weight when administered orally to albino rats weighing between 200 and 300 grams each.

(b) A chemical that has a median lethal dose (LD_{50}) of more than 200 milligrams per kilogram but not more than 1,000 milligrams per kilogram of body weight when administered by continuous contact for 24 hours (or less if death occurs within 24 hours) with the bare skin of albino rabbits weighing between two and three kilograms each.

(c) A chemical that has a median lethal concentration (LC_{50}) in air of more than 200 parts per million but not more than 2,000 parts per million by volume of gas or vapor, or more than two milligrams per liter but not more than 20 milligrams per liter of mist, fume, or dust, when administered by continuous inhalation for one hour (or less if death occurs within one hour) to albino rats weighing between 200 and 300 grams each.

7. Target organ effects. The following is a target organ categorization of effects which may occur, including examples of signs and symptoms and chemicals which have been found to cause such effects. These examples are presented to illustrate the range and diversity of effects and hazards found in the workplace, and the broad scope employers must consider in this area, but are not intended to be all-inclusive.

a. Hepatotoxins .... Chemicals which produce liver damage.
   Signs and Symptoms: .... Jaundice; liver enlargement.
   Chemicals .... Carbon tetrachloride; nitrosamines.
b. Nephrotoxins: .... Chemicals which produce kidney damage.
   Signs and Symptoms: .... Edema; proteinuria.
   Chemicals:............................ Halogenated hydrocarbons; uranium.
c. Neurotoxins: .... Chemicals which produce their primary toxic effects on the nervous system.
   Signs and Symptoms: .... Narcosis; behaviroal changes; decrease in motor functions.
   Chemicals:............................ Mercury; carbon disulfide.
d. Agents which act on the blood of
  hematopoietic system:..................... Decreases hemoglobin function; deprive the body tissues of oxygen.
   Signs and Symptoms: .... Cyanosis; loss of consciousness.
   Chemicals:............................ Carbon monoxide; cyanides.
e. Agents which damage the lung: .... Chemicals which irritate or damage the pulmonary tissue.

STANDARDS AND INTERPRETATIONS

Signs and Symptoms:	....	Cough; tightness in chest; shortness of breath.
Chemicals:	....	Silica; asbestos.
f. Reproductive toxins:	....	Chemicals which affect the reproductive capabilities including chromosomal damage (mutations) and effects on fetuses (teratogenesis).
Signs and Symptoms:	....	Birth defects; sterility.
Chemicals:	....	Lead; DBCP.
g. Cutaneous hazards:	....	Chemical which affect the dermal layer of the body.
Signs and Symptoms:	....	Defatting of the skin; rashes; irritation.
Chemicals:	....	Ketones; chlorinated compounds.
h. Eye hazards:	....	Chemicals which affect the eye or visual capacity.
Signs and Symptoms:	....	Conjunctivitis; corneal damage.
Chemicals:	....	Organic solvents; acids.

APPENDIX B TO § 1910.1200—HAZARD DETERMINATION (MANDATORY)

The quality of a hazard communication program is largely dependent upon the adequacy and accuracy of the hazard determination. The hazard determination requirement of this standard is performance-oriented. Chemical manufacturers, importers, and employers evaluating chemicals are not required to follow any specific mehtods for determining hazards, but they must be able to demonstrate that they have adequately ascertained the hazards of the chemicals produced or imported in accordance with the criteria set forth in this Appendix.

Hazard evaluation is a process which relies heavily on the professional judgment of the evaluator, particularly in the area of chronic hazards. The performance-orientation of the hazard determination does diminish the duty of the chemical manufacturer, importer or employer to conduct a thorough evaluation, examining all relevant data and producing a scientifically defensible evaluation. For purposes of this standard, the following criteria shall be used in making hazard determinations that meet the requirements of this standard.

1. Carcinogenicity: As described in paragraph (d)(4) and Appendix A of this section, a determination by the National Toxicology Program, the International Agency for Research on Cancer, or OSHA that a chemical is a carcinogen or potential carcinogen will be considered conclusive evidence for purposes of this section.

2. Human data: Where available, epidemiological studies and case reports of adverse health effects shall be considered in the evaluation.

3. Animal data: Human evidence of health effects in exposed populations is generally not available for the majority of chemicals produced or used in the workplace. Therefore, the available results of toxicological testing in animal populations shall be used to predict the health effects that may be experienced by exposed workers. In particular, the definitions of certain acute hazards refer to specific animal testing results (see Appendix A).

4. Adequacy and reporting of data. The results of any studies which are designed and conducted according to established scientific principles, and which report statistically significant conclusions regarding the health effects of a chemical, shall be a sufficient basis for a hazard determination and reported on any material safety data sheet. The chemical manufacturer, importer, or employer may also report the results of other scientifically valid studies which tend to refute the findings of hazard.

APPENDIX C TO § 1910.1200—INFORMATION SOURCES (ADVISORY)

The following is a list of available data sources which the chemical manufacturer, importer, or employer may wish to consult to evaluate the hazards of chemicals they produce or import:

— Any information in their own company files such as toxicity testing results or illness experience of company employees.

— Any information obtained from the supplier of the chemical, such as material safety data sheets or product safety bulletins.

— Any pertinent information obtained from the following source list (latest editions should be used):

Condensed Chemical Dictionary
  Van Nostrand Reinhold Co., 135 West 50th Street, New York, NY 10020
The Merck Index: An Encyclopedia of Chemicals and Drugs
  Merck and Company, Inc., 126 E. Lincoln Avenue, Rahway, NJ 07065
IARC Monographs on the Evaluation of the Carcinogenic Risk of Chemicals to Man
  Geneva: World Health Organization, International Agency for Research on Cancer, 1972–1977. (Multivolume work), 49 Sheridan Street, Albany, New York
Industrial Hygiene and Toxicology, by F. A. Patty
  John Wiley & Sons, Inc., New York, NY (Five volumes)
Clinical Toxicology of Commerical Products
  Gleason, Gosselin and Hodge
Casarett and Doull's Toxicology; The Basic Science of Poisons
  Doull, Klaassen, and Amdur, Macmillan Publishing Co., Inc., New York, NY
Industrial Toxicology, by Alice Hamilton and Harriet L. Hardy
  Publishing Sciences Group, Inc., Acton, MA
Toxicology of the Eye, by W. Morton Grant

STANDARDS AND INTERPRETATIONS

Charles C. Thomas, 301–327 East Lawrence Avenue, Springfield, IL

Recognition of Health Hazards in Industry
William A. Burgess, John Wiley and Sons, 605 Third Avenue, New York, NY 10158

Chemical Hazards of the Workplace
Nick H. Proctor and James P. Hughes, J. P. Lipincott Company, 6 Winchester Terrace, New York, NY 10022

Handbook of Chemistry and Physics
Chemical Rubber Company, 18901 Cranwood Parkway, Cleveland, OH 44128

Threshold Limit Values for Chemical Substances and Physical Agents in the Workroom Environment with Intended Changes
American Conference of Governmental Industrial Hygienists, 6500 Glenway Avenue, Bldg. D–5, Cincinnati, OH 4521

Note.—The following documents are on sale by the Superintendent of Documents, U.S. Government Printing Office, Washington, D.C. 20402.

Occupational Health Guidelines
NIOSH/OSHA (NIOSH Pub. No. 81–123)

NIOSH/OSHA Pocket Guide to Chemical Hazards
NIOSH Pub. No. 78–210

Registry of Toxic Effects of Chemical Substances
U.S. Department of Health and Human Services, Public Health Service, Center for Disease Control, National Institute for Occupational Safety and Health (NIOSH Pub. No. 80–102)

The Industrial Environment—Its Evaluation and Control
U.S. Department of Health and Human Services, Public Health Service, Center for Disease Control, National Institute for Occupational Safety and Health (NIOSH Pub. No. 74–117)

Miscellaneous Documents—National Institute for Occupational Safety and Health
1. Criteria for a recommended standard *** Occupational Exposure to "____"
2. Special Hazard Reviews
3. Occupational Hazard Assessment
4. Current Intellligence Bulletins

Bibiliographic Data Bases

Service Provider and File Name

Bibliographic Retrieval Services (BRS), Corporation Park, Bldg. 702, Scotia, New York 12302

AGRICOLA
BIOSIS PREVIEWS
CA CONDENSATES
CA SEARCH

DRUG INFORMATION
MEDLARS
MEDOC
NTIS
POLLUTION ABSTRACTS
SCIENCE CITATION INDEX
SSIE

Lockheed—DIALOG, Lockheed Missiles & Space Company, Inc., P.O. Box 44481, San Francisco, CA 94144
AGRICOLA
BIOSIS PREV. 1972–PRESENT
BIOSIS PREV. 1969–71
CA CONDENSATES 1970–71
CA SEARCH 1972–76
CA SEARCH 1977–PRESENT
CHEMNAME
CONFERENCE PAPERS INDEX
FOOD SCIENCE & TECH. ABSTR.
FOODS ADLIBRA
INTL. PHARMACEUTICAL ABSTR.
NTIS
POLLUTION ABSTRACTS
SCISEARCH 1978–PRESENT
SCISEARCH 1974–77
SSIE CURRENT RESEARCH

SDC—ORBIT, SDC Search Service, Department No. 2230, Pasadena, CA 91051
AGRICOLA
BIOCODES
BIOSIS/BIO6973
CAS6771/CAS7276
CAS77
CHEMDEX
CONFERENCE
ENVIROLINE
LABORDOC
NTIS
POLLUTION
SSIE

Chemical Information System (CIS), Chemical Information Systems Inc., 7215 Yorke Road, Baltimore, MD 21212
Structure & Nomeclature Search System
Acute Toxicity (RTECS)
Clinical Toxicology of Commercial Products
Oil and Hazardous Materials Technical Assistance Data System

National Library of Medicine, Department of Health and Human Services, Public Health Service, National Institutes of Health, Bethesda, MD 20209
Toxicology Data Bank (TDB)
MEDLIN
TOXLINE
CANCERLIT
RTECS

APPENDIX C

SARA TITLE III: CONSOLIDATED HAZARDOUS CHEMICALS LIST AS OF APRIL 4, 1988

The following alphabetical list, although not an official document, was prepared by the EPA in order to have one comprehensive list showing all reporting requirements under the various sections of the law. The list covers the following: SARA 302, Extremely Hazardous Substances (52 FR 13371, revised 52 FR 48072, 48073, and 53 FR 5574); CERCLA Hazardous Substances which are also subject to reporting under Section 304 or Title III (40 CFR Part 302, Table 302.4); SARA Section 313, Toxic Chemicals (53 FR 4500); and RCRA Hazardous Wastes (40 CFR 261.33).

The key to the seven columns in the table is as follows:

Column One—the chemical names in alphabetical order

Column Two—the chemical CAS Number

Column Three—the 302 Column: If a chemical is reportable under Section 302, its threshold planning quantity (TPQ) is presented here. (If the TPQ is in that column, the chemical is reportable under Section 304.)

Column Four—The 304/CERCLA column: If a chemical is reportable under Section 304 and CERCLA, its reportable quantity (RQ) is presented here.

Column Five—The 313 Reporting Requirements: If either an ''X'' or a ''G'' is in this column, the chemical must be reported under Section 313. The ''X'' indicates that the chemical is specifically listed, while the ''G'' means that the chemical is an example of the chemicals included in a generic class. (This is not an exhaustive list of all possible chemical compounds within the 20 categories listed under Section 313.)

Column Six—The RCRA Column: The letter and digit code is the chemical's RCRA waste code.

Column Seven—the de minimus reporting levels.

Note: It is strongly recommended that copies of the chemical lists be secured from the Federal Registers cited above, as those are the official documents with which industry must comply.

KEY TO SYMBOLS IN THE CONSOLIDATED HAZARDOUS CHEMICALS LIST

\# Indicates that the CERCLA reportable quantity is subject to change when assessment of the potential carcinogenicity and/or chronic toxicity is completed; until then the statutory RQ applies. See 50 Federal Register (FR) 13456 (April 4, 1985) and 512 FR 34541 (September 29, 1986).

\#\# Indicates that an adjusted RQ has been proposed but a final adjustment has not been made. See 50 FR 13456 (April 4, 1985).

\#\#\# The EPA may adjust the RQ for methyl isocyanate in a future ruling; until then, the statutory 1-pound RQ applies. See 52 FR 8140 (March 16, 1987).

^ The EPA has proposed to adjust the RQ for radionuclides by establishing RQs in units of curies; until then, the statutory 1-pound RQ applies. See 52 FR 8172 (March 16, 1987).

** Indicates that no RQs have been assigned to this generic or broad class. See 50 FR 13456 (April 4, 1985).

*** The chemical name associated with this CAS Registry number is listed as ''hydrochloric acid'' under CERCLA hazardous substances and the Section 3133 toxic chemicals and as ''hydrogen chloride'' (gas only) under the Section 302(a) extremely hazardous substances.

'' Ferric dextran was designated as a hazardous substance under CERCLA solely because of its listing as a hazardous waste under Section 3001 of RCRA. The EPA recently proposed deleting ferric dextran under RCRA (50 FR 46468, November 8, 1985). The EPA has also proposed delisting ferric dextran from Table 302.4 of 40 CFR 302.4 and thereby removing its designation as a CERCLA hazardous substance. See 51 FR 34541 (September 29, 1986).

'' ' Uranyl acetate and uranyl nitrate are currently being evaluated for their radioactive properties. Their RQs may be changed in future rulemaking adjustments of the RQs of radionuclides. See 51 FR 34541 (September 29, 1986).

O* Applies to inorganic arsenic compounds, except when used in agriculture or as wood preservatives.

O** Standard vacated on technicalities.

Note: OSHA Reference 29 CFR 1910.1000, etc. Revised April 20, 1988.

LIST OF LIST
REVISED 8/23/88

NAME	CAS	SECTION #302 TPQ	SECTION #304 RQ CERCLA	OTHER	EHS	RCRA	TRI#313	AB2588
Acenaphthylene	208-96-8		5000					
Acetaldehyde	75-07-0		1000			U001	0.1 %	1,2,3
Acetaldehyde, trichloro-	75-87-6		1#			U034		
Acetamide	60-35-5						1.0 %	2,3
Acetamide, N-(4-ethoxyphenyl)-	62-44-2		1#			U178		3,5
Acetamide, N-(aminothioxomethyl)-	591-08-2		1000			P002		
Acetamide, N-9H-fluoren-2-yl-	53-96-3		1#			U005	0.1 %	4
Acetic acid	64-19-7		5000					
Acetic acid, ethyl ester (Ethyl acetate)	141-78-6		5000			U112		
Acetic acid, lead salt	301-04-2		5000*			U144	G	
Acetic acid, thallium(I) salt	563-68-8		100			U214	G	
Acetic anhydride	108-24-7		5000					
Acetone	67-64-1		1000			U002	1.0 %	
Acetone cyanohydrin	75-86-5	1,000	10			P069		
Acetone thiosemicarbazide	1752-30-3	1,000/10,000	X					
Acetonitrile	75-05-8		5000			U003	1.0 %	
Acetophenone	98-86-2		5000			U004		
Acetyl bromide	506-96-7		5000					
Acetyl chloride	75-36-5		5000			U006		
2-Acetylaminofluorene	53-96-3		1#			U005	0.1 %	4
Acrolein	107-02-8	500	1			P003	1.0 %	1,2
Acrylamide	79-06-1	1,000/10,000	5000			U007	0.1 %	3
Acrylic acid	79-10-7		5000				1.0 %	
Acrylonitrile	107-13-1	10,000	100*			U009	0.1 %	1,2,3,
Acrylyl chloride	814-68-6	100		1#				
Adipic acid	124-04-9		5000					
Adiponitrile	111-69-3	1,000		1#				
Adriamycin	23214-92-8							3,4,5
AF-2	3688-53-7							3,4
Aflatoxins	*							3,4
Alanine, 3-[p-bis(2-chloroethyl)amino]phenyl-,L-	148-82-3		1#			U150		
Aldicarb	116-06-3	100/10,000	1			P070		
Aldrin	309-00-2	500/10,000	1#			P004	1.0 %	
Allyl alcohol	107-18-6	1000	100			P005		

LIST OF LIST
REVISED 8/23/88

NAME	CAS	SECTION #302 TPQ	SECTION #304 RQ CERCLA	OTHER EHS	RCRA	TRI#313	AB2588
Allyl amine	107-11-9	500		1#			
Allyl chloride	107-05-1		1000			1.0 %	1
Aluminum (fume or dust)	7429-90-5					1.0 %	
Aluminum oxide	1344-28-1					1.0 %	
Aluminum phosphide	20859-73-8	500	100		P006		
Aluminum sulfate	10043-01-3		5000				
2-Aminoanthraquinone	117-79-3					0.1 %	5
4-Aminoazobenzene	60-09-3					0.1 %	3
4-Aminobiphenyl	92-67-1					0.1 %	3,4,5
4-Amino-2-methylanthraquinone	82-28-0					0.1 %	4
2-Amino-5-(5-nitro-2-furyl)1,3,4-thiadizole	712-68-5						3,4
Aminopterin	54-62-6	500/10,000		1#			
Amiton	78-53-5	500		1#			
Amiton oxalate	3734-97-2	100/10,000		1#			
Amitrole	61-82-5		1#		U011		3,4,5
Ammonia	7664-41-7	500	100			1.0 %	2
Ammonium acetate	631-61-8		5000				
Ammonium benzoate	1863-63-4		5000				
Ammonium bicarbonate	1066-33-7		5000				
Ammonium bichromate (Ammonium dichromate)	7789-09-5		1000#			G	
Ammonium bifluoride	1341-49-7		100				
Ammonium bisulfite	10192-30-0		5000				
Ammonium carbamate	1111-78-0		5000				
Ammonium carbonate	506-87-6		5000				
Ammonium chloride	12125-02-9		5000				
Ammonium chloroplatinate	16919-58-7 DE-LISTED						
Ammonium chromate	7788-98-9		1000#			G	
Ammonium citrate, dibasic	3012-65-5		5000				
Ammonium fluoborate	13826-83-0		5000				
Ammonium fluoride	12125-01-8		100				
Ammonium hydroxide	1336-21-6		1000				
Ammonium nitrate (solution)	6484-52-2					1.0 %	
Ammonium oxalate (Ethanedioic acid,ammonium salt)	14258-49-2		5000				
Ammonium oxalate [C2H2O4.2H3N.H2O]	6009-70-7		5000				

LIST OF LIST
REVISED 8/23/88

NAME	CAS	SECTION #302 TPQ	SECTION #304 RQ CERCLA	OTHER EHS	RCRA	TRI#313	AB2588
Ammonium oxalate [C2H2O4.N3H.H2O]	5972-73-6		5000				
Ammonium picrate	131-74-8		10		P009		
Ammonium silicofluoride	16919-19-0		1000				
Ammonium sulfamate	7773-06-0		5000				
Ammonium sulfate (solution)	7783-20-2					1.0 %	
Ammonium sulfide	12135-76-1		100				
Ammonium sulfite	10196-04-0		5000				
Ammonium tartrate [diammonium salt]	3164-29-2		X				
Ammonium tartrate [monoammonium salt]	14307-43-8		5000				
Ammonium thiocyanate	1762-95-4		5000				
Ammonium thiosulfate	7783-18-8		5000				
Ammonium vanadate (Ammonium meta vanadate)	7803-55-6		1000		P119		
Amphetamine	300-62-9	1000		1#			
Amyl acetate	628-63-7		5000				
sec-Amyl acetate	626-38-0		5000				
iso-Amyl acetate	123-92-2		5000				
tert-Amyl acetate	625-16-1		5000				

Name	CAS	Section #302 TPQ	Section #304 RQ CERCLA	OTHER EHS	RCRA	TRI#313	AB2588
Analgesic mixtures containing phenacetin	*						3,4,5
Androgenic (anabolic) steroids	*						3
Aniline	62-53-3	1000	5000		U012	1.0 %	
Aniline, 2,4,6-trimethyl-	88-05-1	500		1#			
o-Anisidine	90-04-0					0.1 %	3,4,5
p-Anisidine	104-94-9					1.0 %	
o-Anisidine hydrochloride	134-29-2					0.1 %	4,5
Anthracene	120-12-7		5000			1.0 %	
Antimony	7440-36-0		5000			1.0 %	
Antimony Compounds	- -0		**			X	
Antimony pentachloride	7647-18-9		1000			G	
Antimony pentafluoride	7783-70-2	500		1#		G	
Antimony potassium tartrate	28300-74-5		100			G	
Antimony tribromide	7789-61-9		1000			G	
Antimony trichloride	10025-91-9		1000			G	
Antimony trifluoride	7783-56-4		1000			G	
Antimony trioxide (Antimony oxide)	1309-64-4		1000			G	

LIST OF LIST
REVISED 8/23/88

NAME	CAS	SECTION #302 TPQ	SECTION #304 RQ CERCLA	OTHER EHS	RCRA	TRI#313	AB2588
Antimycin A	1397-94-0	1,000/10,000		1#			
Antu	86-88-4	500/10,000	100		P072		
Aramite	140-57-8						3,4,5
Azathioprine	446-86-6						3,4,5
Aroclor	88-01-9		X			G	
Aroclor 1016	12674-11-2		10#			G	
Aroclor 1221	11104-28-2		10#			G	
Aroclor 1232	11141-16-5		10#			G	
Aroclor 1242	53469-21-9		10#			G	
Aroclor 1248	12672-29-6		10#			G	
Aroclor 1254	11097-69-1		10#			G	
Aroclor 1260	11096-82-5		10#			G	
Arsenic	7440-38-2		1#		X	0.1 %	1,2,3,
Arsenic acid	7778-39-4		1#		P010	G	
Arsenic acid	1327-52-2		1		P010	G	
Arsenic Compounds	- -0		**			X	
Arsenic disulfide	1303-32-8		5000*			G	
Arsenic pentoxide	1303-28-2	100/10,000	5000*		P011	G	
Arsenic trisulfide	1303-33-9		5000*			G	
Arsenous oxide	1327-53-3	100/10,000	5000*		P012	G	
Arsenous trichloride	7784-34-1	500	5000#			G	
Arsine	7784-42-1	100		1#		G	
Arsine, diethyl-	692-42-2		1#		P038	G	
Asbestos [Friable]	1332-21-4		1#			0.1 %	1,2,3,
Auramine	492-80-8		1#		U014	0.1 %	3,4,5
Azaserine	115-02-6		1#		U015		3,4
Azinophos-methyl	86-50-0	10/10,000	1				
Azinphos-ethyl	2642-71-9	100/10,000		1#			
alpha-BHC	319-84-6		1#				
beta-BHC	319-85-7		1#				
delta-BHC	319-86-8		1				
gamma-BHC (Lindane)	58-89-9	1,000/10,000	1#		U129	0.1 %	
Barium	7440-39-3				X	1.0 %	
Barium compounds	-0					X	

LIST OF LIST
REVISED 8/23/88

NAME	CAS	SECTION #302 TPQ	SECTION #304 RQ			RCRA	TRI#313	AB2588
			CERCLA	OTHER	EHS			
Barium cyanide	542-62-1		10			P013	G	
Benz[a]anthracene	56-55-3		1#			U018		
Benz[c]acridine	225-51-4		1#			U016		
Benz[j]aceanthrylene,1,2-dihydro-3-methyl-	56-49-5		1#			U157		
Benzal chloride	98-87-3	500	5000			U017	1.0 %	
Benzamide	55-21-0						1.0 %	
1,2-Benzanthracene, 7,12-dimethyl-	57-97-6		1#			U094		
Benzenamine, 2-methyl-, hydrochloride	636-21-5		1#			U222	0.1 %	4,5
Benzenamine, 2-methyl-5-nitro-	99-55-8		1#			U181		
Benzenamine, 3-(trifluoromethyl)-	98-16-8	500			1#			
Benzenamine, 4,4'-methylenebis(2-chloro-	101-14-4		1#			U179	0.1 %	3,4,5
Benzenamine, 4-chloro-	106-47-8		1000			P024		
Benzenamine, 4-chloro-2-methyl-',hydrochloride	3165-93-3		1#			U049		
Benzenamine, 4-nitro-	100-01-6		5000			P077		
Benzenamine, N,N-dimethyl-4-phenylazo-	60-11-7		1#			U093	0.1 %	4,5
Benzene	71-43-2		1000*			U019	0.1 %	1,2,3,
Benzene-based dyes	*							3,4,5
Benzene, 1,2,4,5-tetrachloro-	95-94-3		5000			U207		
Benzene, 1,2-dichloro-	95-50-1		100			U070	1.0 %	
Benzene, 1,2-methylenedioxy-4-allyl-	94-59-7		1#			U203	0.1 %	3,4,5
Benzene, 1,2-methylenedioxy-4-propenyl-	120-58-1		1#			U141		
Benzene, 1,2-methylenedioxy-4-propyl-	94-58-6		1#			U090		3,4
Benzene, 1,3,5-trinitro-	99-35-4		10			U234		
Benzene, 1,3-dichloro-	541-73-1		100			U071	1.0 %	
Benzene, 1,4-dichloro-	106-46-7		100			U072	1.0 %	1,2,3
Benzene, 1-(chloromethyl)-4-nitro-	100-14-1	500/10,000			1#			
Benzene, 1-bromo-4-phenoxy-	101-55-3		100			U030		
Benzene, 1-methyl-2,4-dinitro-	121-14-2		1000*			U105	1.0 %	
Benzene, 1-methyl-2,6-dinitro-	606-20-2		1000*			U106	1.0 %	
Benzene, 1-methylethyl-	98-82-8		5000			U055	1.0 %	
Benzene, 2,4-diisocyanatomethyl-	26471-62-5		100			U223		
Benzene, chloro-	108-90-7		100			U037	1.0 %	1,2
Benzene, dimethyl-	1330-20-7		1000			U239	1.0 %	
Benzène, hexachloro	118-74-1		1#			U127	0.1 %	

LIST OF LIST
REVISED 8/23/88

NAME	CAS	SECTION #302 TPQ	SECTION #304 RQ			RCRA	TRI#313	AB2588
			CERCLA	OTHER	EHS			
Benzene, hexahydro-	110-82-7		1000			U056	1.0 %	
Benzene, m-dimethyl-	108-38-3		1000			X	1.0 %	
Benzene, methyl-	108-88-3		1000			U220	1.0 %	2,6
Benzene, o-dimethyl-	95-47-6		1000			U052	1.0 %	
Benzene, p-dimethyl-	106-42-3		1000			X	1.0 %	
Benzene, pentachloro-	608-93-5		10			U183		
Benzene, pentachloronitro-	82-68-8		1#			U185	1.0 %	
Benzenearsonic acid	98-05-5	10/10,000			1#		G	
1,2-Benzenedicarboxylic acid anhydride	85-44-9		5000			U190	1.0 %	2
1,2-Benzenedicarboxylic acid, diethyl ester	84-66-2		1000			U088	1.0 %	

NAME	CAS	SECTION #302 TPQ	SECTION #304 RQ CERCLA	OTHER EHS	RCRA	TRI#313	AB2588
1,2-Benzenedicarboxylic acid [bis(2-ethylhexyl)] ester	117-81-7		1#		U028	0.1 %	1,2,3,
1,3-Benzenediol	108-46-3		5000		U201		
1,2-Benzenediol,4-[1-hydroxy-2-(methylamino)ethyl]-	51-43-4		1000		P042		
Benzenesulfonyl chloride	98-09-9 DE-LISTED		100		U020		
Benzidine	92-87-5		1#		U021	0.1 %	3,4,5
1,2-Benzisothiazolin-3-one,1,1-dioxide, and salts	81-07-2		1#		U202	0.1 %	3,4,5
Benzimidazole, 4,5-dichloro-2-(trifluromethyl)	3615-21-2	500/10,000		1#			
Benzo[a]pyrene	50-32-8		1#		U022		3,4,5
Benzo(b)fluoranthene	205-99-2		1#				3,4,5
Benzo[g,h,i]perylene	191-24-2		5000				
Benzo[j,k]fluorene	206-44-0		100		U120		
Benzo[j]fluoranthanene	205-82-3						3,4
Benzo[k]fluoranthene	207-08-9		1#				3,4
Benzoic acid	65-85-0		5000				
Benzonitrile	100-47-0		5000				
Benzophenone, 4,4'-bis-dimethylamino	90-94-8					0.1 %	4,5
p-Benzoquinone [Quinone]	106-51-4		10		U197	1.0 %	
Benzotrichloride [Benzoic trichloride]	98-07-7	100	1#		U023	0.1 %	4,5
Benzoyl chloride	98-88-4		1000			1.0 %	
Benzoyl peroxide	94-36-0					1.0 %	
1,2-Benzphenanthrene	218-01-9		1#		U050		
Benzyl chloride	100-44-7	500	100*		P028	1.0 %	1
Benzyl cyanide	140-29-4	500		1#	G		
Benzyl violet 4B	1694-09-3						3,4

LIST OF LIST
REVISED 8/23/88

NAME	CAS	SECTION #302 TPQ	SECTION #304 RQ CERCLA	OTHER EHS	RCRA	TRI#313	AB2588
Beryllium	7440-41-7		1#		P015	0.1 %	1,2,3,
Beryllium Compounds	- -0		**			0.1%	
Beryllium chloride	7787-47-5		5000#		G		
Beryllium fluoride	7787-49-7		5000#		G		
Beryllium nitrate [Be.2HNO3]	13597-99-4		5000#		G		
Beryllium nitrate [Be.3H2O.2HNO3]	7787-55-5		5000#		G		
Betel quid with tabacco	*						3
Bicyclo[2.2.1]heptane-2-carbonitrile, 5-chloro-6-	15271-41-7	500/10,000		1#			
[(((methylamino)carbonyl)oxy)imino-	15271-41-7						
Biphenyl	92-52-4					1.0 %	
(1,1'-Biphenyl)-4,4'-diamine,3,3'-dimethyl-	119-93-7		1#		U091	0.1 %	3,4,5
(1,1'-Biphenyl)-4,4'diamine,3,3'dichloro-	91-94-1		1#		U073	0.1 %	3,4,5
(1,1'-Biphenyl)-4,4'diamine,3,3'dimethoxy-	119-90-4		1#		U095	0.1 %	3,4,5
Bitoscanate	4044-65-9	500/10,000		1#			
Bitumens, extract of steam refined	*						3
and air refined bitumens	--						
Bleomycins	*						3
1,4-Butanediol dimethanesulfonate (Myleran)	55-98-1						3,4,5
Boron trichloride	10294-34-5	500		1#			
Boron trifluoride	7637-07-2	500		1#			
Boron trifluoride compound with methyl ether (1:1)	353-42-4	1000		1#			
Bromadiolone	28772-56-7	100/10,000		1#			
Bromine	7726-95-6	500		1#			2
Bromine compounds inorganic	*						2
Bromoacetone	598-31-2		1000		P017		
Bromoehane [Methyl Bromide]	74-83-9	1000	1000		U029	1.0 %	1,2,6
Bromoform	75-25-2		100		U225	1.0 %	
Brucine	357-57-3		100		P018		
Butadiene	106-99-0 DE-LISTED					0.1 %	1,2,3
1,3-Butadiene, 1,1,2,3,4,4-hexachloro-	86-73-3		5000		X		
1-Butanamine, N-butyl-N-nitroso-	924-16-3		1#		U172	0.1 %	3,4,5
Butanoic acid, 4-[bis(2-chloroethyl)amino] benzene-	305-03-3		1#		U035		3,4,5
i-Butanol	71-36-3		5000		U031	1.0 %	
2-Butanone peroxide	1338-23-4		10		U160		

LIST OF LIST
REVISED 8/23/88

NAME	CAS	SECTION #302 TPQ	SECTION #304 R Q CERCLA	OTHER EHS	RCRA	TRI#313	AB2588
2-Butanone	78-93-3		5000		U159	1.0 %	
2-Butene, 1,4-dichloro-	764-41-0		1		U074		
Buterated hydroxyanisole (BHA)	25013-16-5						3
Butyl acetate	123-86-4		5000				
sec-Butyl acetate	105-46-4		5000				
tert-Butyl acetate	540-88-5		5000				
iso-Butyl acetate	110-19-0		5000				
beta-Butly acetone	3068-88-0						3,4
Butyl acrylate	141-32-2					1.0 %	
sec-Butyl alcohol	78-92-2					1.0 %	
iso-Butyl alcohol	78-83-1		5000		U140		
tert-Butyl alcohol	75-65-0					1.0 %	
Butyl benzyl phthalate	85-68-7		100			1.0 %	
Butylamine	109-73-9		1000				
sec-Butylamine (2-Butanamine)	13952-84-6		1000				
iso-Butylamine	78-81-9		1000				
Sec-Butylamine (2-Butanamine, S-)	513-49-5		1000				
tert-Butylamine	75-64-9		1000				
1,2-Butylene oxide	106-88-7					1.0 %	
Butyraldehyde	123-72-8					1.0 %	
iso-Butyraldehyde	78-84-2					1.0 %	
Butyric acid	107-92-6		5000				
iso-Butyric acid	79-31-2		5000				
iso-Butyronitrile	78-82-0	1,000		1#			
C.I. Acid Blue 9, diammonium salt	2650-18-2					1.0 %	
C.I. Acid Blue 9, disodium salt	3844-45-9					1.0 %	
C.I. Acid Green 3	4680-78-8					1.0 %	
C.I. Basic Green 4	569-64-2					1.0 %	
C.I. Basic Red 1	989-38-8					0.1 %	
C.I. Disperse Yellow 3	2832-40-8					1.0 %	
C.I. Food Red 15	81-88-9					0.1 %	
C.I. Food Red 5	3761-53-3					0.1 %	3
C.I. Solvent Orange 7	3118-97-6					1.0 %	
C.I. Solvent Yellow 14	842-07-9					0.1 %	

LIST OF LIST
REVISED 8/23/88

NAME	CAS	SECTION #302 TPQ	SECTION #304 R Q CERCLA	OTHER EHS	RCRA	TRI#313	AB2588
C.I. Solvent Yellow 3	97-56-3					0.1 %	3
C.I. Vat Yellow 4	128-66-5					1.0 %	
Cacodylic acid (Dimethyl arsinic acid)	75-60-5		1#		U136	G	
Cadmium	7440-43-9		1#		X	0.1 %	1,2,3,
Cadmium acetate	543-90-8		100			G	
Cadmium Compounds	- -0		**			X	12345
Cadmium bromide	7789-42-6		100#			G	
Cadmium chloride	10108-64-2		100#			G	
Cadmium oxide	1306-19-0	100/10,000		1#		G	
Cadmium stearate	2223-93-0	1,000/10,000		1#		G	
Calcium arsenate [2AsH3O4.2Ca]	7778-44-1	500/10,000	1000#			G	
Calcium arsenite [AsH3O3.Ca]	52740-16-6		1000#			G	
Calcium carbide	75-20-7		10				
Calcium chromate	13765-19-0		1000#		U032	G	
Calcium cyanamide	156-62-7					1.0 %	
Calcium cyanide	592-01-8		10		P021	G	

Name	CAS	#302 TPQ	CERCLA RQ	EHS RQ	RCRA	TRI#313	AB2588
Calcium dodecylbenzene sulfonate	26264-06-2		1000				
Calcium hypochlorite	7778-54-3		10				
Camphechlor	8001-35-2	500/10,000	1#		P123	0.1 %	3,4,5
Cantharidin	56-25-7	100/10,000		1#			
Captan	133-06-2		10#			1.0 %	
Carbachol chloride	51-83-2	500/10,000		1#			
Carbamic acid, ethyl ester	51-79-6		1#		U238	0.1 %	3,4,5
Carbamic acid, methyl-, O-(((2,4-dimethyl-1, 3-dithiolan-2-y-methylene)amino-	26419-73-8	100/10,000		1#			
2-y-methylene)amino-	26419-73-8 X						
Carbamic acid, methylnitroso-,ethyl ester	615-53-2		1#		U178		3
Carbamide, N-ethyl-N-nitroso-	759-73-9		1#		U176	0.1 %	
Carbamide, N-methyl-N-nitroso-	684-93-5		1#		U177	0.1 %	3,4,5
Carbamide, thio-	62-56-6		1#		U219	0.1 %	
Carbamimidoselenoic acid	630-10-4		1000		P103	G	
Carbamoyl chloride, dimethyl	79-44-7		1#		U097	0.1 %	3,4,5
Carbaryl	63-25-2		100			1.0 %	
Carbofuran	1563-66-2	10/10,000	10				
Carbon black extracts	*						3

LIST OF LIST
REVISED 8/23/88

NAME	CAS	SECTION #302 TPQ	SECTION #304 RQ CERCLA	OTHER EHS	RCRA	TRI#313	AB2588
Carbon disulfide	75-15-0	10,000	100		P022	1.0 %	
Carbon oxyfluoride	353-50-4		1000		U033		
Carbon tetrachloride	56-23-5		5000		U211	0.1 %	1,2,3,
Carbonyl sulfide	463-58-1					1.0 %	
Carbophenothion	786-19-6	500		1#			
Carrageenan (degraded)							3,4
Catechol	120-80-9					1.0 %	
Chloramben	133-90-4					1.0 %	
Chlorambucil	305-03-3		1#		U035	0.1 %	3,4,5
Chloramphenicol	56-75-7						3
Chlorocyclizine hydrochloride	82-93-9						4
Chlordane	57-74-9	1,000	1#		U036	1.0 %	
Chlordane (Technical Mixture and Metabolites)	- -0		**				
Chlorfenvinfos	470-90-6	500		1#			
Chlorinated Benzenes	- -0		**				
Chlorinated Ethanes	- -0		**				
Chlorinated Naphthalene	- -0		**				
Chlorinated fluorocarbon, (Freon 113),	76-13-1					1.0 %	2,6
Ethane,1,1,2-trichloro-1,2,2-trifluoro-	76-13-1					1.0 %	2,6
Chlorine	7782-50-5	100	10			1.0 %	2
Chlorine cyanide	506-77-4		10		P033	G	
Chlorine dioxide	10049-04-4					1.0 %	
Chlormephos	24934-91-6	500		1#			
Chlormequat chloride	999-81-5	100/10,000		1#			
Chlornaphazine	494-03-1		1#		U026		3,4,5
4-Chloro-m-cresol	59-50-7		5000		U039		
Chloroacetaldehyde	107-20-0	Removed	1000		P023		
Chloroacetic acid	79-11-8	100/10,000		1#		1.0 %	
2-Chloroacetophenone	532-27-4					1.0 %	
Chloroalkyl Ethers	0		**				
Chlorobenzene	108-90-7		100		U037	1.0 %	1,2
Ethyl 4,4-Chlorbenzilate	510-15-6		1#		U038	1.0 %	
Chlorodibromomethane	124-48-1		100				
Chloroethane	75-00-3		100			1.0 %	2

LIST OF LIST
REVISED 8/23/88

NAME	CAS	SECTION #302 TPQ	SECTION #304 R Q CERCLA	OTHER EHS	RCRA	TRI#313	AB2588
Chloroethanol	107-07-3	500		1#			
1-(2-chloroethyl)-3-cyclohexyl- 1-nitrosourea (CCNU)	13010-47-4 --						3,4,5
1-(2-chloroethyl)-3-(4-methylcyclohexyl)- 1-nitrosourea (Methyl CCNU)	13909-09-6 --						3
Bis(2-chloroethoxy) methane	111-91-1		1000		U024		
Chloroethyl chloroformate	627-11-2	1000		1#			
Bis-chloroethyl nitrourea	154-93-8						3,4
2-Chloroethyl vinyl ether	110-75-8		1000		U042		
Tris(2-chloroethyl)amine	555-77-1	100		1#			
Chloroform	67-66-3	10,000	5000		U044	0.1 %	1,2,3,
Bis(2-chloroisopropyl) ether	108-60-1		1000		U027	1.0 %	
Chloromethane [Methyl Chloride]	74-87-3		1#		U045	1.0 %	
Chloromethyl ether	542-88-1	100	1#		P016	0.1 %	3
Chloromethyl methyl ether	107-30-2	100	1#		U046	0.1 %	4,5
Bis(chloromethyl) ketone	534-07-6	10/10,000		1#			
beta-Chloronaphthalene	91-58-7		5000		U047		
Chlorophacinone	3691-35-8	100/10,000		1#			
2-Chlorophenol	95-57-8		100		U048	G	
Chlorophenols	-0		**			X	1,2,3
4-Chloro-o-phenylenediamine	95-83-0						3,4,5
4-Chlorophenyl phenyl ether	7005-72-3		5000				
Chlorophenoxy herbicides	*						3
Chloroprene	126-99-8					1.0 %	1,2
Chlorosulfonic acid	7790-94-5		1000				
Chlorothalonil	1897-45-6					0.1 %	
p-Chloro-o-toluidine	95-69-2						3
Chloroxuron	1982-47-4	500/10,000		1#			
Chlorpyrifos	2921-88-2		1				
Chlorthiophos	21923-23-9	500		1#			
Chromic acetate	1066-30-4		1000			G	
Chromic acid	11115-74-5		1000#			G	
Chromic acid (CrH2O4)	7738-94-5		1000#			G	
Chromic chloride	10025-73-7	1/10,000		1#		G	

LIST OF LIST
REVISED 8/23/88

NAME	CAS	SECTION #302 TPQ	SECTION #304 R Q CERCLA	OTHER EHS	RCRA	TRI#313	AB2588
Chromic sulfate	10101-53-8		1000##			G	
Chromium	7440-47-3		1#		X	0.1 %	
Chromium (hexavalent)	18540-29-9						1,2,3,
Chromiun Compounds	-0		**				
Chromous chloride	10049-05-5		1000			G	
Cisplatin	15663-27-1						3
Citrus Red No. 2	6358-53-8						3
Cobalt	7440-48-4	DE-LISTED					
Cobalt Compounds	- -0					X	
Cobalt carbonyl	10210-68-1	10/10,000		1#		G	

Cobalt, ((2,2'-(1,2-ethanediyl-bis-(nitrilomethylidyne))	62207-76-5	100/10,000	1#		G	
bis(6-fluorophenolato))(2-)-N,N',0,0')-(Sp-4-2)-	62207-76-5				G	
Cobaltous bromide	7789-43-7		1000		G	
Cobaltous formate	544-18-3		1000		G	
Cobaltous sulfamate	14017-41-5		1000		G	
Coke Oven Emissionns	-0		1#			12345
Colchicine	64-86-8	10/10,000		1#		
Copper	7440-50-8		5000		1.0 %	2
Copper Compounds	-0		**		X	
Copper cyanide	544-92-3		10	P029	G	
Coumaphos	56-72-4	100/10,000	10			
Coumatetralyl	5836-29-3	500/10,000		1#		
Creosote	8001-58-9		1#		U051	
p-Cresidine	120-71-8				0.1 %	3,4,5
m-Cresol	108-39-4		1000	U052	1.0 %	
p-Cresol	106-44-5		1000*	U052	1.0 %	
o-Cresol	95-48-7	1,000/10,000	1000	U052		
Cresol(s)	1319-77-3		1000	U052	1.0 %	1,2
Cresotes	*					3
Cresylic acid	95-48-7	1,000/10,000	1000	U052	1.0 %	
Crimidine	535-89-7	100/10,000		1#		
Crotonaldehyde	123-73-9	1,000	100	U053		
Crotonaldehyde	4170-30-3	1000	100	U053		
Cumene (Isopropylamine)	98-82-8		5000	U055	1.0 %	

LIST OF LIST

REVISED 8/23/88

| NAME | CAS | SECTION #302 TPQ | SECTION #304 R Q | | RCRA | TRI#313 | AB2588 |
			CERCLA	OTHER EHS			
Cumene Hydroperoxide	80-15-9		10		U096	1.0 %	
Cupferron	135-20-6					0.1 %	4,5
Cupric acetate	142-71-2		100			G	
Cupric chloride	7447-39-4		10			G	
Cupric nitrate	3251-23-8		100			G	
Cupric oxalate	5893-66-3		100			G	
Cupric sulfate	7758-98-7		10			G	
Cupric sulfate ammoniated	10380-29-7		100			G	
Cupric tartrate	815-82-7		100			G	
Cyanide Compounds	- -0		**			X	
Cyanides (soluble cyanide salts)	57-12-5		10		P030	1.0%	
Cyanogen	460-19-5		100		P031	G	
Cyanogen bromide	506-68-3	5000/10,000	1000		U246	G	
Cyanogen iodide	506-78-5	1,000/10,000		1#		G	
Cyanophos	2636-26-2	1,000		1#			
Cyanuric fluoride	675-14-9	100		1#			
Cycasin	14901-08-7						3,4,5
Cyclohexane	110-82-7		1000		U056	1.0 %	
Cyclohexanone	108-94-1		5000		U057		
Cycloheximide	66-81-9	100/10,000		1#			
Cyclohexylamine	108-91-8	10,000		1#			
Cyclophosphamide	50-18-0		1#		U058		3,4
2,4-D Acid	94-75-7		100		U240	1.0 %	
2,4-D Esters	94-11-1		100				
2,4-D Esters	94-79-1		100				
2,4-D Esters	1320-18-9		100				
2,4-D Esters	2971-38-2		100				
2,4-D Esters	1928-61-6		100				
2,4-D Esters	25168-26-7		100				
2,4-Esters	53467-11-1		100				
2,4-D Esters	94-80-4		100				
2,4-D Esters	1928-38-7		100				
2,4-D-Esters	1929-73-3		100				
DDD	72-54-8		1#		U060		

LIST OF LIST
REVISED 8/23/88

NAME	CAS	SECTION #302 TPQ	SECTION #304 RQ CERCLA	OTHER EHS	RCRA	TRI#313	AB2588
DDE	72-55-9		1#				
DDT	50-29-3		1#		U061		3,4,5
DDT and Metabolites	-0		**				
Dacarbazine Bis(p-chlorpenyl)ethane	43 42-03-4						4,5
Daunomycin	20830-81-3		1#		U059		3,4
Decaborane(14)	17702-41-9	500/10,000		1#			
Decabromodiphenyl oxide	1163-19-5					1.0 %	
Demeton	8065-48-3	500		1#			
Demeton-S-methyl	919-86-8	500		1#			
N,N'-Diacetylbenzidine	613-35-4						3
Dialifos	10311-84-9	100/10,000		1#			
Dialkylnitrosamines	*						1
Diallate	2303-16-4		1#		U062	0.1 %	
2,4-Diaminoanisole sulfate	39156-41-7					0.1 %	
2,4-Diaminoanisole	615-05-4					0.1 %	4,5
4,4'-Diaminodiphenyl ether	101-80-4					0.1 %	3
Diaminotoluene [1,2-benzenediamine, 4-methyl]	496-72-0		1#				
Diaminotoluene [1,3-benzenediamine, 2-methyl]	823-40-5		1#		U221		
Diaminotoluene [benzenediamine, ar-methyl]	25376-45-8		1#		U221	0.1 %	
Diaminotoluene [1,3-benzenediamine, 4-methyl]	95-80-7		1#		U221	0.1 %	3,4,5
Diazinon	5333-41-5		1				
Diazomethane	334-88-3					1.0 %	
Dibenz[a,h]acridine	226-36-8						3,4,5
Dibenz[a,j]acridine	224-42-0						3,4,5
Dibenz[a,h]anthracene	53-70-3		1#		U063		3,4,5
7H-Dibenzo[a,e]cabazole	194-59-2						3,4,5
Dibenzofuran	132-64-9			1#		1.0 %	
1,2,7,8-Dibenzopyrene (Dibenzo(a,i)pyrene)	189-55-9		1#		U064		3,4,5
Dibenzo[a,e]pyrene	192-65-4						3,4
Dibenzo[a,h]pyrene	189-64-0						3,4,5
Dibenzo[a,l]pyrene	191-30-0						3,4
Diborane	19287-45-7	100					
1,2-Dibromoethane	106-93-4		1000		U067		1,2,3,
1,2-Dibromo-3-chloropropane	96-12-8		1#		U066	0.1 %	3,4,5

LIST OF LIST
REVISED 8/23/88

NAME	CAS	SECTION #302 TPQ	SECTION #304 RQ CERCLA	OTHER EHS	RCRA	TRI#313	AB2588
Dibutyl phthalate	84-74-2		10		U069	1.0 %	
Dicamba	1918-00-9		1000				
Dichlobenil	1194-65-6		100				
Dichlone	117-80-6		1				
3,5-Dichloro-N-(1,1-dimethyl-2-propynyl)benzamide	23950-58-5		5000		U192		
Dichlorobenzene (mixed)	25321-22-6		100			0.1 %	
Dichlorobenzidine	-0		**				
3,3'-Dichlorobenzidine	91-94-1		1#		U073	0.1 %	3,4,5
Dichlorobromomethane	75-27-4		5000			1.0 %	
Trans-1,4-dichlorobutene	110-57-6	500		1#			
Dichlorodifluoromethane	75-71-8		5000		U075		
1,1-Dichloroethane	75-34-3		1000		U076		
1,2-Dichloroethane	107-06-2		5000		U077	0.1 %	1,2,3,
Dichloroethyl ether	111-44-4	10,000	1#		U025	1.0 %	
1,1-Dichloroethylene (Vinylidene chloride)	75-35-4		5000*		U078	1.0 %	1,2
1,2-Trans-Dichloroethylene	156-60-5		1000		U079		

NAME	CAS	SECTION #302 TPQ	CERCLA RQ	OTHER EHS RQ	RCRA	TRI#313	AB2588
1,2-Dichloroethylene	540-59-0					1.0 %	
Dichloromethylphenylsilane	149-74-6	1000		1#			
2,4-Dichlorophenol	120-83-2		100		U181	1.0 %	
2,6-Dichlorophenol	87-65-0		100		U082		
Dichloropropane	26638-19-7		1000				
1,3-Dichloropropane	142-28-9		1000				
1,1-Dichloropropane	78-99-9		1000				
Dichloropropane - Dichloropropene (mixture)	8003-19-8		100				
1,2-Dichloropropane (Propylene dichloride)	78-87-5		1000		U083	1.0 %	
Dichloropropene	26952-23-8		100				
2,3-Dichloropropene	78-88-6		100				
1,3-Dichloropropene	542-75-6		100*		U084	0.1 %	3
2,2-Dichloropropionic acid	75-99-0		5000				
Dichlorvos	62-73-7	1,000	10			1.0 %	
Dicofol (Kelthane)	115-32-2		10			1.0 %	
Dicrotophos	141-66-2	100		1#			
Dieldrin	60-57-1			1#	P037		
Diepoxybutane	1464-53-5	500		1#	U085	0.1 %	3,4,5

.

LIST OF LIST
REVISED 8/23/88

NAME	CAS	SECTION #302 TPQ	SECTION #304 R Q		RCRA	TRI#313	AB2588
			CERCLA	OTHER EHS			
Diethanolamine	111-42-2					1.0 %	
0,0'-Diethyl S-methyl dithiophosphate	3288-58-2		5000		U087		
Diethyl chlorophosphate	814-49-3	500		1#			
Di(2-ethylhexyl)phthalate (DEHP)	117-81-7		1#		U028	0.1 %	1,2,3,
Diethyl sulfate	64-67-5					0.1 %	3,4,5
Diethyl-p-nitrophenyl phosphate	311-45-5		100		P041		
Diethylamine	109-89-7		100				
Diethylcarbamazine citrate	1642-54-2	100/10,000		1#			
1,4-Diethylene dioxide	123-91-1		1#		U108	0.1 %	1,2,3,
N,N'-Diethylhydrazine	1615-80-1		1#		U086		3,4
Diethylstilbestrol	56-53-1		1#		U089		3,4,5
Digitoxin	71-63-6	100/10,000		1#			
Diglycidyl ether	2238-07-5	1,000		1#			3
Digoxin	20830-75-5	10/10,000		1#			
1,2-Dihydro-3,6-pyridazinedione	123-33-1		5000		U148		
Dimefox	115-26-4	500		1#			
Dimethoate	60-51-5	500/10,000	10		P044		
3,3'-Dimethoxybenzidene	119-90-4		1#		U095	0.1 %	3,4,5
4-Dimethylaminoazobenzene	60-11-7		1#		U093	0.1 %	4,5
trans-2-[Dimethylamino)methylimino]-	5738-54-0						3,4
5-[2-(5-nitro-2-furyl)vinyl]	--						
1,3,4-oxadiazole	--						
Dimethyl phosphorochloridothioate	2524-03-0	500		1#			
Dimethyl phthalate	131-11-3		5000		U102	1.0 %	
Dimethyl sulfate	77-78-1	500	1#		U103	0.1 %	3,4,5
Dimethyl sulfide (Methyl sulfide)	75-18-3	100		1#			
Dimethyl-p-phenylenediamine	99-98-9	10/10,000		1#			
Dimethylamine	124-40-3		1000		U092		2
N,N'-Dimethylaniline	121-69-7					1.0 %	
alpha,alpha-Dimethylbenzylhydroperoxide	80-15-9		10		U096	1.0 %	
Dimethylcarbamoyl chloride	79-44-7		1#		U097	0.1 %	3,4,5
Dimethyldichlorosilane	75-78-5	500		1#			
1,1-Dimethylhydrazine	57-14-7	1,000	1#		U098	0.1 %	3,5
1,2-Dimethylhydrazine	540-73-8		1#		U099		3,4

LIST OF LIST
REVISED 8/23/88

NAME	CAS	SECTION #302 TPQ	SECTION #304 R Q CERCLA	OTHER EHS	RCRA	TRI#313	AB2588
alpha, alpha-Dimethylphenethylamine	122-09-8		5000		P046		
2,4-Dimethylphenol	105-67-9		100		U101	1.0 %	
(Bis-dimethylthiocarbamoyl)disulfide	137-26-8		10		U244		
Dimetilan	644-64-4	500/10,000		1#			
4,6-Dinitro-o-cyclohexylphenol	131-89-5		100		P034		
o-Dinitrobenzene	528-29-0		100				
Dinitrobenzene (mixed)	25154-54-5		100				
m-Dinitrobenzene	99-65-0		100				
p-Dinitrobenzene	100-25-4		100				
Dinitrocresol	534-52-1	10/10,000	10		P047	1.0 %	
Dinitrophenol	25550-58-7		10				
2,5-Dinitrophenol	329-71-5		10				
2,6-Dinitrophenol	573-56-8		10				
2,4-Dinitrophenol	51-28-5		10		P048	1.0 %	
Dinitrotoluene	25321-14-6		1000#				
3,4-Dinitrotoluene	610-39-9		1000*				
Dinoseb	88-85-7	100/10,000	1000		P020		
Dinoterb	1420-07-1	500/10,000		1#			
Dioctyl phthalate	117-84-0		5000		U107	1.0 %	
1,4-Dioxane	123-91-1		1#		U108	0.1 %	1,2,3,
Dioxathion	78-34-2	500		1#			
Diphacinone	82-66-6	10/10,000					
Diphenylhydrazine	-0		**				
Diphenylhydanton	630-93-3						4
1,2-Diphenylhydrazine	122-66-7		1#		U109	0.1 %	4,5
Diphosphoramide, octamethyl-	152-16-9	100	100		P085		
Dipropylamine	142-84-7		5000		U110		
Diquat [C12H12N2.2Br]	85-00-7		1000				
Diquat [C12H12N2]	2764-72-9		1000				
Direct Black 38	1937-37-7					0.1 %	4,5
Direct Blue 6	2602-46-2					0.1 %	4,5
Direct Brown 95	16071-86-6					0.1 %	
Disulfoton	298-04-4	500	1		P039		
Dithiazanine iodide	514-73-8	500/10,000		1#			

LIST OF LIST
REVISED 8/23/88

NAME	CAS	SECTION #302 TPQ	SECTION #304 R Q CERCLA	OTHER EHS	RCRA	TRI#313	AB2588
Dithiobiuret	541-53-7	100/10,000	100		P049		
Diuron	330-54-1		100				
Dodecylbenzenesulfonic acid	27176-87-0		1000				
EPN	2104-64-5	100/10,000		1#			
Emetine, dihydrochloride	316-42-7	1/10,000		1#			
Endosulfan	115-29-7	10/10,000	1		P050		
Endosulfan and Metabolites	-0		**				
Endosulfan sulfate	1031-07-8		1				
alpha-Endosulfan	959-98-8		1				
beta-Endosulfan	33213-65-9		1				
Endothall	145-73-3		1000		P088		

NAME	CAS	SECTION #302 TPQ	CERCLA	OTHER EHS	RCRA	TRI#313	AB2588
Endothion	2778-04-3	500/10,000		1#			
Endrin	72-20-8	500/10,000	1		P051		
Endrin aldehyde	7421-93-4		1				
Endrin and Metabolites	-0		**		X		
Environmental tobacco smoke	*						1,3
Epichlorohydrin	106-89-8	1000	1000*	0.	U041		2,3,4,
Ergocalciferol	50-14-6	1,000/10,000		1#			
Ergotamine tartrate	379-79-3	500/10,000		1#			
Erionite	1318-02-1						3
Estradiol 17 B	50-28-2						4,5
Estrogens, nonsterodial	*						3,4,5
Estrogens, sterdidal	*						3,4,5
Estrone	53-16-7						4,5
Ethanamine, N-ethyl-N-nitroso-	55-18-5		1#		U174	0.1 %	3,4,5
Ethane, 1,1'-oxybis-	60-29-7		100		U117		
Ethane, 1,1,1,2,2,2-hexachloro-	67-72-1		1#		U131	1.0 %	
Ethane, 1,1,1,2-tetrachloro-	630-20-6		1#		U208		
Ethane, 1,1,1-trichloro-2,2-bis(p-methoxyphenyl)-	72-43-5		1		U247	1.0 %	
Ethane, 1,1,2-trichloro-1,2,2-trifluoro-	76-13-1					1.0 %	2,6
Ethane, 1,1,2,2-tetrachloro-	79-34-5		1#		U209	1.0 %	
Ethane, 1,1,2-trichloro-	79-00-5		1#		U227	0.1 %	
Ethane, 1,2-dibromo-	106-93-4		1000*		U067	0.1 %	1,2,3,
1,2-Ethanediyl bis-carbamodithioic acid	111-54-6		5000		U114		

LIST OF LIST
REVISED 8/23/88

NAME	CAS	SECTION #302 TPQ	SECTION #304 R Q		RCRA	TRI#313	AB2588
			CERCLA	OTHER EHS			
Ethanesulfonyl chloride, 2-chloro-	1622-32-8	500		1#			
Ethanethioamide	62-55-5		1#		U219	0.1 %	3,4,5
Ethanol, 1,2-dichloro-, acetate	10140-87-1	1000		1#			
Ethanol, 2,2'-(nitrosoimino)bis-	1116-54-7		1#		U173		3,4,5
Ethenamine, N-methyl-N-nitroso-	4549-40-0		1#		P084	0.1 %	3,4,5
Ethene, 1,1,2,2-tetrachloro- [Perchloroethylene]	127-18-4		1#		U210	1.0 %	1,2,6
Ethene, chloro- (Vinyl chloride)	75-01-4		1#		U043	0.1 %	1,2,3,
Ethion	563-12-2	1000	10				
Ethinylestradiol	57-63-6						4,5
Ethoprophos	13194-48-4	1000		1#			
2-Ethoxyethanol	110-80-5		1*			1.0 %	
Ethyl 4,4'-dichlorobenzilate	510-15-6		1#		U038	1.0 %	
Ethyl acrylate	140-88-5		1000		U113	0.1 %	3
Ethyl chloroformate	541-41-3					1.0 %	
Ethyl methacrylate	97-63-2		1000		U125		
Ethyl methanesulfonate	62-50-0		1#		U119		3,4
Ethyl thiocyanate	542-90-5	10,000		1#	G		
Ethylbenzene	100-41-4		1000			1.0 %	
Ethyl bis(2-chloroethyl)amine	538-07-8	500		1#			
Ethylene	74-85-1					1.0 %	
Ethylene dibromide (Ethylene bromide)	106-93-4		1000		U067	0.1 %	1,2,3,
Ethylene fluorohydrin	371-62-0	10		1#			
Ethylene glycol	107-21-1					1.0 %	
Ethylene oxide	75-21-8	1000	1#		U115	0.1 %	1,2,3,
Ethylenediamine	107-15-3	10,000	5000				
Ethylenediamine tetraacetic acid (EDTA)	60-00-4		5000				
Ethyleneimine	151-56-4	500	1#		P054	0.1 %	
Ethylenethiourea	96-45-7		1#		U116	0.1 %	3,4,5
Bis-d(2-ethylhexyl) adipate	103-23-1					0.1 %	
Ethylmercuric phosphate	2235-25-8	Removed				G	
Etreinate	54350-48-0						4
Famphur	52-85-7		1000		P097		
Fenamiphos	22224-92-6	10/10,000		1#			
Fenitrothion	122-14-5	500		1#			

LIST OF LIST
REVISED 8/23/88

NAME	CAS	SECTION #302 TPQ	SECTION #304 R Q		RCRA	TRI#313	AB2588
			CERCLA	OTHER EHS			
Fensulfothion	115-90-2	500		1#			
Ferric ammonium citrate	1185-57-5		1000				
Ferric ammonium oxalate [C2H2O4.xFexH3N]	55488-87-4		1000				
Ferric ammonium oxalate [3(C2H2O4).FeH3N]	2944-67-4		1000				
Ferric chloride	7705-08-0		1000				
Ferric dextran	9004-66-4		5000''		U139		3,4,5
Ferric fluoride	7783-50-8		100				
Ferric nitrate	10421-48-4		1000				
Ferric sulfate	10028-22-5		1000				
Ferrous ammonium sulfate	10045-89-3		1000				
Ferrous chloride	7758-94-3		100				
Ferrous sulfate [FeH2SO4]	7720-78-7		1000				
Ferrous sulfate [FeH2SO4.7H2O]	7782-63-0		1000				
Fluenetil	4301-50-2	100/10,000		1#			
Fluometuron	2164-17-2					1.0 %	
Fluorene	86-73-7		5000				
Fluorine	7782-41-4	500	10		P056		
Fluoroacetamide	640-19-7	100/10,000	100		P057		
Fluoroacetic acid	144-49-0	10/10,000		1#			
Fluoroacetyl chloride	359-06-8	10		1#			
Fluorouracil	51-21-8	500/10,000		1#			
Fonofos	944-22-9	500		1#			
Formaldehyde	50-00-0	500	1000#		U122	0.1 %	1,2,3,
Formaldehyde cyanohydrin	107-16-4	1000		1#			
Formetanate hydrochloride	23422-53-9	500/10,000		1#			
Formic acid	64-18-8		5000		U123		
Formothion	2540-82-1	100		1#			
Formparanate	17702-57-7	100/10,000		1#			
2-(2-Formylhydrazine)-4-(5- nitro-2-furyl)thiazole	3570-75-0 --						3,4
Fosthietan	21548-32-3	500		1#			
Freon 113	76-13-1					1.0 %	2,6
Fuberidazole	3878-19-1	100/10,000		1#			
Fulminic acid, mercury(II)salt	628-86-4		10		P065	G	

LIST OF LIST
REVISED 8/23/88

NAME	CAS	SECTION #302 TPQ	SECTION #304 R Q		RCRA	TRI#313	AB2588
			CERCLA	OTHER EHS			
Fumaric acid	110-17-8		5000				
Furan	110-00-9	500	100		U124		
Furan, tetrahydro-	109-99-9		1000		U213		
2-Furancarboxaldehyde	98-01-1		5000		U125		
2,5-Furandione	108-31-6		5000		U147	1.0 %	1,2
Gallium trichloride	13450-90-3	500/10,000		1#			
Gasoline vapors	*						2
Glu-P-1 (2-Amino-6-methyldipyrido [1,2-a:3',2'-d]imidazole)	67730-11-4 --						3
Glu-P-2 (2-Aminidipyridol [1,2-a:3',2'-d]imidazole	67730-12-5 --						3
D-Glucopyranose, 2-deoxy-2-(3-methyl-3-nitrosoureido)-	18883-66-4		1#		U206		3,4,5
Glutraldehyde	111-30-8						6
Glycidylaldehyde	765-33-4		1#		U126		
Glycol Ethers	- 0					X	6

NAME	CAS	SECTION #302 TPQ	CERCLA	OTHER EHS	RCRA	TRI#313	AB2588
Griseofulvin	126-07-8						3
Guanidine, N-nitroso-N-methyl-N'-nitro-	70-25-7			1#	U163		3
Gyromitrin Acetalhyde methylformylhydrazone	16568-02-8						
Haloethers	-0			**			
Halomethanes	-0			**			
Heptachlor	76-44-8			1#	P059	1.0 %	
Heptachlor and Metabolites	-0			**			
Heptachlor epoxide	1024-57-3			1#			
Hexachloro-1,3-butadiene	87-68-3			1#	U128	1.0 %	
Hexachlorobenzene	118-74-1			1#	U127	0.1 %	
alpha-Hexachlorocyclohexane (HCCH)	319-84-6			1#			
beta-Hexachlorocyclohexane	319-85-7			1#			
gamma-Hexachlorocyclohexane (Lindane)	58-89-9	1,000/10,000		1#	U129	0.1 %	
Hexachlorocyclohexanes	*						3,4,5
Hexachlorocyclopentadiene	77-47-4	100		1#	U130	1.0 %	2
Hexachloroethane (1,1,1,2,2,2-)	67-72-1			1#	U131	1.0 %	
Hexachloronaphthalene	1335-87-1	De-listed				1.0 %	
Hexachlorophene	70-30-4			100	U132		
Hexachloropropene	1888-71-7			1000			

LIST OF LIST
REVISED 8/23/88

NAME	CAS	SECTION #302 TPQ	SECTION #304 R Q CERCLA	OTHER EHS	RCRA	TRI#313	AB2588
Hexaethyl tetraphosphate	757-58-4		100		P062		
Hexamethylenediamine, N,N'-dibutyl-	4835-11-4	500		1#			
Hexamethylphosphoramide	680-31-9					0.1 %	3,4,5
Hydrazine	302-01-2	1,000		1#	U133	0.1 %	3,4,5
Hydrazine sulfate	10034-93-2					0.1 %	4,5
Hydrazobenzene	122-66-7			1#	U109	0.1 %	4,5
Hydrochloric acid ***	7647-01-0	500	5000			1.0 %	2
Hydrocyanic acid (Hydrogen cyanide)	74-90-8	100	10		P063	1.0 %	2
Hydrogen fluoride	7664-39-3	100	100		U134	1.0 %	2
Hydrogen peroxide	7722-84-1	1000		1#			
Hydrogen selenide	7783-07-5	10		1#		G	
Hydrogen sulfide	7783-06-4	500	100		U135		2
Hydroquinone	123-31-9	500/10,000		1#		1.0 %	
Indeno(1,2,3-cd)pyrene	193-39-5			1#	U137		3,4,5
IQ (2-Amino-3-methylimidaz	76180-96-6						3
[4,5-f]quinoline	--						
Isotretinoin	4759-48-2						4
Iron dextran complex (ferric form only)	9004-66-4		5000**		U139		3,4,5
Iron, pentacarbonyl- (Iron carbonyl)	13463-40-6	100		1#			
Isobenzan	297-78-9	100/10,000		1#			
Isocyanic acid, 3,4-dichlorophenyl ester	102-36-3	500/10,000		1#			
Isodrin	465-73-6	100/10,000	1#		P060		
Isofluorphate	55-91-4	100	100		P043		
Isophorone	78-59-1		5000				
Isophorone diisocyanate	4098-71-9	100		1#			
Isoprene	78-79-5		100				
Isopropanolamine dodecylbenzene sulfonate	42504-46-1		1000				
Isopropyl alcohol (mfg.-strong acid processes)	67-63-0					0.1 %	
Isopropyl benzene	98-82-8		5000		U055	1.0 %	
Isopropyl chloroformate	108-23-6	1,000		1#			
Isopropyl formate	625-55-8	500		1#			
4,4'-Isopropylidenediphenol	80-05-7					1.0 %	
Isopropylmethylpyrazolyl dimethylcarbamate	119-38-0	500		1#			
Kepone	143-50-0		1#		U142		3,4

LIST OF LIST
REVISED 8/23/88

NAME	CAS	SECTION #302 TPQ	SECTION #304 R Q CERCLA	OTHER EHS	RCRA	TRI#313	AB2588
Lactonitrile	78-97-7	1000		1#			
Lasiocarpine	303-34-4		1#		U143		
Lead	7439-92-1		1#		X	1.0 %	1
Lead Fluoborate	13814-96-5		100		G		
Lead Compounds	-0		**			X	1,6
Lead arsenate [AsH3O4.xPb]	7645-25-2		5000#		G		
Lead arsenate [3(AsH3O4).2Pb]	10102-48-4		5000#		G		
Lead arsenate [AsH3O4.Pb]	7784-40-9		5000#		G		
Lead chloride	7758-95-4		100		G		
Lead fluoride	7783-46-2		100	G			
Lead iodide	10101-63-0		100		G		
Lead nitrate	10099-74-8		100		G		
Lead phosphate	7446-27-7		1#		U145	G	
Lead stearate [2(C18H36O2).Pb]	1072-35-1		5000*		G		
Lead stearate [C18H36O2.Pb]	7428-48-0		5000		G		
Lead stearate [dibasic]	52652-59-2		5000		G		
Lead stearate [C36H70O6.Pb]	56189-09-4		5000		G		
Lead subacetate	1335-32-6		1#		U146	G	
Lead sulfate [H2SO4.Pb]	7446-14-2		100		G		
Lead sulfate [H2SO4.xPb]	15739-80-7		100		G		
Lead sulfide	1314-87-0		5000*		G		
Lead thiocyanate	592-87-0		100		G		
Leptophos	21609-90-5	500/10,000		1#			
Lewisite	541-25-3	10		1#			
Lindane ("gamma-BHC")	58-89-9	1,000/10,000	1#		U129	0.1 %	
Lithium chromate	14307-35-8		1000#			G	
Lithium hydride	7580-67-8	100		1#			
Malathion	121-75-5		100				
Maleic acid	110-16-7		5000				
Maleic anhydride	108-31-6		5000		U147	1.0 %	1,2
Malononitrile	109-77-3	500/10,000	1000		U149		
Maneb	12427-38-2					1.0%	
Manganese	7439-96-5					1.0 %	1,2
Manganese Compounds	- -0						

LIST OF LIST
REVISED 8/23/88

NAME	CAS	SECTION #302 TPQ	SECTION #304 R Q CERCLA	OTHER EHS	RCRA	TRI#313	AB2588
Manganese, tricarbonyl methylcyclopentadienyl	12108-13-3	1000#		1#		G	
Mechlorethamine	51-75-2	10		1#		0.1 %	3,4,5
Melamine	108-78-1					1.0 %	
Melphalan	148-82-3		1#		U150		3,4,5
Mephosfolan	950-10-7	500		1#			
Mercuric acetate	1600-27-7	500/10,000		1#		G	
Mercuric chloride	7487-94-7	500/10,000		1#		G	2
Mercuric cyanide	592-04-1		1			G	
Mercuric nitrate	10045-94-0		10			G	
Mercuric oxide	21908-53-2	500/10,000		1#		G	
Mercuric sulfate	7783-35-9		10			G	
Mercuric thiocyanate	592-85-8		10			G	
Mercurous nitrate	7782-86-7		10##			G	
Mercurous nitrate	10415-75-5		10			G	

NAME	CAS	SECTION #302 TPQ	SECTION #304 RQ CERCLA	OTHER EHS	RCRA	TRI#313	AB2588
Mercury	7439-97-6		1		U151	1.0 %	1,2
Mercury Compounds	-0		**			X	
Mestranol	72-33-3						3,5
Methacrolein diacetate	10476-95-6	1000		1#			
Methacrylic anhydride	760-93-0	500		1#			
Methacrylonitrile	126-98-7	500	1000		U152		
Methacryloyl chloride	920-46-7	100		1#			
Methacryloyloxyethyl isocyanate	30674-80-7	100		1#			
Methamidophos	10265-92-6	100/10,000		1#			
Methane, bromo	74-83-9	1000	1000		U029	1.0 %	1,2,6
Methane, chloro (Methyl chloride)	74-87-3		1#		U045	1.0 %	
Methane, dibromo-	74-95-3		1000		U068	1.0 %	
Methane, dichloro- (Methylene dichloride)	75-09-2		1000		U080	1.0 %	1,2,3,
Methane, iodo-	74-88-4		1#		U138	0.1 %	5
Methane, trichlorofluoro-	75-69-4		5000		U121		
Methanesulfonyl fluoride	558-25-8	1000		1#			
Methanol	67-56-1		5,000		U154	1.0 %	2
Methapyrilene	91-80-5		5000		U155		
Methidathion	950-37-8	500/10,000		1#			
Methiocarb	2032-65-7	500/10,000	10				

LIST OF LIST

REVISED 8/23/88

NAME	CAS	SECTION #302 TPQ	SECTION #304 RQ CERCLA	OTHER EHS	RCRA	TRI#313	AB2588
Methomyl	16752-77-5	500/10,000	100		P066		
Methoxychlor	72-43-5		1#		U247	1.0 %	
2-Methoxyethanol	109-86-4					1.0 %	
Methoxyethylmercuric acetate	151-38-2	500/10,000		1#		G	
5-Methoxysoralen	4484-20-8						3
Methyl 2-chloroacrylate	80-63-7	500		1#			
Methyl acrylate	96-33-3					1.0 %	
Methyl bromide (Bromomethane)	74-83-9	1000	1000		U029	1.0 %	1,2,6
Methyl chloride (Chloromethane)	74-87-3		1#		U045	1.0 %	
Methyl chloroform (1,1,1-trichloroethane)	71-55-6		1000		U226	1.0 %	1,2,6
Methyl chloroformate	79-22-1	500	1000		U156		
Methyl disulfide	624-92-0	100		1#			
Methyl iodide (Iodomethane)	74-88-4		1#		U138	0.1 %	5
Methyl ethyl ketone	78-98-3		5000		U159	1.0%	
Methyl isobutyl ketone	108-10-1		5000		U161	1.0 %	
Methyl isocyanate	624-83-9	500	1###		P064	1.0 %	2
Methyl isothiocyanate	556-61-6	500		1#			
Methyl mercaptan	74-93-1	500	100		U153		
Methyl mercury (Dimethyl mercury)	593-74-8						4
Methyl methacrylate	80-62-6		1000		U162	1.0 %	2,8
Methyl methansulfonate	66-27-3						3
2-Methyl-1-nitroanthraquinone	129-15-7						3
(uncertain purity)	--						
3-Methyl-nitrosaminoproplonitrile	50153-49-3						3
4-(Methyl-nitrosoamino)-1-((3-pyridyl)-	64091-91-4						3
1-butanone (NNK)	--						
Methyl phenkapton	3735-23-7	500		1#			
Methyl phosphonic dichloride	676-97-1	100		1#			
Methyl tert-butyl ether	1634-04-4					1.0 %	
Methyl thiocyanate	556-64-9	10,000		1#			
Methyl vinyl ketone	78-94-4	10		1#			
1-Methylbutadiene	504-60-9		100		U186		
Methylene Bis(2-chloroaniline) (MBOCA)	101-14-4		1#		U158	0.1 %	3,4,5
4,4'-Methylene bis(N,N dimethyl) benzenamine	101-61-1					0.1 %	5

LIST OF LIST
REVISED 8/23/88

NAME	CAS	SECTION #302 TPQ	SECTION #304 R Q		RCRA	TRI#313	AB2588
			CERCLA	OTHER EHS			
Methylene bis(phenylisocyanate) (MBI)	101-68-8					1.0 %	
Methylene bromide (Dibromomethane)	74-95-3		1000		U068	1.0 %	
Methylene chloride (Methylene dichloride)	75-09-2		1000		U080	1.0 %	1,2,3,
4,4'-Methylene dianiline	101-77-9					0.1 %	5
Methylhydrazine	60-34-4	500	10		P068	1.0 %	
Methylmercuric dicyanamide	502-39-6	500/10,000		1#		G	
Methylthiouracil	56-04-2		1#		U164		3
Methyltrichlorosilane	75-79-6	500		1#			
Metolcarb	1129-41-5	100/10,000		1#			
Metronidazole	443-48-1						3,4,5
Mevinphos	7786-34-7	500	10		X		
Mexacarbate	315-18-4	500/10,000	1000				
Michler's ketone	90-94-8					0.1 %	4,5
Mineral fibers	*						2
Mineral oils	*						3,5
Mirex	2385-85-5						3,4,5
Mitomycin C	50-07-7	500/10,000	1#		U010		3
Molybdenum trioxide	1313-27-5					1.0 %	
Monocrotaline	315-22-0						3
Monocrotophos	6923-22-4	10/10,000		1#			
Monoethylamine	75-04-7		100				
Monomethylamine	74-89-5		100				
5-(Morphollnommethyl)-3-[(5-nitro furfurylldene)amino]-2-oxazolldinone	139-91-3 --						3
Muscimol	2763-96-4	10,000	1000		P007		
Mustard gas	505-60-2	500		1#		0.1 %	3,4,5
Nafenoplin	377-11-9						,4,5
Naled	300-76-5		10				
Naphthalene	91-20-3		100		U165	1.0 %	2
1,4-Naphthalenedione	130-15-4		5000		U166		
Naphthenic acid	1338-24-5		100				
1-Naphthylamine	134-32-7		1#		U167	0.1 %	
2-Naphthylamine	91-59-8		1#		U168	0.1 %	3,4,5
alpha-Naphthylamine	134-32-7		1#		U167	0.1 %	

LIST OF LIST
REVISED 8/23/88

NAME	CAS	SECTION #302 TPQ	SECTION #304 R Q		RCRA	TRI#313	AB2588
			CERCLA	OTHER EHS			
beta-Naphthylamine	91-59-8		1#		U168	0.1 %	3,4,5
Nickel	7440-02-0	Removed	1#			0.1 %	1,2,3,
Nickel ammonium sulfate	15699-18-0		5000#			G	
Nickel compounds	-0		**			X	3
Nickel carbonyl	13463-39-3	1	1#		P073	G	
Nickel chloride (No longer used-see 7718-54-9)	37211-05-5		5000#			G	
Nickel chloride [Cl2Ni]	7718-54-9		5000			G	
Nickel cyanide	557-19-7		1#.		P074	G	
Nickel hydroxide	12054-48-7		1000#			G	
Nickel nitrate	14216-75-2		5000#			G	
Nickel sulfate	7786-81-4		5000#			G	
Nicotine	54-11-5	100	100		P075		

Name	CAS	Section #302 TPQ	Section #304 RQ	RCRA	TRI#313	AB2588
Nicotine sulfate	65-30-5	100/10,000	1#			
Niridazole	61-57-4					3
Nitric acid	7697-37-2	1000	1000		1.0 %	
Nitric oxide	10102-43-9	100	10	P076		
Nitrilotriacetic acid	139-13-9				0.1 %	4,5
N-Nitro di-N-propylamine	621-64-7		1#	U111	0.1 %	3,4,5
5-Nitroacenaphthene	602-87-9					3
5-Nitro-o-anisidine	99-59-2				0.1 %	5
Nitrobenzene	98-95-3	10,000	1000	U169	1.0 %	1 ,2
4-Nitrobiphenyl	92-93-3				0.1 %	
Nitrocyclohexane	1122-60-7	500	1#			
Nitrofen (TOK)	1836-75-5				0.1 %	3,4,5
1-[(5-Nitrofurfurylidend)amino]	555-84-0					3
2-imidazolidinone	--					
N-[4-(5-Nitro-2-furyl)	531-82-8					3
2-thiazolyl]acetamide	--					
Nitrogen dioxide [same as 10102-44-0]	10544-72-6		10	P078		
Nitrogen dioxide [same as 10544-72-6]	10102-44-0	100	10	P078		
Nitrogen Mustard	51-75-2	10	1#		0.1 %	3,4,5
Nitrogen mustard N-oxide	302-70-5					3,4
Nitrogen oxide	10102-43-9	100	10	P078		
Nitroglycerine	55-63-0		10	P018	1.0 %	

LIST OF LIST
REVISED 8/23/88

NAME	CAS	SECTION #302 TPQ	SECTION #304 RQ			RCRA	TRI#313	AB2588
			CERCLA	OTHER	EHS			
o-Nitrophenol	88-75-5		100				1.0 %	
Nitrophenol (mixed)	25154-55-6		100					
m-Nitrophenol	554-84-7		100					
p-Nitrophenol	100-02-7		100			U170	1.0 %	
Nitrophenols	-0		**					
2-Nitropropane	79-46-9		1#			U171	0.1 %	3,4,5
Nitrosamines	-0		**					
N-Nitroso di-N-Butylamine	924-16-3		1#			U172	0.1 %	3,4,5
N-Nitoso di-ethylamine	4549-40-0		1#			P084	0.1 %	3,4,5
N-Nitrosomethylethylamine	10595-95-6							3
(N-Methyl-N-nitrosoureathane)	--							
N-Nitroso-N-Methylurea	684-93-5		1#			U177	0.1 %	3,4,5
N-Nitroso-N-ethylurea	759-73-9		1#			U176	0.1 %	
3-Nitroso-N-methyl-N'-nitroquanidine	70-25-7		1#			U163		3
N-Nitrosodiethanolamine	1116-54-7		1#			U173		3,4,5
N-Nitrosodiethylamine	55-18-5		1#			U174	0.1 %	3,4,5
Nitrosodimethylamine	62-75-9	1,000	1#			P082	0.1 %	3,4,5
N-Nitrosodiphenylamine	86-30-6		100				1.0 %	
p-Nitrosodiphenylamine	156-10-5						0.1 %	5
N-Nitrosomethylvinylamine	4549-40-0		1#			P084	0.1 %	3,4,5
N-Nitrosomorpholine	59-89-2						0.1 %	1,2,3,
N-Nitrosonornicotine	16543-55-8						0.1 %	3,4,5
N-Nitrosopiperidine	100-75-4		1#			U179	0.1 %	3,4,5
N-Nitrosodi-N-propylamine	621-64-7		1#			U111	0.1 %	3,4,5
3-Nitrosopyrrolidine	930-55-2		1#			U180		3,4,5
N-Nitrososarcosine	13256-22-9							3,4,5
Nitrotoluene	1321-12-6		1000					
p-Nitrotoluene	99-99-0		1000					
m-Nitrotoluene	99-08-1		1000					
o-Nitrotoluene	88-72-2		1000					
Norbormide	991-42-4	100/10,000	1#					
Norethisterone	68-22-4							3,5
Octachloronaphthalene	2234-13-1						1.0 %	
Oil Orange SS	2646-17-5							3

LIST OF LIST
REVISED 8/23/88

NAME	CAS	SECTION #302 TPQ	SECTION #304 R Q CERCLA	OTHER EHS	RCRA	TRI#313	AB2588
Osmium tetroxide	20816-12-0	De-listed	1000		P087	1.0 %	
Ouabain	630-60-4	100/10,000		1#			
Oxamyl	23135-22-0	100/10,000		1#			
1,2-Oxathiolane, 2,2-dioxide	1120-71-4		1#		U193	0.1 %	3,4,5
Oxetane, 3,3-bis(chloromethyl)-	78-71-7	500		1#			
Oxydisulfoton	2497-07-6	500		1#			
Oxymethhholone	434-07-1						3,4,5
Ozone	10028-15-6	100		1#			
Panfuran S (Dihydroxymethylfuratrizine)	794-93-4						3,4
Paraformaldehyde	30525-89-4		1000				
Paraldehyde	123-63-7		1000				
Paraquat	1910-42-5	10/10,000		1#			
Paraquat methosulfate	2074-50-2	10/10,000		1#			
Parathion	56-38-2	100	1#		P089	1.0 %	
Parathion-methyl	298-00-0	100/10,000	100		P071		
Paris green	12002-03-8	500/10,000	100#				
Pentaborane	19624-22-7	500		1#			
Pentachloroethane	76-01-7	De-listed	1#		U184		
Pentachlorophenol	87-86-5	De-listed	10*		U242	1.0 %	
Pentadecylamine	2570-26-5	100/10,000		1#			
Peracetic acid	79-21-0	500		1#		1.0 %	
Perchloroethylene [1,1,2,2-tetrachloroethene]	127-18-4		1#		U210	1.0 %	1,2,6
Perchloromethylmercaptan	594-42-3	500	100		P118		
Phenacetin	62-44-2		1#		U178		3,5
Phenanthrene	85-01-8		5000				
Phenazopyridine hydrochloride	94-78-0						3,4,5
Phenobarbitol	50-06-6						3
Phenol	108-95-2	500/10,000	1000		U188	1.0 %	1,2
Phenol, 2,2'-thiobis(4,6-dichloro)-	97-18-7	100/10,000		1#			
Phenol, 2,2'-thiobis[4-chloro-6-methyl]-	4418-66-0	100/10,000		1#			
Phenol, 2,3,4,6-tetrachloro-	58-90-2		10		U212	G	
Phenol, 2,4,5-trichloro-	95-95-4		10#		U230	1.0 %	
Phenol, 3-(1-methylethyl)-, methylcarbamate	64-00-6	500/10,000		1#			
Phenol,2,4,6-trichloro	88-06-2		10#		U231	0.1 %	1,4

LIST OF LIST
REVISED 8/23/88

NAME	CAS	SECTION #302 TPQ	SECTION #304 R Q CERCLA	OTHER EHS	RCRA	TRI#313	AB2588
Phenoxarsine, 10,10'-oxydi-	58-36-6	500/10,000		1#		G	
Phenyl dichloroarsine	696-28-6	500	1#		P036	G	
p-Phenylenediamine	106-50-3					1.0 %	
Phenylhydrazine hydrochloride	59-88-1	1,000/10,000		1#			
Phenylmercury acetate	62-38-4	500/10,000	100		P092	G	
2-Phenylphenol	90-43-7					1.0 %	
Phenylsilatrane	2097-19-0	100/10,000		1#			
Phenylthiourea	103-85-5	100/10,000	100		P093		
Phenytoin	57-41-0						3,4,5
Phorate	298-02-2	10	10		P094		
Phosacetim	4104-14-7	100/10,000		1#			
Phosfolan	947-02-4	100/10,000		1#			
Phosgene	75-44-5	10	10		P095	1.0 %	2
Phosmet	732-11-6	10/10,000		1#			
Phosphamidon	13171-21-6	100		1#			

NAME	CAS	SECTION #302 TPQ	CERCLA	OTHER EHS	RCRA	TRI#313	AB2588
Phosphine (Hydrogen phosphite)	7803-51-2	500	100		P096		
Phosphonothioic acid, methyl-, O-ethyl O-(4-	2703-13-1	500		1#			
Phosphorothioic acid,o,o-dimethyl-S-(2methylthi)ethyl est (methylthio)phenyl)		500		1#			
Phosphonothioic acid, methyl-, S-(2-(bis(1-methylethyl) amino)ethyl)O-ethyl ester	50782-69-9	100		1#			
Phosphonothioic acid, methyl-,O-(4-nitrophenyl) O- phenyl ester	2665-30-7	500		1#			
Phosphoric acid	7664-38-2		5000			1.0 %	
Phosphoric acid, dimethyl 4-(methylthio) phenyl ester	3254-63-5	500		1#			
Phosphorous trichloride	7719-12-2	1000	1000				
Phosphorus	7723-14-0	100	1			1.0 %	2
Phosphorus oxychloride	10025-87-3	500	1000				
Phosphorus pentachloride	10026-13-8	500		1#			
Phosphorus pentasulfide	1314-80-3		100		U189		
Phosphorus pentoxide	1314-56-3	10		1#			
Phthalate Esters	-0		**				
Phthalic anhydride	85-44-9		5000		U190	1.0 %	2
Physostigmine	57-47-6	100/10,000		1#			

LIST OF LIST
REVISED 8/23/88

NAME	CAS	SECTION #302 TPQ	CERCLA	OTHER EHS	RCRA	TRI#313	AB2588
Physostigmine, salicylate (1:1)	57-64-7	100/10,000		1#			
2-Picoline	109-06-8		5000		U191		
Picric acid	88-89-1					1.0 %	
Picrotoxin	124-87-8	500/10,000		1#			
Piperidine	110-89-4	1000		1#			
Piprotal	5281-13-0	100/10,000		1#			
Pirimifos-ethyl	23505-41-1	1000		1#			
Polybrominated Biphenyls (PBBs)	- -0					X	3,4,5
Polychlorinated Biphenyls (PCBs)	1336-36-3		10*			0.1 %	1,2,3,
Polynuclear Aromatic Hydrocarbons	-0		**				1,2
Ponceau 3R	3564-09-8						3
Progesterone	57-83-0						3,4,5
Potassium arsenate (AsH304K)	7784-41-0		1000#			G	
Potassium arsenite (AsH304.xK)	10124-50-2	500/10,000	1000#			G	
Potassium bichromate	7778-50-9		1000#			G	
Potassium bromate	7758-01-2						3
Potassium chromate	7789-00-6		1000#			G	
Potassium cyanide	151-50-8	100	10		P098	G	
Potassium hydroxide	1310-58-3		1000				
Potassium permanganate	7722-64-7		100			G	
Potassium silver cyanide	506-61-6	500	1		P099	G	
Procarbazine hydrochloride	366-70-1						3,4,5
Progestins	*						3
Promecarb	2631-37-0	500/10,000		1#		G	
1-Propanamine	107-10-8		5000		U197		
Propane sultone	1120-71-4			1#	U193	0.1 %	3,4,5
1-Propanol, 2,3-dibromo-, phosphate (3:1)	126-72-7			1#	U235	0.1 %	
Propargite	2312-35-8		10				
Propargyl alcohol	107-19-7		1000		P102		
Propargyl bromide	106-96-7	10		1#			
beta-Propiolactone	57-57-8	500		1#		0.1 %	3,4,5
Propionaldehyde	123-38-6					1.0 %	
Propionic acid	79-09-4		5000				
Propionic acid, 2-(2,4,5-trichlorophenoxy)	93-72-1		100		U233		

LIST OF LIST
REVISED 8/23/88

NAME	CAS	SECTION #302 TPQ	SECTION #304 RQ CERCLA	OTHER EHS	RCRA	TRI#313	AB2588
Propionic anhydride	123-62-6		5000				
Propionitrile	107-12-0	500	10		P101		
Propionitrile, 3-chloro-	542-76-7	1000	1000		P027		
Propiophenone, 4-amino-	70-69-9	100/10,000		1#			
Propoxur	114-26-1					1.0 %	
Propyl chloroformate	109-61-5	500		1#			
Propylene (Propene)	115-07-1					1.0 %	2
Propylene oxide	75-56-9	10,000	100			0.1 %	1,2,3
Propyleneimine	75-55-8	10,000	1#		P067	0.1 %	
Propylthiouracil	51-52-5						3,4,5
Prothoate	2275-18-5	1,000/10,000		1#			
Pseudocumene (1,2,4-trimethylbenzene)	95-63-6	Removed				1.0 %	
Pyrene	129-00-0	1,000/10,000	5000				
Pyrethrins	121-29-9		1				
Pyrethrins	121-21-1		1				
Pyrethrins	8003-34-7		1				
Pyridine	110-86-1		1000		U196	1.0 %	
Pyridine, 2-methyl-5-vinyl-	140-76-1	500		1#			
Pyridine, 4-amino-	504-24-5	500/10,000	1000		P008		
Pyridine, 4-nitro-, 1-oxide	1124-33-0	500/10,000		1#			
Pyriminil	53558-25-1	100/10,000		1#			
Quinoline	91-22-5		5000			1.0 %	
Quinone	106-51-4		10		U197	1.0 %	
Quintozone [Benzene, penta chloro nitro-]	82-68-8		1#		U185	1.0 %	
Radionucides	-0		1^				1,2
Reserpine	50-55-5		5000		U200		5
Saccharin [Manufacture only]	81-07-2		1#		U202	0.1 %	3,4,5
Salcomine	14167-18-1	500/10,000		1#			
Sarin	107-44-8	10		1#			
Selenium	7782-49-2		100		X	1.0 %	2
Selenium Compounds	-0		**			X	2,5
Selenium dioxide	7446-08-4		1000		U204		
Selenium disulfide	7488-56-4		1#		U205	G	
Selenium oxychloride	7791-23-3	500		1#		G	

LIST OF LIST
REVISED 8/23/88

NAME	CAS	SECTION #302 TPQ	SECTION #304 RQ CERCLA	OTHER EHS	RCRA	TRI#313	AB2588
Selenous acid	7783-00-8	1000/10,000	10		U204	G	
Semicarbazide hydrochloride	563-41-7	1000/10,000		1#			
Shale oil	*						3
Silane, (4-aminobutyl)diethoxymethyl-	3037-72-7	1,000		1#			
Silica, crystaline	*						3
Silver	7440-22-4		1000		X	1.0 %	
Silver Compounds	-0		**			X	
Silver cyanide	506-64-9		1#		P104	G	
Silver nitrate	7761-88-8		1			G	
Sodium	7440-23-5		10				

NAME	CAS	SECTION #302 TPQ	CERCLA	OTHER EHS	RCRA	TRI#313	AB2588
Sodium arsenate (AsH304.xNa)	7631-89-2	1,000/10,000	1000#			G	
Sodium arsenite (AsHO2Na)	7784-46-5	500/10,000	1000#			G	
Sodium azide (Na[N3])	26628-22-8	500	1000		P105		
Sodium bichromate	10588-01-9		1000#			G	
Sodium bifluoride	1333-83-1		100				
Sodium bisulfite	7631-90-5		5000				
Sodium cacodylate	124-65-2	100/10,000		1#		G	
Sodium chromate	7775-11-3		1000#			G	
Sodium cyanide (Na(CN))	143-33-9	100	10		P106	G	
Sodium dodecylbenzene sulfonate	25155-30-0		1000				
Sodium fluoride	7681-49-4		1000				
Sodium fluoroacetate	62-74-8	10/10,000	10		P058		
Sodium hydrosulfide (Sodium bisulfide)	16721-80-5		5000				
Sodium hydroxide	1310-73-2		1000			1.0 %	2
Sodium hypochlorite (ClHO.5Na)	10022-70-5		100				
Sodium hypochlorite (ClHO.Na)	7681-52-9		100				
Sodium methylate (Sodium methoxide)	124-41-4		1000				
Sodium nitrite	7632-00-0		100				
Sodium pentachlorophenate	131-52-2	100/10,000		1#			
Sodium o-phenylphenate	132-27-4						3
Sodium phosphate, dibasic (H304P.12H2O.2Na)	10039-32-4		5000				
Sodium phosphate, dibasic (H304P.2Na)	7558-79-4		5000				
Sodium phosphate, dibasic (H304P.xH2O.2Na)	10140-65-5		5000				
Sodium phosphate, tribasic (H6O18P6.6Na)	10124-56-8		5000				

LIST OF LIST
REVISED 8/23/88

NAME	CAS	SECTION #302 TPQ	SECTION #304 R Q CERCLA	OTHER EHS	RCRA	TRI#313	AB2588
Sodium phosphate, tribasic (H304P.10H2O.3Na)	10361-89-4		5000				
Sodium phosphate, tribasic (H304P.12H2O.3Na)	10101-89-0		5000				
Sodium phosphate, tribasic (H304P.3Na)	7601-54-9		5000				
Sodium phosphate, tribasic (H309P.3Na)	7785-84-4		5000				
Sodium phosphate, tribasic (H5O10P3.5Na)	7758-29-4		5000				
Sodium selenate (H204Se.2Na)	13410-01-0	100/10,000		1#		G	
Sodium selenite (H203Se.2Na)	10102-18-8	100/10,000	100			G	
Sodium selenite (disodium penta hydrate)	7782-82-3		100			G	
Sodium sulfate (solution)	7757-82-6					1.0 %	
Sodium tellurite	10102-20-2	500/10,000		1#			
Sterigmatocystin	10048-13-2						3
Stannane, acetoxytriphenyl-	900-95-8	500/10,000		1#			
Streptozotocin	18883-66-4		1#		U206		3,4,5
Strontium chromate	7789-06-2		1000#			G	
Strontium sulfide	1314-96-1		100		P107		
Strychnine	57-24-9	100,10,000	10		P108		
Strychnine, sulfate	60-41-3	100/10,000		1#			
Styrene (MONOMER)	100-42-5		1000			1.0 %	
Styrene oxide	96-09-3					1.0 %	3
Sulfallate	95-06-7						3,4,5
Sulfotep	3689-24-5	500	100		P109		
Sulfoxide, 3-chloropropyl octyl	3569-57-1	500		1#			
Sulfur dioxide	7446-09-5	500		1#			
Sulfur monochloride (Sulfur chloride)	12771-08-3		1000				
Sulfur tetrafluoride	7783-60-0	100		1#			
Sulfur trioxide	7446-11-9	100		1#			
Sulfuric Acid (No longer used - see 7664-93-9)	17107-61-8						
Sulfuric acid	7664-93-9	1000	1000			1.0 %	
Sulfuric acid-fuming [Oleum]	8014-95-7		1000				
2,4,5-T amines	1319-72-8		5000				
2,4,5-T amines	2008-46-0		5000				
2,4,5-T amines	6369-96-6		5000				
2,4,5-T amines	6369-97-7		5000				
2,4,5-T amines	3813-14-7		5000				

LIST OF LIST
REVISED 8/23/88

NAME	CAS	SECTION #302 TPQ	SECTION #304 R Q		RCRA	TRI#313	AB2588
			CERCLA	OTHER EHS			
2,4,5-T esters	2545-59-7		1000				
2,4,5-T esters	61792-07-2		1000				
2,4,5-T esters	25168-15-4		1000				
2,4,5-T esters	93-79-8		1000				
2,4,5-T salts	13560-99-1		1000				
2,4,5-T	93-76-5		1000		U232		
2,4,5-TP acid esters	32534-95-5		100				
Tabun	77-81-6	10		1#			
Talc containing asbestiform fibers	*						3
Tars	*						3,4,5
Tellurium	13494-80-9	500/10,000		1#			
Tellurium hexafluoride	7783-80-4	100		1#			
Tepp	107-49-3	100	10		P111		
Terbufos	13071-79-9	100		1#			
Terephthalic acid	100-21-0					1.0 %	
1,1,2,2-Tetrachloro ethane	79-34-5		1#		U209	1.0 %	
2,3,7,8-Tetrachlorodibenzo-p-dioxin (TCDD)	1746-01-6		1#				3,4,5
Tetrachlorvinphos	961-11-5					1.0 %	
Tetraethyllead	78-00-2	100	10		P110	G	
Tetraethyltin	597-64-8	100		1#		G	
Tetramethyl lead	75-74-1	100		1#		G	
Tetranitromethane	509-14-8	500	10		P112		
Thalldomide	50-35-1						4
Thallic oxide	1314-32-5		100		P113	G	
Thallium	7440-28-0		1000			1.0 %	
Thallium Compounds	-0		**			X	
Thallium(I) nitrate	10102-45-1		100		U217	G	
Thallium(I) selenide	12039-52-0		1000		P114	G	
Thallous carbonate	6533-73-9	100/10,000	100		U215	G	
Thallous chloride	7791-12-0	100/10,000	100		U216	G	
Thallous malonate	2757-18-8	100/10,000		1#		G	
Thallous sulfate	7446-18-6	100/10,000	100		P115	G	
Thallous sulfate	10031-59-1	100/10,000	100		P115	G	
Thioacetamide	62-55-5		1#		U218	0.1 %	3,4,5

LIST OF LIST
REVISED 8/23/88

NAME	CAS	SECTION #302 TPQ	SECTION #304 R Q		RCRA	TRI#313	AB2588
			CERCLA	OTHER EHS			
Thiocarbazide	2231-57-4	1,000/10,000		1#			
4,4'-Thiodianiline	139-65-1					0.1 %	3
Thiofanox	39196-18-4	100/10,000	100		P045		
Thionazin	297-97-2	500	100		P040		
Thiophenol	108-98-5	500	100		P014		
Thiosemicarbazide	79-19-6	100/10,000	100		P116		
Thiourea	62-56-6		1#	1	U219	0.	3,4,5
Thiourea, (2-chlorophenyl)-	5344-82-1	100/10,000	100		P026		
Thiourea, (2-methylphenyl)-	614-78-8	500/10,000		1#			
Thorium dioxide	1314-20-1					1.0 %	4,5
Titanium tetrachloride	7550-45-0	1000		1#		1.0 %	
Tobacco products, smokeless	*						3
Toluene	108-88-3		1000		U220	1.0 %	2,6
alpha-chlorinated toluenes	*						3
Toluene 2,4-diisocyanate	584-84-9	500	100			0.1 %	2,3,5

Name	CAS	Section #302 TPQ	CERCLA	OTHER EHS	RCRA	TRI#313	AB2588
Toluene 2,6-diisocyanate	91-08-7	100	100			0.1 %	2,3,5
o-Toluidine	95-53-4		1#			0.1 %	3,4,5
p-Toluidine	106-49-0		1#		U353		
o-Toluidine hydrochloride	636-21-5		1#		U222	0.1 %	4,5
Toxaphene	8001-35-2	500/10,000	1#		P123	1.0%	
Tresoulfan	299-75-2						3,4
Triamiphos	1031-47-6	500/10,000		1#			
Triaziquone	68-76-8					0.1 %	
Triazofos	24017-47-8	500		1#			
Trichloro(chloromethyl)silane	1558-25-4	100		1#			
Trichloro(dichlorophenyl)silane	27137-85-5	500		1#			
Trichloroacetyl chloride	76-02-8	500		1#			
1,2,4-Trichlorobenzene	120-82-1		100			1.0 %	
1,1,1-Trichloroethane (Methyl chloroform)	71055-6		1000		U226	1.0 %	
1,1,2-Trichloroethane	79-00-5		1#		U227	1.0 %	
Trichloroethylene	79-01-6		1000*		U228	1.0 %	1,2
Trichloroethylsilane	115-21-9	500		1#			
Trichloronate	327-98-0	500		1#			
Trichlorophenol	25167-82-2		10#				

LIST OF LIST
REVISED 8/23/88

NAME	CAS	SECTION #302 TPQ	SECTION #304 RQ		RCRA	TRI#313	AB2588
			CERCLA	OTHER EHS			
2,3,4-Trichlorophenol	15950-66-0		10#				
3,4,5-Trichlorophenol	609-19-8		10*				
2,3,5-Trichlorophenol	933-78-8		10*				
2,3,6-Trichlorophenol	933-75-5		10*				
2,4,5-Trichlorophenol	95-95-4		10#		U230	1.0 %	
2,4,6-Trichlorophenol	88-06-2		10#		U231	0.1 %	1,4
Trichlorophenylsilane	98-13-5	500		1#			
Trichlorophon	52-68-6	De-listed	100			1.0 %	
Triethanolamine dodecylbenzene sulfonate	27323-41-7		1000				
Triethoxysilane	998-30-1	500		1#			
Triethylamine	121-44-8		5000				
Trifluralin	1582-09-8					1.0 %	
Trimethylamine	75-50-3		100				
Trimethylbenzene	95-63-6	De-listed				1.0 %	
Trimethylchlorosilane	75-77-4	1,000		1#			
Trimethylolpropane phosphite	824-11-3	100/10,000		1#			
Trimethyltin chloride	1066-45-1	500/10,000		1#		G	
Triphenyltin chloride	639-58-7	500/10,000		1#		G	
Tris (2,3-dibromopropyl) phosphate (3:1)	126-72-7			1#	U235	0.1 %	
Tris(1-azuiridinyl)phosphine sulfide (Thiotepa)	52-24-4 / --						3,4,5
Trp-P-1 (3-amino-1,4-dimetthyl-5H-pyrido[4,3-b]indole)	62450-06-0 / --						3
Trp-P-2 (3-Amino-1-methyl-5H pyrido[4,3-b]indole)	62450-07-1 / --						3
Trypan blue	72-57-1		1#		U236		3
Uracil, 5-[bis(2-chloroethyl)amino]-	66-75-1		1#		U237		3
Uranyl acetate	541-09-3		100'''				
Uranyl nitrate	10102-06-4		100'''				
Uranyl nitrate	36478-76-9		100'''				
Urethane [Ethyl carbamate]	51-79-6		1#		U238	0.1 %	3,4,5
Valinomycin	2001-95-8	1,000/10,000		1#			
Valproate	99-66-1						4

LIST OF LIST
REVISED 8/23/88

NAME	CAS	SECTION #302 TPQ	SECTION #304 RQ CERCLA	OTHER EHS	RCRA	TRI#313	AB2588
Vanadium (fume or dust)	7440-62-2					1.0 %	
Vanadium pentoxide	1314-62-1	100/10,000	1000		P120		
Vanadyl sulfate (Vanadium sulfate)	27774-13-6		1000				
Vinyl Chloride (monomer)	75-01-4		1#		U043	0.1 %	1,2,3,
Vinyl acetate (monomer)	108-05-4	1000	5000			1.0 %	
Vinyl bromide	593-60-2					0.1 %	3
Vinylidene chloride (monomer)	75-35-4		5000*		U078	1.0 %	1,2
Warfarin	81-81-2	500/10,000	100		P001		4
Warfarin sodium	129-06-6	100/10,000		1#			
m-Xylene	108-38-3		1000		X	1.0 %	
o-Xylene	95-47-6		1000			1.0 %	
p-Xylene	106-42-3		1000		X	1.0 %	
Xylene	1300-71-6		1000				
Xylenes	*						1,2,6
2,6-Xylidine	87-62-7					1.0 %	
Zylylene dichloride	28347-13-9	100/10,000		1#			
Zinc	7440-66-6		1000			1.0 %	2
Zinc acetate	557-34-6		1000		G		
Zinc ammonium chloride	52628-25-8		1000		G		
Zinc ammonium chloride (C14Zn.2H4N)	14639-97-5		5000##		G		
Zinc ammonium chloride (C15Zn.3H4N)	14639-98-6		5000##		G		
Zinc Compounds	-0		**		X		
Zinc borate	1332-07-6		1000		G		
Zinc bromide	7699-45-8		1000		G		
Zinc carbonate	3486-35-9		1000		G		
Zinc chloride	7646-85-7		1000		G		
Zinc cyanide	557-21-1		10		P121	G	
Zinc fluoride	7783-49-5		1000		G		
Zinc formate	557-41-5		1000		G		
Zinc hydrosulfite	7779-86-4		1000		G		
Zinc nitrate	7779-88-6		1000		G		
Zinc oxide	1314-13-2						2
Zinc phenolsulfonate	127-82-2		5000		G		
Zinc phosphide	1314-84-7	500	100		P122	G	

LIST OF LIST
REVISED 8/23/88

NAME	CAS	SECTION #302 TPQ	SECTION #304 RQ CERCLA	OTHER EHS	RCRA	TRI#313	AB2588
Zinc silicofluoride	16871-71-9		5000			G	
Zinc sulfate	7733-02-0		1000			G	
Zinc, dichloro(4,4-dimethyl-5((((methylamino) carbonyl) oxy)imino)pentanenitrile,-	58270-08-9	100/10,000		1#		G	
Zineb	12122-67-7					1.0 %	
Zirconium nitrate	13746-89-9		5000				
Zirconium potassium fluoride	16923-95-8		1000				
Zirconium sulfate	14644-61-2		5000				
Zirconium tetrachloride	10026-11-6		5000				

STCW&WON REVISED 8/23/88 (BillD)

APPENDIX D

FORM R REQUIRED FOR SECTION 313 TOXIC CHEMICAL RELEASE REPORTING; EXCERPT FROM EPA 560/4-88-005

INSTRUCTIONS FOR COMPLETING
SPECIFIC SECTIONS OF EPA FORM R

The following are specific instructions for completing each part of EPA Form R. The number designations of the parts and sections of these instructions correspond to those in Form R unless otherwise indicated.

Instructions for Completing All Parts of the Form:

1. Type or print information on the form in the units and format requested.

2. Use place-holding zeros (e.g., if the CAS number is 108-88-3, the entry should read 000108-88-3).

3. Much of the information requested on the form is required. Some information is optional for the first year, as described in the instructions. Do not leave required information blank. If the required information does not apply to you, enter not applicable [N/A] in the space provided. If several spaces are provided and your information does not fill them all, enter not applicable [N/A] in the next blank space in the sequence.

4. Do not submit an incomplete form. The certification statement (Part I) specifies that the report is complete as submitted.

5. When completing Part IV (Supplemental Information) or additional pages for Part II of the form, number or letter the additional information sequentially from the prior sections of the form.

An example of a completed Form R for a hypothetical facility reporting under Title III, section 313 is included in Appendix D.

PART I. FACILITY IDENTIFICATION INFORMATION

1.1 Does This Report Contain Trade Secret Information?

Answer this question only after you have completed the rest of the report. The specific identity of the toxic chemical being reported in Part III, Sections 1.2 and 1.3, may be designated as trade secret. If you are making a trade secret claim, answer by marking the "yes" box and proceed to Section 1.2. (See Part III, Section 1, of these instructions for specific instructions on trade secrecy claims.) If the answer is no, proceed to Section 1.3.

1.2 Is This a Sanitized Copy?

Answer this question only after you have completed the rest of the report. Answer yes if this copy of the report is the public "sanitized" version of a report where the chemical identity is claimed trade secret in Part III, Section 1.4, of the report. Otherwise, answer no.

1.3 Reporting Year

In Section 1.3, you must enter the year to which the reported information applies, not the year in which you are submitting the report.

2. Certification

The certification statement must be signed by the owner or operator, or a senior official with management responsibility for the person (or persons) completing the form. The owner, operator, or official must certify the accuracy and completeness of the information reported on the form by signing and dating the certification statement. Each report must contain an original signature. Print or type the name and title of the person who signs the statement in the space provided. This certification statement applies to all the information supplied on the form, and should be signed only after the form has been completed.

3. Facility Identification

3.1 Facility Name and Location

You must enter the name of your facility (plant site name or appropriate facility designation), street address, city, county, state, and zip code in the space provided. You may not use a post office box number for this location information. The address provided should be the location where the chemicals are manufactured, processed, or otherwise used.

3.2 Full or Partial Facility Indication

You must indicate whether your report is for the covered facility as a whole or for part of a covered facility. Check box a. if this report contains information about a chemical for an entire covered facility. Check box b. if the report contains information about a chemical but for only part of a covered facility. Thresholds should be figured for an entire facility.

Section 313 requires reports by "facilities" defined as "all buildings, equipment, structures, and other stationary items which are located on a single site or on contiguous or adjacent sites and which are owned or operated by the same person."

The SIC code system defines business "establishments" as "distinct and separate economic activities [which] are performed at a single physical location." Under section 372.30(c) of the reporting rule you may choose to submit a separate Form R for each establishment, or for groups of establishments, in your covered facility. This allows you the option of reporting separately on the activities involving a toxic chemical at each establishment, or group of establishments (e.g., part of a covered facility), rather than submitting a single Form R for that chemical for the entire facility. You may do this provided that all releases of the toxic chemicals from the covered facility are reported. However, if an establishment or group of establishments does not manufacture, process, or otherwise use a toxic chemical, then you do not have to submit a report on that chemical from that establishment or group of establishments.

3.3 Technical Contact

You must enter the name and telephone number (including area code) of a technical representative whom EPA or State officials may contact for clarification of the information reported on the form. This person does not have to be the person who prepares the report or signs the certification statement. However, this person must have detailed knowledge of the report to be able to respond to questions.

3.4 Public Contact

You must enter the name and telephone number of a person who can respond to questions from the public about the report. If you choose to designate the same person as both the technical and the public contact, you may enter "same as 3.3" in this space. If no public contact is designated in Section 3.4, EPA will treat the technical contact as the public contact.

3.5 Standard Industrial Classification (SIC) Code

You must enter the appropriate 4-digit primary Standard Industrial Classification (SIC) code for your facility (see Table I on page 22). If the report covers more than one establishment, enter the primary 4 digit SIC code for each establishment. You are only required to enter SIC codes for establishments within the facility that fall within SIC codes 20 to 39. Refer to Table I for a listing of these SIC codes. Use the supplemental information sheet (Part IV) if you need to enter more than three SIC codes.

3.6 Latitude and Longitude

Enter the latitudinal and longitudinal coordinates of your facility. You must supply latitude and longitude for calendar year 1987 reports if the information is readily available to you. Sources of these data include EPA permits (e.g., NPDES permits), county property records, facility blueprints, and site plans. If these geographic coordinates are not readily available to you for calendar year 1987 reports, enter not applicable [N/A].

Instructions on the development of coordinates can be found in Appendix A. All facilities are required to provide this information in reports submitted for the calendar year 1988 and subsequent years. Use leading place holding zeros.

3.7 Facility Dun and Bradstreet Number

You must use the number assigned by Dun and Bradstreet for your facility or each establishment within your facility. This may be available from your facility's treasurer or financial officer. If none of your establishments have been assigned Dun and Bradstreet Numbers, indicate this in Section 3.7 by entering not applicable [N/A] in box a. If only some of your establishments have been assigned Dun and Bradstreet numbers, enter those numbers in Section 3.7. Use leading place holding zeros. For more than two establishments, use the supplemental information sheet (Part IV).

3.8 EPA Identification Number

If your facility has been assigned EPA Identification Numbers, you must enter those numbers. The EPA I.D. Number is a 12-digit number assigned to facilities covered by hazardous waste regulations under the Resource Conservation and Recovery Act (RCRA). Facilities not covered by RCRA are not likely to have an assigned I.D. Number. If your facility does not have an I.D. Number, enter not applicable [N/A] in box a. If your facility has more than two numbers, use the supplemental information sheet (Part IV).

3.9 NPDES Permit Numbers

You must enter the numbers of any permits your facility holds under the National Pollutant Discharge Elimination System (NPDES). This 9-digit permit number is assigned to your facility by EPA or the State under the authority of the Clean Water Act. If your facility has more than two permits, use the supplemental information sheet (Part IV). If your facility does not have a permit, enter not applicable [N/A] in box a.

3.10 Name of Receiving Stream or Water Body

You must enter the name of each surface water body or receiving stream to which the chemical being reported is directly discharged. Report the name of each receiving stream or water body as it appears on the NPDES permit for the facility. If you do not have a permit, enter the name of the off-site stream or water body to allow for the evaluation of watersheds. Enter not applicable [N/A] if you do not discharge any listed toxic chemicals to surface water bodies. If your facility discharges the toxic chemical to more than three receiving streams or water bodies, use the supplemental information sheet (Part IV).

3.11 Underground Injection Well Code (UIC) Identification Number

If your facility has a permit to inject chemical-containing waste which includes the toxic chemical into Class 1 deep wells, you must enter the Underground Injection Control (UIC) 12-digit identification number assigned by EPA or by the State under the authority of the Safe Drinking Water Act. If your facility does not hold such a permit, enter not applicable [N/A] in this space.

4. Parent Company Information

You must provide information on your parent company. For purposes of this form, a parent company is defined as a company which directly owns at least 50 percent of the voting stock of another company.

4.1 Name of Parent Company

You must enter the name of the corporation or other business entity that is your parent company. If you have no parent company enter not applicable [N/A].

4.2 Parent Company's Dun & Bradstreet Number

If applicable, you must enter the Dun and Bradstreet Number for your parent company. The number may be obtained from the treasurer or financial officer of the company. If your parent company does not have a Dun and Bradstreet number, enter not applicable [N/A]. Use leading place holding zeros.

PART II. OFF-SITE LOCATIONS TO WHICH TOXIC CHEMICALS ARE TRANSFERRED IN WASTES

This section requires a listing of all off-site locations to which you transfer wastes containing the toxic chemical. The information that you enter in this section relates to data to be reported in Part III, Section 6, of the form. List only publicly owned treatment works (POTW) and off-site treatment or disposal facilities. Do not list locations to which products containing the toxic chemical are shipped for sale or distribution in commerce or for further use. Also, do not list locations to which wastes containing the chemical are sold or sent for recovery, recycling, or reuse of the toxic chemical.

1. Publicly Owned Treatment Works (POTW)

You must enter the name and address of the POTW to which your facility discharges wastewater containing any toxic chemical you are reporting. If you do not discharge wastewater containing reported toxic chemicals to a POTW, enter not applicable [N/A]. If you discharge wastewater containing toxic chemicals to more than one POTW, use additional copies of Part II.

2. Other Off-Site Locations

In the block next to the heading "Other off-site location," enter a number. For the first such off-site location enter "1" in the block. Continue numbering the off-site locations in ascending order. This is the block number required by Part III, Section 6. If your facility transfers any toxic chemical to more than three off-site locations, use additional copies of Part II and continue numbering these locations in ascending order. Check the box at the bottom of each page if additional pages of Part II are attached.

In the spaces provided you must enter the name and address of each location (other than POTWs) to which you ship or transfer wastes containing the toxic chemical. Also enter the RCRA I.D. Number (EPA I.D. Number) for each such location, if known to you. If the facility does not have a RCRA I.D number, enter not applicable [N/A] in this space. Such information may be found on the Uniform Hazardous Waste Manifest which is required by RCRA regulations. You must also indicate in the space provided whether the location is owned or controlled by your facility or your parent company.

░░░░░░░░░░░░░   EXAMPLE   ░░░░░░░░░░░░░

Your facility is involved in chrome plating of metal parts, which are shipped to an off-site warehouse not owned by your company for distribution. Your facility produces an aqueous plating waste which is treated on-site to recover chromium sludge. The effluent from the on-site treatment plant, which contains chromium compounds, a listed toxic chemical, is piped to a POTW. The chromium sludge is transferred to an off-site privately-owned recovery firm. Chromium is recovered from the sludge by an ion exchange process. Your facility also produces a solid waste containing chromium, which is sent to an off-site permitted landfill owned by your facility.

You must report the locations of the POTW and the permitted landfill in Sections 1 and 2 of Part II of the form. Do not report the location of the warehouse or give any information about the on-site treatment plant in this section. Indicate that the landfill is under the control of your facility. You are not required to report the location of the off-site privately-owned recovery firm or provide any information concerning off-site recovery.

PART III. CHEMICAL SPECIFIC INFORMATION

1.1 Trade Secret Block

If appropriate, you must indicate that a trade secret claim is being made for the specific chemical identity by checking the box in Section 1.1. If you are claiming chemical identity of the toxic chemical as a trade secret (i.e., the information in Sections 1.2 and 1.3 of Part III), you must attach a completed trade secret substantiation form to the report, as set forth in the trade secret rule in 40 CFR Part 350. When the chemical identity is claimed trade secret, you must also provide a generic name in Section 1.4.

Note: If you complete and submit your Toxic Chemical Release Inventory Reporting Form before the trade secret rule is in effect, you are still required to substantiate your claim that the specific chemical identity is a trade secret. Accordingly, you should follow the provisions of the proposed trade secret rule and use the proposed trade secret substantiation form which appeared in the FEDERAL REGISTER of October 15, 1987 (52 FR 38312-38377).

1.2 CAS Registry Number

You must enter the Chemical Abstracts Service (CAS) registry number that appears in Table III on page 28 for the chemical being reported. Use leading place holding zeros. If you are reporting one of the chemical categories in Table III(c) of the rule (e.g., copper compounds), enter [N/A] in the CAS number space. CAS numbers for chemicals required under section 313 are cross-referenced with an alphabetical list of trade names and chemical names in Table III of these instructions and section 372.65 of the rule.

1.3 Chemical or Chemical Category Name

You must enter in the space provided the name of the chemical or chemical category as it is listed in Table III. If more than one name is listed, you may use either name.

1.4 Generic Chemical Name

You must complete Section 1.4 if you are claiming the specific chemical identity of the toxic chemical as a trade secret, and have marked the trade secret block in Section 1.1. Enter a generic name that is descriptive of the chemical structure. You must limit the generic name to seventy characters (e.g., numbers, letters, spaces, punctuation) or less.

2. Mixture Component Identity

Do not complete this section if you have completed Section 1 of Part III.

Use this section in the following specific case:

1. You use a particular mixture or trade name product in excess of 10,000 pounds or you process such a product in excess of the applicable "process" threshold for the year;

2. You determine that the mixture contains a covered toxic chemical but the only identity you have for that chemical is a generic name;

3. You know either the specific composition of that toxic chemical component or a maximum concentration figure;

4. You determine by multiplying the composition figure by the total annual amount of the whole mixture used (or processed) that you exceed the use or process threshold for that individual, generically identified mixture component. You would then enter that generic component name in Section 2.

⬛⬛⬛⬛⬛⬛⬛⬛ EXAMPLE ⬛⬛⬛⬛⬛⬛⬛⬛

Your facility uses 20,000 pounds of a solvent which your supplier has told you contains eighty percent "chlorinated aromatic," their generic name for a chemical subject to reporting under section 313. You therefore know that you have exceeded the use threshold for some listed toxic chemical. You would enter the name "chlorinated aromatic" in the space provided in Section 2.

3. Activities and Uses of the Chemical at the Facility

This section requires an indication of whether the chemical is manufactured (including imported), processed, or otherwise used at the facility for which the form is being filed and the general nature of such activities and uses at the facility during the calendar year. Report activities that take place only at your facility, not activities that take place at other facilities involving your products. You must mark all the appropriate blocks in this section that apply. If you are a manufacturer, you must check at least one of a or b, and at least one of c, d, e, or f. Refer to the definitions of "manufacture," "process," and "otherwise used" in the general information section of these instructions or section 372.3 of the rule for explanations supplementing those provided below.

3.1 Manufacture

a. Produce - A chemical included in this category is produced at the facility.

b. Import - A chemical included in this category is imported by the facility into the territory of the United States.

c. For on-site use/processing - A chemical included in this category is manufactured and then further processed or otherwise used at the same facility.

d. For sale/distribution - A chemical in this category is manufactured specifically for sale or distribution outside the manufacturing facility.

e. As a byproduct - A chemical in this category is produced coincidentally during the production, processing, use, or disposal of another chemical substance or mixture, and following its production, is separated from that other chemical substance or mixture.

f. As an impurity - A chemical in this category is produced coincidentally with another chemical substance, and is processed, used, or distributed with it.

3.2 Process (incorporative-type activities)

a. **As a reactant** - A natural or synthetic chemical used in chemical reactions for the manufacture of another chemical substance or of a product. Includes, but is not limited to, feedstocks, raw materials, intermediates, and initiators.

b. **As a formulation component** - A chemical added to a product or product mixture prior to further distribution of the product that aids the performance of the product in its use. Examples include, but are not limited to, additives, dyes, reaction diluents, initiators, solvents, inhibitors, emulsifiers, surfactants, lubricants, flame retardants, and rheological modifiers.

c. **As an article component** - A chemical substance that becomes an integral component of an article distributed for industrial, trade, or consumer use.

d. **Repackaging only** - Processing or preparation of a chemical or product mixture for distribution in commerce in a different form, state, or quantity.

3.3 Otherwise Used (non-incorporative-type activities)

a. **As a chemical processing aid** - A chemical that is added to a reaction mixture to aid in the manufacture or synthesis of another chemical substance but does not intentionally remain in or become part of the product or product mixture. Examples of such chemicals include, but are not limited to, process solvents, catalysts, inhibitors, initiators, reaction terminators, and solution buffers.

b. **As a manufacturing aid** - A chemical whose function is to aid the manufacturing process that does not become part of the resulting product. Examples include, but are not limited to, lubricants, metalworking fluids, coolants, refrigerants, and hydraulic fluids.

c. **Ancillary or other use** - A chemical in this category is used at a facility for purposes other than as a chemical processing aid or manufacturing aid as described above. Includes, but is not limited to, cleaners, degreasers, lubricants, and fuels.

░░░░░░░░░░░ **EXAMPLE** ░░░░░░░░░░░░░░░

In the example below, it is assumed that the threshold quantities for manufacture, process, or otherwise use (75,000 pounds, 75,000 pounds, and 10,000 pounds respectively for 1987) have been exceeded and the reporting of listed chemicals is therefore required.

(1) Your facility receives toluene and naphthalene, both listed toxic chemicals, from an off-site location. You react the toluene with air to form benzoic acid and react the naphthalene with sulfuric acid, which forms phthalic acid and also produces sulfur dioxide fumes. Your facility <u>processes</u> toluene and naphthalene. Both are used as <u>reactants</u> to produce benzoic acid and phthalic acid, chemicals not on the section 313 list.

The phthalic acid and benzoic acid are reacted to form a reaction intermediate. The reaction intermediate is dissolved in sulfuric acid, which precipitates terephthalic acid (TPA). Fifty percent of the TPA is sold as a product, and fifty percent is further processed at your facility into polyester fiber. The TPA is treated with ethylene glycol to form an intermediate product, which is condensed to polyester.

Your company <u>manufactures</u> terephthalic acid, a listed chemical, both for <u>sale/distribution,</u> as a commercial product, and for <u>on-site</u> <u>use/processing</u> as a feedstock in the polyester process. Because it is a <u>reactant</u>, it is also <u>processed</u>.

Your facility also <u>uses</u>, as well as <u>processes</u>, sulfuric acid, a listed substance, as it serves as a process solvent to precipitate terephthalic acid.

(2) The intermediate product from which the polyester is prepared contains dimethyl phthalate, a listed substance. The method of reporting this substance depends on its eventual disposition in the polyester production process:

    (a) If the dimethyl phthalate is <u>removed</u> from the intermediate product <u>before</u> it is reacted to form polyester fiber, then dimethyl phthalate is <u>manufactured</u> at your facility as a <u>byproduct</u>.

    (b) If it is incorporated into the polyester fiber in an <u>unreacted</u> form, then it is manufactured at your facility as an <u>impurity</u>.

    (c) If the dimethyl phthalate participates in the reaction to form polyester fiber without leaving the process, then it is <u>processed</u> as a <u>reactant</u> (intermediate), as are the ethylene glycol and terephthalic acid in the process.

Sections of Form R completed, assuming that 2(c) represents your process, are illustrated on the following page.

(3) Your facility operates a fume scrubber that uses sodium hydroxide solution and recovers the sulfur dioxide fumes from the phthalic acid production process as sodium sulfate solution. Both sodium solutions are listed chemicals. Your facility <u>manufactures</u> sodium sulfate as a <u>byproduct</u> and <u>processes</u> sodium hydroxide as a <u>reactant</u>.

(4) Your facility applies C.I. disperse yellow 3, a listed chemical, to the finished polyester fiber as a dye, which is incorporated into the polyester fiber product and remains in the product after it is sold. Your facility <u>processes</u> the C.I disperse yellow 3 as an <u>article component</u>.

(Important: Type or print; read instructions before completing form.)   **Page 3 of 5**

EPA FORM R
PART III. CHEMICAL SPECIFIC INFORMATION

(This space for EPA use only.)

1. CHEMICAL IDENTITY

1.1 ☐ Trade Secret (Provide a generic name in 1.4 below. Attach substantiation form to this submission.)

1.2 CAS # [0] [0] [0] [1] [3] [1] - [1] [1] - [3] (Use leading zeros if CAS number does not fill space provided.)

1.3 Chemical or Chemical Category Name
    Dimethyl Phthalate

1.4 Generic Chemical Name (Complete only if 1.1 is checked.)

2. MIXTURE COMPONENT IDENTITY (Do not complete this section if you have completed Section 1.)

2. Generic Chemical Name Provided by Supplier (Limit the name to a maximum of 70 characters (e.g., numbers, letters, spaces, punctuation)).

3. ACTIVITIES AND USES OF THE CHEMICAL AT THE FACILITY (Check all that apply.)

3.1 Manufacture:
- a. ☐ Produce
- b. ☐ Import
- c. ☒ For on-site use/processing
- d. ☐ For sale/distribution
- e. ☐ As a byproduct
- f. ☐ As an impurity

3.2 Process:
- a. ☒ As a reactant
- b. ☐ As a formulation component
- c. ☐ As an article component
- d. ☐ Repackaging only

3.3 Otherwise Used:
- a. ☐ As a chemical processing aid
- b. ☐ As a manufacturing aid
- c. ☐ Ancillary or other use

---

4. Maximum Amount of the Chemical On Site at Any Time During the Calendar Year

You must insert the appropriate code (see below) that indicates the maximum quantity of the chemical (e.g.,in storage tanks, process vessels, on-site shipping containers) at your facility at any time during the calendar year. If the chemical was present at several locations within your facility, use the maximum total amount present at the entire facility at any one time.

Range Code	Weight Range in Pounds From...	To....
01	0	99
02	100	999
03	1,000	9,999
04	10,000	99,999
05	100,000	999,999
06	1,000,000	9,999,999
07	10,000,000	49,999,999
08	50,000,000	99,999,999
09	100,000,000	499,999,999
10	500,000,000	999,999,999
11	1 billion	more than 1 billion

If the toxic chemical was present at your facility as part of a mixture or trade name product, to determine the maximum quantity of the chemical present at the facility you must calculate only the weight of the toxic chemical, not the weight of the entire mixture or trade name product. See section 372.30(b) of the reporting rule for further information on how to calculate the weight of the chemical in the mixture or trade name product. For chemical categories, include all chemicals in the category when calculating the weight of the toxic chemical.

5. Releases of the Chemical to the Environment

In Section 5 you must account for the total aggregate releases of the toxic chemical from your facility to the environment for the calendar year. Releases to the environment include emissions to the air, discharges to surface waters, and releases to land and underground injection wells. Check the box on the last line of the section if you use Part IV, supplemental information sheet. If you have no releases to a particular media (e.g., stack air), enter not applicable [N/A]. Do not leave blank.

All air releases of the chemical from the facility must be covered. In case of doubt about whether an air release is a point or non-point release, it is important that the release be included as one or the other rather than omitted. Do not enter information on individual emission points or releases. Enter only the total release.

5.1 Fugitive or non-point air emissions.

These are releases to the air that are not released through stacks, vents, ducts, pipes, or any other confined air stream. You must include (1) fugitive equipment leaks from valves, pump seals, flanges, compressors, sampling connections, open-ended lines, etc.; (2) evaporative losses from surface impoundments; (3) releases from building ventilation systems; and (4) any other fugitive or non-point air emissions.

5.2 Stack or point air emissions.

These are releases to the air that are through stacks, vents, ducts, pipes, or other confined air streams. You must include storage tank emissions. Air releases from air pollution control equipment would generally fall in this category.

5.3 Discharges to water

You must enter the applicable letter code for the receiving stream or water body from Section 3.10 of Part 1 of the form. Also, you must enter the total annual amount of the chemical released from all discharge points at the facility to each receiving stream or water body. You must include process outfalls such as pipes and open trenches, releases from on-site wastewater treatment systems, and the contribution from stormwater runoff if applicable (see instructions for column C below). Do not include "indirect" discharges to surface waters such as to a POTW or off-site wastewater treatment facility in this section of the form. These must be reported in Section 6.

5.4 Underground injection

You must enter the total annual amount of the chemical that was injected into all wells, including Class I, at the facility.

5.5 Releases to land

You must report quantities of the chemical that were landfilled, impounded, or otherwise disposed of at the facility. Do not report land disposal at off-site locations in this section.

You must enter the appropriate disposal code from the following list:

Disposal Codes

D02	Landfill
D03	Land Treatment/Application/Farming
D05	Surface Impoundment (to be closed as a Landfill)
D99	Other Disposal

Three lines are provided in this section of the form to accommodate various types of land disposal.

For the purpose of this form, a surface impoundment is considered "final disposal." Quantities of the chemical released to surface impoundments that are used merely as part of a wastewater treatment process generally must not be reported in this section of the form. However, if the impoundment accumulates sludges containing the chemical, you must include an estimate in this section unless the sludges are removed and otherwise disposed of (in which case they should be reported under the appropriate section of the form). For the purposes of this reporting, storage tanks are not considered to be a type of disposal and are not to be reported in this section of the form. "Other disposal" includes spills and leaks.

A. Total Release

Only releases of the toxic chemical to the environment for the calendar year are to be reported in this section of the form. The total releases from your facility do not include transfers or shipments of the chemical from your facility for sale or distribution in commerce or of wastes to other facilities for treatment or disposal (see Section 6.1.). Both routine releases, such as fugitive air emissions, and accidental or non-routine releases, such as chemical spills, must be included in your estimate of the quantity released.

A.1 Reporting Ranges

For reports submitted for calendar years 1987, 1988 and 1989 only, you may take advantage of range reporting for releases that are less than 1,000 pounds for the year to an environmental medium. You may mark one of the three boxes, 0, 1-499, or 500-999, corresponding to releases of the chemical to any environmental medium (i.e., any line item). However, you do not have to use these range check boxes. You have the option of providing a specific figure in column A.2 as described below.

For releases of 1,000 pounds or more for the year to any medium, you must provide an estimate in pounds per year in column A.2. Any estimate provided in column A.2 is required to be accurate to no more than two significant figures. Beginning with reports for calendar year 1990, you may not use ranges to report; you must report in column A.2.

A.2 Enter Estimates

You must provide your estimates of releases in pounds for the year in column A.2. This estimate is required to be rounded to no more than two significant figures.

Calculating Releases - To provide the release information required in both Sections A.1 and A.2 in this section of the form, you must use all readily available data (including relevant monitoring data and emissions measurements) collected at your facility pursuant to other provisions of law or as part of routine plant operations, to the extent you have such data for the toxic chemical.

When relevant monitoring data or emission measurements are not readily available, reasonable estimates of the amounts released must be made using published emission factors, material balance calculations, or engineering calculations. You may not use emission factors or calculations to estimate releases if more accurate data are available.

No additional monitoring or measurement of the quantities or concentrations of any toxic chemical released into the environment, or of the frequency of such releases, is required for the purpose of completing this form, beyond that which is required under other provisions of law or regulation or as part

<u>of routine plant operations.</u>

You must estimate as accurately as possible the quantity in pounds of the chemical or chemical category that is released annually to each environmental medium. Do not include the quantity of components of the waste stream other than the toxic chemical in this estimate. If the toxic chemical was present at your facility as part of a mixture or trade name product, you must calculate the releases of the chemical only. Do not include releases of the other components of the mixture or trade name product. If you only know about or are only able to estimate the releases of the mixture or trade name product as a whole, you must assume that the toxic chemical is released in proportion to its concentration in the mixture or trade name product. See section 372.30(b) of the reporting rule for further information on how to calculate the concentration and weight in the mixture or trade name product.

If you are reporting a chemical <u>category</u> listed in Table III and section 372.65(c) of the reporting rule rather than a specific chemical, you must combine the release data for all chemicals in the listed chemical category (e.g., all glycol ethers or all chlorophenols) and report the aggregate amount for that chemical category. Do not report releases of each individual chemical in that category separately. For example, if your facility releases 3,000 pounds per year of 2-chlorophenol, 4,000 pounds per year of 3-chlorophenol, and 4,000 pounds per year of 4-chlorophenol, you should report that your facility releases 11,000 pounds per year of chlorophenols. (Other than for listed chemical categories in Table III and section 372.65(c) of the rule, each form must report on an individual chemical.)

For listed chemicals with the qualifier "solution," such as sodium sulfate, in concentrations of 1 percent (or 0.1 percent in the case of a carcinogen) or greater, the chemical concentrations must be factored into threshold and release calculations because threshold and release amounts relate to the amount of <u>chemical</u> in solution, not the amount of solution.

For metal compound categories (e.g., chromium compounds), report releases of <u>only</u> the parent metal. For example, a user of various inorganic chromium salts would report the total chromium released in each waste type regardless of the chemical form (e.g., as the original salts, chromium ion, oxide, etc.), and exclude any contribution to mass made by other species in the molecule.

▓▓▓▓▓▓▓▓▓▓▓▓▓   EXAMPLE   ▓▓▓▓▓▓▓▓▓▓▓▓▓▓▓▓

Your facility disposes of 14,000 pounds of lead chromate ($PbCrO_4 \cdot PbO$) and 15,000 pounds of zinc dichromate ($ZnCr_2O_7 \cdot 3H_2O$) in an on-site landfill. You transfer 16,000 pounds of lead selenate ($PbSeO_4$) to an off-site land disposal facility. You would therefore be submitting four separate reports on the following: lead compounds, zinc compounds, selenium compounds, and chromium compounds. However, the quantities you would be reporting would be the pounds of "parent" metal being released or transferred offsite. All quantities are based on mass balance calculations (see Section 5B for information on Basis of Estimate and Section 6C for treatment/disposal codes and information on transfers of chemical wastes). You would calculate releases of lead, zinc, chromium, and selenium by first determining the percentage by weight of these metals in the materials you use as follows:

Lead Chromate ($PbCrO_4 \cdot PbO$) -
Molecular weight = 546.37
Lead   2 Pb - Molecular weight = 207.2 x 2 = 414.4
Chromate 1 Cr - Molecular weight = 51.996

Lead chromate is therefore (% by weight)
(414.4/546.37) = 75.85% lead and
(51.996/546.37) = 9.52% chromium

You can then calculate the total amount of the metals that you must report.

14,000 pounds of lead chromate contains:

14,000 x 0.7585 = 10,619 lbs of lead
14,000 x 0.0952 = 1,332.8 lbs of chromium

Similarly, zinc dichromate is (65.38/335.4) = 19.49% zinc and (51.996 x 2/335.4) = 31.01% chromium, and lead selenate is (207.2/350.17) = 59.17% lead and (78.96/350.17) = 22.55% selenium.

The total pounds of lead, chromium, zinc, and selenium released or transferred from your facility are as follows:

Lead

(release)
0.7585 x 14,000 = 10,619.0 lbs from lead chromate
(round to 11,000 lbs)
(transfer)
0.5917 x 16,000 = 9,467.2 lbs from lead selenate
(round to 9,500 lbs)

As an example, the releases and transfers of <u>lead</u> should be reported as illustrated on the next two pages.

Chromium

(release)
0.0952 x 14,000 = 1,332.8 lbs from lead chromate
(round to 1,300 lbs)
(release)
0.3100 x 15,000 = 4,650.0 lbs from zinc dichromate
(round to 4,700 lbs)

Zinc

(release)
0.1949 x 15,000 = 2,923.5 lbs from zinc dichromate
(round to 2,900 lbs)

Selenium

(transfer)
0.2255 x 16,000 = 3,608.0 lbs of selenium from lead selenate
(round to 3,600 lbs)

1. CHEMICAL IDENTITY	
1.1	☐ Trade Secret (Provide a generic name in 1.4 below. Attach substantiation form to this submission.)
1.2	CAS # ☐☐☐☐☐☐☐ - ☐ N - A (Use leading zeros if CAS number does not fill space provided.)
1.3	Chemical or Chemical Category Name Lead Compounds
1.4	Generic Chemical Name (Complete only if 1.1 is checked.)

---

5. RELEASES OF THE CHEMICAL TO THE ENVIRONMENT

You may report releases of less than 1.000 lbs. by checking ranges under A.1.		A. Total Release (lbs/yr)				B. Basis of Estimate (enter code)	
		A.1 Reporting Ranges			A.2 Enter Estimate		
		0	1–499	500–999			
5.1 Fugitive or non-point air emissions	5.1a				N/A	5.1b ☐	
5.2 Stack or point air emissions	5.2a				N/A	5.2b ☐	
5.3 Discharges to water 5.3.1 ☐ (Enter letter code from Part I Section 3.10 for stream(s).)	5.3.1a				N/A	5.3.1b ☐	C. % From Stormwater 5.3.1c N/A
5.3.2 ☐	5.3.2a					5.3.2b ☐	5.3.2c
5.3.3 ☐	5.3.3a					5.3.3b ☐	5.3.3c
5.4 Underground injection	5.4a				N/A	5.4b ☐	
5.5 Releases to land 5.5.1 D 0 2 (enter code)	5.5.1a				11,000	5.5.1b C	
5.5.2 ☐☐☐ (enter code)	5.5.2a				N/A	5.5.2b ☐	
5.5.3 ☐☐☐ (enter code)	5.5.3a					5.5.3b ☐	

☐ (Check if additional information is provided on Part IV-Supplemental Information.)

EPA Form 9350-1(1-88)

EPA FORM **R**. Part III (Continued)   Page 4 of 5

6. TRANSFERS OF THE CHEMICAL IN WASTE TO OFF-SITE LOCATIONS

You may report transfers of less than 1,000 lbs. by checking ranges under A.1.		A. Total Transfers (lbs/yr)			B. Basis of Estimate (enter code)	C. Type of Treatment/ Disposal (enter code)
		A.1 Reporting Ranges		A.2 Enter Estimate		
		0 1–499 500–999				
6.1 Discharge to POTW				N/A	6.1b ☐	
6.2 Other off-site location (Enter block number from Part II, Section 2.)	1			9,500	6.2b C	6.2c M 7 2
6.3 Other off-site location (Enter block number from Part II, Section 2.)	☐			N/A	6.3b ☐	6.3c
6.4 Other off-site location (Enter block number from Part II, Section 2.)	☐				6.4b ☐	6.4c

☐ (Check if additional information is provided on Part IV-Supplemental Information)

B. Basis of Estimate

For each release estimate you are required to indicate the principal method by which the quantity was derived. Enter the letter code to identify the method which applies to the largest portion of the total estimated quantity.

For example, if 40 percent of stack emissions of the reported substance were derived using monitoring data, 30 percent by mass balance, and 30 percent by emission factors, you would enter the code letter "M" for monitoring. The codes are as follows:

   M - Based on monitoring data or measurements for the toxic chemical as released to the environment and/or off-site facility.

   C - Based on mass balance calculations, such as calculation of the amount of the toxic chemical in streams entering and leaving process equipment.

   E - Based on published emission factors, such as those relating release quantity to throughput or equipment type (e.g., air emission factors).

   O - Based on other approaches such as engineering calculations (e.g., estimating volatilization using published mathematical formulas) or best engineering judgment. This would include applying an estimated removal efficiency to a wastestream even if the composition of stream before treatment was fully characterized by monitoring data.

EPA requires that releases be rounded to no greater than two significant figures. If the monitoring data, mass balance, or emission factor used to estimate the release is not specific to the toxic chemical being reported, the estimate should be reported as based on

engineering calculations or judgment.

If a mass balance calculation yields the flow rate of a wastestream, but the quantity of reported chemical in the wastestream is based on solubility data, report "O" because "engineering calculations" were used as the basis of estimate of the quantity of the chemical in the wastestream.

If the concentration of the chemical in the wastestream was measured by monitoring equipment and the flow rate of the wastestream was determined by mass balance, then the primary basis of estimate is "monitoring" (M) even though a mass balance calculation also contributed to the estimate. "Monitoring" should be indicated because monitoring data was used to estimate the concentration of the wastestream.

Mass balance (C) should only be indicated if it is used to calculate directly the mass (weight) of chemical released. Monitoring data should be indicated as the basis of estimate only if the chemical concentration is measured in the wastestream being released into the environment as opposed to measured in other process streams containing the chemical.

C. Percent From Stormwater

This column only relates to Section 5.3 - Discharges to Water. If your facility has monitoring data on the amount of the chemical in stormwater runoff, you must include that quantity of the chemical in your water release in column A and indicate the percentage of the total quantity (by weight) of the chemical contributed by stormwater in column C (5.3c).

If your facility has monitoring data on the chemical and an estimate of flow rate, you must use this data to determine the percent stormwater.

If you have monitored stormwater but did not detect the chemical, enter zero (0) in column C. If your facility has no stormwater monitoring data for the chemical, enter not applicable [N/A] in this space on the form.

############## EXAMPLE ##############

Bi-monthly stormwater monitoring data shows that the average concentration of zinc from a biocide containing a zinc compound in the stormwater discharges from your facility is 1.4 milligrams per liter, and the total annual stormwater discharge from the facility is 7.527 million gallons. The total amount of zinc discharged to surface water through the plant wastewater discharge (non-stormwater) is 250 pounds per year. The total amount of zinc discharged with stormwater is:

(7,253,000 gallons stormwater) x
    3.785 liters/gallon   = 27,452,605 liters
                                    stormwater
(27,452,605 liters stormwater) x
    1.4 mg.zinc/liter)   = 38,433.6 g zinc
                          =   84.7 lbs zinc

The total amount of zinc discharged from all sources of your facility is:

250   lbs zinc from wastewater
_84.7_ lbs zinc from stormwater
334.7 lbs zinc total

Report 330 lbs. of zinc in total.

The percentage of zinc discharged through stormwater is:

    87.9/337.9 x 100   = 26%

###

If your facility does not have periodic measurements of stormwater releases of the chemical but has submitted chemical specific monitoring data in permit applications, then these data must be used to calculate the percent contribution from stormwater. Flow rate data can be estimated by multiplying the annual amount of rainfall times the land area of the facility times the runoff coefficient.

The runoff coefficient represents the fraction of rainfall that does not infiltrate into the ground but runs off as stormwater. The runoff coefficient is directly related to land uses located in the drainage area. (See table below.)

Description of Land Area	Runoff Coefficients
Business	
Downtown areas	0.70-0.95
Neighborhood areas	0.50-0.70
Industrial	
Light areas	0.50-0.80
Heavy areas	0.60-0.90
Railroad yard areas	0.20-0.40
Unimproved areas	0.10-0.30
Streets	
Asphaltic	0.70-0.95
Concrete	0.80-0.95
Brick	0.70-0.85
Drives and walks	0.70-0.85

Roofs	0.75-0.95
Lawns; Sandy Soil:	
Flat, 2%	0.05-0.10
Average, 2-7%	0.10-0.15
Steep, 7%	0.15-0.20
Lawns; Heavy Soil:	
Flat, 2%	0.13-0.17
Average, 2-7%	0.18-0.22
Steep, 7%	0.25-0.35

You should choose the most appropriate runoff coefficient for your site or you may use the following weighted-average coefficient that takes into account different types of land use at your facility:

$$\text{Weighted-average runoff coefficient} = \frac{\text{Area}_1 C_1 + \text{Area}_2 C_2 + ... A_i C_i}{\text{Total Site Area}}$$

    where C_i = runoff coefficient for a specific land use of Area_i.

################## EXAMPLE ##################

Your facility is located in a semi-arid region of the United States which has an annual precipitation (including snowfall) of 12 inches of rain. (Snowfall should be converted to the equivalent inches of rain; assume one foot of snow is equivalent to one inch of rain.) The area covered by your facility is 42 acres (about 170,000 square meters or 1,829,520 square feet). The area of your facility is 50 percent unimproved area, 10 percent asphaltic streets, and 40 percent concrete pavement.

The total stormwater runoff at your facility is therefore calculated as follows:

Land Use	%Area	Runoff Coefficient
Unimproved area	50	0.20
Asphaltic streets	10	0.85
Concrete pavement	40	0.90

$$\text{Weighted-average runoff coefficient} = \frac{(50\%)(0.20) + (10\%)(0.85) + (40\%)(0.90)}{100\% \text{ Area}}$$

                          = 0.545

Rainfall x land x runoff = stormwater
            area   coefficient   discharge

1 foot x 1,829,520 ft^2 x 7.48 gal/ft^3 x 0.545 =
                          7,458,221 gallons/year

Total stormwater runoff = 7.458 million gallons/year

###

6. Transfers of the Chemical in Waste to Off-Site Locations

You must report in this section the total annual quantity of the chemical sent to any of the off-site disposal, treatment, or storage facilities for which you have provided an address in Part II.

Line 6.1 is for transfers to a POTW. Lines 6.2

through 6.4 are provided for transfers to other off-site locations, including privately owned wastewater treatment facilities.

Enter, from Section 2 of Part II, the block number that corresponds to the off-site location to which you transferred waste containing the chemical. If you need additional space (i.e., you ship waste to more than three off-site locations), check the box at the bottom of Section 6 and use the supplemental information sheet (Part IV).

A.   Total Transferred

You must follow the instructions for providing estimates as presented in the instructions for column A of Section 5 above. You must enter the amount in pounds of only the toxic chemical that is being transferred; do not enter the total poundage of wastes, including mixtures or trade name products containing the chemical. As with Section 5, you may report in ranges only for calendar years 1987, 1988, and 1989, if the total amount transferred is less than 1,000 pounds. Enter not applicable [N/A] if you have no transfers off-site.

B.   Basis of Estimate

You must identify the basis for your estimate. Follow the instructions and use the same codes as presented in the instructions for column B of Section 5.

C.   Type of Treatment/Disposal for Off-Site Locations

You must enter one of the following codes to identify the type of treatment or disposal method used by the off-site location for the chemical being reported. You may have this information in your copy of EPA Form SO, Item S of the Annual/Biennial Hazardous Waste Treatment, Storage, and Disposal Report (RCRA). Applicable codes for this section are as follows:

M10   Storage Only
M20   Reuse as Fuel/Fuel Blending
M40   Solidification/Stabilization
M50   Incineration/Thermal Treatment
M61   Wastewater Treatment (Excluding POTW)
M69   Other Treatment
M71   Underground Injection
M72   Landfill/Disposal Surface Impoundment
M73   Land Treatment
M79   Other Land Disposal
M90   Other Off-Site Management
M91   Transfer to Waste Broker
M99   Unknown

7.   Waste Treatment Methods and Efficiency

In Section 7, you must provide the following information related to the chemical for which releases are being reported: (A) the general wastestream types containing the chemical being reported; (B) the waste treatment methods (if any) used on all wastestreams containing the chemical; (C) the range of concentrations of the chemical in the influent to the treatment method; (D) whether sequential treatment is used; (E) the efficiency or effectiveness of each treatment method in removing the chemical; and (F) whether the treatment efficiency figure was based on actual operating data. You must use a separate line in Section 7 for each treatment method used on a wastestream. This section is to be used to report only treatment of wastestreams at your facility, not treatment off-site. If you do not treat wastes on-

site, enter not applicable [N/A] in 7.1.b.

A.   General Wastestream

For each waste treatment method report you must indicate the type of wastestream containing the chemical that is treated. Enter the letter code that corresponds to the general wastestream type:

A = Gaseous (including gases, vapors, airborne particulates)
W = Wastewater (aqueous waste)
L = Liquid waste (non-aqueous waste)
S = Solid waste (including sludges and slurries)

If a waste is a mixture of water and organic liquid, you must report it under wastewater unless the organic content exceeds 50 percent. Slurries and sludges containing water must be reported as solid waste if they contain appreciable amounts of dissolved solids, or solids that may settle, such that the viscosity or density of the waste is considerably different from that of process wastewater.

B.   Treatment Method

Codes for treatment methods are included in Table II on page 27 of these instructions. You must enter the code for each treatment method used on a wastestream containing the toxic chemical, regardless of whether this treatment method actually removes the specific chemical. Treatment methods must be reported for each type of waste being treated (i.e., gaseous wastes, aqueous wastes, liquid non-aqueous wastes, and solids).

Wastestreams containing the chemical may have a single source or may be aggregates of many sources. For example, process water from several pieces of equipment at your facility may be combined prior to treatment. Report treatment methods that apply to the aggregate wastestream as well as treatment methods that apply to individual wastestreams. If your facility treats various wastewater streams containing the chemical in different ways, the different treatment methods must each be listed separately.

Your facility may have several pieces of equipment performing a similar service. It is not necessary to enter four lines of data to cover four scrubber units, for example, if all four are treating wastes of similar character (e.g., sulfuric acid mist emissions), have similar influent concentrations, and have similar removal efficiencies. If, however, any of these parameters differ from one unit to the next, each scrubber must be listed separately.

C.   Range of Influent Concentration

The form requires an indication of the range of concentration of the toxic chemical in the wastestream (i.e., the influent) as it typically enters the treatment equipment. You must enter in the space provided one of the following code numbers corresponding to the concentration of the chemical in the influent:

1 = Greater than 1 percent
2 = 100 parts per million (0.01 percent) to 1 percent (10,000 parts per million)
3 = 1 part per million to 100 parts per million
4 = 1 part per billion to 1 part per million
5 = Less than 1 part per billion

Note that parts per million (ppm) is milligrams/kilogram (mass/mass) for solids and liquids; cubic centimeters/cubic meter (volume/volume) for gases; milligrams/liter for solutions or dispersions of the chemical in water; and milligrams of chemical/kilogram of air for particulates in air. If you have particulate concentrations (at standard temperature and pressure) as grains/cubic foot of air, multiply by 1766.6 to convert to parts per million; if in milligrams/cubic meters, multiply by 0.773 to obtain parts per million. (Note: Factors are for standard conditions of $0^{\circ}C$ ($32^{\circ}F$) and 760 mmHg atmospheric pressure.)

D. Sequential Treatment?

You may use various treatment steps in a sequence but only be able to estimate the treatment efficiency of the overall treatment process. If this is the case, you must enter codes for all of the treatment steps in the process. You must check the column D "sequential treatment?" box for all of these steps in the same sequence. With respect to information that must be supplied in columns C and E, you must provide the range of influent concentrations (column C) in connection with the first step of the sequential treatment. Then provide the treatment efficiency (column E) in connection with the last step in the treatment. You do not need to complete columns C or E for any intermediate step in the sequence.

E. Treatment Efficiency Estimate

In the space provided, you must enter the number that indicates the percentage of the toxic chemical that is removed from the wastestream. The treatment efficiency (expressed as percent removal) represents any destruction, biological degradation, chemical conversion, or physical removal of the chemical from the wastestream being treated. This efficiency must represent the mass or weight percentage of chemical destroyed or removed, not just changes in volume or concentration of the chemical or the wastestream. The efficiency indicated for a treatment method must refer only to the percent conversion or removal of the listed toxic chemical from the wastestream, not the percent conversion or removal of other wastestream constituents (alone or together with the listed chemical), and not the general efficiency of the method for any wastestream.

For some treatments, the percent removal will represent removal by several mechanisms, as in secondary wastewater treatment, where a chemical may evaporate, be biodegraded, or be physically removed in the sludge.

Percent removal must be calculated as follows:

$$\frac{(I - E)}{I} \times 100$$

where I = mass of the chemical in the influent wastestream and E = mass of the chemical in the effluent wastestream.

The mass or weight of chemical in the wastestream being treated must be calculated by multiplying the concentration (by weight) of the chemical in the wastestream times the flow rate. When calculating or estimating percent removal efficiency for various wastestreams, the percent removal must compare the gaseous effluent from treatment to the gaseous influent, the aqueous effluent from treatment to the aqueous influent, and similarly for organic or non-aqueous liquid and solid waste. However, some treatment methods may not result in a comparable form of effluent wastestream. Examples are incineration or solidification of wastewater. In these cases, the percent removal of the chemical from the influent wastestream would be reported as 100 percent because the wastestream does not exist in a comparable form after treatment. Some of the treatments listed in Table II do not destroy, chemically convert, or physically remove the chemical from its wastestream. Some examples include fuel blending and evaporation. For these treatment methods, an efficiency of zero must be reported.

For metal compounds, the reportable concentration and treatment efficiency must be calculated based on the weight of the parent metal and not the weight of the metal compounds. Metals are not destroyed but can only be physically removed or chemically converted from one form into another. The treatment efficiency reported must only represent physical removal of the parent metal from the wastestream, not the percent chemical conversion of the metal compound. If a listed treatment method converts but does not remove a metal (e.g., chromium reduction), the method must be reported, but the treatment efficiency must be reported as zero.

All data available at your facility must be utilized to calculate treatment efficiency and influent chemical concentration. You are not required to collect any new data for the purposes of this reporting requirement. If data are lacking, estimates must be made using best engineering judgment or other methods.

F. Based on Operating Data?

This column requires you to indicate "Yes" or "No" to whether the treatment efficiency estimate is based on actual operating data. For example, you would check "Yes" if the estimate is based on monitoring of influent and effluent wastes under typical operating conditions.

If the efficiency estimate is based on published data for similar processes or on equipment supplier's literature, or if you otherwise estimated either the influent or effluent waste comparison or the flow rate, you must check "No."

EXAMPLE

Your facility produces several different waste streams treated at on-site and transferred to off-site facilities. You have previously indicated the location of the off-site facilities in Section 2, Part II of the form and have indicated the quantity of each reported chemical transferred to off-site facilities in Section 6, Part III of the form, using a separate form for each chemical.

One wastestream generated by your facility is the aqueous waste containing lead chromate, zinc dichromate, and lead selenate discussed in a previous example in these instructions. In this example, the waste is transferred to off-site facilities after on-site wastewater treatment. The on-site wastewater treatment plant precipitates metal sludges. The wastewater is first treated with sulfuric acid and sodium disulfate to reduce the hexavalent chromate to trivalent chromium. The wastewater is then treated with lime to raise the pH. This precipitates chromium hydroxide, zinc hydroxide, and lead hydroxide, but does not remove the selenium. The selenium is removed from the wastewater by an ionic exchange. The chromium, zinc, and lead hydroxide sludge (solid) waste is transferred to an off-site land disposal facility and the selenium-containing ion exchange resin is transferred to an off-site facility for metal recovery (off-site recovery should not be reported). The treated wastewater is sent to a POTW after neutralization. You would indicate the following treatment methods for the on-site treatment of each of the lead, zinc, chromium, and selenium compounds:

C21 -   Chromium Reduction
C01 -   Chemical Precipitation -- Lime or Sodium Hydroxide
R22 -   Metals Recovery -- Ion Exchange
C11 -   Neutralization

All sequential treatment steps must be indicated for all the metal compound categories reported even if the treatment method does not affect the particular metal. For example, ionic exchange must be reported as a treatment method for lead, zinc, chromium, and selenium compounds, even though the method only affects the selenium compound.

You would indicate the percent removal of chromium, lead, zinc, and selenium, by subtracting the amount of each metal in the wastewater discharge from the amount of each metal in the wastewater before treatment, and dividing by the amount of each metal in the wastewater before treatment.

You would indicate a discharge to a POTW in Section 6, Part III and indicate the location of the POTW in Section 1, Part II. You would also indicate the release of the metal sludge to an off-site land disposal facility in Section 6, Part III.

8. Optional Information on Waste Minimization

Information provided in Part III, Section 8, of the form is optional. This section allows you to identify waste minimization efforts relating to the reported toxic chemical that may not have been reflected in your responses to previous sections of the form. Waste minimization means reduction of the amount of the chemical in wastes that are generated. Treatment or disposal does not minimize waste; recycle or reuse of a waste should be counted as waste minimization. Waste minimization applies to air emissions and wastewater as well as to liquid or solid materials that are released, disposed of, or treated. For example, a program to recycle material from reactor cleaning could reduce the amount of a listed chemical in wastewater prior to treatment. This reduction might not show up in annual reports of release to receiving streams (due to effective treatment, for example), but would be captured in this section.

A. Type of modification

Enter one code from the following list that best describes the type of waste minimization activity:

M1 - Recycling/reuse on-site
M2 - Recycling/reuse off-site
M3 - Equipment/technology modifications
M4 - Process procedure modifications
M5 - Reformulation/redesign of product
M6 - Substitution of raw materials
M7 - Improved housekeeping, training, inventory control
M8 - Other waste minimization technique

B. Quantity of the chemical in the wastestream prior to treatment/disposal

Enter the pounds of the toxic chemical in all wastes in the reporting year and the pounds in all wastes in the year prior to the reporting year. Alternatively, to protect confidential information, you may wish to enter only the percentage by which the weight of the chemical in the wastes has changed. This figure may be calculated using the following formula:

$$\frac{(\text{toxic chemical in wastes in reporting year} - \text{toxic chemical in wastes in prior year})}{\text{toxic chemical in wastes in prior year}} \times 100$$

The resulting figure may be either negative or positive (i.e., if the amount of waste generated has been reduced, a negative number should be reported).

C. Index

Enter the ratio of reporting year production to production in the year prior to the reporting year. This index should be calculated to most closely reflect activities involving the chemical. The index provides a means for users of the data to distinguish the effects of changes in business activity from the effects specifically of waste minimization efforts. It is not necessary to indicate the units on which the index is based. Examples of acceptable indices include:

- Amount of chemical produced in 1987/amount of chemical produced in 1986. For example, a company manufactures 200,000 pounds of a chemical in 1986 and 250,000 pounds of the same chemical in 1987. The index figure to report would be 1.3 (1.25 rounded).
- Amount of paint produced in 1987/amount of paint produced in 1986.
- Number of appliances coated in 1987/number of appliances coated in 1986.
- Square feet of solar collector fabricated in 1987/square feet of solar collector fabricated in 1986.

D. Reason for action

Finally, enter the codes from the following list that best describe the reason for initiating the waste minimization effort:

R1 - Regulatory requirement for the waste.
R2 - Reduction of treatment/disposal costs.
R3 - Other process cost reduction.
R4 - Self-initiated review
R5 - Other (e.g., discontinuation of product, occupational safety, etc.).

(Important: Type or print; read instructions before completing form.)

Page 1 of 5

U.S. Environmental Protection Agency

⊕EPA   **TOXIC CHEMICAL RELEASE INVENTORY REPORTING FORM**

Section 313, Title III of The Superfund Amendments and Reauthorization Act of 1986

EPA FORM

R

PART I.   FACILITY IDENTIFICATION INFORMATION

(This space for EPA use only.)

1.

1.1 Does this report contain trade secret information?

☐ Yes (Answer 1.2)   ☐ No (Do not answer 1.2)

1.2 Is this a sanitized copy?

☐ Yes   ☐ No

1.3 Reporting Year

---

2. CERTIFICATION (Read and sign after completing all sections.)

I hereby certify that I have reviewed the attached documents and that, to the best of my knowledge and belief, the submitted information is true and complete and that the amounts and values in this report are accurate based on reasonable estimates using data available to the preparers of this report.

Name and official title of owner/operator or senior management official

Signature

Date signed

---

3. FACILITY IDENTIFICATION

3.1

Facility or Establishment Name

Street Address

City

County

State

Zip Code

3.2

This report contains information for: (check one)

a. ☐ An entire covered facility.

b. ☐ Part of a covered facility.

3.3 Technical Contact

Telephone Number (include area code)

(   )   −

3.4 Public Contact

Telephone Number (include area code)

(   )   −

3.5 a. SIC Code   b.   c.

3.6

Latitude

Deg.   Min.   Sec.

Longitude

Deg.   Min.   Sec.

Where to send completed forms:

U.S. Environmental Protection Agency
P.O. Box 70266
Washington, DC 20024−0266
Attn: Toxic Chemical Release Inventory

3.7 Dun & Bradstreet Number(s)

a.   −   −   b.   −   −

3.8 EPA Identification Number (RCRA I.D. No.)

a.   b.

3.9 NPDES Permit Number(s)

a.   b.

3.10 Name of Receiving Stream(s) or Water Body(s)

a.

b.

c.

3.11 Underground Injection Well Code (UIC) Identification No.

---

4. PARENT COMPANY INFORMATION

4.1 Name of Parent Company

4.2 Parent Company's Dun & Bradstreet No.

−   −

EPA Form 9350−1 (1−88)

(Important: Type or print; read instructions before completing form.)

EPA FORM R
PART II. OFF-SITE LOCATIONS TO WHICH TOXIC CHEMICALS ARE TRANSFERRED IN WASTES

(This space for EPA use only.)

---

1. PUBLICLY OWNED TREATMENT WORKS (POTW)

Facility Name

Street Address

City | County

State | Zip | | | | | | - | | | |

---

2. OTHER OFF-SITE LOCATIONS - Number these locations sequentially on this and any additional page of this form you use.

☐ **Other off-site location**

EPA Identification Number (RCRA ID. No.) | | | | | | | | | | | | |

Facility Name

Street Address

City | County

State | Zip | | | | | | - | | | |

Is location under control of reporting facility or parent company? ☐ Yes ☐ No

☐ **Other off-site location**

EPA Identification Number (RCRA ID. No.) | | | | | | | | | | | | |

Facility Name

Street Address

City | County

State | Zip | | | | | | - | | | |

Is location under control of reporting facility or parent company? ☐ Yes ☐ No

☐ **Other off-site location**

EPA Identification Number (RCRA ID. No.) | | | | | | | | | | | | |

Facility Name

Street Address

City | County

State | Zip | | | | | | - | | | |

Is location under control of reporting facility or parent company? ☐ Yes ☐ No

☐ Check if additional pages of Part II are attached.

EPA Form 9350-1 (1-88)

(Important: Type or print; read instructions before completing form.)

EPA FORM R **PART III. CHEMICAL SPECIFIC INFORMATION**	(This space for EPA use only.)

1. CHEMICAL IDENTITY

1.1 ☐ Trade Secret (Provide a generic name in 1.4 below. Attach substantiation form to this submission.)

1.2 CAS # ☐☐☐☐☐☐☐ – ☐☐ – ☐ (Use leading zeros if CAS number does not fill space provided.)

1.3 Chemical or Chemical Category Name

1.4 Generic Chemical Name (Complete only if 1.1 is checked.)

2. **MIXTURE COMPONENT IDENTITY** (Do not complete this section if you have completed Section 1.)

Generic Chemical Name Provided by Supplier (Limit the name to a maximum of 70 characters (e.g., numbers, letters, spaces, punctuation)).

3. ACTIVITIES AND USES OF THE CHEMICAL AT THE FACILITY (Check all that apply.)

3.1 Manufacture:
a. ☐ Produce   b. ☐ Import   c. ☐ For on-site use/processing
d. ☐ For sale/distribution   e. ☐ As a byproduct   f. ☐ As an impurity

3.2 Process:
a. ☐ As a reactant   b. ☐ As a formulation component   c. ☐ As an article component
d. ☐ Repackaging only

3.3 Otherwise Used:
a. ☐ As a chemical processing aid   b. ☐ As a manufacturing aid   c. ☐ Ancillary or other use

4. MAXIMUM AMOUNT OF THE CHEMICAL ON SITE AT ANY TIME DURING THE CALENDAR YEAR

☐☐ (enter code)

5. RELEASES OF THE CHEMICAL TO THE ENVIRONMENT

You may report releases of less than 1,000 lbs. by checking ranges under A.1.		A. Total Release (lbs/yr)				B. Basis of Estimate (enter code)	
		A.1 Reporting Ranges			A.2 Enter Estimate		
		0	1–499	500–999			
5.1 Fugitive or non-point air emissions	5.1a					5.1b ☐	
5.2 Stack or point air emissions	5.2a					5.2b ☐	
5.3 Discharges to water 5.3.1 ☐ (Enter letter code from Part I Section 3.10 for streams(s).)	5.3.1a					5.3.1b ☐	C. % From Stormwater 5.3.1c
5.3.2 ☐	5.3.2a					5.3.2b ☐	5.3.2c
5.3.3 ☐	5.3.3a					5.3.3b ☐	5.3.3c
5.4 Underground injection	5.4a					5.4b ☐	
5.5 Releases to land 5.5.1 ☐☐ (enter code)	5.5.1a					5.5.1b ☐	
5.5.2 ☐☐ (enter code)	5.5.2a					5.5.2b ☐	
5.5.3 ☐☐ (enter code)	5.5.3a					5.5.3b ☐	

☐ (Check if additional information is provided on Part IV–Supplemental Information.)

EPA Form 9350-1 (1-88)

EPA FORM **R**, Part III (Continued)

6. TRANSFERS OF THE CHEMICAL IN WASTE TO OFF-SITE LOCATIONS

You may report transfers of less than 1,000 lbs. by checking ranges under A.1.		A. Total Transfers (lbs/yr)			B. Basis of Estimate (enter code)	C. Type of Treatment/ Disposal (enter code)
		A.1 Reporting Ranges		A.2 Enter Estimate		
		0 / 1–499 / 500–999				
6.1 Discharge to POTW					6.1b ☐	
6.2 Other off-site location (Enter block number from Part II, Section 2.) ☐					6.2b ☐	6.2c ☐☐☐
6.3 Other off-site location (Enter block number from Part II, Section 2.) ☐					6.3b ☐	6.3c ☐☐☐
6.4 Other off-site location (Enter block number from Part II, Section 2.) ☐					6.4b ☐	6.4c ☐☐☐

☐ (Check if additional information is provided on Part IV–Supplemental Information)

7. WASTE TREATMENT METHODS AND EFFICIENCY

A. General Wastestream (enter code)	B. Treatment Method (enter code)	C. Range of Influent Concentration (enter code)	D. Sequential Treatment? (check if applicable)	E. Treatment Efficiency Estimate	F. Based on Operating Data? Yes No
7.1a ☐	7.1b ☐☐	7.1c ☐	7.1d ☐	7.1e ___ %	7.1f ☐ ☐
7.2a ☐	7.2b ☐☐	7.2c ☐	7.2d ☐	7.2e ___ %	7.2f ☐ ☐
7.3a ☐	7.3b ☐☐	7.3c ☐	7.3d ☐	7.3e ___ %	7.3f ☐ ☐
7.4a ☐	7.4b ☐☐	7.4c ☐	7.4d ☐	7.4e ___ %	7.4f ☐ ☐
7.5a ☐	7.5b ☐☐	7.5c ☐	7.5d ☐	7.5e ___ %	7.5f ☐ ☐
7.6a ☐	7.6b ☐☐	7.6c ☐	7.6d ☐	7.6e ___ %	7.6f ☐ ☐
7.7a ☐	7.7b ☐☐	7.7c ☐	7.7d ☐	7.7e ___ %	7.7f ☐ ☐
7.8a ☐	7.8b ☐☐	7.8c ☐	7.8d ☐	7.8e ___ %	7.8f ☐ ☐
7.9a ☐	7.9b ☐☐	7.9c ☐	7.9d ☐	7.9e ___ %	7.9f ☐ ☐
7.10a ☐	7.10b ☐☐	7.10c ☐	7.10d ☐	7.10e ___ %	7.10f ☐ ☐
7.11a ☐	7.11b ☐☐	7.11c ☐	7.11d ☐	7.11e ___ %	7.11f ☐ ☐
7.12a ☐	7.12b ☐☐	7.12c ☐	7.12d ☐	7.12e ___ %	7.12f ☐ ☐
7.13a ☐	7.13b ☐☐	7.13c ☐	7.13d ☐	7.13e ___ %	7.13f ☐ ☐
7.14a ☐	7.14b ☐☐	7.14c ☐	7.14d ☐	7.14e ___ %	7.14f ☐ ☐

☐ (Check if additional information is provided on Part IV–Supplemental Information.)

8. OPTIONAL INFORMATION ON WASTE MINIMIZATION

(Indicate actions taken to reduce the amount of the chemical being released from the facility. See the instructions for coded items and an explanation of what information to include.)

A. Type of modification (enter code)	B. Quantity of the chemical in the wastestream prior to treatment/disposal			C. Index	D. Reason for action (enter code)
	Current reporting year (lbs/yr)	Prior year (lbs/yr)	Or percent change		
☐☐	_____	_____	____ %	☐☐.☐	☐☐

EPA Form 9350-1 (1–88)

(Important: Type or print; read instructions before completing form.) Page 5 of 5

EPA FORM R
PART IV. SUPPLEMENTAL INFORMATION
Use this section if you need additional space for answers to questions in Parts I and III.
Number or letter this information sequentially from prior sections (e.g., D,E, F, or 5.54, 5.55).

(This space for EPA use only.)

ADDITIONAL INFORMATION ON FACILITY IDENTIFICATION (Part I – Section 3)

3.5 SIC Code

3.7 Dun & Bradstreet Number(s)

3.8 EPA Identification Number(s) RCRA I.D. No.)

3.9 NPDES Permit Number(s)

3.10 Name of Receiving Stream(s) or Water Body(s)

ADDITIONAL INFORMATION ON RELEASES TO LAND (Part III – Section 5.5)

Releases to Land	A. Total Release (lbs/yr)			B. Basis of Estimate (enter code)
	A.1 Reporting Ranges		A.2 Enter Estimate	
	0 1–499 500–999			
5.5____ ☐☐☐ (enter code)	5.5____a			5.5____b ☐
5.5____ ☐☐☐ (enter code)	5.5____a			5.5____b ☐
5.5____ ☐☐☐ (enter code)	5.5____a			5.5____b ☐

ADDITIONAL INFORMATION ON OFF–SITE TRANSFER (Part III – Section 6)

	A.Total Transfers (lbs/yr)			B. Basis of Estimate (enter code)	C. Type of Treatment/ Disposal (enter code)
	A.1 Reporting Ranges		A.2 Enter Estimate		
	0 1–499 500–999				
6.____ Discharge to POTW	6.____a			6.____b ☐	
6.____ Other off-site location (Enter block number from Part II, Section 2.) ☐	6.____a			6.____b ☐	6.____c. ☐☐☐
6.____ Other off-site location (Enter block number from Part II, Section 2.) ☐	6.____a			6.____b ☐	6.____c. ☐☐☐

ADDITIONAL INFORMATION ON WASTE TREATMENT (Part III – Section 7)

A. General Wastestream (enter code)	B. Treatment Method (enter code)	C. Range of Influent Concentration (enter code)	D. Sequential Treatment? (check if applicable)	E. Treatment Efficiency Estimate	F. Based on Operating Data? Yes No
7.___a ☐	7.___b ☐☐☐	7.___c ☐	7,___d ☐	7.___e ____%	7.___f ☐ ☐
7.___a ☐	7.___b ☐☐☐	7.___c ☐	7,___d ☐	7.___e ____%	7.___f ☐ ☐
7.___a ☐	7.___b ☐☐☐	7.___c ☐	7,___d ☐	7.___e ____%	7.___f ☐ ☐
7.___a ☐	7.___b ☐☐☐	7.___c ☐	7,___d ☐	7.___e ____%	7.___f ☐ ☐
7.___a ☐	7.___b ☐☐☐	7.___c ☐	7,___d ☐	7.___e ____%	7.___f ☐ ☐

EPA Form 9350–1 (1–88)

APPENDIX E

STATUS OF STATE ACTIONS: SERC CHAIRS AND LEPC DESIGNATION

Status of State Actions

ALABAMA:

SERC Chair:

Director, Emergency Management Agency Director, Department of Environment Management

Address and Phone
Alabama Emergency Management Agency
520 S. Court St.
Montgomery, AL 36130
(205) 834-1375
(Emergency Planning)

Alabama Department of Environmental Management
1751 Federal Drive
Montgomery, Alabama 36130
(205) 271-7700
(Notification and Data Management)

LEPC Designation
67 Counties established as LEPDs

ALASKA:

SERC Chair

Commissioner or designee, Department of Environmental Conservation (Chair), and Commissioner or designee, Department of Military and Veterans Affairs (Co-Chair)

Address and Phone
Alaska State Emergency Response Commission
c/o Department of Environmental Conservation
P.O. Box O
Juneau, Alaska 99811-1800
(907) 465-2600

LEPC Designation
5 existing regions established by the Division of Emergency Service for emergency response planning

---

ARIZONA:

SERC Chair

Director, Division of Emergency Services

Address and Phone
Arizona Emergency Response Commission
Division of Emergency Services
5636 E. McDowell Road
Phoenix, Arizona 85008

LEPC Designation
15 Counties established as LEPDs

ARKANSAS

SERC Chair

Director, Arkansas Department of Pollution Control and Ecology

Address and Phone
Arkansas Department of Pollution Control and Ecology
Post Office Box 9583
Little Rock, Arkansas 72219
(501) 562-7444

LEPC Designation
77 districts established as LEPDs

CALIFORNIA:

SERC Chair

Director, Governor's Office of Emergency Services

Address and Phone
Chemical Emergency Planning and Response Commission
c/o Governor's Office of Emergency Services
Hazardous Materials Division
2800 Meadowview Road
Sacramento, California 95832
(916) 427-4201

LEPC Designation
Established 6 existing Emergency Services Regions as LEPDs

COLORADO:

SERC Chair

Director, Division of Disaster Emergency Services, Department of Public Safety, and Director, Division of Hazardous Materials and Waste, Department of Health

Address and Phone
Colorado Department of Public Safety
Division of Disaster Emergency Services
Camp George West
1500 Golden Road
Golden, Colorado 80401
(303) 273-1622
(Emergency Planning)

Colorado Department of Health
Division of Hazardous Materials and Waste Management
4210 East 11th Avenue
Denver, Colorado 80220
(303) 331-4600
(Chemical Inventory and Community Right-to-Know)

LEPC Designation
63 counties established as LEPDs

CONNECTICUT:

SERC Chair

Deputy Commissioner, Department of Environmental Protection

Address and Phone
Connecticut State Emergency Response Commission
Department of Environmental Protection
165 Capitol Avenue
Hartford, Connecticut 06106
(203) 566-4856

LEPC Designation
169 towns as Local Emergency Planning Districts

DELAWARE:

SERC Chair

Secretary, Department of Public Safety

Address and Phone
Delaware State Emergency Response Commission
Department of Public Safety
Post Office Box 818
Dover, Delaware 19903
(302)736-4321

LEPC Designation
Established the entire state as one Local Emergency
Planning District

FLORIDA:

SERC Chair

Secretary, Department of Community Affairs (Chair), and Director, Division of Emergency Management, Department of Community Affairs (Alternate)

Address and Phone
Florida State Emergency Response Commission
Department of Community Affairs
Division of Emergency Management
1720 South Gadsden Street
Tallahassee, Florida 32301
(904) 488-1900

LEPC Designation
11 established as Local Emergency Planning Districts

GEORGIA:

SERC Chair

Commissioner, Department of Natural Resources

Address and Phone
Georgia Department of Natural Resources
Floyd Towers East
Suite 1252
205 Butler Street S.W.
Atlanta, Georgia 30334
(404) 656-3500

LEPC Designation
Designated the entire State to serve as the Local Emergency Planning District

HAWAII:

SERC Chair

Director, Department of Health

Address and Phone
Hawaii Emergency Response Commission
Department of Health
Division of Environmental Health
P.O. Box 3378
Honolulu, Hawaii 96801
(808) 548-5832

LEPC Designation
Established 4 counties to serve as Local Emergency Planning Districts

IDAHO:

SERC Chair

President, Idaho Mining Association

Address and Phone

LEPC Designation
Established 6 existing State Department of Transportation districts to serve as Local Emergency Planning Districts

ILLINOIS:

SERC Chair

Director, Emergency Services and Disaster Agency

Address and Phone
Illinois Emergency Services and Disaster Agency
110 East Adams Street
Springfield, Illinois 62706
(217) 782-2700

LEPC Designation
Established 103 counties as LEPDs

INDIANA:

SERC Chair

Director, Office of Public Relations, Department of Environmental Management

Address and Phone
Indiana Emergency Response Commission
Department of Environmental Management
Office of Environmental Response
5500 West Bradbury Avenue
Indianapolis, Indiana 46241
(317) 243-5176

LEPC Designation
Established 92 counties as LEPDs

IOWA:

SERC Chair

Director, Disaster Services Division, Public Defense Dept.

Address and Phone
Iowa State Emergency Response Commission
301 East 7th Street
Des Moines, Iowa 50319
(515) 281-6175

LEPC Designation
Established 99 counties as LEPDs

KANSAS:

SERC Chair

Lt. Governor

Address and Phone
Kansas State Emergency Response Commission
c/o Right-to-Know Program
Bureau of Air Quality and Radiation Control
Kansas Department of Health and Environment
Forbes Field, Building 728
Topeka, Kansas 66620
(913) 296-1690

LEPC Designation
Established 105 counties as LEPDs

KENTUCKY:

SERC Chair

Executive Director, Kentucky Disaster and Emergency Services, Department of Military Affairs

Address and Phone
Kentucky Disaster and Emergency
ATTN: KYERC
Boone Center
Frankfort, Kentucky 40601
(502) 564-8680

LEPC Designation
Established 120 counties as LEPDs

LOUISIANA: *SERC Chair*

The Commission is chaired by a private citizen, and the Department of Public Safety and Corrections serves as lead agency.

Address and Phone
Louisiana Emergency Response Commission
c/o Department of Public Safety and Corrections
P.O. Box 66614
Baton Rouge, Louisiana 70896
(504) 925-6113

LEPC Designation
Designated 64 parishes as LEPDs

MAINE: *SERC Chair*

Director, Maine Emergency Management Agency, Department of Defense and Veterans' Services

Address and Phone
Maine Emergency Management Agency
Department of Defense and Veterans' Services
State Office Building
Station 72
Augusta, Maine 04333
1-800-452-8735 (Maine only)

LEPC Designation
Established 16 counties as LEPDs

MARYLAND: *SERC Chair*

Secretary, Department of Public Safety and Correctional Services

Address and Phone
SARA
State Emergency Response Commission
c/o Science and Health Advisory Group
201 W. Preston Street
Maryland Department of Environment
Baltimore, Maryland 21201
(301) 225-5780

LEPC Designation
Established 23 counties as LEPDs

MASSACHUSETTS: *SERC Chair*

Secretary, Executive Office of Public Safety

Address and Phone
Massachusetts Emergency Response Commission
Executive Office of Public Safety
One Ashburton Place
Boston, Massachusetts 02108
(General Information)
(617) 727-7775

Massachusetts Civil Defense Agency and Office of Emergency
Preparedness
400 Worcester Road
Framingham, Massachusetts 01701
(Emergency Notification, Planning and Training)
(617) 875-1381

Massachusetts Department of Environmental Quality Engineering
SARA Title III
One Winter Street
Boston, Massachusetts 02108
(Chemical Inventory and Right-to-Know)
(617) 292-5810

LEPC Designation
Established 4 regions as LEPDs

MICHIGAN:

SERC Chair

Director, Department of Natural Resources

Address and Phone
Michigan Emergency Planning and Community
Right-to-Know Commission
Michigan Department of Natural Resources
Post Office Box 30028
Lansing, Michigan 48909

LEPC Designation
Established 83 counties as LEPDs

MINNESOTA:

SERC Chair

Elected annually from the Commission membership. Commissioner,
Department of Public Safety, is chair for this year.

Address and Phone
Minnesota Department of Public Safety
Room B-5, State Capitol
St. Paul, Minnesota 55155
(612) 296-0481

LEPC Designation
Established 1 Local Emergency Planning District and Committee for the
State of Minnesota until July 1, 1988, which will be divided into seven
regional committees and districts.

MISSISSIPPI:

SERC Chair

Director, Mississippi Emergency Management Agency

Address and Phone
Mississippi Emergency Response Commission
P.O. Box 4501
Fondren Station
Jackson, Mississippi 39216-0501
(601) 960-9000

LEPC Designation
Established 82 counties as LEPDs

MISSOURI:

SERC Chair

Director, Department of Natural Resources

Address and Phone
Missouri Emergency Response Commission
Title III Liaison Officer
P.O. Box 3133
Jefferson City, Missouri 65102

LEPC Designation
Established 114 counties and two cities as LEPDs

MONTANA:

SERC Chair

Assistant Administrator, for Environmental Health, Department of Health and Environmental Sciences and

Administrator, Division of Disaster and Emergency Services

Address and Phone
Governor's Office
Capitol Station
Helena, Montana 59620
(406) 444-3111

LEPC Designation
Established the entire state as a Local Emergency Planning District

---

NEBRASKA:

SERC Chair

Director, Department of Environmental Control

Address and Phone
Nebraska Department of Environmental Control
Technical Services Section
Call No. 98922, Statehouse Station
301 Centennial Mall South
Lincoln, Nebraska 68509-8922

LEPC Designation
Established 10 regional planning districts

NEVADA:

SERC Chair

Director of Aviation, McCarran International Airport; and Director, Department of Motor Vehicles and Public Safety.

Address and Phone
Nevada State Emergency Response Commission
Department of Motor Vehicles and Public Safety
Director's Office
555 Wright Way
Carson City, Nevada 89711
(702) 885-5375

LEPC Designation
Established 17 counties as LEPDs

NEW HAMPSHIRE: *SERC Chair*

Director, Governor's Office of Emergency Management

Address and Phone
New Hampshire Emergency Response Commission
c/o Governor's Office of Emergency Management
State Office Park South
107 Pleasant Street
Concord, New Hampshire 03301
(603) 271-2231

LEPC Designation
Established the entire state as an LEPD

NEW JERSEY: *SERC Chair*

Superintendent, New Jersey State Police and Director, State Office of
Emergency Management; and

Commissioner, New Jersey Department of Environmental Protection.

Address and Phone
New Jersey State Police
Emergency Management Section
Division Headquarters
Box 7068 River Road
West Trenton, New Jersey 08628-0068
(609) 882-2000

New Jersey Department of Environmental Protection
Division of Environmental Quality
Bureau of Hazardous Substances Information
Title III
CN027
Trenton, New Jersey 06825

LEPC Designation
Established 21 counties as LEPDs

NEW MEXICO: *SERC Chair*

Director, Technical Emergency Support Division, Department of Public
Safety

Address and Phone
Department of Public Safety
Technical Emergency Support Division
P.O. Box 1628
Santa Fe, New Mexico 87504-1628
(505) 827-3375

LEPC Designation
Established 33 counties as LEPDs

NEW YORK: *SERC Chair*

Commissioner, New York Department of Health, by appointment of the
Governor.

Address and Phone
New York State Emergency Response Commission
Public Security Building
State Campus
Albany, NY 12226-5000
(518)457-2222

LEPC Designation
Established 57 counties as LEPDs

NORTH CAROLINA: *SERC Chair*

Director, Division of Emergency Management

Address and Phone
North Carolina Emergency Response Commission
116 West Jones Street
Raleigh, North Carolina 27603-1335
(919)733-3867

LEPC Designation
Established 6 existing emergency response regions as Title II Local
Emergency Planning Districts

NORTH DAKOTA: *SERC Chair*

Director, Division of Emergency Management, State Emergency
Operations Center

Address and Phone
North Dakota Health Department
Environmental Engineering Division
Room 304
Post Office Box 5520
Bismarck, North Dakota 58502-5520
(701)224-2348
(Notifications and Chemical Inventory)

North Dakota Division of Emergency Management
Post Office Box 5511
Bismarck, North Dakota 58502-5511
(701)224-2111
(Emergency Planning)

LEPC Designation
Established 53 counties as LEPDs

OHIO: *SERC Chair*

Assistant Director, Ohio Environmental Protection Agency

Address and Phone
Ohio Environmental Protection Agency
SARA Title III
P.O. Box 1049
Columbus, Ohio 43266-0149
(614) 481-4300

LEPC Designation
86 counties formed districts and two counties joined together in one district, resulting in 87 planning districts

---

OKLAHOMA:

SERC Chair

Secretary of Safety and Security

Address and Phone
Oklahoma Department of Civil Defense
Post Office Box 53365
Oklahoma City, Oklahoma 73152
(405) 521-2481

LEPC Designation
Established 77 counties as LEPDs

OREGON:

SERC Chair

Assistant to the Governor for Natural Resources

Address and Phone
Oregon State Emergency Response Commission
c/o State Fire Marshal
3000 Market Street Plaza
Suite 534
Salem, Oregon 97310
(503) 378-3473

LEPC Designation
Designated the entire state to serve as the Title III Local Emergency Planning District

---

PENNSYLVANIA:

SERC Chair

Lieutenant Governor

Address and Phone
Pennsylvania Emergency Response Commission
c/o Pennsylvania Emergency Management Agency
P.O. Box 3321
Harrisburg, Pennsylvania 17105
(717) 783-8150

LEPC Designation
Established 67 counties as LEPDs

PUERTO RICO:

SERC Chair

Chair of the existing Puerto Rico Environmental Quality Board

Address and Phone
Puerto Rico Environmental Quality Board
Office of the Governor
Box 11488
San Juan, Puerto Rico 00910

(809) 725-5140, ext. 204 or 214
(809) 722-1175, 722-2173

LEPC Designation
Established 9 existing Civil Defense Emergency Zones as LEPDs

---

RHODE ISLAND:

SERC Chair

Director, Rhode Island Emergency Management Agency

Address and Phone
Rhode Island Emergency Management Agency
State House
Providence, Rhode Island 02903
(401) 272-3121

LEPC Designation
Established 8 Mutual Aid Agreements boundaries as LEPDs

SOUTH CAROLINA:

SERC Chair

Director, Division of Public Safety Programs, Executive Policy and Programs Office

South Carolina Emergency Response Commission
Division of Public Safety Programs
Office of the Governor
1205 Pendleton Street
Columbia, South Carolina 29201
(803) 734-0442

LEPC Designation
Established 46 counties as LEPDs

SOUTH DAKOTA:

SERC Chair

Chairman, Board of Minerals and Environment

Address and Phone:
South Dakota Emergency Response Commission
Department of Water and Natural Resources
Office of Air Quality and Solid Waste
523 E. Capitol Street, Room 217
Pierre, South Dakota 57501
(605) 773-3153

LEPC Designation
Established 6 emergency planning regions as LEPDs

TENNESSEE:

SERC Chair

Director, Emergency Management Agency

Address and Phone
Tennessee Emergency Response Council
c/o Tennessee Emergency Management Agency
3042 Sidco Drive

Nashville, Tennessee 37204-1502
(615) 252-3300

LEPC Designation
Established 95 counties as LEPDs

TEXAS:

SERC Chair

Director, Department of Public Safety and Chair of existing Council

Address and Phone
Texas State Emergency Response Council
Division of Emergency Management
Post Office Box 4087
Austin, Texas 78773-0001
(512)465-2138

LEPC Designation
Established 254 counties as LEPDs

UTAH:

SERC Chair

Commissioner, Department of Public Safety, and Executive Director, Department of Health

Address and Phone
Utah Department of Public Safety
Post Office Box 8100
1543 Sunnyside Avenue
Salt Lake City, Utah 84108-0110
(801)533-5271
(Emergency Planning)

Utah Department of Health
288 North, 1460 West
Post Office Box 16690
Salt Lake City, Utah 84106-0690
(801) 538-6121
(Chemical Inventory and Community Right-to-Know)

LEPC Designation
Established 13 Local Emergency Planning Districts in the state

---

VERMONT:

SERC Chair

Commissioner, Department of Labor and Industry

Address and Phone
Vermont Emergency Response Commission
Department of Labor and Industry
120 State Street
State Office Building
Montpelier, Vermont 05602
(802)828-2286

LEPC Designation
Six of Vermont's fourteen counties formed their own planning districts

VIRGINIA:

SERC Chair

Executive Director, Department of Waste Management

Address and Phone
Virginia Emergency Response Council
c/o Department of Waste Management
James Monroe Building, Eleventh Floor
101 North Fourteenth Street
Richmond, Virginia 23219
(804) 225-2667

LEPC Designation
Established 74 counties, 25 cities and eight towns with populations of 5000 or more as LEPDs

---

WASHINGTON:

SERC Chair

Director, Department of Community Development

Address and Phone
Washington State Emergency Response Commission
Department of Community Development
9th and Columbia Building
GH-51
Olympia, Washington 98504
(206) 753-2200

LEPC Designation
Established 39 counties and 25 cities as LEPDs

WEST VIRGINIA:

SERC Chair

Director, Department of Natural Resources

Address and Phone
West Virginia Emergency Response Commission
Department of Natural Resources
1800 E. Washington Street
Charleston, West Virginia 25305
(304) 348-2755

LEPC Designation
Established 55 counties as LEPDs

WISCONSIN:

SERC Chair

Administrator, Division of Emergency Government, Department of Administration

Address and Phone
Wisconsin Division of Emergency Government
Department of Administration
4802 Sheboygan Avenue
Post Office Box 7865
Madison, Wisconsin 53707
(608) 266-3232

LEPC Designation
Established 72 counties as LEPDs

WYOMING:

SERC Chair

Private Citizen

Address and Phone
Wyoming Emergency Response Commission
c/o Emergency Management Agency
P.O. Box 1709
Cheyenne, Wyoming 82003
(307) 777-7566

LEPC Designation
Established 23 counties as LEPDs

Source: National Governor's Association, *The Emergency Planning and Community Right-to-Know Act: A status of State Actions.*
(Washington, D.C.: National Governors Association) April 1988.

APPENDIX F

OHIO HAZARDOUS MATERIALS CROSS REFERENCE

THE PLAN CROSS REFERENCE

Cross reference for the hazardous materials emergency response plan.

For planning element details, see *NRT-1*, Part 5, *Planning Guide, which describes what sort of information should be included in each element. These issues need to be addressed in the plan.*

Planning Element	*Local Plan Reference*
	Section Part Page

A. *Introduction*

   1. Incident Information Summary—
Develop a format for recording essential information about the incident. _____

   2. Promulgation Document—
statement of plan authority _____

   3. Legal Authority and Responsibility
for Responding

     a. Authorizing legislation and regulations _____

       1. Federal (e.g., CERCLA,
SARA, Clean Water Act,
National Continguency
Plan, and Disaster Relief
Act) _____

       2. State _____

       3. Regional _____

       4. Local _____

     b. Mandated agency responsibilities _____

     c. Letters of agreement _____

4. Table of Contents—All sections of the plan should be listed here and clearly labeled with a tab for easy access.

   _____

5. Abbreviations and Definitions— Frequently used abbreviations, acronyms, and definitions should be gathered here for easy reference.

   _____

6. Assumptions/Planning Factors— Appropriate maps should be included in this section. Maps should show water intake, environmentally sensitive areas, major chemical manufacturing or storage facilities, population centers, and the location of response resources.

   _____

  a. Geography and Maps

    1. Sensitive environmental areas.

   _____

    2. Land use (actual and potential in accordance with local development codes).

   _____

    3. Water supplies

   _____

    4. Public transportation networks (roads, trains, buses, school buses).

   _____

    5. Population density of affected areas.

   _____

    6. Particularly sensitive institutions (e.g., schools, hospitals, nursing homes).

   _____

  b. Climate/Weather Statistics (Averages)

   _____

  c. Time Variable (e.g., rush hour, vacation season, annual events).

   _____

  d. Particular Characteristics of Each Facility and the Transportation Routes for Which the Plan is Intended.

   _____

    1. On-site details.

   _____

    2. Neighboring population.

   _____

    3. Surrounding terrain.

   _____

4. Known impediments (tunnels, bridges). _____

5. Other areas at risk. _____

e. Assumptions—Assumptions are the advance judgments concerning what would happen in the ase of an accidental spill or release. For example, planners might assume that a certain percentage of local residents on their own will evacuate the area along routes other than specified evacuation routes.

    1. Vulnerability analysis. _____

    2. Risk analysis. _____

7. Concept of Operations

a. Governing Principles—The plan should include brief statements of precisely what is expected to be accomplished if an incident should occur. _____

    1. Block diagram illustrating relationships among response groups should be included. _____

    2. Include a complete response management reporting chain. _____

    3. Show the capability for 24-hour, protracted operations. _____

b. Organizational Roles and Responsibilities _____

    1. Municipal government. _____

        a. Chief elected official. _____

        b. Emergency management director. _____

        c. Community emergency coordinator (Title III of SARA) _____

        d. Communications personnel _____

        e. Fire service _____

Local Plan Reference

Section   Part   Page

    a. Response capabilities

    b. Procedure for using out-
       side resources

  c. Explain the relationship of this
    plan to other plans and list the
    other plans.

8. Instructions on Plan Use

  a. Planning Element—Purpose:
    This should be a clear and suc-
    cinct statement of when and
    how the plan is meant to be
    used. It is appropriate to list
    those facilities and transpor-
    tation routes explicitly con-
    sidered in the plan.

  b. Plan Section—Plan Distribution

    1. List of organizations/
      persons receiving plan. Or-
      ganizations receiving copies
      should sign and list the date
      of receipt.

      The entire plan should be
      available to the public; it
      can be stored at a library,
      the local emergency man-
      agement agency, or some
      other public place. The plan
      should be distributed to all
      persons responsible for re-
      sponse operations. The plan
      distribution list should ac-
      count for all organizations
      receiving such copies of the
      plan. This information is es-
      sential when determining
      who should be sent revi-
      sions and updates to the
      plan.

    2. Plan maintenance should be
      provided for:

      a. Update as needed

      b. Annual review and cer-
        tification for currency

      c. Plans and approved
        changes distributed ap-
        propriately

    d. Revisions dated and
changes marked   _____

9. Record of Amendments

    a. Change record sheet to include:

      1. Signature of person receiving amendments   _____

      2. Date received amendments   _____

      3. Page number of amendments   _____

      4. Instructions on how to replace the amended pages   _____

B. *Emergency Assistance Telephone Roster*

1. List of telephone numbers for:

    a. See the list in NRT-1 for guidance.   _____

C. *Response Functions*

1. Initial Notification of Response Agencies   _____

    a. Emergency classification system established.   _____

    b. Notification systems keyed to emergency classification system.   _____

    c. Five levels of initial accident notification established: _____

      1. Incident location to local emergency agency.   _____

      2. Local emergency management agency to emergency service organizations.   _____

      3. Emergency service organizations to their personnel.   _____

      4. Local, state and federal officials.   _____

      5. Special facilities.   _____

    d. 24-hour emergency response hotline telephone numbers.   _____

    e. Documentation of accident notification provided for.   _____

Local Plan Reference

Section   Part   Page

   f. Notification of emergency classification levels to special facilities provided for, including:

     1. School districts

     2. Private schools

     3. Day care centers

     4. Hospitals

     5. Nursing homes

     6. Industries

     7. Detention centers

     8. Other (specify)
- NATIONAL RESPONSE CENTER (800-424-8802; 202-426-2675 or 202-267-2675 in Washington, D.C., area)

   g. Other agencies (with telephone numbers) to notify immediately (e.g., hospitals, health department, Red Cross)

2. Direction and Control

   a. Procedures for notifying key officials in the event of an emergency.

   b. Describe who is in charge for each emergency or disaster situation on scene and off and where direction and control will emante from (EOC or in disaster situations where field forces are used as the on-scene commander).

   c. Lines of succession to assure continuous leadership, authority, and responsibility in key positions.

   d. Chain of command (block diagram).

   e. Identifying the circumstances under which predelegated authorities would become effective and when they would be terminated.

f. Criteria for activating an EOC. _____

g. Identifying the official responsible for managing the EOC during emergency periods. _____

h. Identifying, by title or position in the plan, personnel assigned to the EOC in the event of a crisis situation. _____

i. List roles and responsibilities of each. _____

j. Describing EOC functions, layout, concept of operations, duties of staff, use of displays and message forms, and bring the EOC to full readiness on a continuous 24-hour basis for communications and other emergency functions. _____

k. Ensuring EOC staff members can be recalled on short notice. _____

l. An alternate EOC (either fixed or mobile) to serve as a backup if the primary EOC is not able to function. _____

m. Ensure that the EOC workers are trained to acknowledge/ authenticate reports. _____

n. Make provisions for logistical support for food, water, lighting, fuel, etc., to support EOC staff and personnel deployed to the disaster site. _____

o. Establish a central coordinating point(s) for obtaining, analyzing, reporting, and retaining (e.g., events log) disaster-related information (casualty information, property damage, fire status, number of evacuees, radiation dose, etc.) for EOC staff and/or field forces. _____

p. Identifying alternate sites for departments or agencies having emergency functions. _____

Local Plan Reference

Section   Part   Page

q. Method of establishing an on-scene Command Post.

_____

r. Who will maintain the on-scene Command Post?

_____

s. Communications network between Command Post and response teams.

_____

t. Method of activating Emergency Response Teams.

_____

u. Who has advisory roles and what are the roles?

_____

v. 1. Levels of response based on incident history.

_____

2. List of priorities for Response Actions.

_____

w. Who makes the technical recommendations on response actions to the lead agency?

_____

x. Who has veto powers?

_____

y. Who is responsible for requesting outside assistance?

_____

z. Response Action Checklists.

_____

3. Communications (among Responders) Any form(s) of exchanging information or ideas for emergency response under other entities, either internal or external to the existing organizational structure.

_____

a. Show provisions exist for:

_____

1. 24-hour a day notification to include 24-hour communications links.

_____

2. Communications with contiguous state and local governments.

_____

3. Communications with federal agencies.

_____

4. Communications with local EOCs and facility or company.

_____

    5. Alerting and activating
       emergency personnel.

  b. Are there communication links
    for fixed and mobile medical
    support facilities?

  c. Explain the periodic testing of
    entire emergency commu-
    nications system.

  d. Have provisions been made for:

    1. Incident to local commu-
       nications system not vulner-
       able to adverse environmen-
       tal conditions and traffic
       overloading established?

    2. Reliable primary and
       backup means of commu-
       nications established?

    3. Primary and alternate indi-
       vidual, by title, respon-
       sible for communication
       links?

  e. Coordination:

    1. Have procedures been es-
       tablished for coordination of
       information during a re-
       sponse?

    2. Has one organization been
       designated to coordinate
       communications activities?

  f. Clearinghouse Functions:

    1. Has a central clearinghouse
       for hazardous materials in-
       formation been established
       with access by the public
       and private sectors?

4. Warning Systems and Emergency
   Public Notification—Methods for
   Alerting the Public

  a. Establish a means to warn the
    public in the event of a disaster
    situation, defining responsibili-
    ties of agencies or personnel
    and describing activation
    procedures.

b. Develop an emergency classification and action level scheme consistent with that established by the facility and the state.

c. Describe the continuous 24-hour warning point to alert key officials and activate the public warning system.

   1. List of essential data to be passed on (e.g., health hazards precautions for personal protection, evacuation routes and shelters, hospitals to be used).

   2. Time requirements for alerting the public specified.

   3. Special alert is provided for:

      a. Remote areas.

   4. Siren locations and coverage illustrated.

   5. Means for monitoring alert system coverage established.

   6. Alternate alert system established.

   7. Alert system testing provided for.

d. Warning special locations, such as schools, hospitals, nursing homes, major industries, institutions, and places of public assembly.

e. List methods of warning the hearing impaired and non-English-speaking groups where appropriate.

5. Public Information/Community Relations

   a. List an information office which is the official point of contact for the media during an emergency.

b. List an authoritative spokesperson designated as the public information officer (PIO).

_____

c. How does the PIO coordinate with the departments or agencies the release of information to the public?

_____

d. The distribution of emergency public information materials using all sources available, such as newspapers, radio, television, etc.

_____

e. Describe the preparation of EPI guidance materials based on all hazards affecting the jurisdiction (pamphlets, magazines, etc).

_____

f. Provide for disseminating prescripted emergency information materials available for use by the media.

_____

g. Provide for disseminating EPI materials for the visually impaired and non-English-speaking groups, if appropriate.

_____

h. What written or oral agreements are available with the information media for dissemination of emergency public information and emergency warnings?

_____

i. List points of contact for release of public information in an emergency.

_____

j. Include EBS operational area planning requirements.

_____

k. Provide details on disseminating essential information to the public, including the appropriate protective actions to be taken.

_____

l. List methods for authenticating all sources of information being received and varified for accuracy.

_____

m. List methods for clearing information with the chief executive before release to the media.

_____

Local Plan Reference

Section   Part   Page

n. List methods for addressing rumor control.

o. What procedures are in place for informing the public about places of contact for missing relatives, continued emergency services, restricted areas, etc.?

p. Provide announcements urging residents to share their homes with evacuees.

6. Resource Management

a. List the personnel needed for emergency response.

b. Have response equipment requirements been identified for a given level of response capability?

c. Are the following types of equipment available?

1. Personal protective equipment

2. First aid and other medical emergency equipment

3. Emergency vehicles available for hazardous materials response

4. Sampling equipment (air, water, soil, etc.) and other monitoring devices (e.g., explosivity meters, oxygen meters)

5. Analytical equipment of facilities available for sample analyses

6. Firefighting equipment/ other equipment and material (bulldozers, boats, helicopters, vacuum trucks, tank trucks, chemical retardants, foam)

d. Are sufficient quantities of each type of equipment available on a sustained basis?

e. Is all available equipment capable of operating in the local environmental conditions?

f. Are up-to-date equipment lists maintained? Are they computerized?

g. Are equipment lists available to all responders?

h. Are these lists broken down into the various types of equipment (e.g., protective clothing, monitoring instruments, medical supplies, transportation equipment)?

i. Is there a mechanism to ensure that the lists are kept up-to-date?

j. Have procedures necessary to obtain equipment on a 24-hour basis been identified?

k. Does a program exist to carry out required maintenance of equipment?

l. Are there maintenance and repair records for each piece of equipment?

m. Have mutual aid agreements been established for the use of specialized response equipment?

n. Is sufficient communications equipment available for notifying personnel or to transmit information? Is the equipment of various participating agencies compatible?

o. Is transportation equipment available for moving equipment rapidly to the scene of an incident, and its state of readiness assured?

p. Have facilities capable of performing rapid chemical analysis been identified?

q. Do adequate facilities exist for storage and cleaning/reconditioning of response equipment?

_____

r. Have locations or facilities been identified for the storage, treatment, recycling, and disposal of wastes resulting from a release?

_____

s. Do facilities exist that are capable of providing medical treatment to persons injured by chemical exposure?

_____

t. Have facilities and procedures been identified for housing persons requiring evacuation or temporary relocation as a result of an incident?

_____

u. Have facilities been identified that are suitable for command centers.?

_____

7. Health and Medical

_____

a. Provisions for medical treatment have been made in the following areas:

_____

1. Inoculating individuals if warranted by the threat of disease.

_____

2. Determining the need for contaminated and exposed individuals for treatment and care, including decontamination.

_____

3. Expanding mortuary services in an emergency.

4. Establishing and operating emergency medical care centers for essential workers in the hazardous area following the evacuation of the general population.

_____

5. Provide for health/medical care at shelter/congregate care facilities.

_____

6. Health/medical services in reception and care facilities.

_____

7. Obtain emergency medical support and hospital care during and after an emergency.

8. Reducing the patient population in hospitals, nursing homes, and other health care facilities if evacuation is necessary, and continuing medical care for those that cannot be evacuated.

9. Identifying hospitals, nursing homes, and other facilities that could be expanded into emergency treatment centers for disaster victims.

10. Crisis augmentation of health/medical personnel (e.g., nurses' aides, paramedics, Red Cross personnel and other trained volunteers).

b. Provisions for ambulance service in the following areas have been made:

1. Transport and care of individuals from the disaster site to medical facilities.

2. Noninstitutionalized population needing ambulance transportation confidentiality listed.

3. Methodology for compiling above list described.

4. Ambulance reserve for injured persons and unforeseen requests established.

5. Means for requesting ambulance transportation specified.

6. Priority for use of ambulances established.

7. Percentage of institutionalized population needing am-

bulance transportation estimated.

8. Response Personnel Safety

   a. Establish standard operating
   procedure for entering and leaving sites.

   b. Accountability for personnel entering and leaving the sites has
   been planned for.

   c. Establish decontamination
   procedures.

   d. List recommended safety and
   health equipment that is
   available.

   e. Establish personal safety precautions.

   Care must be taken to choose
   equipment that protects the worker
   from the hazard present at the site
   without unnecessarily restricting
   the capacities of the worker. Although the emphasis in equipment
   choices is commonly focused on
   protecting the worker from the
   risks presented by the hazardous
   material, impaired vision, restricted
   movements, or excessive heat can
   put the worker at equal risk.

9. Personal Protection of Citizens

   a. Indoor Protection.

      1. List hazard-specific personal
      protection to also include:

         a. An emergency manage-
         ment system and
         decision-making criteria
         for determining when an
         indoor protection
         strategy should be used.

         b. A system for warning
         and advising the public.

         c. A system for determin-
         ing when a cloud has
         cleared a particular
         area.

d. A system for advising people to leave a building at an appropriate time.

_____

e. Public education on the value of indoor protection and on expedient means to reduce ventilation.

_____

b. Evacuation Procedures

_____

1. Discuss all evacuation procedures to include:

_____

a. Title of person and alternate(s) who can order/recommend an evacuation.

_____

b. Vulnerable zones where evacuation could be necessary and a method for notifying these places.

_____

c. Provisions for a precautionary evacuation.

_____

d. Methods for controlling traffic flow and providing alternate traffic routes.

_____

e. Shelter locations and other provisions for evacuations (e.g., special assistance for hospitals).

_____

f. Agreements with nearby jurisdictions to receive evacuees.

_____

g. Agreements with hospitals outside the local jurisdictions.

_____

h. Protective shelter for relocated populations.

_____

i. Reception and care of evacuees.

_____

j. Reentry procedures.

_____

2. Maps (drawn to the same scale) with evacuation routes and alternatives clearly identified should be prepared for each risk zone in the area. Maps should indicate precise routes to another location where special populations (e.g., from schools, hospitals,nursing homes, homes for the physically or mentally disabled) can be taken during an emergency evacuation, and the methods of transportation during the evacuation.

3. Consideration of when and how evacuees will return to their homes should be part of this section.

4. This section on evacuation should include a description of how other agencies will coordinate with the medical community.

5. Copies of evacuation procedures should be provided to all appropriate agencies and organizations (e.g., Salvation Army, churches, schools, hospitals) and could periodically be published in the local newspaper(s).

c. Other Public Protection Strategies to be outlined are:

1. Relocation

2. Water supply protection.

3. Sewage system protection.

10. Fire and Rescue

a. List the following in detail:

1. Chain of command among firefighters.

2. List of available support systems.

   _____

3. List of all tasks for fire-fighters.

   _____

4. The deployment of fire/rescue personnel and equipment in the event of an emergency.

   _____

5. Fire protection in emergency shelters.

   _____

6. Providing decision makers advice on the hazards associated with hazardous materials.

   _____

7. Rescuing injured people during emergency operations.

   _____

8. Alerting all emergency support services of the dangers associated with technological hazards and fire during emergency operations.

   _____

b. This section should also identify any mutual aid or Good Samaritan agreements with neighboring fire departments, hazmat teams, and other support systems.

   _____

11. Law Enforcement

   _____

a. List in detail the following:

   _____

1. Chain of command for law enforcement officials.

   _____

2. List of all tasks for law enforcement personnel.

   _____

3. Traffic control during an emergency.

   _____

4. Relocating and housing prisoners in the event of an emergency.

   _____

5. The use of law enforcement personnel to assist in movement to shelter or evacuate.

   _____

6. Security for critical facilities and resources.

   _____

7. Law enforcement in reception centers, lodging and feeding facilities, and emergency shelters.

8. The protection of property and damaged areas.

9. Evacuating disaster areas during emergency operations.

10. Limiting access to the evacuation area during response and recovery operations.

b. This section should include maps that indicate control points where police officers should be stationed in order to expedite the movement of responders toward the scene and of evacuees away from the scene, to restrict unnecessary traffic from entering the scene, and to control the possible spread of contamination.

12. Ongoing Incident Assessment

a. Discuss the makeup and duties of the field monitoring teams.

b. Provision for environmental assessment, biological monitoring, and contamination surveys should be included in this plan.

c. Food/water controls should be established in this plan.

d. Discuss the following areas:

1. Hazardous Materials Response Teams with rapid, 24-hour capability.

2. Hazardous Material Team Procedures.

a. Identification of hazardous materials.

b. First aid and life saving.

c. Method of obtaining specific information in-

volved hazardous mate-
rials.

   d. Accident description
and potential hazards.

   e. Hazardous materials
survey instruments.

   f. Dose projection techniques.

   g. Area control
procedures.

   h. Environmental sampling
procedures.

   i. Methods of obtaining
meteorological infor-
mation.

   j. Provisions for communications between Haz-
ardous Material Teams
and central assessment
control point.

   k. Accident site chain of
command.

   l. Inclement weather hazard assessment

   m. Record keeping and
documentation of acci-
dent assessment.

13. Human Services

   a. List the agencies providing human services. Coordinate the
activities of organizations such
as the Red Cross, Salvation
Army, local church groups, and
others that will help people during a hazardous materials emergency.

   b. List the human services tasks of
each agency.

14. Public Works

   a. List all tasks for public works
personnel to include:

      1. Clearance of debris in an
emergency.

2. Backup electrical power to the EOC.

3. Preparation and maintenance of a resource list that identifies source, location and availability of earth-moving equipment, dump trucks, road graders, fuel, etc., that could be used to support disaster response/recovery operations.

4. The repair and restoration of essential services and vital facilities.

5. A potable water supply during an emergency.

6. Restoring utilities to critical and essential facilities.

7. Sanitation services during an emergency.

15. Others

   a. If the preceding list of functions does not adequately cover the various tasks to be performed during emergency responses, additional response functions can be developed.

D. *Containment and Cleanup*

   1. Techniques for Spill Containment and Cleanup

      a. Outline the following:

         1. Containment and mitigation actions.

         2. Cleanup methods.

         3. Restoration of the surrounding environment.

         4. Criteria for reentry established, including:

            a. Acceptable residual levels.

            b. Existing and potential conditions.

    c. State and industry rec-
       ommendations. _____

    d. Selective reentry op-
       tions described. _____

5. Continued monitoring/
   sampling _____

6. Means for informing evacuees of reentry _____

7. Services similar to those for
   evacuation provided, including: _____

    a. Traffic control _____

    b. Transportation assis-
       tance _____

8. Postaccident surveying and
   decontamination tech-
   niques. _____

9. Decontamination of
   property and disposition of
   contaminated product
   procedures. _____

10. Inspection, inventory, and
    return of equipment. _____

2. Resources for Cleanup and Disposal _____

  a. Provide for and discuss: _____

    1. Cleanup disposal contrac-
      tors and services provided. _____

    2. Cleanup material and
      equipment _____

    3. Communications equipment _____

    4. Provision for long-term site
      control during extended
      cleanups _____

    5. Emergency transportation
      (e.g., aircraft, four-wheel-
      drive vehicle, boats) _____

    6. Cleanup personnel _____

    7. Personal protective
      equipment _____

    8. Approved disposal sites _____

b. This section is similar to the Yellow Pages of the telephone book. It provides plan users with the following important information:

    1. What types of resources are available (public and private)

    2. How much is stockpiled

    3. Where it is located (address and telephone number)

    4. What steps are necessary to obtain the resources

c. Organizations that may have resources for use during a hazardous materials incident include:

    1. Public agencies (e.g., fire, police, public works, public health, agriculture, fish and game)

    2. Industry (e.g., chemical producers, transporters, storers, associations, spill cleanup contractors, construction companies)

    3. Spill/equipment cooperatives

    4. Volunteer groups (ham radio operators, four-wheel-drive vehicle clubs)

d. Resource availability will change with time, so keep this section of the plan up-to-date

E. *Documentation and Investigative Follow-Up*

1. Include a list of required reports.

2. Explain the reasons for requiring the reports.

3. Show the format for reports.

4. Explain methods for determining whether the response mechanism worked properly.

5. Discuss provision for cost recovery to include

   a. Documentation of damages, losses and costs provided for

   b. Consolidation and review of records

   c. Critique and report of overall emergency operations.

F. *Procedures for Testing and Updating Plan*

   1. Testing the plan

      a. Make provisions for regular tabletop, functional, and full-scale exercises.

      b. List the organization in charge of the exercise.

      c. Explain the types of exercises.

      d. List the frequency of exercises.

      e. Include a procedure for evaluating performance, making changes to plans, and correcting identified deficiencies in response capabilities as necessary.

   2. Updating the plan

      a. List and discuss the following topics:

         1. Training for planners

         2. Title and organization of persons responsible for hazardous materials response planning

         3. Designation of emergency planning coordinator

         4. How often the plan should be audited and what mechanisms will be used to change the plan

         5. Distribution of revisions

         6. Detailed list of supporting plans

Local Plan Reference

Section   Part   Page

7. List of procedures to implement the plan

8. Table of Contents and Cross Reference

9. Review by the State Emergency Response Commission

10. State Emergency Response Commission recommendations

11. Review of plans by Regional Response Teams (RRT)

12. Distribution of plans

13. Telephone numbers

b. Following are examples of information that must be regularly checked for accuracy:

1. Identity and phone numbers of response personnel.

2. Name, quantity, properties, and location of hazardous materials in the community. (If new hazardous materials are made, used, stored or transported in the community, revise the plan as needed.)

3. Facility maps.

4. Transportation routes.

5. Emergency services available

6. Resource availability.

G. *Hazards Analysis (Summary)*

1. Identify the hazardous materials hazards of the area.

2. Include an analysis of vulnerability.

3. Include an analysis of risk.

4. Individual data sheets and maps for each facility and transportation route of interest could be included

in this section. Similar data could be included for recurrent shipments of hazardous materials through the area. This section will also assess the probability of damage and/or injury. In communities with a great deal of hazardous materials activity, the hazards analysis will be too massive to include in the emergency plan. In that case, all significant details should be summarized here.

H. *Training*

   1. Programs should be established for initial training and periodic retraining of all personnel who have responsibilities for responding to accidents involving hazardous materials to teach:

      a. Hazardous materials, types, recognition and contamination.

      b. DOT and NRC regulations on transportation of hazardous materials, including labeling, placarding, shipping papers and packaging requirements.

      c. Relative hazard of hazardous materials.

      d. General responsibilities of carriers, shippers and licensees in emergencies.

      e. Training for specific problems which may be encountered.

      f. Types and quantities of hazardous materials typically used or transported.

      g. Familiarity with major manufacturers and industries dealing with hazardous materials.

   2. Provision should be made for using applicable training programs of manufacturers and users to supplement state and local government emergency training programs.

   3. Each state and local response organization should participate in and

receive training. Where mutual aid agreements exist, the training should also be offered to the other organizations who are part of the agreement.

4. Specific training should be provided to those individuals with specific roles in response such as first aid, rescue, security, traffic control, firefighting and medical personnel. Topics should include such items as protective measures, assessment, communications, relationship to federal response capabilities, decontamination and cleanup.

5. Emphasis should be given to training and encouraging smaller rural hospitals located near major highways to develop response plans.

I. *References*

1. Laboratory, Consultant, and Other Technical Support Resources

   a. Include a telephone directory of technical support services including

      1. Laboratories (environmental and public health).

      2. Private consultants.

      3. Colleges or universities (chemistry departments and special courses)

      4. Local chemical plants.

2. Technical Library

   a. Include a list of references, their location, and their availability to include:

      1. General planning references.

      2. Specific references for hazardous materials.

      3. Technical references and methods for using national data bases.

      4. Maps.

APPENDIX G

GLOSSARY

Absolute Pressure. The true pressure. It equals atmospheric plus gauge pressure and is abbreviated "psia."

Absolute Zero. The lowest point on the Kelvin scale, at which there is a total absence of heat: $-459.67°F$ or $-273.15°C$. The temperature at which all molecular motion ceases.

Absorbent Material. Used to soak up liquid hazardous materials. Commercially bagged clay, kitty litter, or Zorbal.

Absorption. The taking in of toxic materials by contact with the skin. Where one material actually penetrates the inner structure of another. Contrast with *Adsorption*.

Acid. A chemical compound that contains one or more hydrogen ions that liberate hydrogen gas on contact with certain metals, and is very active chemically.

Acid Gas. A gas that forms an acid when dissolved in water.

Acid or Ammonia Suits. Special protective clothing that prevents toxic or corrosive substances or vapors from coming in contact with the body.

Active Ingredient. A chemical that has pesticidal action. Active ingredients are listed in order on a pesticide label as percentage by weight or as pounds per gallon of concentrate. See *Inert Ingredients*.

Acidity. The degree to which the pH of a substance is below 7.

Activity. Refers to chemical activity, the speed with which the element will seek out ways to satisfy the octet rule.

Acute Poisoning. Poisoning by a single exposure to a toxic chemical.

Additive. Any material mixed with a plastic or resin to modify its properties.

Adsorption. Where on substance is attracted to and held on the surface of another. Contrast with *Absorption*.

Aerator. Device for introducing air into dry bulk solids to improve flowability.

AFFF. Aqueous-film-forming-foam. An extinguishing agent designed to flow over a burning liquid. Can be used on certain pesticides.

Air-Reactive Materials. Substances that will ignite at normal temperatures when exposed to air.

Air-Supplied Suit. Protective suit providing a completely enclosed environment.

Alcohol. The hydrocarbon derivative whereby a hydroxyl radical (–OH) is substituted for a hydrogen atom and has the general formula R–OH.

Alcohol Foam. Blankets fires in the same manner as conventional foam, but is intended for use with liquids which are soluble in water, such as alcohol and acetone. It must be applied more carefully than regular foam because the mechanical strength of the bubbles is less.

Aldehyde. A hydrocarbon derivative with the general formula R–CHO.

Alkali. Any compound which forms the hydroxide ion.

Alkali Metals. The elements of Group IA.

Alkaline Earth. The elements of Group IIA.

Alkalinity. The degree to which the pH of a substance is above 7.

Alkanes. An analogous series of saturated hydrocarbons with the general formula C_nH_{2n+2}.

Alkenes. An analogous series of unsaturated hydrocarbons with the general formula C_nH_{2n}. The alkenes all contain just one double bond between carbon atoms.

Alkyl. The general name for a radical of an alkane. An alkyl halide is a halogenated hydrocarbon whose hydrocarbon backbone originated as an alkane.

Alkynes. An analogous series of unsaturated hydrocarbons with the general formula C_nH_{2n-2}. The alkynes all contain just one triple bond between carbon atoms.

Alloy (Metal). A physical mixture of two or more materials.

Alloy (Plastic). A blend of polymers and/or copolymers.

Allotrope. A different form of the same substance. One of several possible forms of a substance.

Alpha Particle. The largest of the common radioactive particles, having a mass of 4 amu. It is identical to the nucleus of the helium atoms, travels only 3 or 4 inches, and is stopped by a sheet of paper.

Alpha Rays. Made up of very large particles which are the same as the nucleus of the helium atom.

Amine. The hydrocarbon derivative whereby an amine group (NH_2) is substituted for a hydrogen atom and has the general formula $R-NH_2$.

Ammonium Nitrate. Fertilizer used on crops and usually found in farm supply occupancies. Can be in bulk or bags. It is a strong oxidizer, enhances combustion, and can explode.

AMU. Atomic mass unit. The unit of weight used to state atomic or molecular weights of atoms or molecules. The proton and the neutron both weigh 1 amu.

Anhydrous. Without water.

Anhydrous Ammonia. Nitrogen/hydrogen-based compressed liquefied gas (without water).

Analogous Series. A series of compounds that have similar differences between compounds. That is, in an analogous series of hydrocarbon compounds, each compound is different from the one succeeding it (one more carbon atom in the chain) or the one preceding it (one less carbon atom in the chain) by a specific "unit," or part of the compound, like one carbon and two hydrogens.

Analogue. A compound in one analogous series that has something in common with a compound in another analogous series; for example, methyl chloride is an analogue of methyl fluoride.

Anion. A negatively charged ion.

Aromatic. The name originally given to cyclical compounds containing the benzene ring, because the first benzene-type compounds isolated smelled good.

Article. A manufactured item which:
1. Is formed to a specific shape or design during manufacture;
2. Has end use function(s) dependent, in whole or in part, upon its shape or design during end use; and
3. Does not release, or otherwise result in exposure to, a hazardous chemical under normal conditions of use.

Asphyxiant. (1) A substance that can cause death by displacing air inside enclosures. (2) A substance that interferes with the respiratory process. A gas that is essentially nontoxic but can cause unconsciousness or death by lowering the concentration of oxygen in the air or by totally replacing the oxygen in breathing air.

Asphyxiating Materials. Substances that can cause death by displacing the oxygen in the air.

Atmospheric Pressure. The pressure caused by the weight of the air elevated above the earth's surface. At sea level it equals 14.7 pounds per square inch (psi).

Atmospheric Tank. Storage tank for moderately volatile liquids stored near normal atmoshperic pressure.

Atom. The smallest particle of an element that can exist. The smallest particle of an element that can still be identified as the element.

Atomic Number. The number of protons in the nucleus.

Atomic Weight. The total number of protons and neutrons in the nucleus. A fractional atomic weight is due to the averaging of the weights of all the isotopes of the element.

Atomization. Reduction of a substance to minute particles.

Autoignition Temperature. The minimum temperature to which a substance must be heated in order to initiate or cause self-sustained combustion independently of the heated element. Same as ignition temperature.

Backdraft. The term given to a type of explosion caused by the sudden influx of air into a mixture of gases heated to above the ignition temperature of at least one of them.

Bactericide. A pesticide used to control bacteria.

Base. A chemical compound that contains the hydroxide ion, is the chemical opposite of an inorganic acid, and is very active chemically.

Beta Particle. Same size as an electron, but may be charged positively or negatively, can travel up to 100 feet, and needs special protection in addition to turnout gear.

Beta Rays. Rays made up of electrons; smaller than alpha rays.

Bi-. The prefix meaning two.

Binary Compound. A compound that contains the atoms or ions of two elements. It may contain more than one atom or ion of an element, but only two elements may be represented in the compound.

Blasting Agent. A mixture of materials, usually ammonium nitrate and fuel oil, that is used instead of an explosive in certain applications. It does not contain any explosives and is so insensitive to heat and shock that special procedures are required to cause it to explode.

Blasting Cap. A device containing a primary and/or a secondary explosive, and used to detonate the main charge.

BLEVE. (1) An acronym for Boiling Liquid Expanding Vapor Explosion. Normally concerned with fires involving compressed gases in cylinders. (2) A major container break, into two or more pieces, at a moment when the contained liquid is at a temperature well above its boiling point at normal atmospheric pressure. (3) Boiling Liquid Expanding Vapor Explosion. A container failure with a release of energy, often rapidly and violently, accompanied by a release of gas to the atmosphere and propulsion of the container or its pieces.

Blood Axphyxiant. A substance that interferes with the ability of the red blood cells to carry oxygen to the cells of the body and to release it to those cells.

Boiling Point. (1) The temperature at which a substance changes from a liquid to a gas within the body of the liquid, varying in accordance with altitude and pressure. (2) The temperature at which the vapor pressure of a liquid equals the atmospheric pressure. The temperature at which a liquid vaporizes. (3) The temperature at which a liquid boils, given in either degrees Celsius or degrees Fahrenheit, at a pressure of 760 mm of mercury (Hg), 1 atm, or 14.7 psia (absolute). (4) The temperature at which the vapor pressure of the liquid just equals the atmospheric pressure.

Booster Explosive. See *Secondary Explosive.*

Boyle's Law. The volume occupied by a given mass of gas varies inversely with the absolute pressure if the temperature stays the same, or $PV =$ Constant. When the temperature and mass of a gas are kept constant, the product of the pressure and volume is equal to a constant.

Branching. When a carbon atom attaches itself to another carbon atom that has two or three other carbon atoms attached to it, a *branch,* or side chain, is formed. When the carbon attaches to another carbon that has only one other carbon attached to it, a straight chain is formed rather than branched.

Brisance. The sharp, shattering effect an explosive has on its surroundings. Also referred to as the ''explosive power'' of an explosive.

BTU. An acronym for British Thermal Unit. The BTU designates the quantity of heat, whereas temperature measures the intensity of heat. The amount of heat necessary to raise 1 pound of water 1°F from 63°F to 64°F.

Butane. One of the paraffin hydrocarbons (C_4H_{10}).

Calorie. The amount of heat (energy) required to raise the temperature of 1 gram of water 1°C.

Carbon Dioxide. A gas stored in cylinders and applied through a fixed or semifixed system or from a portable extinquisher. It is useful for inerting a closed area or for putting out small local fires.

Carbon Monoxide. A highly toxic, flammable gas that is a by-product of incomplete combustion. This gas is very dangerous.

Carbonaceous. A compound having a carbon atom in the chemical structure.

Carbonyl. The functional group with the structural formula

Carboy. A glass or plastic bottle encased in a wooden crate.

Carcinogen. A cancer-causing agent.

Catalyst. A substance that, when present, affects the rate of a chemical reaction. An additive that speeds up a reaction but is not consumed by the reaction.

Catalytic Combustion. A process employed by many combustible gas and vapor detectors; measures by passing vapors over a heated filament to detect the resistance of the filament in direct proportion to the presence of vapors.

Cation. A positively charged ion.

Caustic. Any strongly alkaline substance that has a corrosive effect on tissue. Usually refers to bases.

Chain. The way carbon atoms react with each other and with covalent bonds between them, resembling a chain with carbon atoms as the links.

Chain Length. The number of repeating monomer units in a polymer molecule.

Charles' Law. This Law states that the volume of a given mass of gas is directly proportional to its absolute temperature if the pressure is kept constant. If the volume of a gas is kept constant and the temperature is increased, the pressure increases in direct proportion to the increase in absolute temperature.

Chemical. Any element, chemical compound or mixture of elements and/or compounds.

Chemical Action. The reaction of a chemical with another substance.

Chemical Manufacturer. An employer in SIC Codes 20 through 39 with a workplace where chemical(s) are produced for use or distribution.

Chemical Name. The scientific designation of a chemical in accordance with the nomenclature system developed by the International Union of Pure and Applied Chemistry (IUPAC) or the Chemical Abstracts Service (CAS) rules of nomenclature, or a name which will clearly identify the chemical for the purpose of conducting a hazard evaluation.

Chemical Property. Property of a material related to toxicity, flammability or chemical reactivity.

Chemical Reaction. Where a chemical change occurs when two or more substances are brought together and energy is either absorbed or liberated. The types of chemical reactions are oxidation, reduction, ionization, combustion, polymerization, hydrolysis and condensation.

Chemical Resistance. The ability of a material to resist chemical reaction with active chemicals.

Chemistry. The science of matter, energy and reactions.

CHEMTREC. (1) The Chemical Transportation Center (Emergency), a telephone hotline for emergencies;

phone: (800) 424-9300. (2) CHEMical TRansportation Emergency Center. Provides assistance during a hazardous materials emergency:
1. Relays action information in regard to the specific chemical.
2. Will contact the manufacturer or other experts for additional information or on-site assistance.

Chronic Poisoning. Poisoning that occurs over a period of time as a result of repeated exposure to sublethal doses.

Class A Combustibles. Ordinary combustibles, which leave a residue after burning.

Class B Combustibles. Flammable liquids and gases.

Class C Combustibles. Class A or B fires that occur in or near electrical equipment.

Class D Combustibles. Combustible metals that are easily oxidized.

Class A Explosive. A material or device that presents a maximum hazard through detonation.

Class B Explosive. A material or device that presents a flammable hazard and functions by deflagration.

Class C Explosive. A material or device that contains restricted quantities of either a Class A or B explosive, or both, but presents a minimum hazard.

Class A Poison. A poisonous gas or liquid of such nature that a very small amount of the gas, or vapor of the liquid, mixed with air, is dangerous to life.

Class B Poison. Highly toxic material. A substance that is known to be so toxic to human life that it provides a severe health hazard during transportation.

Classification. An artificial grouping of objects or incidents into like categories. In reference to fire, the classification is as follows:
Class A: Fires in combustibles and flammable gases or liquids.
Class B: Fires in combustible solids, such as wood, paper and cardboard.
Class C: Fires involving energized electrical equipment.
Class D: Fires involving combustible metals such as magnesium

CFR. Code of Federal Regulations. The formal name given to those books or documents that contain the specific regulations provided for by the law.

Combination. The change that occurs when two chemicals are combined and the result is a different chemical.

Combustible Gas Indicator (CGI). A device, usually portable, which measures the presence of flammable gases and vapors.

Combustible Liquid. A liquid with a flash point at 100°F or higher.

Combustible Metal. A metal that will burn.

Combustible Solid. A material which ignites relatively easy and is subject to rapid flame propagation at moderate temperatures. (1) (Often called ''fire''.) An exothermic chemical reaction is caused by light, heat and rapid oxidation of fuel, accompanied by flames. Rapid oxidation or chemical combination, usually accompanied by heat or light. (2) A very rapid oxidation reaction, usually accompanied by the liberation of heat and light.

Combustion Explosion. (1) Sudden fracture of a container or structure accompanied by a shock wave due to overpressure created by the attempt of a gas within the container to expand. (2) Reaction produced by heated gas or vapors within an enclosure.

Commission. The State Emergency Response Commission created by the governor of each state.

Common Name. (1) The name originally given to a compound when it was discovered, prior to the adoption of an organized system of assigning proper names. (2) Any designation or identification such as code name, code number, trade name, brand name or generic name used to identify a chemical other than by its chemical name.

Common Name of Pesticide. Well-known made-up name accepted by the Environmental Protection Agency to identify the active ingredients in a pesticide. It is listed under the active ingredient statement on the label.

Complex Ion. Two or more atoms, bound together chemically, that have collectively gained or lost one or more electrons and are now electrically charged.

Compound. A substance which consists of two or more elements that have united chemically. A pure substance composed of two or more elements.

Compound (Chemical). A chemical combination of two or more elements, either the same of different, that is electrically neutral.

Compressed Gas. (1) Any material or mixture having in the container absolute pressure exceeding 40 psi. A gas that, at normal atmospheric temperatures, exists solely in the gaseous state inside its container. A gas that is under pressure, either while in the gaseous state or liquefied. (2) Any material or mixture whose container pressure exceeds 40 psi at 70°F (21.11°C) or whose absolute pressure exceeds 104 psia at 130°F (54.44°C).

Compressed Gas in Solution. A nonliquefied gas that is dissolved in a solvent at high pressures.

Compressed Liquified Gas. Gas which, at normal atmospheric temperatures, exists partly in the gaseous and partly in the liquid state under pressure within its container.

Concentration. The percentage of an acid or base dissolved in water.

Condensation. Going from the gaseous to the liquid state. The process by which a gas or vapor is transformed into a liquid.

Conduction. A method of heat transfer whereby molecules of the substance transfer heat to one another by direct contact. Heat transfer through the movement of atoms within a substance. The transfer of heat through a medium.

Conflagration. A massive fire front that crosses over natural and manmade barriers to involve large numbers of occupancies.

Convection. A method of heat transfer whereby the molecules that are heated circulate throughout the medium. Heat transfer from one place to another by actual motion of the hot material.

Corrosion. The destructive attack of a metal by chemical or electrochemical reaction with its environment.

Corrosive. Any material that will attack and destroy, by chemical action, any living tissue with which it comes in contact.

Corrosive Material. A liquid or solid that causes destruction of human skin tissue or a liquid that has a strong corrosive effect on steel or aluminum.

Covalent Bond. The sharing of two electrons between the atoms of two nonmetallic elements.

Covalent Compound. A compound containing atoms bonded together by covalent bonds.

Cracking. The breaking of covalent bonds, usually between carbon atoms.

Critical Pressure. The pressure required to liquefy a gas at its critical temperature.

Critical Temperature. The temperature above which it is impossible to liquefy a gas.

Crude Oil. Raw produce of an oil well made up of organic hydrocarbons.

Cryogenic. Gases that must be cooled to a very low temperature in order to bring about a change from a gaseous to a liquid state.

Cryogenic Gas. A gas with a boiling point at −150°F or lower.

Cryogenics. Pertains to gases that are liquefied and stored at temperatures approaching absolute zero. Substances having temperatures below −150°F (−101.1°C). The study of the behavior of matter at temperatures of −150°F and below.

Curie. A measure of radioactivity. The amount of radioactive material that will give 37 billion disintegrations per second.

Cyclical. The structure of certain molecules where there is no end to the carbon chain; the molecule is a closed structure resembling a ring, where what would be the last carbon in the chain is bonded to the first. There are cyclical compounds in which the closed structure contains the atoms of other elements in addition to carbon.

Cytotoxin. A poison that attacks a specific organ.

Dash Method. A method of showing the configuration of an atom's upaired electrons by using a dash for every unpaired electron. The dash, when used around the symbol of one element, is *not* a covalent bond.

Decomposition. Reducing a substance to a less complex form. Breaking down a substance to a less complex form. This can be accomplished by the introduction of heat, the addition of neutralized chemicals, or biodegradation.

Deflagrate. To burn very rapidly. The speed of reaction of deflagration is much faster than that of ordinary combustion but slower than that of detonation.

Deflagration. The intense burning rate of some explosives, such as black powder.

Density. The ratio of the weight of a mass to the unit volume.

Derivative. A compound made from a hydrocarbon by substituting another atom or group of atoms for one of the hydrogen atoms in the compound.

Detonation. (1) A wave that passes along the body of an explosive, instantaneously converting it to a gas. (2) Same definition as that of an explosion in many cases. Technically, the major difference is that a detonation is preopagated by a shock wave and travels at supersonic speeds.

Di-. The prefix meaning two.

Diatomic. Two atoms, as in a diatomic molecule, which contains two atoms bound covalently to each other.

Diffusion Flame. The flame produced by the spontaneous mixture of fuel vapors or of gases and air.

Diluent. A liquid or solid material capable of diluting an active ingredient. Any liquid or solid material used to carry or dilute an active ingredient.

Dilution. The act of adding water to a water-soluble material to lessen its concentration, thereby weakening it.

Distillation. Going from the liquid to the gaseous to the liquid state.

Dose. The total quantity of ionizing radiation.

Dose Rate. The amount of ionizing radiation to which a person has been exposed over a period of time.

Dosimeter. An instrument used for measuring total accumulated exposure to ionizing radiation. Designed for measuring accumulated exposure doses of gamma radiation to emergency response personnel.

DOT. Department of Transportation; the administrative body of the executive branch of the federal government responsible for transportation policy, regulation and enforcement.

Dot Method. A method of showing the configuration of an atom's valence electrons.

Double Bond. Where two atoms share two pairs of electrons between them.

Dry Chemical. A special fire-extinguishing chemical, either sodium, potassium bicarbonate or monosodium phosphate powder, usually available from a semifixed or portable extinguisher.

Duet Role. A special case of the octet rule. To reach stability, an atom (or ion) must have two electrons in its only orbital.

Electron. A subatomic particle that has essentially no weight and an electrical charge of -1.

Element. A pure substance that cannot be broken down into simpler substances by chemical means. The simplest form of a substance and the basic building block of chemistry.

Emergency Planning District. An emergency planning district or joint emergency planning district.

Emergency Services. Those professionals in a community whose primary function is to protect the community in an emergency.

Emergency Support Forces. Any of a range of professionals who provide support for the emergency services during specific emergencies (e.g., emergency pipeline company service men, technical experts).

Emergency Suit. Any "free-entry" protective clothing which is capable of protecting the wearer upon entering a fire up to a temperature of 1,000°F.

Employee. A worker who may be exposed to hazardous chemicals under normal operating conditions or foreseeable emergencies, including but not limited to production workers, line supervisors and repair or maintenance personnel. Office workers, ground maintenance personnel, security personnel and nonresident management are generally not included unless their job performance routinely involves potential exposure to hazardous chemicals.

Employer. A person engaged in a business where chemicals are either used or produced for use or distribution.

Emulsion. A mixture in which one liquid is suspended as tiny drops in another liquid such as oil in water.

Endothermic. The absorption of heat. A chemical reaction that absorbs heat.

Endothermic Reaction. A reaction in which heat is absorbed.

Energy. The capacity to do work.

EPA Registration Number. The number that appears on the pesticide label to identify the pesticide product. May appear as "EPA Reg. No."

Ester. The hydrocarbon derivative with the general formula:

$$O$$
$$\parallel$$
$$R—C—O—R$$

Ethane. One of the paraffin hydrocarbon substances (C_2H_6).

Ether. A hydrocarbon derivative with the general formula R–O–R.

Etiologic Agent. A living microorganism that may cause human diseases. A microorganism, or its toxin, that causes or may cause human disease.

Evaporation. The process by which molecules of a liquid escape through the surface of the liquid into the air above. The changing of a liquid to a vapor.

Exothermic. A chemical reaction that emits heat. The liberation of heat.

Exothermic Reaction. A reaction that produces heat.

Expansion Ratio. The determination of how many volumes of a gas or vapor are produced by the evaporation of one volume of liquid.

Explosion. A sudden, violent release of mechanical, chemical or nuclear energy from a confined region. An explosion is propagated by a heat wave and travels at subsonic speeds. Often used interchangeably with *Detonation.*

Explosive. A chemical that cuases a sudden, almost instantaneous release of pressure, gas and heat when subjected to sudden shock, pressure or high temperature.

Explosive Limits. Percent, by volume in air, of gas vapors which can ignite and/or explode. Same as *Flammable Limits.*

Explosive Train. The building up of sufficient brisance to detonate the main charge. Usually uses a primary explosive to detonate a secondary explosive, which in turn detonates the main charge.

Exposures. People, property or the environment that are or that may be exposed to the harmful affects of a hazardous material.

Extremely Flammable. A liquid pesticide that has a flash point of 20°F (−6.67°C) or lower, determined by the closed cup or Seta flash test.

Facility. All buildings, equipment, structures and other stationary items that are located on a single site or on contiguous or adjacent sites and that are owned or operated by the same person or by any person who controls, is controlled by, or is under common control with such person.

Family Effect. Each element in the "family" or group has very similar chemical properties due to the number of electrons in the outer ring.

Fire Point. The lowest temperature of a liquid at which vapors are emitted rapidly enough to support combustion.

Fire-Proximity Suit. Special clothing capable of protecting the wearer in close proximity to a fire.

Fissile. Radioactive material that may be able to undergo a nuclear fission reaction.

Flame Impingement. The points where flames contact the surface of a container.

Flame Spread. The speed at which a flame will cross over the surface of a material.

Flammable Compressed Gas. Any flammable material or mixture in a container having a pressure exceeding 40 psi at 100°F (37.78°C).

Flammable Gas. Any gas that will burn. Any compressed gas that will burn.

Flammable Limits. (1) Percent, by volume in air, of gases or vapors needed to support ignition. (2) The range of gas or vapor concentrations (percent by volume in air) that will burn or explode if an ignition source is present. Limiting concentrations are commonly called the "lower explosive limit (LEL)" and the "upper explosive limit (UEL)." Below the LEL, the mixture is too lean to burn, and above the UEL it is too rich to burn.

Flammable Liquid. Any liquid having a flash point below 100°F (37.78°C), determined by tests prescribed in the Federal Regulations. Also, a liquid pesticide that has a flash point between 20°F and 80°F, determined by the closed cup or Seta flash test. Note: This is the EPA definition for pesticide labeling. It varies from the NFPA and DOT definitions.

Flammable Material. A substance that is capable of being easily ignited and of burning rapidly.

Flammable Range. The proportion of gas or vapor in air that is between the upper and lower flammable limits.

Flammable Solid. Any solid material, other than an explosive, which is likely to cause fires through friction, absorption of moisture, spontaneous chemical changes, or retained heat from manufacturing or processing, or which can be ignited readily and, when ignited, burns vigorously and persistently.

Flammability (of Liquids). Standard based on the flash point of liquid; liquids with flash points less than 100°F are termed "flammable liquids."

Flash Point. (1) Lowest temperature at which liquid vapors can be made to ignite in a laboratory test. The minimum temperature of a liquid at which it gives off vapors sufficient to form an ignitable mixture with the air. (2) The minimum temperature at which a spark or flame will cause an instantaneous flash in the vapor space above a liquid. (3) The temperature at which the substance gives off flammable vapors which, in contact with a spark or flame, will ignite. (4) The lowest temperature at which a liquid will give off sufficient flammable vapor for ignition to occur. Values can be determined by the open cup or closed cup method. In general, the open cup value is about 10°F to 15°F (−12.22° to −9.44°C) higher than the closed cup value.

Flashover. Where heat radiated back to the floor by superheated gases near the ceiling causes the entire room to burst into flame almost instantaneously.

Forbidden Explosive. An explosive that may not be transported by common carrier.

Formula. The shorthand used to signify what elements or ions are present in a compound, and how many of each. Although the compound may be ionic, the charges on the ions are never shown in a formula.

Frangible Disc. A safety release device that will burst at a predetermined pressure.

Free Radical. A molecular fragment created by the breaking of a molecule into two or more parts by breaking covalent bonds. An atom or group of atoms bound together chemically that has at least one unpaired electron. It is formed by the introduction of energy to a covalently bonded molecule and is formed when that molecule is broken apart by the energy. It cannot exist free in nature, and therefore must react quickly with other free radicals present.

Freezing Point. The temperature in degrees Celsius or Fahrenheit at which a liquid solidifies.

Fuel. A material composed of carbon, hydrogen and other elements which accompany the combustion process. Anything that will burn.

Fuel Oils. Any of a number of moderately to slightly flammable, volatile products of petroleum.

Full Protective Clothing. Clothing that prevents gases, vapors, liquids and solids from coming in contact with the skin. Full protective clothing includes the helmet, self-contained breathing apparatus, coat and pants customarily worn by fire fighters (turnout or bunker coat and pants), rubber boots, gloves, bands around the legs, wrist and waist, as well as covering for the neck, ears, and other parts of the head not protected by the helmet, breathing apparatus or face mask.

Fumigation. The use of chemicals in a gaseous form to destroy noxious insects.

Functional Group. An atom or group of atoms bound together chemically that has an unpaired electron and, on attachment to the hydrocarbon backbone, imparts special properties to the new compound formed.

Fungicide. A pesticide that controls or inhibits fungus growth.

Fusible Plug. A safety relief device in the form of a plug of low-melting metal. The plug closes the safety relief device channel under normal conditions and is intended to yield or melt at a set temperature to permit the escape of gas.

Fusion. Conversion of a substance from a solid to a liquid state.

Gamma Rays. (1) A form of electromagnetic radiation similar to X-rays. (2) The most dangerous form of common radiation particles because of the speed at which it moves and the great distances it can cover.

Gas. (1) In general, applies to all aeriform bodies, whose smallest particles exhibit the tendency to fly apart from each other in all directions. A state of matter defined as a fluid with a vapor pressure not exceeding 40 psia at 100°F. (2) A substance existing in a gaseous state at normal atmospheric temperature and pressure.

Gasoline. Highly flammable, volatile hydrocarbon fuel product of petroleum.

Gauge Pressure. The pressure read on a gauge, which does not take atmospheric pressure into account. The abbreviation for this pressure reading is psig.

Geiger Counter. A device that may be used to detect low levels of nuclear radiation.

General Formula. The general way of writing a molecular formula for an analogous series of compounds that will give the actual molecular formula for any member of the series as long as one knows the number of carbon atoms in the compound. This number is substituted for the letter n in the formula.

Glycerol. A series of substituted hydrocarbons with three hydroxyl radicals substituted for hydrogen atoms.

Glycol. A hydrocarbon derivative with two hydroxyl radicals substituted for two hydrogens.

Gram. The weight of 1 cubic centimeter of water at 4°C.

Gram-Calorie. One gram-calorie is the amount of heat necessary to raise 1 gram of water 1°C from 14.5°C to 15.5°C.

Half-Life. (1) The time required for half of a given amount of a radioactive substance to change into the next element. (2) The time required for a radioactive material to undergo enough disintegrations to reduce its mass to half of its original mass.

Halide. A halogenated compound.

Halogenated. A compound that has had a halogen atom substituted for another atom. A halogenated hydrocarbon has had at least one hydrogen removed and a halogen put in its place.

Halogenation. The chemical reaction whereby a halogen is substituted for another atom, usually a hydrogen atom.

Halogens. The elements of Group VIIAA: fluorine, chlorine, bromine, iodine, and astatine.

Halon (1211, 1301). Two of the halogenated control agents used in fighting flammable liquids and electrical fires; fluorine-based halogens.

Hazard Class. A group of materials, designated by the DOT, that share a common major hazardous property such as radioactivity or flammability.

Hazard Warning. Any words, pictures, symbols, or any combination thereof appearing on a label or other appropriate form of warning which convey the hazards of the chemical(s) in the container(s).

Hazardous Chemical. Any chemical which is a physical or health hazard.

Hazardous Materials. (1) A substance in a quantity or form that may pose an unreasonable risk to health or property when transported in commerce. (2) A substance or material which has been determined by DOT to be capable of posing an unreasonable risk to health, safety or property when transported in commerce and has been so designated. (3) A substance or material in a quantity or form that may pose an unreasonable risk to health, safety or property when stored, transported or used in commerce. (Note: This is the DOT definition.)

Health Hazard. A chemical for which there is statistically significant evidence, based on at least one study conducted in accordance with established scientific principles, that acute or chronic health effects may occur in exposed employees. The term "health hazard" includes chemicals which are carcinogens, toxic or highly toxic agents, reproductive toxins, irritants, corrosives, sensitizers, hepatoxins, nephrotoxins, neurotoxins, agents which act on the hematopoietic system, and agents which damage the lungs, skin, eyes or mucus membranes.

Heat. A condition caused by the rapid movement of molecules. A form of energy. The total amount of vibration in a group of molecules.

Heat Measurement. Measurement of the range of heat intensity.

Heat of Fusion. The quantity of heat that must be supplied to a material at its melting point to convert it completely to a liquid at the same temperature.

Heat of Vaporization. The quantity of heat that must be supplied to a liquid at its boiling point to convert it completely to a gas at the same temperature.

Hemotoxin. A poison that affects the circulatory system.

Heptane. One of the paraffin group hydrocarbons (C_7H_{16}).

Herbicide. Pesticide that controls plant life.

Hexane. One of the paraffin group hydrocarbons(C_6H_{14}).

High-Expansion Foam. Detergent base foam which expands at a ratio of 1,000 to 1. It is low-water-content foam.

High Explosive. An explosive that is *relatively* insensitive to heat and shock, and that usually detonates rather than deflagrates. Usually divided into primary or initiating, secondary, and main charge explosives.

Hydrocarbon. A covalent compound containing only hydrogen and oxygen. A compound that consists primarily of hydrogen and carbon atoms. Any organic substance whose composition is based on hydrogen and carbon.

Hydrocarbon Backbone. The molecular fragment that remains after a hydrogen is removed from a hydrocarbon. The hydrocarbon portion of a hydrocarbon derivative. A hydrocarbon with one or more hydrogens removed. A hydrocarbon radical.

Hydrocarbon Derivative. A compound that begins as a hydrocarbon and has a hydrocarbon removed from the chain and a functional group attached to the place where the hydrogen was removed.

Hydrogen Ion. H^{+1}. A hydrogen atom that has lost its electron.

Hydronium Ion. H_3O^{+1}. The hydrogen ion dissolved in water.

Hydroxide Ion. OH^{-1}. The ion associated with bases.

Hydroxyl. The functional group of the alcohols. The structural formula is $-O-H$.

Hygroscopic. The ability of a substance to absorb moisture from the air. Capable of absorbing moisture from its surroundings.

Hypergolic. (1) Any substance that spontaneously ignites on contact with another. (2) The property of reacting with another substance immediately upon coming in contact with that substance. Both materials must be hypergolic. An example is materials that are used in a solid fuel rocket engine, which can be counted on to react and burn, producing thrust, without depending upon an ignition device that might fail.

Hypergolic Materials. Materials that ignite on contact with one another.

ICC. Interstate Commerce Commission. An independent federal government agency in the executive branch (not affiliated with DOT) charged with administering acts of Congress affecting rates and routes for the transport of interstate commerce.

Identity. Any chemical or common name which is indicated on the MSDS for the chemical. The identity used permits cross references to be made among the required list of hazardous chemicals, the label and the MSDS.

Ignition Continuity. The continuation of burning caused by the radiated heat of the flame.

Ignition Source. Anything producing a flame, spark, friction or static electricity.

Ignition Temperature. (1) The temperature at which a substance must be heated in order to sustain its own combustion process. (2) The temperature at which a fuel or substance ignites and the flame is self-propagating. (3) The minimum temperature to which a substance must be raised before it will ignite. (4) The minimum temperature in degrees Fahrenheit or Celsius required to ignite gas or vapor without the presence of a spark or flame. Values provided in reference texts are only approximate because they change substantially with changes in geometry, gas, or vapor concentrations and in the presence of catalysts.

Immediate Danger Area. The perimeter of a hazardous material leak, spill, explosion, fire or similar emergency.

Immediate Use. The hazardous chemical will be under the control of and used only by the person who transfers it from a labeled container and only within the work shift in which it is transferred.

Impermeable. Cannot be penetrated by liquid or vapor.

Importer. The first business with employees within the Customs Territory of the United States which receives hazardous chemicals produced in other countries for the purpose of supplying them to distributors or manufacturing purchasers within the United States.

Incident Commander. The person who has the responsibility for total operations in a hazardous materials emergency.

Incident Factors. Considerations evaluated by the commander in a (hazardous material) emergency size-up.

Incipient Fires. Fires in the beginning stages.

Individual Container. A cargo container, such as a box or drum, used to transport materials in small quantities.

Inert. Any substance that will not react chemically. A substance that is relatively inactive.

Inert Element. An element lacking chemical or biological action.

Inert Gases. The elements of Group VIII: helium, neon, argon, krypton, xenon, and radon. Also known as the *Noble Gases*.

Inert Ingredient. Material in a pesticide formulation that generally has no pesticidal activity but could be flammable or combustible.

Ingestion. The taking in of toxic materials through the mouth.

Inhalation. The taking in of toxic materials by breathing through the nose or mouth.

Inhibitor. Also called a "stabilizer." A substance used to prevent a chemical reaction from starting. Any substance added to unstable material to prevent a violent reaction.

Initiating Explosive. See *Primary Explosive*.

Initiator. A substance used to start a chemical reaction.

Inorganic. A chemical compound which does not contain carbon.

Inorganic Acid. An acid that contains the anion of a salt. Also known as a "mineral acid."

Inorganic Chemistry. The branch of chemistry dealing with compounds that do not contain carbon.

Inorganic Polymer. A polymer without carbon in its backbone.

Input Heat. The amount of heat required to produce the evolution of vapors from a solid or liquid.

Inverse Square Law. The amount of radiation absorbed falls off as the inverse square of the distance from the source of radiation.

Ion. An atom or group of atoms bound together chemically that have gained or lost one or more electrons and are electrically charged according to the number of electrons gained or lost.

Ionic Bond. The electrostatic attraction of oppositely charged ions.

Ionic Compound. A chemical combination of oppositely charged ions, which are held together by the electrostatic attraction of opposite charges.

Ionization. The process by which an atom or group of atoms bound together chemically gains or loses one or more electrons and becomes an ion. In reference to an acid, the degree to which the acid gas or liquid acid forms ions when it dissolves in water.

Irritant. A substance that is not classified as a poison but might produce dangerous or intensely irritating fumes.

Irritating Material. A liquid or solid substance that, on contact with fire or on exposure to air, gives off dangerous or intensely irritating fumes, but not including any poisonous Class A material.

ISO. International Organization of Standardization.

Isomer. A compound with the same molecular formula as another compound but a different structural formula. That is, a compound may possess exactly the same elements, and exactly the same number of atoms of those elements as another compound, but those atoms are arranged in a different order than those of the other compound.

Isotope. An element with the same number of protons but a different number of neutrons. An atom of the same element with a different number of neutrons in its nucleus.

Jet Fuel. Any of a number of flammable, combustible fuel products of petroleum.

Ketone. A hydrocarbon derivative with the general formula

Kinetic Molecular Theory. A theory that states that all molecules are in constant motion at any temperature above absolute zero. Further, as energy is absorbed by the molecules, their speed of motion or vibration increases, and as energy is withdrawn, molecular motion decreases.

Label. Any written, printed or graphic material displayed on or affixed to containers of hazardous chemicals.

Latent Heat. The amount of heat absorbed or released by a substance as it passes from a liquid to a gas or from a solid to a liquid state.

Latent Heat of Vaporization. The amount of heat absorbed by a liquid as it converts from a liquid to a vapor or gas.

LC$_{50}$. The lethal concentration of a gas, vapor, dust, or fume in air that kills half of the test animals during the observation period.

LD$_{50}$. The lethal dose of a pesticide's active ingredient taken by mouth or absorbed by the skin which is expected to cause death in 50% of the test animals during the observation period. The lethal dose is measured in milligrams per kilogram of body weight.

LD$_{100}$. The lethal dose of an active ingredient taken by mouth.

Light Ends. A term used to describe petroleum products that have a low flash point and high pressure (vapors).

Liquid. (1) The state of a substance characterized by free molecular movement, without the tendency of the molecules to separate from each other, and taking the shape of the container when so enclosed. (2) A fluid with a vapor pressure no higher than 40 psia.

Liquified Gas. A gas that has been converted to a liquid by pressure and/or cooling.

Liquified Natural Gas (LNG). Cryogenic form of natural gas.

Liquified Petroleum Gas. Compressed liquefied hydrocarbon gas, composed mainly of propane and butane.

Local Emergency Planning Committee. The local emergency planning committee of an Emergency Planning District, joint Emergency Planning District, or joint Interstate Planning District.

Low Explosive. An explosive that is sensitive to heat and shock, and that usually deflagrates rather than detonates, unless confined. Also called a "propellant."

Lower Explosive Limits. See *Flammable Limits.*

Lower Flammable Limits. The concentration of a gas or vapor in air below which it cannot be ignited.

Lower Limit of Flammability. The smallest percentage of a flammable gas or vapor, by volume in air, needed for an ignitable mixture.

Main Charge. The high explosive that does the most damage to the surroundings.

Main Group. Those elements of the groups with an *A* after the roman numberal. The vertical columns headed by hydrogen, beryllium, aluminum, carbon, nitrogen, oxygen, fluorine, and helium. Also known as the "representative elements."

Manufacturing Purchaser. An employer who purchases a hazardous chemical for use in the workplace.

Material Safety Data Sheet (MSDS). Written or printed material concerning a hazardous chemical which is prepared in accordance with paragraph (g) of this section.

Matter. That which has weight and occupies space.

Melting Point. The temperature in degrees Fahrenheit or Celsius at which a solid becomes a liquid.

Mer. The repeating molecular unit in any polymer.

Metals. The elements to the left of and below the line on the Periodic Table in the text.

Methane. One of the paraffin group hydrocarbons (CH_4).

Miscible. Two or more liquids that can be mixed and will remain mixed under normal conditions.

Mixture. (1) A combination of chemicals that contains two or more substances that do not lose their individual identities. (2) A substance made up of two or more compounds physically mixed together. A mixture may also contain elements and compounds mixed together.

Model Statute. A drafted piece of legislation to be submitted to a legislative body for consideration and ultimate adoption.

Molecular Formula. Where the molecule is represented by a written formula, using chemical symbols, listing which atoms and how many of them are in the molecule, without showing how they are bonded to each other.

Molecular Weight. The total weight of all atoms in a molecule.

Molecule. A combined group of atoms. The smallest particle of a compound that can still be recognized as the compound. Two or more atoms bound together chemically by covalent bonds and electrically neutral.

Mono-. The prefix meaning one.

Monomer. A simple, small molecule that has the special capability of reacting with itself to form a polymer.

Multiple Bond. A double or triple covalent bond.

Mutual Aid. An agreement among fire departments to provide equipment and services in an emergency.

Natural Gas. A utility gas composed mainly of methane, used for heating, cooking, and water heating.

Natural Gasoline. In commerce, a fuel liquid composed mainly of the heavier paraffin group hydrocarbons, used to supplement the combustion properties of petroleum-based gasolines.

Neo-. A prefix given to an isomer of another compound. It exists in compounds that were named long ago and is used only where the compound is best known by its common name.

Neurotoxin. A poison that attacks the nervous system.

Neutralization. The chemical reaction whereby an acid or base reacts with another material and the resulting pH is 7. The classic neutralization reaction involves an inorganic acid plus a base: HCl + NaOH $->$ NaCl + HOH (water).

Neutron. A nuclear particle that has an atomic weight of 1.0 and is electrically neutral.

NFPA 704. National Fire Protection Association Pamphlet 704, which describes a system for marking hazardous materials in terms of their health hazard, flammability, and reactivity.

NFPA 704M. Pamphlet which describes a system for identifying fire hazards.

NHTSA. National Highway Traffic Safety Administration of DOT; responsible for establishing motor vehicle safety standards and regulations for new vehicles. Formerly called the National Highway Safety Bureau (NHSB).

Nitrophenols. Synthetic organic pesticides containing carbon, hydrogen, nitrogen and oxygen that are used as wood preservatives, fungicides or disinfectants. Affect the liver and central nervous system in the human body.

Noble Gases. The elements of Group VIII: helium, neon, argon, krypton and xenon.

Nonflammable Gas. A compressed gas not classified as flammable.

Nonliquified Gas. A gas that is entirely gaseous at a temperature of 70°F (21.11°C).

Nonmetals. The elements to the right of an above the line on the Periodic Table.

Normal. The designation given to a straight chain compound that has isomers. The designation in the molecular formula ia an *n-* in front of the formula.

NOS. Not otherwise specified.

NOS or NOIBN. Notations designated "Not Otherwise Specified" or "Not Otherwise Identified By Name" and appearing on shipping papers when the materials conform to a hazardous material definition but not listed by generic name in the regulations. Example: Flammable NOS.

Nucleus. A subatomic particle that contains all the positive charge and essentially all the weight of the atom.

Octet Rule. To reach stability, each atom must have eight electrons in its outermost ring. The fulfillment of the octet rule is what causes ionization.

Odorant. A mercaptan or sulfur-based substance added to flammable gases in distribution to provide a warning of the gas's presence to consumers.

Oil and Hazardous Materials—Technical Assistance Data System (OHM—TADS). Organization within the EPA that provides information on some hazardous substances to emergency teams responding to spills.

Orbitals. The "rings" around the nucleus that contain the orbiting electrons.

Organic. Chemical compound containing carbon; some may occur in nature, while others are produced by chemical synthesis.

Organic Acid. An acid containing the carboxyl (COOH) group. The exceptions are those benzene ring compounds containing the hydroxyl (OH) functional group and hydrocyanic acid.

Organic Chemistry. The branch of chemistry that deals with compounds containing carbon.

Organic Peroxide. (1) An organic derivative of the inorganic compound hydrogen peroxide. (2) A group of highly dangerous hazardous materials. Used as initiators for thermoplastics and curing agents for thermosets, they are highly reactive oxidizing agents that burn, and they can start their own decomposition process when contaminated, heated or shocked. (3) An organic compound which contains the bivalent –O–O– structure and which may be considered a structural derivative of hydrogen peroxide in which one or both of the hydrogen atoms has been replaced by an organic radical.

Organic Phosphate Insecticide. Organic insecticides, i.e., HETP (Hexaethyl Tetraphosphate) and TEPP (Tetraethyl Pyrophosphate).

Organochlorine Compounds. Synthetic organic pesticides that contain chlorine, carbon and hydrogen.

Organochlorine Compounds (Chlorinated Hydrocarbons). Synthetic organic pesticides that contain chlorine, carbon and hydrogen. These pesticides affect the central nervous system. Examples: DDT and Endrin.

Organophosphates. Synthetic organic pesticides that contain carbon, hydrogen and phosphorus. Highly toxic to humans because they prevent proper transmission of nerve impulses. Examples: Parathion and Malation.

ORMs. (1) Materials that do not meet the definitions of hazardous materials but require some regulation. (2) Other Regulated Materials that do not meet the definitions of hazardous materials but possess enough characteristics of hazards in transport to require some regulation.

Oxidation. The chemical combination of a substance with oxygen.

Oxidizer. A substance containing oxygen that gives it up readily, or the halogens, which support combustion. Releases oxygen under decomposition and supports combustion.

Oxidizing Ability. The ability to yield oxygen readily to stimulate combustion.

Oxidizing Agent. Any material containing oxygen that will give it up readily, plus the halogens. Also known as *Oxidizers*.

Oxidizing Material. A substance that yields oxygen readily to stimulate the combustion of organic matter.

Oxyacid. An acid that contains an oxygen-containing anion.

Oxyanion. A complex anion that contains oxygen.

Oxygen. An element which readily unites with materials.

Oxysalt. An ionic compound containing an oxyanion.

Paired Electrons. Electrons that are close to each other and tend to be attracted to each other in pairs. Paired electrons form a covalent bond only when they are shared by two atoms.

Paraffin Series. An older name given to the alkanes.

Pentane. One of the paraffin group hydrocarbons (C_5H_{12}).

Periodic Table. A systematic arrangement of all the known elements, by atomic number, which demonstrates the periodicity, or regular repeating, of chemical properties of the elements.

Permissible Explosive. An explosive that may be used in mines.

Peroxide. The hydrocarbon derivative with the general formula R–O–O–R. Also, the name of the peroxide radical which has the structural formula –O–O–.

Pesticide. A chemical or mixture of chemicals used to destroy, prevent or control any living organism considered to be a pest.

Petrochemical. Any of a group of chemical substances manufactured from petroleum products.

pH. Refers to the acidity or alkalinity of a substance. A pH of 1 to 7 is acidic, and a pH from 7 to 14 is alkaline. A pH of 7 is neutral. Technically, pH is the logarithm of the reciprocal of the concentration of hydrogen ions in solution.

Phenyl. The general name for the radical of benzene.

Physical Hazard. A chemical for which there is scientifically valid evidence that it is a combustible liquid, a compressed gas, an explosive, a flammable, an organic peroxide, an oxidizer, pyrophoric, unstable (reactive) or water-reactive.

Physical Properties. Any property of an organic substance related to its form and behavior in a given environment. Properties of a material that relate to the physical states common to all substances: that is, a solid, a liquid or a gas.

Placards. (1) Square diamond markers required on transporting vehicles. (2) Ten- and 3/4-inch (273.0-mm) square diamond markers required on the transporting vehicle, such as a truck, tank car or freight container 640 cubic feet (19.2 cubic meters) or more.

Plastic. ASTM definition: ''A material that contains as an essential ingredient an organic substance of large molecular weight, is solid in its finished stated, and, at some stage in its manufacture or in its processing into finished articles, can be shaped by flow.'' This definition excludes inorganic plastic and includes rubbers and elastomers.

Poison. Any substance that causes injury, illness, or death to living tissue by chemical means.

Poly-. A prefix meaning many. A polymer means many (poly) parts (mer).

Polymer. A ''giant'' molecule made up of thousands of tiny molecules linked together in a long chain.

Polymerizable. The ability of a small molecule, usually called a ''monomer,'' to react with itself to form a very large molecule called a ''polymer.'' When this occurs in an uncontrolled way, the monomer may react explosively.

Polymerization. (1) A chemical reaction in which the molecules link together to form long chain molecules. (2) The process by which monomers combine with themselves to form giant molecules called ''polymers.'' This is a reaction in a controlled atmosphere (inside a large vat called a ''reactor''). When the reaction is in a runaway (uncontrolled) mode, the result is instant polymerization, which in large quantities is accompanied by a violent and destructive explosion.

Positron. A positively charged electron.

Precipitate. The result when a solution of one chemical is combined with a solution of another chemical and an insoluble material is produced.

Pressure. A force applied over a given area.

Pressure Vessel. A type of liquid storage container used to hold highly flammable, volatile liquids and liquefied gases under pressure.

Pressurized Gas. A gas that is still in the gaseous state but is under higher pressure than 14.7 psia.

Primary Explosive. A very sensitive high explosive that is used to detonate a secondary explosive in an explosive train. Also called an ''initiating explosive.''

Propane. One of the LP-gas paraffin group hydrocarbons (C_3H_8).

Propellant. See *Low Explosive*.

Proper Name. A system of naming organic compounds according to the longest carbon chain in the compound.

Proportioning. The occurrence of intermolecular collisions between oxygen and hydrocarbon molecules.

Proton. A nuclear particle that has an atomic weight of 1.0 and an electrical charge of +1.

Psia. Pressure expressed in pounds per square inch absolute. Add approximately 14.7 to gauge reading to obtain the absolute reading. See *Absolute Pressure*.

Psig. Pressure expressed in pounds per square inch gauge. Gauge pressure is the difference between atmospheric pressure and pressure being measured.

PSTN. Pesticide Safety Team Network. Regional teams of the National Agricultural Chemical Association designed to deal with pesticide incidents.

Public Information Officer. Individual on the Command Post Staff responsible for providing information to the news media.

Pyrolysis. Breakdown of molecules by heat. Pryolysis of polymers can produce shorter chain (lower molecular weight) polymers or the original monomer.

Pyrophoric. Any substance which ignites spontaneously upon contact with the atmosphere. Capable of igniting spontaneously when exposed to dry or moist air at or below 130°F (54.44°C). The ability to react in air.

Pyrophoric Liquids. Any liquid that ignites spontaneously in dry or moist air or below 130°F.

Quenchant. Any substance that absorbs another.

Rad. The transfer of heat with no medium.

Radiation. Heat transfer by electromagnetic waves. The transfer of heat with no medium.

Radical. An atom or group of atoms bound together chemically that has one or more unpaired electrons. Since it cannot exist in nature, it reacts very quickly with another radical that is present to form a new compound. Also know as a "free" radical.

Radioactive. Capable of spontaneously emitting ionizing radiation.

Radioactive Material. Any material or combination of materials that spontaneously emits ionizing radiation and has a specific activity greater than 0.002 microcuries per gram.

Radioactivity. The spontaneous disintegration of unstable nuclei accompanied by emission of nuclear radiation.

Radioisotopes. Artificially radioactive elements.

RBE. Relative Biological Effectiveness. The conversion of the number of rads of gamma radiation to the number of rads of a different form of radiation that will produce the same biological effect.

Reactants. The chemical compounds that are brought together in a chemical reaction.

Reactive. Capable of or tending to react chemically with other substances.

Reactive Materials. Substances capable of or tending to react chemically with other substances.

Reactivity. The ability of one substance to undergo a chemical combination with another substance.

Reducing Agent. A fuel that becomes chemically changed by the oxidizing process.

Release. Any spilling, leaking, pumping, pouring, emitting, emptying, discharging, injecting, escaping, leaching, dumping, or disposing of into the environment including, without limitation, the abandonment or discarding of barrels, containers, and other closed receptacles that contained any hazardous chemical, hazardous substance, extremely hazardous substance or toxic chemical,

Rem. A unit or biological dose of radiation.

Repellent. A chemical which drives insects or other pests away from a treated person.

Reportable Leak. Any of several conditions cited in 49 CFR 191 and CFR 195 defined by the Secretary of Transportation.

Representative. The elements of the long Groups on the Periodic Table.

Resonance. A phenomenon whereby a structure, to satisfy the rules of covalent bonding, should be fluctuating (resonating) back and forth between two alternate molecular structures, both of which are "correct" for the molecule. It is a way of explaining what cannot be explained using the rules of covalent bonding.

Respiratory Paralyzer. Any substance that causes the respiratory system to shut down.

Rings. The paths around the nucleus in which the orbiting electrons travel.

Rodenticide. A pesticide used to control rodents.

Roentgen. A unit of exposure to gamma or X-ray radiation.

Rupture Disc. A safety relief device in the form of a metal disc that closes the relief channel under normal conditions. The disc bursts at a set pressure to permit the escape of gas. A safety device which fails at a predetermined pressure and thus protects a pressure vessel from being overpressurized.

SADT. Self-Accelerating Decomposition Temperature. A property of most organic peroxides. The temperature at which the decomposition of the molecule becomes self-feeding and irreversible.

SAE. Society of Automotive Engineers.

Safety Relief Valves. A device on pressure cargo tanks containing an operating part that is held in place by spring force. Valves open and close at set pressures.

Salt. An ionic compound formed by a metal and a nonmetal.

Saturated. A hydrocarbon possessing only single covalent bonds between carbon atoms.

Secondary Explosive. A sensitive high explosive that is used to detonate the main charge in an explosive train if the brisance of the primary explosive is not high enough to cause the detonation. Also called a "booster explosive." May also be used as an initiating explosive.

Self-Accelerating Decomposition Temperature. The temperature above which the decomposition of an unstable material proceeds by itself, independently of the external temperature.

Self-Contained Breathing Apparatus. Type of emergency equipment including a mask and a portable air supply.

Shielding. Any material or obstruction that absorbs radiation.

Simple Asphyxiant. A material that is not toxic, or has a very low order of toxicity, but kills by diluting or displacing the oxygen needed for breathing.

Size-Up. Emergency command procedure in which incident factors are evaluated by the Commander to determine the control objectives.

Solubility. Indication of a substance's ability to mix with water.

Solution. Mixture of one or more substances in another substance in which all ingredients are completely dissolved.

Solvent. A liquid that will dissolve a substance to form a solution. Examples: water, petroleum distillate, xylene and methanol.

Specific Gravity. (1) Ratio of the density of a substance compared to that of another standard substance (e.g., pure water, hydrogen) when both densities are obtained by the weighing the substances in air. (2) The ratio of the weight of a volume of the product to the weight of an equal volume of water. In the case of liquids of limited solubility, the specific gravity indicates whether the product will sink or float on water. For example, if the specific gravity is greater than 1, the product will sink; if the specific gravity is less than 1, the product will float. (3) The ratio between the amount of heat necessary to raise the temperature of a substance and the amount of heat necessary to raise the same weight of water the same number of degrees.

Specific Heat. A measure of the ability of a substance to absorb heat.

Spontaneously Combustible. A material that proceeds without constraint by internal impulse or outside energy to kindle or set a fire. A solid material that can decompose in the absence of air, generally causing ignition or deflagration.

Spring-Loaded Valve. A safety relief device that is set to operate by opening to relieve pressure, and then to reseal when the pressure drops to below the spring's rated strength.

Stabilization. The stage of an incident when the immediate problem has been controlled or extinguished.

Standard Transportation Commodity Code (or STCC Code Number). A listing of code numbers in general use by carriers for categories of articles being shipped

Straight Chain. The configuration of the molecule of a hydrocarbon when a carbon atom attaches itself to another carbon atom that has only one other carbon atom already attached to it.

Strength. The degree to which an acid ionizes in water. Strong acids ionize nearly 100%.

Stress. A state of tension put on or in a shipping container by internal chemical action, external mechanical damage, or external flames or heat.

Structural Effect. The effect upon certain properties of an analogous series of compounds by *branching*. Properties like boiling point. flash point, ignition temperature, and others change as branches are added to compounds, including isomers.

Structural Formula. A drawing of the molecule showing all of its atoms and how they are bonded to every other atom.

Sublimation. The change of a liquid from the solid to the gaseous state without becoming a liquid.

Sublime. To change from the solid state directly to the vapor state, bypassing the liquid state.

Substituted. A compound that has had one or more of its atoms removed and atoms of other elements put in their place in the molecule. A substituted hydrocarbon is one that has had a hydrogen removed and another atom substituted for it.

Symbol. The chemical shorthand used instead of writing out the name of an element.

Snythesize. To make a molecule to duplicate a molecule made in nature.

Synthetic. Made by humans as opposed to being made in nature.

Systemic Poison. Any substance that interferes with any vital bodily process.

Tank Farm. Type of large liquids storage installation.

Technical Assistance. Personnel, agencies or printed materials that provide technical information on the handling of hazardous materials.

Temperature. The condition of an object that determines whether heat will flow to or from another object. A measure of how fast a group of molecules are moving.

Teratogen. A substance which may cause abnormal development in unborn animals.

Thermometer. A device for measuring heat intensity.

Threshold Limit Value. The concentration of a toxic substance that can be tolerated with no ill effects.

Tissue Asphyxiant. Any substance that can be carried by the red blood cells to tissue cells and, upon release, render the tissue cells incapable of ever again accepting oxygen, thus killing them.

TLV. Threshold Limit Value. The amount of a substance to which an average person in average health may be exposed in a 40-hour work week. The values may be averaged over time. The TLV is also referred to as the "Time Weighted Average (TWA)."

Toxic. (1) Poisonous, relating to a toxin or caused by a toxin. Materials that can be poisonous if inhaled, swallowed or absorbed into the body through cuts or breaks in the skin. (2) Anything harmful, destructive, deadly or poisonous to the body.

Toxic Materials. Substances that can be poisonous if inhaled or swallowed.

Toxicity. Poisonous property of a substance. The ability of a chemical substance to produce injury once it reaches a susceptible site in or near the body.

Trade Secret. Any confidential formula, pattern, process, device, information or compilation of information (including a chemical name or other unique chemical identifier) that is used in an employer's business and gives the employer an opportunity to obtain an advantage over competitors who do not know or use it.

Transmutation. Changing one element into another by a nuclear reaction.

Tri-. The prefix meaning three.

Triple Bond. Where two atoms share three pairs of electrons between them.

Unit. A molecular fragment that repeats itself in a series.

Unpaired Electrons. Electrons that can react or pair up with electrons of another atom to form a covalent bond.

Unsaturated. A hydrocarbon that has at least one multiple bond between two carbon atoms somewhere in the molecule.

Unstable (reactive). A chemical which in the pure state, or as produced or transported, will vigorously polymerize, decompose, condense or become self-reactive under conditions of shock, pressure or temperature.

Unstable elements. Elements that emit particles and decay to form other elements (radioactive elements.)

Unstable Materials. Substances capable of rapidly undergoing chemical changes or decomposition.

Upper Explosive Limits. See *Flammable Limits*.

Upper Flammable Limit. The maximum concentration of a gas or vapor in air above which it is not possible to ignite the gas or vapor.

Upper Limit of Flammability. The largest percentage of gas or vapor, by volume in air, which produces an ignitable mixture.

Utilities Coordination Committee (UCC). A voluntary association of utilities, usually established for safety planning.

Valence Electrons. The electrons in the outermost ring. The configuration of these electrons determine the chemistry of each element.

Valence Ring. The outermost ring of the atom.

Vapor. Gases released with or without the aid of heat by substances that, under ordinary circumstances, are either in a solid or a liquid state. Diffuse, gaseous matter produced by heating a liquid to and beyond the boiling point.

Vapor Density. The relative mass of a vapor compared to a fixed standard (usually in air). This is actually a specific gravity rather than a true density, because it equals the ratio of the weight of a vapor or gas (with no air present) compared to the weight of an equal volume of air at the same temperature and pressure. Values less than 1 indicate that the vapor or gas tends to rise, and values greater than 1 indicate that it tends to settle. However, temperature effects must be considered.

Vapor Pressure. The pressure exerted by a vapor that is in equilibrium with its liquid form. The pressure exerted by the molecules of a liquid leaving the liquid and entering the void space of a closed container. The equilibrium pressure of the saturated vapor above the liquid, measured in millimeters of mercury (760 mm Hg = 14.7 psia) at 20°C (68°F) unless another temperature is specified. Conversion is done as follows:

$$\text{psi} = \frac{\text{mm Hg} \times 14.7}{760}$$

Vapor Recovery Hood. A collecting device installed over tank vents for the collection of vapors generated during tank loading.

Vapor Recovery Line. A line which connects the vapor recovery hood to a convenient location for attachment to a vapor recovery hose.

Vaporization. Going from a liquid to a gaseous state or from a solid to a gaseous state.

Vents. Devices which control or limit tank pressure. Some types are pressure relief, vacuum relief, fusible (opens at elevated temperature), Christmas tree (slang for a combination vent) and Frangible Vent.

Viscosity. The tendency of a liquid to flow as expressed in SAE ratings.

Volatilization. Changing a liquid to a vapor.

Water Foam. Either mechanical or chemical foam is produced by a special foam nozzle or by a fixed system. It is used to form a blanket over a surface of burning liquids. It is effective only with liquids which are not appreciably soluble in water.

Water Fog. A finely divided mist produced by either a high- or low-velocity fog nozzle. It is used to knock down flames and cool hot surfaces.

Water-Reactive. Materials, generally flammable solids, that react in varying degrees when mixed with water or in contact with humid air. The reaction of a substance when it comes into contact with water. It may produce hazardous vapors or any other hazardous material, or release energy such as heat.

Water-Reactive Materials. Substances, generally flammable solids, that react in varying degrees when mixed with water.

Water Solubility. The ability of a liquid or solid to mix with or dissolve in water.

Weight Effect. As the molecular weight (calculated by adding up the atomic weights of all the atoms in the molecule) of compounds in an analogous series is increased or decreased, certain properties, including flash point, boiling point, and water solubility, change.

Wettable Powder. A finely ground pesticide dust that mixes with water to form a suspension for application. This formulation may not burn, but it may release toxic fumes under fire conditions.

X-Rays. Electromagnetic radiation of high energy possessing wavelengths shorter than those of ultraviolet radiation.

INDEX